SKETCHES OF URBAN AND CULTURAL

LIFE IN NORTH AMERICA

W9-ACI-995

Sketches of Urban and Cultural Life in North America

by

Friedrich Ratzel

Translated and edited by Stewart A. Stehlin

Rutgers University Press
NEW BRUNSWICK AND LONDON

This book originally appeared as *Städte- und Culturbilder aus Nordamerika* (Leipzig: F. A. Brockhaus, 1876).

Portions of this work dealing with the Centennial Exposition in Philadelphia and the Smithsonian Institution in Washington, D.C., have appeared in slightly altered form in *Pennsylvania History* 44 (1977) and *Records of the Columbia Historical Society* 50 (1980).

Library of Congress Cataloging-in-Publication Data

Ratzel, Friedrich, 1844–1904.
[Städte- und Culturbilder aus Nordamerika. English]
Sketches of urban and cultural life in North America / by Friedrich Ratzel ; translated and edited with an introduction by Stewart A. Stehlin.
p.   cm.
Translation of: Städte- und Culturbilder aus Nordamerika.
Bibliography: p.
ISBN 0-8135-1327-8 ISBN 0-8135-1328-6 (pbk.)
1. United States—Description and travel—1865–1900. 2. City and town life—United States—History—19th century. 3. United States—Civilization—1865–1919. 4. Ratzel, Friedrich. 1844–1904—Journeys—United States. I. Stehlin, Stewart A., 1936–
II. Title.
E168.R2213 1988   87-37588
973.8—dc19   CIP

British Cataloging-in-Publication information available

To
BAYRD STILL,
colleague and friend,
who first urged me to undertake this
translation and bring this work to the
attention of English-speaking readers

Contents

Illustrations

All photographs courtesy of the Library of Congress, Washington, D.C., unless otherwise stated.

Photographs

Map

Introduction

The importance of some books is recognized immediately upon publication, some books are duly appreciated only after later works by the same author become successes, still others remain neglected and must wait for their time to come. Friedrich Ratzel's work, *Städte- und Culturbilder aus Nordamerika* (Sketches of Urban and Cultural Life in North America), published in 1876, can perhaps be most readily classified as belonging to the last category. His name is well known in the fields of geography and anthropology but much less so, if at all, in the fields of urban or cultural history. Neither is his a familiar name like Tocqueville, Chevalier, Dickens, Bryce, or the acerbic Mrs. Trollope,[1] nor does the reader ever encounter quotations from Ratzel's travel account of America as he does from those of the other Europeans. Moreover, Ratzel's work is not excerpted or even listed in most anthologies of notable travelers to the United States.[2]

There are perhaps several reasons for this omission: Ratzel was an unknown young journalist at the time of his visit; he wrote in an easy flowing style, which caused some critics to regard his monograph as impressionistic observations written for the general public and so to overlook the value of his comments; his larger, more scholarly works, including one on America, began to appear within a few years after the *Sketches*, thus tending to overshadow it; and perhaps historiographically most significant, he wrote about cities and their importance at a time when scholars had not come to understand the importance of urban history for comprehending modern society and when the general public was mainly interested in learning about the United States in broad terms and seeking to understand its political institutions. Since Ratzel's visit to America a little over one hundred years ago, the growth of large cities has become a hallmark of modern civilization not only in the United States but all over the world. Urban history has taken its place as a legitimate academic discipline, and scholars are busy examining primary sources about the various stages of urban development. The time has come to reexamine this too little-known work of Ratzel to learn what he has to say about the beginnings of the era of big cities.

Ratzel was born in Karlsruhe, Germany, on August 30, 1844. Having begun work as a pharmacist, he soon realized a broader interest in the natural sciences and returned to school. After completing his university studies in the field of zoology, where he was introduced to Darwin's ideas about natural selection in the struggle for survival and about the influence of environment on the species, in 1869 he submitted a series of articles to the *Kölnische Zeitung* about the zoology of the Mediterranean region. The newspaper's editors, recognizing the journalistic ability of this new contributor, invited him to write further articles on his travels through other regions of Europe, such as Hungary, Romania, and Italy. After the Franco-Prussian War, in which Ratzel served as a volunteer from his home state of Baden, he undertook further studies in the early 1870s at Munich, where he was introduced to geology and ethnography, and in his writings he began to stress the importance of geographical location for a nation's development. In 1873 he began a trip lasting for several years, which took him from one end of the United States to the other and then on to Mexico and Cuba.

Having completed his *Wanderjahre*, he returned to Europe in 1875 with notebooks filled with observations made during his trip. He completed further studies in Munich and began an academic career first at the Polytechnicum (*Technische Hochschule*) in Munich and then later, after 1886, at the University of Leipzig as professor of geography. He remained in Leipzig, teaching until his death in 1904.

Throughout his career, Ratzel was a prodigious scholar, publishing such major works as his important study of the United States, *Die Vereinigten Staaten von Nordamerika* (1878–1880), which dealt in systematic form with the physical and cultural geography of the country he had visited, and a work on anthropology, *Anthropologie* (1882–1891), in which he analyzed the influence of situation, space, seas, rivers, and other physical phenomena on human development. In another important book, *Politische Geographie* (1897), he analyzed the relation of politics and the structure of the state to geographic forces. These ideas—including that of *Lebensraum*, which Ratzel suggested in this study and developed in another work, *Der Lebensraum* (1901)—were picked up and embroidered upon in the twentieth century by the Haushofer school of *Geopolitik*; this in turn caused much misinterpretation and criticism of Ratzel for his use of this concept and linked him with all the unfortunate associations and meanings given this word later on in this century. Today his influence is still great among geographers. Also, as interest develops in cultural anthropology and as the importance of this discipline becomes more and more apparent, his contribution to this field will have to be reevaluated.[3]

All of his scholarly contributions and his reputation as an academic, however, lay in the future when in 1872, satisfied with the work the twenty-eight-year-old Ratzel was doing for the *Kölnische Zeitung*, the editors of that paper decided to offer him an even greater task, a trip to the New World. His employer was a large, independent newspaper located in the Rhineland, one of Germany's growing urban industrial complexes. The journal was widely respected and was read throughout all of Germany, thus giving its correspondents a large reading public. The editors believed that their readers would be interested in learning about developments then occurring within the industrializing society in America, and about what had transpired there since the devastating disruption in the political, economic, and social fabric caused by the Civil

War. Ratzel was given complete freedom to select and choose the topics to report upon, with money being no object; all bills were to be paid by the newspaper.

The young newspaperman readily accepted the offer and spent a great deal of time reading all he could about North America to prepare for his trip. From August 1873 until October 1874, he traveled the length and breadth of the United States, sending articles back to his paper. Two years later, Ratzel revised and selected some of his essays about the United States, which were published in book form by the prestigious publishing house of F. A. Brockhaus in Leipzig. The book, the *Sketches*, was printed in two parts and consisted of twenty-one essays of varying length dealing with aspects of American geography and descriptions of life in more than eighteen cities; Ratzel dealt with such topics as urban society, city planning, education, architecture, race relations, economic developments, and the importance of transportation facilities. In contrast to many books by American authors at that time and to municipal centennial histories, which described buildings, spoke of the accomplishments of public officials, and served as advertisements for the city, Ratzel's essays tell us not only about the architecture of a given place, but about the street life, the manner in which people lived, and the reasons for a city's development. In other words, the *Sketches* was a much more ambitious and fuller view of urban life than Americans were generally writing in that period.

On his visit to America, he spent several weeks in New York where, armed with many introductory letters, he met with numerous Americans and German-Americans. In October he went on to Boston where he was introduced to such well-known scholars as the naturalist Louis Agassiz and took time to study and praise the educational facilities at Harvard. While there he also made good use of the numerous scholarly facilities in the area, and his research resulted in a whole series of articles for his newspaper. Working his way down the East Coast, he commented on aspects of city life that particularly impressed him in each place, such as the preparations for the Centennial Exposition in Philadelphia and the collections of the Smithsonian Institution in Washington and its methods of disseminating research findings to all parts of the country. He visited Richmond, Charleston, Savannah, and parts of Florida, where he predicted large numbers of people would soon come and settle for health reasons and because of the warm climate. Traveling across the South by train and boat, he stopped in New Orleans, then went up the Mississippi by steamboat and on to the metropolises of the Midwest, Cincinnati, St. Louis, and Chicago, where again he was impressed with the growth and expansion of the latter city, especially after the great fire of 1871. The last leg of his American tour took him by train to Denver and over the Rocky Mountains to San Francisco, where he rounded out his journey with an impressive description of San Francisco Bay that complemented his description of New York Bay at the beginning of the book.[4] He had, in other words, not restricted himself to one general geographic area, as many other travelers had, but chose to visit what he considered important sections of the country from east to west and north to south and to observe city life in all stages of development from the most advanced on the East Coast to the newest along the western frontier.[5]

Critics have sometimes objected to a somewhat ponderous style in some of his later works, but no one can say this about his *Sketches*, since the book, based on his newspaper articles, was written for both the general public and the more educated reader in a journalistic style that, while assuming a certain basic general knowledge, is informative and illustrative and at the same time vivid, lively, and easy to read. In fact, precisely the easy flow of the narrative may help to account for the neglect the book received from the more scholarly journals at the time of publication. Nevertheless, where reviews did appear, such as in the Leipzig *Illustrirte Zeitung*, one of the oldest leading German illustrated weeklies, credit was given for the carefully depicted scenes of city life that in their own way give us a view of American society in general. The importance of the city for America, which according to the reviewer, Ratzel admirably demonstrates, was in itself reason enough to recommend the book.[6]

In contrast to eastern Europeans, but like the English and French, Germans knew quite a bit about the New World by the mid-nineteenth century.[7] There were numerous informative pamphlets about America for those contemplating emigration, some statistical reports, and a number of works written by Germans who had been to the United States, including the books of Maximilian von Wied, prince of the house of Wied, the historian Friedrich von Raumer, the great naturalist Alexander von Humboldt, and Germans who had emigrated to America, such as the eminent scholar Francis Lieber and the writer and politician Francis J. Grund. But although many Germans had come to visit the United States, they did not rival either the English or the French in the sheer number of books written that sought to interpret America for their readers. Nevertheless, what the Germans did publish was characterized in general by a philosophical impartiality, which made the German writings a middle ground between the enthusiastic and urbane French and the negative or sneering English reportage.[8]

Moreover, German interest in and connections to the United States remained great. In 1854, 215,000 people, or over one-half of the total immigrants to the United States that year, came from Germany. By 1873 the number was still as high as 150,000, or just about one-third of all immigrants.[9] During this period, America had made tremendous strides in growth and in acquisition of wealth, and the immigrants were sending back tales that formed the basis for the myth in Germany of America as the land of unlimited possibilities (*das Land der unbegrenzten Möglichkeiten*). An American scholar, writing a decade before Ratzel visited America, emphasized the closeness of the relationship between the people of both countries when he stated, "No Europeans, in our own day, have had more reason to regard North America with hopeful interest than the Germans. . . . In the sphere of intellectual and of utilitarian life, a mutual understanding and sympathy, and a community of political interests, have tended to bring the two nations into nearer relations."[10] Thus it was only natural that a people with an already established connection to the New World would be anxious to update their information about American life and society. Many of the early German immigrants had come from the Rhineland and western Germany, and a prominent Rhenish newspaper, such as the *Kölnische Zeitung*, could thus reasonably expect strong public interest in Ratzel's reporting.

What makes Ratzel different from any other German or, for that matter, any other foreign visitor, is his fascination with the city. For him, it became the theme around which he would organize his observations and analysis. His analysis of the impact of the city on the totality of American life is unusually perceptive for something written as early as the mid-1870s. Unlike other commentators, who depict America as still basically a rural nation filled with fields of grain and impressive natural wonders, Ratzel focuses on the population flow to the cities, especially to the large cities. He is intrigued by the process of urbanization and its concomitant social factors—the primary schools, city layout, mass transit, and the manner in which the nation is drawn together by an all-encompassing railroad system. The pragmatic way in which Americans overcame the physical obstacles to lay track from one ocean to the other was, he feels, a tribute to their practical ability to modernize. He is fascinated by the transcendence of these large networks and systems—the education system, the economic system, the transportation system—all of which are integrating factors that serve to replace the age of the small entrepreneur and the rugged individual with larger entities and bigger organizations, which find their base and source of strength in the large cities. He rightly perceives the magnetism of large urban centers for the Americans of the 1870s. As one editor of a Midwestern newspaper stated in 1871, a person preferred to be "the most insignificant member of some great community rather than a very important member of a small one. . . . Better to be the 1/1,000,000,000 of New York than the 1/1 of Aroostook County." In 1899 this opinion was confirmed by the economist Edmund J. James, who stated that the increase in the number of cities with populations of 200,000 or more made the late nineteenth century "not only the age of cities, but the age of great cities."[11] This had in fact been Ratzel's perception some twenty-five years before.

True, he generally follows the standard travel route, stopping at those places a visitor was expected to see,[12] but he does it with a thoroughness that takes in life in all parts of the country, distinguishing differences from section to section, noting the similarities. Travelers in a foreign land can easily fall into the trap of simply passing on information supplied to them by the local inhabitants in casual conversation. Ratzel, however, utilizing the American predilection for statistics, spent much time gathering facts and figures from printed sources and speaking to qualified persons about specific topics, so that his comments could be made with a reasonable degree of accuracy. More than just descriptions of plants, wildlife, and geological formations in this country such as one might expect from a trained naturalist, more than just opinions about American customs, society, and city life such as one usually reads in travel accounts, Ratzel's emphasis is on the relation of nature to man's potential for developing it, and on the significance of geography for urban growth. In almost Braudelian terms, our German traveler observes and comments on the geography, the advantage of a city's site for industry and trade, the natural resources, the climate, and the produce of the land as contributory to the growth of human settlements. What impresses him most is that the United States had so many large cities with populations of over 100,000 inhabitants, and that the metropolises were growing so rapidly.

In his preface, Ratzel immediately indicates his interest in the city and the direction his discussion is to follow. Two trends, he states, were especially significant for the nineteenth century: the growth of large cities and the narrowing of the gap between city and countryside. Urban influences, he explains, had extended into the rural areas, as agriculture became more mechanized, as education and knowledge were disseminated from the large cities, as rural populations tended to migrate to the city, and as towns tended to emulate large cities. For Ratzel, progress throughout the world would be defined in terms of the growth of large urban civilizations, and in this sense he believes the United States, ahead of Europe, was the precursor of what was to occur throughout the modern world. Because of its rapid urban growth and the number of these large cities spread across the huge expanse of land, America was the forerunner of a development he saw Europe beginning to experience. He points out that America had over 4,000,000 people living in cities of 100,000 or more while Germany, with a greater population, had a little more than 2,000,000 in cities of similar size, and even France (including Paris) had only 3,000,000. He does not mention England, which was then more urbanized than the United States, but England's urban population was concentrated in London and a few manufacturing centers. Moreover, in the decades prior to Ratzel's visit, the proportional increase of England's large-city dwellers was slower and the number of these metropolises smaller than in the United States. Thus England's example does not invalidate his assertion about the rapidity and extent of America's urban development.[13]

In describing American cities, he makes frequent comparisons to those in Europe, especially in Germany, stating that American ones contain more hustle and bustle, fewer unemployed, more single family dwellings, etc. He calls attention to how these new metropolises differed from their European counterparts by noting five characteristics generally present: 1) the frequent use of the grid plan or systematic layout of the city, most notably in Philadelphia, which was in turn used as a model by other cities in the American West; 2) the amount of heavy traffic found in the city streets; 3) the predominant number of small private homes; 4) the division of business and residential areas; and 5) the space allotted to parks filled with greenery.

The grid plan he believes was very sensible, allowing for wider avenues, which in turn facilitate commerce as well as the installation of sewage, gas, and water systems. He is thus practical enough to see that many urban amenities were facilitated by this layout. The traffic in the city, although noisy and unsettling, connotes for him a vital and flourishing culture and prosperous economy. Moreover, forethought had been given to accommodate traffic by a system of trolleys or mass transit, which he feels was a great improvement over municipal transportation facilities in many European cities. Like the steam engine, he says, this mode of travel brought everyone closer together. Although there had been discussions about developing the trolley system on the continent, little had been done to put it into operation."The Americans are right," he notes, "when they say that appropriately broad streets in which a trolley line can be built are a fundamental prerequisite of a big city" (p.28). The ease with which one could travel from place to place, from home to business, encouraged people to live farther out from the center, to build their own homes, which, while tending to divide business from residential areas, provided for independent dwellings in the fresh air. In Europe, business and residential areas were generally not separate, with many shopkeepers living above or not far from their place of business. In other words, Ratzel is already sensitive to the idea of suburban living, even before it was to become more prevalent in Europe.

As for the parks, he remarks that even people familiar with the Bois de Boulogne in Paris or the Prater in Vienna would have been surprised to see the space allotted by the city planners to such areas of greenery as Central Park in New York or Fairmount Park in Philadelphia. Even cemeteries were beautifully laid out in America and seemed to him to be as much places for the living to come, relax, and reflect, as they were places of rest for the dead. By the 1880s, the situation was to be reversed and America would be sending observers to study new ideas about city planning in Germany; but until the 1870s, when Ratzel was writing, many European urban centers, with the notable exception of Haussmann's reconstruction of Paris during the Second Napoleonic Empire, had developed haphazardly with little forethought to a systematically planned city that took into account all the needs of the inhabitants. Older European parks consequently had an aristocratic tradition, belonging to or having been established by royalty or nobility. In America, Ratzel was seeing cities, and large cities at that, which had developed within a generation, seeking to solve some of the problems created by rapid growth with systematic planning, by making provisions for traffic and public recreational areas.

In recording his findings, Ratzel also interrelates cities throughout the narrative and weaves into each separate and individual analysis a comparative thread that allows a reader to see the entire network of associations and developments stretching from coast to coast and from the industrial hub of America out to the broader reaches of world trade, commerce, and culture. It is this comprehensiveness of observation that gives his work one of its unique qualities. Moreover, Ratzel makes comparisons between American cities, offering, for example, New York's ethnic cosmopolitanism as a reason for its growing faster than its sister metropolises; or, sensing a deficiency in what were in general good ideas in urban design, he makes recommendations for a city's improvement, such as cutting a diagonal road through Philadelphia's grid plan in order to improve traffic conditions.

Taking into consideration the geographic site, the overall economic development of an area, and the competition among several cities, Ratzel also occasionally makes predictions about the future of an urban center; he diagnoses the disadvantages Cincinnati had to face in competition with St. Louis and Chicago and foresees that they would outpace the Ohio metropolis in growth. In the South he observes that large cities were generally lacking, that industry and education were slow in starting, and that hence the South still lagged behind the North. But with the war over and unity secured, these problems, he suggests, would eventually be overcome. Although his basic purpose was to inform, not to instruct, and his methods were exemplative not theoretical, Ratzel nonetheless illustrates what had been done in America, hints at what could be done in Europe, and suggests what should be done in any urbanizing, modernizing society.

Although primarily considered a geographer, our German visitor, attentive to origins and changes in a city's life, places his analysis in a historical framework and seeks the reasons for this rapid growth of the American city. Besides natural increase, he understandably attributes it to European and rural immigration, which in turn he regards as a factor of modernization. In addition, in each of his sketches, he begins with an analysis of the geographic location and its advantages for urban growth; he traces its historical development and indicates in most cases how geographic factors were helpful for commerce and industry, which then in consequence were largely instrumental in spurring urban development. The other element for growth that he stresses is the importance of the means of transportation, especially the railroad, in spreading urban culture and ideas, causing large cities to grow closer together, aiding smaller cities and towns to imitate the great metropolises, and lessening the differences between town and country. This interacting process in turn strengthened urban influences, since the newly improved and enlarged transportation facilities took the teacher, the salesman, and the newspaper from the city into the countryside. The railroads expanding in the West, the canals connecting the Great Lakes with natural waterways, and great rivers like the Mississippi and the Missouri carrying a large share of the nation's products to waiting markets are all cited as examples to support his argument. When he is not observing cities and the life of their inhabitants, he is frequently writing of his journey on the railroad in the South or over the Rockies or on a steamboat up the Mississippi, always stressing the value of good transportation and its potential and use for furthering trade, cultural integration, and urban growth. Modernized, efficient, and speedy transportation, he says, was a phenomenon the emerging new society would have to reckon with as a factor of growth.

Educated as a naturalist and experienced as a journalist, an individual with a scholarly sensitivity to detail and factual bases for impressions and observations, Ratzel was more knowledgeable than many other travelers, for he was trained as a researcher who viewed things with a professional eye. Although scientists, scholars, and journalists had visited our shores before, in Ratzel we see the qualities of all three combined in one person who by acknowledging the importance of large cities in America pointed to one of the essential aspects then being identified with modern society throughout the western world. In addition, recent events in Germany and the proclamation of the German Empire in 1871 no doubt influenced or helped focus his interest on the city and its interrelation with industrialization, commercial expansion, the growth of economic wealth, improved facilities for research, and technological improvement: these were important elements in the modernizing process to which a state like Germany, having completed its political unification, could then turn its attention.

The similarities for future institutional, economic, and social development in both countries must have been evident. Like the United States, Germany had just gone through a war of unification, which not only consolidated the country politically but helped unify the monetary system, the weights and measures, civil and commercial law, tariffs, etc.—all prerequisites for a more efficient state. What Bismarck had called the tragedy of the ages—the disunity among the German states—had been surmounted. Like the United States, Germany in the Bismarckian era of the 1870s needed and received a period of undisturbed peace to consolidate, coordinate, and grow. Like the United States, which in 1870 was trying to put the agony of the Civil War behind it and rebuild a sense of nationhood, Germany in this period was also trying to put the upheaval of its three wars of unification behind it and to develop a more concrete sense of German nationalism.[14]

Like the United States, Germany also had large iron and coal deposits, so necessary for industrialization, and had cities favorably located on the waterways, the Rhine, the Elbe, the Oder, and the Weser, which controlled the center of the continent. Moreover, its railroad system, developing since the 1820s, had made a major contribution toward bringing the individual German states closer together and therefore toward national unity. As the economic historian J. H. Clapham was later to remark, the impact of the railroads on German life had something American about it "just as there was a technical likeness between German and American railway methods."[15] The decade 1865–1875 saw the completion of virtually all essential railway lines in Germany, just as in America the same period saw the completion of the transcontinental railroad link. German unification also provided the potential for greater urban growth, first by its stimulus to commerce and industry, and second by enlarging the area from which cities could attract workers to swell their ranks. During this period, Germany's coal production tripled, and steel production in the early years of the Empire more than tripled. Exports rose from 2.5 to 3.5 billion marks. As a consequence, these basic industries spurred on others such as the textile and chemical industries, and a very rapid population growth assisted this development by providing a ready and inexpensive labor force. All of these German developments in commerce, industry, and technological progress were centered in and around large cities. In 1871 Germany had only eight cities of over 100,000 inhabitants, by 1900 there were thirty-three, and by 1910 there were forty-eight.[16] Between 1870 and 1900, what Ratzel sensed, the worldwide extension of modern urban societies, and what he observed taking place in America, was also becoming a reality in Germany.

Ratzel was no doubt impressed by these similarities and also by the rapidity with which urbanization was taking place in both countries. In 1890 three of the eight largest cities in the western world were American, and their annual rate of increase from 1850 to 1890 was prodigious: New York's population had increased fourfold, Philadelphia had doubled in size, but most impressive were the cities that had only recently become thriving metropolises, such as Chicago, which in its early years during the 1850s had increased thirty-six times in size. The European centers that came close to this were Berlin, whose population had increased five times, and Vienna, which had tripled in size, as compared to Paris and London whose population had only doubled; the slowness in proportional growth of the latter two, however, was in part due to their already considerable size.[17] Undoubtedly, Ratzel was impressed by the growth of German cities as well as by other factors conducive to modernization and expansion and by developments caused or furthered by the recent unification. A man such as Ratzel, who was initially aware of the importance of geographic factors and whose theories were only reinforced by his American experiences, would naturally want to share his observations with his fellow Germans as a basis of comparison and as a means of highlighting what could be done in Germany, which was then in a period of national self-concern, undergoing its period of great industrial, commercial, and urban expansion. He was able to point out the reasons why and how it was happening by observing the phenomenon in America, where it had occurred a little earlier and a bit faster than in Europe.

Tocqueville, in his famous book on the United States published between 1835 and 1840, defines American society especially in terms of its character and its institutions, but also its environment. Ratzel, who was familiar with and refers to Tocqueville's work, approaches his subject from the opposite direction. While paying heed to the first two aspects, he gives greater prominence to the third—to the environment. Whereas Tocqueville is the analyst of American political institutions, Ratzel is the analyst of American urban life; whereas Tocqueville discusses the leveling and equalizing effect of democratic institutions upon society, Ratzel stresses the practical effect of such tendencies on society, as for example in his discussion of New York's trolleys, which had no class-segregated cars and were used by rich and poor alike. Man's environment and his use of it were changing his mode of living and ushering in a new urban society. Tocqueville sees the political future in terms of democracy that, whether in favor of it or not, one had to live with and so must understand. Ratzel's vision of the social future is an urban one, which was constantly expanding the frontiers of its influence; and in order to allay some of the anxiety about the direction in which modernization was going, he tries to identify some of its characteristics as seen in the United States.

Whereas the historian Frederick Jackson Turner some twenty years later in *The Significance of the Frontier in American History* (1893) and in other works was to disregard or at least omit the city as an important consideration for the growth of the American frontier, placing emphasis instead on the yeoman farmer, Ratzel visualizes the reverse, positing for his time the novel view of the superiority of urban life developing all over America, an urban frontier so to speak. The city was not the end but the spearhead of the frontier. Whereas Turner might view the city as jeopardizing the American character, Ratzel sees it as a crucial and beneficial influence, one whose culture was fast penetrating and dominating rural traditions and values. The "cities," he asserts, "bring out the greatest, best, and most typical aspects of a people" (p. 3). The strength of America's greatness emanated from the cities, the source of knowledge, wealth, and industrialization. As the frontier progressed, so did the cities, which in turn sent railroads and other means of communication toward the next frontier.

Ratzel shows a preference for the East Coast, devoting more than half of the book to Eastern cities. It was, however, here that large-city life was most developed and where its accomplishments could best be evaluated. For each city he carefully selects aspects that illustrate urban life as a whole but also are indicative of the place he is then visiting—New York for its board of health, Cambridge for its academic life, Philadelphia for its newspaper publishing. Having established his basic premises about urban life in these chapters, he goes on to describe other cities in briefer fashion, concentrating on their unique contributions. That he found little to praise at that time in a Western city like Denver is understandable insofar as he was unable yet to detect the clear outlines of a future metropolis in what was then still very much a frontier settlement. That he devotes more than three-quarters of the book to descriptions of areas that extend scarcely beyond the Mississippi tells us more about American urban geography at that time than about his preferences. In the Far West of the 1870s there were few large cities that were "musts" for the visitor except for San Francisco, in which he duly arrived by way of the Pacific Railroad. Metropolises like Los Angeles, Dallas, and Phoenix were still to develop in the future in a manner that would only serve to support Ratzel's thesis.

The subjects selected for comment by Ratzel within each city are of interest not only for what they tell us about America in the 1870s but also for what they say about Europe. Many things we now take for granted—a predominance of female teachers in elementary schools, a college president chosen not for his educational but his administrative abilities, a government bureau for predicting the weather, broad streets and rational layouts facilitating traffic—were in large part new to many European readers and were held up for admiration and possible emulation by the author. It requires a foreigner to remind us of the novelty of these things to which we have routinely become accustomed.

Moreover, his comments about city life of little more than a hundred years ago also give us an opportunity to reflect on what things have and have not changed since Ratzel visited our shores. His verbal portraits of cosmopolitan life and culture are reminders of a world we have lost, of a time that today's Americans can perceive only from surviving fragments of nineteenth-century American life preserved in our architecture, cinema, literature, or other arts. Many of these descriptions, some of which are very far removed from our everyday experience, such as trips to health springs, become all the more intrinsically interesting and valuable as historical depictions for contemporary readers. When one walks through the downtown area of many large American cities today, Ratzel's comments about the deserted quality of the urban commercial district after sundown and on weekends, the streets filled with sidewalk vendors, the high cost of labor, or the ubiquity of aggressive advertising ring as true for many metropolises as they did one hundred years ago. On the other hand, his comments also serve to highlight what has changed. Few Americans today would characterize our public schools as maintaining a stricter discipline than that of European schools, and the statement that the American people have a greater love of nature and are closer to it than are the Europeans, as demonstrated by the beautiful parks and green borders along most of America's urban streets, is a subject that at least can still be seriously debated.

True, there are certain topics associated with urban living and the suffering that life in a large city brings to many people—unemployment, the breakdown of family values and life styles, the rise of crime—he does not address, some of which, as he mentions in his preface, he neglected because of space limitations. Since he generally only comments on matters he had carefully studied, he also perhaps believed that he did not have sufficient knowledge (be the reason lack of facts, time, or interest) for conclusions on such subjects, or perhaps that Europe would not profit from either positive or negative examples of the American experience in these areas. He does, however, remark on overcrowding in tenement housing as well as on the problem of sanitation and disease control, which American cities were combating with their municipal health bureaus. In this respect he again believes that America was ahead of Germany: "Some big cities in Germany are suffering considerably more from the problem of overcrowding and provide in every respect poorer housing for their lower classes than does New York, but one pays unquestionably more attention to this here than elsewhere" (note, p. 35).

He does not remain uncritical of life in American cities, for he cites many things he dislikes such as the dirty streets, the lack of taste in architecture, which he says cannot be compensated for by magnificence or wealth, and the dangers of a too practical society that gives small heed to aesthetic values or is occupied with the acquisition of material gain at the expense of encouraging philosophy and the arts among the general public. He is also aware of contemporary social currents and problems within American society, including the role of women and the attitude toward blacks. He is pleased to see that women are represented in the teaching profession and attend university lectures more so than in Europe. While disapproving of the insipid, heavily made-up women, so often met in America by the European traveler, he pays tribute to the American women who in search of education and learning have pursued a course of reading and discussion that enables them to discourse on a wider range of subjects than many of their counterparts in Europe and thus to merit the position of respect women have attained within American society. His comments on blacks, however, are mixed and reflect some general nineteenth-century impressions of blacks as generally indolent and untidy. His comments are, no doubt, in part conditioned by the people with whom he spoke. But he also shows admiration for the noble character of some blacks he met and for the oratory and style of black politicians whom, despite white allegations to the contrary, he finds to be as good at speaking as their white colleagues. If the black legislators were at times inept or corrupt, they were doing no worse than their former masters whom they had as models of right conduct. Ratzel expresses sympathy for the blacks' long years of oppression and shows understanding for their sometimes "droll misgovernment" in the Reconstruction South, and he hopes for a solution to the race problem, fearing that when the whites regained control, the blacks would once more be reduced to an abject state.

He also takes the opportunity of pointing to problems that were either not addressed or solved by Americans themselves until much later, such as the renovation and reconstruction of downtown Boston, the unsuitability of San Francisco's peninsular location for dealing with any large-scale influx of traffic, and the needs of educating the blacks, especially in the South, all of which became public concerns in the twentieth century. In his last chapter, entitled "Ruins," with a caption stating that America is aging rapidly, Ratzel gives a most perceptive warning about a serious American problem. In a very philosophical mood, he pauses, after all the things he has viewed, all the bright spots in the American scene, to reflect on some of the negative consequences of American growth. There are dangers, he says, to an overrapid development. In these last few pages, in almost Spenglerian terms, the author describes the ghost towns, the abandoned sites, the debris he has observed along the railroads, the refuse of a young, disposable society that had resorted to the destructive exploitation of its natural resources. He warns that too rapid modernization and urbanization also have their pitfalls, since they can only bring waste, and that speed for speed's sake should by no means be the criterion for development. Rather, he explains, new growth should be carefully channeled and adequate measures taken to avert the dangers that are inherent in these processes. These last pages can be read in almost allegorical terms as a portrait of the decline of a civilization after too rapid modernization, America is in too much of a hurry and lives too rapidly. If it does not take time, Ratzel suggests, to conserve and make prudent decisions, nature will once more return, overwhelm the ruins left by man, and restore the places where humans once lived and worked to landscapes where nothing is any longer in a hurry. Ratzel, therefore, is one of the first travelers to add an ecological note to his writings.[18] Europe was supposed to profit not only by America's progress but also from its mistakes.

Ratzel at times is too romantic, too philosophic, too much a representative of the nineteenth century for our late twentieth-century tastes. These things, however, are more than compensated for by his keen observations and insightful analysis backed up by statistics or factual documentation. His conversational tone, which in word choice and syntax seems at times quaint, even archaic, to our ear and eye works to its own advantages by providing the historical imprint for a period tableau. Likewise, Ratzel's bold facts and depictions of the uncanny stages in the development of a young nation make him appear at times like a hard-hitting newspaperman out to get his story. Moreover, his narrative is by no means monotonous, for he varies his style: at times he pauses to be contemplative, as when describing the destruction in the South, at times he is conversational, as when explaining his encounters with boarding-house life in Alabama, at times he is analytically comparative, as when contrasting certain conditions in Europe and America, at times prophetic, as when envisioning the future potential of various metropolises, and at times narrative, as when elaborately using words to describe grand scenes for an age that had no camera to take the place of close observation. It is difficult to forget his panoramic description of New York Bay, which encompasses the vista, the excitement, and the combination of natural grandeur and human potential; of his trip up the Hudson, which parallels in words what painters such as Thomas Cole, Frederick Edwin Church, or John Frederick Kensett depicted on their canvases; or of the dramatic destructiveness of nature seen in the Mississippi valley after the disastrous spring flood of 1874.

Whether this book is considered a detailed set of one man's ideas and personal observations or a history of social and cultural development in the decade after the Civil War, it is a document of absorbing interest. Moreover, it is not only of value for giving us a European view of a period in American history for which we have few German accounts of significance but also is of importance for its timeliness. Ratzel came to America when it was in transition from a simpler to a more complex way of life, from a rural to an urban society, from an agrarian to an industrial, more centralized and integrated nation. He was here to perceive and to record his perceptions whether they were about the effects of the Civil War, the efforts at rebuilding, or the racial problems with blacks, Chinese, and Indians. He was here to see the increase and importance of railroad traffic and to chronicle the decline in river traffic and to enable his reader, via his essays, to travel on both the old and the new modes of transportation. He was here to observe, firsthand, historical events such as the preparations for the nation's centennial, the disgruntlement in the South with Reconstruction policies, the rebuilding of Chicago after the terrible fire of 1871, the

American public schools in dramatic transition with the beginning of the systematization of education, the emergence of the modern American university, and the increasing problem of teaching poor children. He was here at a time when the Federal Government was unifying its administrative agencies in order to provide better and more efficient services. It was in the 1870s that the U.S. Weather Bureau was created to provide accurate prognostications for most of the country; it was the decade when flood control along the Mississippi was put under Federal supervision, when several competing Federal agencies engaged in scientific surveys, such as the Hayden Reports, were combined and superceded by the U.S. Geological Survey, and when stirrings of ecological concern prompted the creation of the world's first national park at Yellowstone. Ratzel was here at a time that was alive with change and a sense of growth, progress, and vitality as America prepared to enter its second century of existence, and his narrative indicates some of these changes and reflects some of the currents of that dynamic period in our history.

One wonders what Ratzel's evaluation of American cities would be today, for there is still much dirt to be found in them, still the hustle, bustle, and noise of traffic, and innumerably more problems than he visualized. Fortunately, however, there are measures underway in many urban centers to preserve or restore those elements Ratzel found so good in the culture and life of the urban civilization—to replant trees and provide greenery in the inner cities, to cut down on the noise, and to prevent waste, to cite but a few worthwhile efforts. Ratzel's account of his visit in 1873–1874 was indeed then farsighted. He provided his contemporaries with a vision of the future age and has also given readers of today an insight into our own cultural development and into those aspects of culture we should foster and encourage, as well as into those we should attempt to change. He sensed as a foreigner so early what historians were to analyze later, that the nineteenth century was becoming the era of large cities, that instead of a wilderness or a country of farmlands, America was becoming a nation of large metropolises, and that urbanization was becoming a factor in the modernizing process of the entire western world. He gives us then a clear, precise, yet lively account of the nature and dimensions of America's large-city growth, of how its culture pervaded the entire society and was eventually to dominate the rural, and of what it was like to live in cities affected by this growth. Perhaps only someone coming from a country experiencing similar developments and equipped with the scholar's love of detail and accuracy and the journalist's skill in observation and narration would with interest, admiration, and a little bit of envy, have been able to identify and describe this development so early and so well.

In translating this book I have tried to keep as close to the German text as possible. Small mistakes of a factual nature, where they do not disturb the sense of the narrative, have been left in the text to show what Ratzel actually said. I have at times, for example's sake, added a note to indicate a correction without burdening the text with excessive notes. Mindful, however, of St. Paul's dictum that the "letter killeth but the spirit giveth life," I have corrected minor errors and inconsistencies and altered several colloquial expressions to convey the meaning more effectively to a twentieth-century audience. I have also divided up many long paragraphs and sentences into smaller units and eliminated some redundant phrases to provide a smoother flow in the narrative. Nevertheless, I have still chosen to keep some of the author's long sentences, parenthetic phrases, and, to our ears, quaint expressions in order to retain a bit of the nineteenth-century flavor. A modern reader might be tempted to blame the writer, the translator, or the German language for the long, thought-filled sentences. One has only to glance at the works of Dickens or Trollope to be reminded of the similarities in the descriptive writing of native English speakers of that century. To alter all of Ratzel's syntax would render the translation too contemporary.

Ratzel's methods of expressing weights and distances proves to be quite varied. At different times he uses centners, tons, feet, meters, kilometers, and English statute, geographic, and German Imperial miles—whatever most conveniently conveys his intention in a given sentence. I have retained Ratzel's terminology, but whenever not stated in measurements generally familiar to today's reader, I have also added in parentheses the more commonly recognized terms such as statute miles, feet, etc.[19] The author's original usage has been preserved, however, to show how, in an age when units of weights and measures were not yet standardized, Ratzel and some of his readers could, or perhaps were obliged to, reckon in not one but in several systems of measurement.

There are many people to whom I owe a debt of gratitude for their aid in bringing this book to completion. Of these I would like to single out my colleague at New York University, Bayrd Still, who first suggested to me that this book be translated into English and whose advice and encouragement over the years have been a great source of comfort. In addition, there are many other colleagues and friends who were generous with their time and suggestions, either to offer information about Ratzel and the historical background for this book, or to explain a difficult or obscure German or specialized term: Paul Becker, Maximilian Bucher, Irmgard Deuerlein, Ursula Huber, and Daniel Walkowitz. The staff of New York University's Bobst Library was most cooperative in helping me track down some obscure references in the text. The Faculty of Arts and Science Dean's Office of New York University very generously provided me with funds to help defray expenses in preparing the pictures and the map. Daniel Halford, Brian Hotaling, Eugene Richie, Frederick Schult, and Robert Tomes, despite their busy schedules, generously gave of their time to read the manuscript. Demetrios Mihailidis and Gerard Sheridan assisted with some of the technical aspects of preparing this manuscript. To all of these people I wish to express my sincere and heartfelt thanks. Lastly, as with past research projects, I wish to thank my mother for her advice and encouragement and for her patience and willingness in typing the drafts of this work.

STEWART A. STEHLIN
New York, N.Y.
October 1987

SKETCHES OF URBAN AND CULTURAL

LIFE IN NORTH AMERICA

Ratzel's travel route in 1873–1874

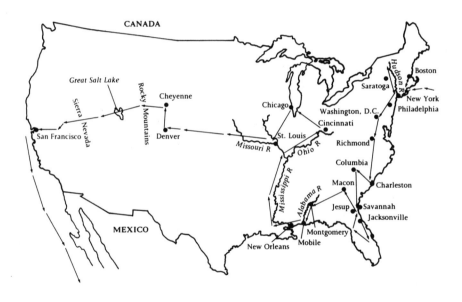

NOTE: RATZEL VISITED MORE PLACES THAN DEPICTED IN HIS BOOK AND AT TIMES TOOK A MORE COMPLICATED ROUTE THAN SHOWN HERE. I HAVE SIMPLIFIED HIS TRAVEL ROUTE AND OMITTED SOME PLACES NOT MENTIONED IN THE *SKETCHES*. FOR ADDITIONAL SITES THAT RATZEL VISITED SEE GÜNTHER BUTTMAN, *FRIEDRICH RATZEL* (STUTTGART, 1977), PP. 43–46 AND MAP ON P. 45.

Preface

The following chapters present impressions about cities, urban life, and related subjects I gathered during a trip to the United States in 1873–1874. During those years the great majority of the chapters appeared as articles in the *Kölnische Zeitung*. They now appear here before the public in a revised and considerably expanded form and, taken together, give a general view of the character and importance of the large and small cities of that land. A study of urban life in North America can also be of considerable significance for cultural history. The facts offered here were checked with care, and this little work, without attempting to be an exhaustive inquiry, can claim to present the subject accurately.

The journey upon which these sketches of urban life are based was made on behalf of the *Kölnische Zeitung*. If my travel impressions are significant and important enough to have any value, I would attribute that first of all to a freedom of movement, which permitted me to stay a while where I considered it necessary and to bypass places where nothing attracted me. And for this freedom I am thankful to the directors of the *Kölnische Zeitung* who believed in the value of my trip.

Several important questions, such as social conditions, city government, the press, the role of the Germans in cities where they are found in great numbers, as St. Louis, Chicago, and Cincinnati, have merely been touched upon in this little work. Space was too limited, because of so many other subjects, to treat these problems with the thoroughness their importance demanded.

The life of a people is blended, compressed, and accelerated in cities, with the result that it not only becomes richer and more productive but also that its characteristics become clearer and present a lasting testimony to posterity. Cities bring out the greatest, best, and most typical aspects of a people. Not only in today's world do cities collect and bring together the most significant things which civilization has produced, that is, the best in science, art, industry, wealth, endeavor, and talent, but they have done this in every age; therefore it can be said that the history of big cities comprises the history of the world. Their names alone—Thebes, Babylon, Jerusalem, Athens, Rome—are like chapter headings of the most important epochs in world history; bright titles that summarize everything these epochs say and mean, and any one of them, whenever spoken aloud, almost magically evokes an entire world in our minds. Out of the interaction of the spirits of bygone days in these cities arises what we call history. The countryside has no history, often for thousands of years, for one generation plows, sows, and harvests there just like the next. One has only to look at Rome where, despite the most important changes the city has experienced, the shepherd of the Campagna has remained with only slight modification an old Roman peasant.[1]

In modern times, however, several factors have worked to lessen the division between the city and the country. Better transportation facilities make it possible for countries with many cities or completely urbanized areas to import their grain and meat products from predominantly agricultural regions which lack urban development and also remove the need for people to live as close as possible to one another in order to interact in business, trade, or intellectual pursuits. The dwellings of the rural inhabitants are becoming as urbanized as their life styles. Agriculture through mechanization is beginning to resemble industry, and the curse of working by the sweat of the brow to earn one's bread is losing its onerous, all-too-literal meaning even for the farmer. All this contributes to bringing the small cities and villages closer together.

On the other hand, however, large cities are growing more quickly today and in greater numbers than ever before. Just as the small amount and slower means of travel in earlier times fostered the growth of small- and middle-size cities, today's incomparably more abundant and more rapid transportation facilities favor big cities. There is something basic to the nature of these facilities which tends to bring them together at several important geographic points while bypassing less important ones, consolidating the secondary arteries into fewer but more effective main arteries. For this reason no century before ours has seen the growth of so many large cities. Metropolises must develop when the world's traffic increases, and this has been demonstrated not simply in Europe but even more clearly on those continents where transport systems found untapped riches and slumbering forces to awaken and into which they then breathed an almost unbelievable life. One has only to remember that at the beginning of this century North America did not contain one single city of 100,000 inhabitants or more while it now has fourteen.[2] During the same period, along the entire periphery of the Pacific Ocean, great world trade centers have arisen from the tiniest beginnings or from virtually nothing: Singapore, Hong Kong, Shanghai, San Francisco, Melbourne, Sydney—not to mention the South American ones. If we consider then these great events overseas as well as a series of similar occurrences on a somewhat smaller scale which are taking place all around us in Europe, then we cannot doubt that the drive to develop large cities and the lessening of the difference between city and country are two of the most important "trademarks" of our time.

North America, this wonderland of modern civilization, has also run ahead of the Old World with regard to these two tendencies. In Europe every seed of civilization must with great difficulty work itself out of the thick sterile underbrush which has been allowed to continue growing for centuries, to work itself out of dirt and dust, and then it is often enough choked before it sees the light of day. But in North America it grows in fresh, unspoiled, virgin soil as luxuriantly as corn or wheat in the black soil of the prairies. It does just as much good for seeds of thought as normal biological seeds to have an undisturbed period of growth, for they both are tender and susceptible to disturbing influences and both respond most positively to good care. That is the reason this youthfully vigorous people has surpassed us so quickly in the development of modern inventions. With a vigor and determination for which we Europeans have no example, they have learned how to harness steamships, railways, the telegraph system, and agricultural machines to their uses.

Moreover, they have also transplanted accomplishments of a higher intellectual order to their virgin soil with no less decisiveness and perseverance, and these are thriving equally well. All levels of instruction, from the university to the basic primary school, the education of the general public, the manner in which inexpensive books and newspapers as well as the living word are disseminated, all offer proof for this statement. In the Eastern states, where the wealth that has been amassed here for some time has already made life more comfortable for thousands, the cultivation of the arts and sciences has already assumed an important role. Given these circumstances, it is evident that in this country the new tendencies in urban growth will manifest themselves more clearly than in Europe because here in America the cities are the centers of every important cultural development. In this regard North America is the forerunner of Europe. The fact alone that more than 4,000,000 people live there in cities of over 100,000 inhabitants, while for example in Germany with a larger population only 2,100,000, and in rich France with its metropolis, Paris, only 3,100,000 live in cities of this size, only emphasizes the significance of the cities for this young land. North American cities not only resemble one another in the essential features all cities more or less possess but also resemble European cities in many incidental characteristics. Conversely, in many respects they also exhibit individualistic traits, which are so strongly pronounced in certain external aspects of city life that the physiognomy of North American cities takes on a definitely foreign appearance for us. This applies less to the newer cities than to the older ones. In the latter, one still finds sections that lack very little for them to look completely European—although these areas are generally already so completely engulfed by newer structures that only in a few instances do they still determine the character of the city.

The old Puritan city of Salem in Massachusetts, the former Spanish St. Augustine on the east coast of Florida, and, of the big cities, Quebec in Canada are the most prominent of the few really old cities of North America. Boston, New York, and New Orleans contain old sections that resemble our old cities with narrow, winding little streets. But only in Boston do these streets, reinforced by the city's hilly terrain, contribute to the general character of the city. Other cities that cannot be considered new, like Philadelphia and Charleston, were laid out from the very beginning in a broad and regular manner.

The new cities of the West, however, which have come to prominence in the last fifty years, as well as the newer parts of all older cities, are like model cities, laid out spaciously, airily, and regularly. Unfortunately, the good intentions for the city layout were not completely realized in some instances because of difficulties with the sites. For example, the hilly areas of Cincinnati and San Francisco restrict traffic in many directions, and all the splendor of the newer sections of New Orleans do not compensate for the disadvantage of the city's swampy site at the mouth of the Mississippi.

Apart from unessential local peculiarities, when one considers the overall impression of the larger American cities, four characteristics can definitely be cited. They are: the broad, straight streets, the heavy traffic, the small size of the average house, and the sharp division between business and residential areas. The great number of small-sized houses is especially striking in really big cities like New York and Philadelphia, the latter standing unique among the big cities of the world in this regard. The reason for such buildings stems from a healthy preference for private family dwellings and certainly contributes a great deal to the physical and psychological well-being of the inhabitants. But in the long run, this method of building homes cannot continue to the degree that it is now being employed. In New York the number of huge tenement houses, which make better use of land and capital investment, are increasing rapidly from year to year. In addition, the separation of commercial and residential buildings according to specifically defined areas, which are often far away from one another, must contribute to the well-being of the inhabitants, alleviate the commercial traffic problem, and promote a comfortable, healthy, and reasonable life style. This separation is so practical that it appears to have been carried out even in the smaller cities. It presupposes, however, good and numerous means of transportation, which in the form of horse-drawn trolley cars is not lacking in a middle-sized or large city. Even cities of upwards of twenty thousand inhabitants and very frequently also smaller ones have this means of transportation. In turn, the trolleys presuppose broad, straight streets if they are going to carry out their function properly. Likewise, the installation of gas conduits and drainage systems, which already are much more extensively in use here than in Europe, as well as water mains, upon which the Americans put such high value, are also facilitated by the systematic layout of the cities.

The friendly rural character prevails in the smaller cities because of the attractiveness and neatness of the houses, which are usually built out of whitewashed wood or covered with this material, the little gardens, which without exception surround them, and the rows of shade trees, which are rarely missing from a street. A trace of this idyllic picture is still preserved even in the middle of New York, Boston, and most especially in Philadelphia by the rows of trees lining the streets, the small lawns in front of the houses, and the climbing plants on their balconies. Even in San Francisco, despite the dry sandy soil, they have at least planted eucalyptus trees, which require little water. On the other hand, here in America many fewer flowers are placed in the windows than in Germany.

Nevertheless, it is the beautiful parks and public gardens, even more than these green and shady borders along the streets, that give us an idea of the closeness to nature of American culture and its inhabitants' love of nature—something one would scarcely have expected if it did not keep recurring as the most marked theme in their recent literature.[3] They have spent huge sums in the more important cities for parks and public gardens, and even Europeans who are familiar with the Prater or the Bois de Boulogne[4] will be astonished by the size and magnificence of Fairmount Park in Philadelphia or of Central Park in New York. For my taste, Fairmount Park offers the most beauty that one can expect in a park, since it not only has mile-long expanses of wooded area and lawn of all kinds, but right in the middle there is also a wide river and a murmuring brook running between green-covered banks. The entire area is imperceptibly beautified nature. Moreover, the new cities of Cincinnati and St. Louis already have beautiful park grounds too.

Like these public parks and gardens, the cemeteries in all reasonably important cities of North America are also magnificent, generously endowed and, to some extent, tastefully laid out and maintained. By and large, one sees here the attempt to obliterate the melancholy character of rows of graves through all possible means of landscaping and artistic ornamentation. This simple purpose, offering the dead an undisturbed place of rest, is much less important than making cemeteries pleasant places of reflection and relaxation for the living. In the larger cities, all, as in New York, or at least some of the cemeteries are situated on the most beautiful sites. From the famous Greenwood Cemetery near New York, one enjoys a view of New York, Brooklyn, and the ocean—a view that perhaps can only be rivaled by that of Vienna of all the great cities.[5] In Boston, Mt. Auburn Cemetery has a much more beautiful location and display of greenery than the Boston Common or the Public Garden, and in Washington and Richmond the cemeteries have the cities' most attractive observation points and park grounds. In this respect the South does not lag behind the North. An abundance of fine monuments exists here also—too many perhaps not to give the impression of pretentiousness and of mounds of piled up stone. Nevertheless, in a cemetery like Greenwood or Mt. Auburn, thick groves of the most beautiful trees alternate with flower beds, little lakes alternate with hills, and all sorts of slopes, lawns, hedges, and the like are arranged in the most natural manner. Paths lined with magnolia, linden, oak, and chestnut trees (most of which have name placards on them like the streets in the cities of the living) crisscross each other in every direction. One row of vaults leads into the actual burial chambers through Egyptian temple gates, another through a colonnade, and still another through chapels, while the most costly monuments, both beautiful and impressive because of their oddness, crowd around in large numbers. All this forms a particularly attractive setting, which above all brightens and enriches the dull life of the big city.

Less attractive than these places of rest and relaxation, with which American cities surely leave their European sisters far behind, are their large and grandiose so-called "beautiful" public structures. For a long time the people here decorated these structures with only Greek and Roman columns as can still be seen on the majority of buildings more than thirty years old, especially in Philadelphia, Boston, and Washington. This true republican style was even popular for church architecture. But more recently the Americans have experimented with all possible and impossible styles and have a special liking for entirely new combinations. With very little finesse they seek to produce the desired effect by means of originality or every kind of the most absurd ornamental overloading. Architectural unrest and exaggeration are seen in most edifices which are supposed to be significant, and one has to search for simple beauty and nobility in modest, unassuming works. Often one can still console onself mostly by the stone used in building, of which North America can boast an excellent and abundant variety, be it granite, marble, or sandstone.

As is well known, bridge building has celebrated some of its greatest triumphs in North America. In truth, it is these achievements which make the greatest impression on the visitor. The new Mississippi bridge at St. Louis and the Ohio bridges at Louisville and Cincinnati[6] definitely enhance the general appearance of these cities more than all their church steeples and splendid houses. The giant bridge now rising on pilings between New York and Brooklyn will add a new element to the already splendid skyline of New York's harbor which will surpass all others in grandeur.[7] The insignificant fact that all river steamers, whether big or small, are painted white is also worth mentioning. In the vicinity of bustling cities situated on big rivers—such as New York, Philadelphia, Cincinnati, and St. Louis—large numbers of these bright vessels give the river scene a cheerful character—as opposed to the impression which our black, smoke-covered, dirt-ladened boats produce. Also what appears to be trivial yet in reality is important is that in the big cities of the East they prefer to burn only Pennsylvania anthracite coal, which does not cause soot. This is why Philadelphia, despite its large industry, has not in the least become blackened. Cincinnati, which burns a coal that produces a great deal of soot, looks much older and gloomier than any of the big eastern cities, and this applies even more so to Pittsburgh.

The population of all American cities, with the exception of the Southern ones where the Negroes sport their indolence, is distinguished by their versatile, active, and industrious life style. You can scarcely go along the street without noticing these characteristics, which are as evident in the small cities as in the larger ones. A visitor is also struck by the degree of respectability in both dress and behavior one encounters. One would not be wrong in saying that the population of the big cities is as a rule youthful in comparison to those in the small towns and the rural sections, which in general is due to the influx of young immigrants from both Europe and the farm areas. The huge market for inexpensive newspapers, magazines, and books offered for sale at every street corner seems to corroborate the fact that a medium-level education is fairly widespread in this country. The education of the populace, however, does not prevent the churches from enjoying good attendance, and American cities have on the whole more churches than do German ones.

Schools of every sort indicate by their number, size, and facilities that the primary education system is well supported here. In the large cities a public library has been established either by private funding or by the community itself and is accessible to everyone. On the other hand, with the exception of New York and New Orleans, which in this regard are the most Europeanized cities, the theater here, in regard both to the edifices and the performances, is insignificant. Music enjoys moderate but quickly growing support among the public. Places of amusement such as beer gardens and coffee houses are only to be found in those cities where there is a large German element, and then only in proportion to the wealth and *joie de vivre* of the local inhabitants. Nevertheless, there has been an increase in these establishments, and they are no longer inferior to those back in the old country.

Finally, we can now ask what the consequences of this great urban development are for the country as a whole, since they are no less important than the development itself. Two factors that play an important role in American life are the extraordinarily active communication between the various areas and the effort to lessen as much as possible the difference between town and country. This causes the influence of urban life and its products to have a much greater effect on everything that happens in that country than we can imagine. In the large food-producing centers of the land, no progress, discovery, or improvement is made, no undertaking suggested, no idea announced that does not resound in the most distant corners of the land, in the last farmhouse of a mountain valley. Nowhere can you escape the messengers of the big cities who carry news of that concentrated urban life out to distant places, i.e., the newspapers, the books, the traveling lecturers and teachers, the wandering merchants and artisans, the representatives of every conceivable organization, the surveyors, the road and railway builders. One has only to think of several million copies of the weekly editions of city newspapers and magazines, which are disseminated throughout the country and endeavor to do as much as possible to bring the rural inhabitants into close contact with the events and views of the urban populace, to get some idea of the importance of the cities for the general life pulse and progress of this young nation, especially in maintaining a certain uniformity in the level of education and in the common interests so essential for the Republic. One could also believe that there is something dangerous about the almost naturally irresistible attraction and influence of the new metropolises. But isn't it normal for every anxiety to be overridden by the wish to bring culture to the nation as quickly as possible and by the belief that in this period of enormous growth and development the unbroken activity of urban life serves, so to speak, as the flywheel whose driving energy becomes indispensable as long as it does not come to a standstill?

Enough of these suggestions and broad outlines. The reader is now kindly invited to discover for himself the more specific details from the following pages.

Part I

CHAPTER ONE

New York

SITE AND GROWTH OF THE CITY. ITS COMMERCIAL IMPORTANCE.

GENERAL CULTURAL SIGNIFICANCE FOR AMERICA.

In that corner of New York between Lake Ontario and Lake Champlain and the St. Lawrence River, the Adirondack Mountains, with their many lakes and streams, send most of their plentiful waters directly into these larger bodies, so that the mountains are a source for only one important river, which flows southward. This river, with three arms being fed by numerous springs and large and small inland lakes, flows in a steady southward direction through the rolling New York countryside and by Troy (above Albany) already comes so near to sea level that the ebb and flood tides of the ocean affect it. From here, more than 30 German miles (about 140 statute miles) above the estuary, it becomes a broader and deeper river, which can carry the largest river steamers, and allows the large sailboats to travel up to a point approximately 8 (37 statute) miles farther upstream.

The coastline where this river, the Hudson, empties into the Atlantic is deeply indented. True, there is not the abundance of islands, channels, and headlands here that makes the more southerly area between the 29th and 35th parallels on the coast of Pennsylvania, Delaware, Virginia, and North Carolina one of the world's most richly endowed areas of bays and harbors. But the mainland extends into the ocean here in such an extraordinarily fortuitous way that the natural formation creates one of the world's largest and best harbors. This natural formation results from three factors: a forking of the river close to its mouth; the position of two of the islands situated at the estuary, i.e., Long Island and Staten Island, which enclose the bay in the east and west respectively, leaving only two gateways open; and the position of the shorelines converging from northeast and southwest. The bay of New York, with its northwesterly entrance through Long Island Sound and its southerly one through the so-called Narrows, is a harbor that no human ingenuity could have bettered, in any event not in such large proportions.

New York, which is situated with its suburbs at the mouth of this river, occupies the southern half of an island cut off from the mainland partly by a little river, the Harlem River, emptying into the Hudson here, and partly by the East River, a connecting link between Long Island Sound and the bay. This island, partly surrounded by river and partly by sea, was named Manhattan by the Indians. Its elongated form measures almost 3 geographical (almost 14 statute) miles in length and not quite one-half (almost 2.3 statute) mile at its greatest width. In relation to the Hudson, which flows in a southwesterly direction to the sea, it extends from southwest to northeast with a total area of 1.33 geographical (about 28 statute) square miles. At present its natural contours, covered with every kind of house and building, are hard to recognize. However, the description of the first settlers tells us that the southern portion, which today is the center of the city, was covered with "wooded hills and pretty green valleys" and also contained a number of swamps as well as a deep pond; that the northern part consisted of higher, rockier ground covered with open forest; and that the soil was abundantly fertile and the forest full of game. In general the ground descends on both of the island's long sides so that the higher area runs like a backbone along the island's axis. This area became very significant because later the city's main street, Broadway, developed here, and as it extended northwards, Central Park and the planned major streets in the northern part of the city also took shape here.

On the other side of the water that flows around Manhattan, there were just as few places as on the island itself that the immigrants did not deem suitable for farming or trade. Thus, shortly after the colony on Manhattan was founded, settlements sprang up and prospered on the other side of the Hudson as well as on the tip of Long Island, which lies opposite New York. Then, with time, as New York developed into a more important city and steamship traffic developed on the none-too-wide branches of the river, these settlements became so closely connected with the island city that they eventually became actual parts of the city itself, although never at any time all belonging to the state of New York (the right bank of the Hudson opposite New York City is part of the state of New Jersey). Thus the city of Brooklyn, with about 400,000 inhabitants in 1870, developed on the tip of Long Island opposite New York, and the cities of Hoboken and Jersey City, with a combined population of over 100,000, developed on the western edge of the Hudson estuary. Even the smaller islands in the area of the bay increased in population and developed socially and intellectually along with the metropolis until they also became integrated into that wonderful urban center that has been created there. Today, New York proper, the city in Manhattan, can no longer be separated from these areas, which have gradually become attached to it. If one speaks of the development, significance, or future of New York, one does not think of the city of one million inhabitants, which actually carries that name, but of the entire urban complex around the Hudson estuary, which soon will have a population of two million, and will one of these days probably unite to form the political unit that the nature of things already seems to have predestined.[1] Soon one of the largest bridges that has ever been built will connect New York City and Brooklyn,[2] while some twenty steamships travel from shore to shore and numerous big and small steam and sailing ships take care of other internal traffic within this tripartite coastal and island city.

It is only right that New York, without doubt the heart of the entire structure, would give its name to the entire complex, for its wealth and activity are concentrated there. Brooklyn is a more residential area, while Jersey City and Hoboken serve more for the railway traffic and industry, and the development of New York proper really gave them their significance. To understand how New York came to be what it is today, one must try to trace its evolution from its very beginnings. As always, with whatever develops into something great among man's creations, the contribution of the internal and external attributes of the work alone do not explain why a thing has evolved as it has. Influences, which often work from afar and are completely coincidental, enter into the developmental process in incalculable ways, advancing or retarding it without essentially being recognized, affecting it to such a degree that the finished product and its development and growth process seem to us like a puzzle. To name but one very important factor, it is often merely a small alteration in the temporal succession of external influences, a dislocation of their order, which becomes decisive. If we take two similar plants and expose one to heat today and to cold tomorrow and expose the other to these conditions in the reverse order or in the same order a few days later, the difference can be ruinous for the one and beneficial for the other. Similarly, favorable events within a country affect various aspects of a nation's growth in differing degrees, depending on whether or not these aspects of growth offer the pertinent influences a receptive soil. These influences bypass parts of a nation's evolution, fructify others, and sometimes concentrate their effects so strongly on one aspect that here or there growth takes place, which later appears marvelous but inexplicable. This phenomenon is especially noticeable in urban development.

Soon after the discovery of the Hudson River (1609), the island of Manhattan became a center for the barter trade, particularly in furs, which the Dutch at that time carried on with the Indians. A permanent settlement of colonists who cleared and cultivated the land, however, was only founded in the beginning of the 1620s, when in 1623 thirty families sent by the Dutch West India Company landed here. Mostly Protestant Walloons who had left Europe because of religious persecution, they were similar to the Puritans who had immigrated to New England a few years before. The surrounding territory was named New Holland and the colony itself, New Amsterdam. The first houses stood on the southern end of Manhattan in the area now occupied by the grass- and tree-covered areas known as the Battery and Bowling Green and where the buildings that provided the first shelter for immigrants are still located.[3] Year after year the number of colonists grew. Shipbuilding and the fur trade employed many hands and at the beginning of the 1630s the yearly exports from Manhattan already amounted to more than 100,000 gulden, whereas the population in the year 1653 was given at something over 1,000.

The immigrants were then predominantly Dutch, and ever so often there were also a few Germans. But from the time the colony fell to England (1664) and received the name New York, the British element coming from the mother country as well as from the neighboring colonies began to become stronger and soon left the mark of its energy, its indefatigable activity, and its love of freedom on this Dutch colony, just as it was later to do in the French colonies located now in the northern and southern parts of the Union's territory. At the end of the century, considering the sparse population density of the North American colonies at that time, the city of New York possessed a goodly population of not quite five thousand people; at the end of the first half of the eighteenth century it had ten thousand souls, and at the beginning of the Revolutionary War the figure had more than doubled. The growth from ten thousand to twenty-two thousand inhabitants within twenty-four years and the beginning of the city's rapid rise in prosperity are connected with the general development of the resources of the colonies and with the great expansion of British North American territorial possessions brought about by the Peace of Paris in 1763.[4] Nevertheless, during this time New York still ranked behind Boston and Philadelphia. Only after the end of the Revolutionary War did New York begin to catch up to and then soon entirely surpass them with a population increase of more than thirty thousand people in every decade from 1790 to 1820.

In the period after the end of the war, all the states of the Union experienced extraordinary development, and especially those whose geographical position enabled them to enjoy the benefits of the commerce and trade, which was suddenly freed from all foreign restrictions. The American states now reaped all the advantages that had been denied up until then because of ridiculous English artificial limitations,[5] and in this new era of free competition New York's natural assets automatically began to prevail, most particularly its central location and its superb harbor. Some of the considerations that encouraged this natural development of New York were: that by 1807 a steamboat had successfully traveled up the Hudson, that four years later steam ferries were traveling between New York and Jersey City, that at the beginning of the 1830s the Hudson railroad, which had opened up the interior of the United States, was growing rapidly and increasingly by way of New York, and finally that the colonization of the West was more actively pursued from year to year and the quantity of movable wealth increased beyond all expectations.

Without doubt, the most important of these considerations was the connection of the sea with Lake Erie by means of a canal, which was opened in 1825 and extended the fine waterway that runs into the interior by means of the Hudson into the fertile lake area. By means of this canal, which is 76 geographical miles (351 statute miles) long from Buffalo to where it joins the Hudson and which, including a later enlargement, cost the state over $40,000,000, New York became the most easily accessible coastal town for the northern and Midwestern states of the interior. Thus the gigantic boom these states experienced, especially after the introduction of the railroad, could not fail directly to affect their shipping port. Like the heat at the center of a flame, the prosperity of the widely scattered distant areas still farther to the west was most perceptible here on the Atlantic Coast. Though New York saw its population rise to 110,000, 203,000, and 298,000 in the decades of the 1830s, 1840s, and 1850s, it saw only an intensified reflection of the population growth that was doubling in Ohio and Illinois during these decades. Boston, which has only overland connections with the interior, and Philadelphia, for which the shortest routes to the West are built through the Alleghenies and is less favorably located for trade with Europe, both fell behind New York, which knew how to utilize the benefits of its natural advantages in every possible way. In the race with these two very dangerous rivals, a very important element, which tipped the scales in New York's favor, was the cosmopolitan character it had assumed in comparison to either the Puritan or the Quaker city. It did not close the door to foreign elements among its population, elements that felt more at home here than in the other cities where the older residents kept themselves apart from the foreigners, who along with some disturbing things nevertheless still brought with them technical knowledge in various fields and a desire to succeed. In a later phase in New York's growth this consideration became a matter of consequence.

Clearly, in view of the importance Europe has for America, this American metropolis had to be one of the great commercial centers on the Atlantic Coast. Nevertheless, America was the colony, while Europe remained the older, accomplished center of civilization. America's natural resources had been so little used, its population relatively still so sparse, that cultivation of the soil and mining were the predominant occupations here. Exportation of raw materials and importation of factory products made trade the next most important occupation. Approximately 60 percent of the imports and between 40 percent and 50 percent of the exports pass through New York, and in the last few years it has also become the center of the most industrialized region of the entire continent.

The wealth, the spirit, and the workers that such a fast-growing city has brought together here are things that, apart from the accomplishments they produce, possess in themselves an expanding, self-begetting power. They prove the old saying: to him that has, is given. If one river ever becomes larger than the other ones, it soon grows at a much faster rate because it contains more water, because the flow of water down to the sea becomes stronger. Only one in a hundred streams becomes a river, and a little advantage can be the decisive factor. Thus the flow of transportation is quite similar. Activity and intelligence follow capital, create something new, and thereby attract other things, while the results of this interplay beneficially continue to develop further. Even natural disadvantages can be compensated for in this manner. For example, although ten railroad lines come into New York, until now, the insular character of the city has allowed only one of them, the Hudson River Line, to go directly into the city via a bridge over the eastern branch of the Hudson, while the others have to pick up their passengers and freight on the mainland by using ferries. Still in the long run this has not been any great obstacle for the growth of the city.

It is therefore a natural consequence of the preceding expansion of this city that the Pacific Railroad, which has epoch-making significance for world trade, put its eastern terminal in New York; it was just as natural as making San Francisco, the capital of the West, the other terminal.[6] Both cities, the one facing the Atlantic Ocean and Europe, the other facing the Pacific, Asia, and Polynesia, frequently perform a similar task for the land to which they belong, for they are above all the gates of entry and departure for an enormous traffic and trade. A railway that has set for itself the task of surmounting the wedge, which in the form of the American continent lies shoved between the opposite ends of the Old World, must select these gates as points of entry and departure if it wants to become an internationally significant railroad line. Even if someday a canal through Central America links the Atlantic and Pacific oceans more closely, as the Panama Railroad is already doing—and this idea is definitely a possibility in the distant future—this railway line, along with the parallel lines that must eventually be built, will always be of primary importance for New York, for every road, every canal, every rail line that brings the West nearer means a definite gain and a step forward for New York. It is also likely that trade with Asia will one day be very important for North America. New York, then, could become a center for many things, even for European-Asian commerce.

There is no doubt that New York has won for itself a position of great importance for the entire hemisphere. Anyone traveling in Central or South America already notices the influence that America's greatest city exerts over the entire area between Cape Horn and Hudson Bay. In Europe we do not have any one city of so far-reaching, decisive preponderance as this. In this regard, perhaps the Paris of a former era could best be compared with New York. To name a single example I need only mention that the few decently printed illustrated weeklies worth reading (*Mundo Nuevo* and *Siglo XIX*),[7] which are read throughout all Spanish America, are written and printed in New York, as are numerous books for the young as well as technical journals. Wealthy South and Central Americans, when they want to give their children a first-class education, prefer to send them to New York. That this city is the training school for young businessmen is self explanatory. The custom to enjoy one's riches and leisure in New York instead of in Paris or Madrid is becoming increasingly popular in South and Central America. Every year, shopping as well as curiosity causes thousands of Cubans, Mexicans, and South Americans to come to New York, and this influx of visitors is rising to such a degree that one can say that every new railroad, every new steamboat line that is opened in these countries only enhances New York's position as the metropolis of that portion of the world with the most potential.

As far as one can gaze into the future here, one sees only progress and prosperity. The entire country is in a state of development, rivals are no longer to be feared, and the power of attraction, which great commercial centers all over the world exert, seems for the time being unlimited here. Restrictive influences are less likely to be found in a people who love freedom and who, because they are in a dominant position in relation to all their neighbors and masters of their own fate, are thus able to maintain their freedom.

From a general viewpoint it can be said that today the great trading centers can no longer lose their importance as easily as in former centuries. They are presently relatively more powerful, their wealth in terms of money, activity, knowledge, and experience is less variable, and the trade routes have become institutionalized. It is no longer possible to monopolize certain advantages in order to protect oneself against this rising power of the great world metropolises unless some very powerful natural advantages are already present.

GENERAL IMPRESSION. LITTLE THAT IS OLD. SITE ON A NARROW ISLAND CAUSES A PARTICULAR DEVELOPMENT. BROADWAY. STREET LIFE. ATMOSPHERE OF A FAIR IN ITS SIDE STREETS. RESIDENTIAL STREETS.

To say something meaningful about one's general impression of a large city is certainly very difficult, for one is dealing with a complex phenomenon. In every large city, I can think of streets that portray scenes so full of life that they look like anthills and others, sometimes very close by, that depict scenes of gaping emptiness. I know homes that are so cheery and surrounded by greenery that one could transpose them to a mountain valley and others where smoke and soot, billowing away, showering the area from hundreds of smokestacks, have taken away all the color; sections with a bad name and sections with an aristocratic reputation, streets filled with dawdlers and the sections where the moneyed class live, squares on which pigs could usefully and pleasurably graze and others that are filled with magnificent lawns, flowers, and trees. All these contrasts are found in every large city, for wherever so many people with so many varied interests live close together, the populace divides itself according to class, wealth, and occupation, and these larger divisions contain many small ones, each possessing its own decisive character and making its own impression on the observer. Something that people share in common or that unifies them can be found more readily in the intellectual and social character of the populace, especially in our old, large cities, which have had the time to place their stamp upon their inhabitants. But this is lacking in a city like New York, which is so young, has grown in the last seventy years from sixty thousand to almost one million inhabitants, and is receiving such a huge, uninterrupted stream of immigrants from all parts of the world.*

*OF GREAT SIGNIFICANCE FOR NEW YORK IS ITS LOCATION AND THE SURROUNDING AREAS ONE SEES UPON ENTERING THE HARBOR. I HAVE TAKEN THE FOLLOWING CITATION ABOUT THIS FROM MY DIARY:

"FINALLY THE LAST DAY OF OUR JOURNEY BEGAN. EARLY IN THE MORNING A STRETCH OF THE LONG ISLAND COAST APPEARED TO OUR RIGHT, A BRIGHT STRIP OF SAND DUNES AND ABOVE IT A FLAT PLATEAU. IT WAS A FINE DAY, 'AMERICAN WEATHER' AS MY COMPANIONS ABOARD CALLED IT WITH PATRIOTIC PRIDE. TODAY EVERONE WAS CROWDED TOGETHER ON DECK, HAPPY BECAUSE OF THE END OF THE LONG TRIP AND ANXIOUS IN ANTICIPATION OF WHAT WAS TO COME. EVEN BREAKFAST, WHICH USUALLY WAS TAKEN LEISURELY AS A PLEASANT PASTIME, LASTED MUCH TOO LONG TODAY. EVERYONE CUT IT SHORT FOR THE FIRST TIME IN ORDER NOT TO MISS ANY OF THE NEW THINGS, WHICH EVERY MINUTE WERE INCREASINGLY BEING SIGHTED UP ON DECK. THE NUMBER OF PASSING SHIPS GREW VERY RAPIDLY, AND IF ONE HAD COUNTED THE SAILING BOATS AND STEAMSHIPS, WHICH COULD BE SEEN NEAR AND FAR, ONE WOULD HAVE OBTAINED A FIRSTHAND IDEA OF WHAT WAS MEANT BY THE TERM A 'MAIN THOROUGH-FARE OF WORLD TRADE.' TO THE LEFT, SANDY HOOK CAME INTO SIGHT, A HIGHER, WOODED LANDSTRIP ON THE POINT OF A NARROW PENINSULA THAT JUTS OUT TOWARD THE ENTRANCE OF NEW YORK BAY. LATER ON STATEN ISLAND CAME CLOSER ON THIS SIDE AND LONG ISLAND ON THE OTHER, AND BEFORE WE HAD TRAVELED THROUGH THE NARROWS, WHICH HEM IN THE OCEAN HERE AT THE ENTRANCE TO THE BAY, THE COASTLINES WERE ALREADY SO CLEARLY PERCEPTIBLE THAT THE HOUSES OF THEIR CITIES AND VILLAGES CLEARLY STOOD OUT FROM THE DARKNESS ALONG THE WATER'S EDGE. THESE WHITE-WALLED HOUSES, STANDING SOMETIMES SINGLY, SOMETIMES CLUSTERED TOGETHER, GLISTENED IN THE MORNING LIGHT ACROSS THE WATER, STANDING THERE AS IF THROWN UP BY THE SEA LIKE SNOW-WHITE, BLEACHED MUS-SELS AND SHELLS.

THE FURTHER WE TRAVELED THE MORE NUMEROUS BECAME THE HOUSES WE SAW ON THE LAND AND THE SHIPS ON THE WATER; PARTICULARLY LARGE NUMBERS OF LITTLE SCREW STEAM-ERS USED IN HARBORS DARTED BACK AND FORTH; OTHERS WERE BUSY HAULING SAILBOATS OUT OF THE HARBOR; AND STILL OTHERS, CONSIDERABLY LARGER, WERE FILLED WITH PASSENGERS, SUCH AS FERRIES GOING TO A DESTINATION ON LONG ISLAND OR TO THE NEARBY COAST OF NEW JERSEY. ABOVE ALL, THE LITTLE SAILBOATS AND ROWBOATS, WHICH ROCKED AND HURRIED ABOUT LIKE WATERFOWL, WERE MOST FREQUENTLY SIGHTED. MOREOVER, THE SEA IS STILL SO WIDE ON ALL SIDES HERE THAT THE ACTIVITY ON ITS SURFACE AND ON ITS BANKS APPEARS DOUBLY IMPRESSIVE. AND AS THE CITY ITSELF DREW NEARER, WITH BROOKLYN ON THE OTHER SIDE AND THE CITY'S SOUTHERN TIP ON THIS SIDE OF ONE OF THE BRANCHES OF THE SEA, WHICH ENTERS INTO THE HARBOR, IT LOOKED VERY LARGE INDEED, AND WHEN SOME ISLANDS WITH FORTIFICATION AND IMPOSING BUILDINGS ON BOTH SIDES APPEARED AND THE SHIPS ALL AROUND ALONG THE SHORELINES BECAME INCREASINGLY MORE NUMEROUS, ALL OF A SUDDEN THE FIELD OF VISION TURNED INTO A SINGLE PICTURE OF MAGNIFICENT, RICH PROPORTIONS."

Nevertheless, precisely because of its relative youth, New York has a better opportunity of leaving behind a definite general impression of itself than do those cities that develop over many centuries and that, because of the social and cultural requirements that vary according to the period in which these cities arise, contain sections that together form very divergent aggregates of the inner and outer parts, of the old and new suburbs, of the city. New York has the advantage over the others of an unrestricted expansion on virgin soil, of a thought-out, unified conception adopted to modern needs, and there are therefore very few parts of the city that do not give the impression of a completely modern and very new city.[8] I have walked around New York for weeks without observing any monuments of a former time other than the simple gravestones of the long-forsaken cemetery of Trinity Church, which surrounds it like a garden on lower Broadway—gravestones, however, that speak only of three generations. Anyone who searches may find some more things, but they are already very much hidden from view, and the few streets found in this area that are not straight and wide, the remains of old New York, will in a short time be all that is left to tell that there was a time when everything was not yet built here according to a well-laid plan of only rectangular city blocks. The fact that business and trade are concentrated in the older section of the city, where the value of land and houses has risen very quickly and higher than in other sections, explains why precisely here the old, almost without exception, must make room for the new and the newer for the newest. The value of a building is subject to change to the same degree as the land on which it stands. The higher the land value rises, the higher are the rents that it must bring, so that the size and magnificence of the houses, at least in the big cities, are generally a good indication of the value of the land. For that reason there is practically no one in New York who wants to swim against the stream and try to hold onto the past. In addition, the air is so clean here in the city that the houses seem hardly discolored by smoke, even decades later, and the city contains a generous amount of large and small grass plots, trees, and tree groves. New York is indeed a more youthful and modern city than even its exact age would lead us to expect.

What I have just described, then, is one characteristic of New York the visitor notices immediately and is generally found everywhere when one looks at the external appearance of the city. Other traits lie deeper and can be truly recognized and understood only if one begins to study more closely the form, the location, and the development of the city.

Of prime significance is first of all the location of the city on the long, narrow island of Manhattan, eight times as long as it is wide, and on the average not even one-half a geographical mile (about 2.3 statute miles) wide. This gives New York a shape that is not at all natural for a city of such size. Large cities expand as much as possible equally in all directions, but this one grows in a straight line from south to north. It does not have the heart of its transportation network located at its geographical center but rather in the southern parts of the city, nor does it have any radial or circular streets but only longitudinal ones with crossroads constructed at right angles, of which the former are more important for transportation than the latter. The side streets, running east to west from shore to shore, are busy streets especially because of the heavy traffic that New York carries on with surrounding areas on the mainland and with the islands, and also because of the docks and warehouses that lie along the shore on the periphery and are naturally part of a commercial city. Just as naturally, the longitudinal streets that intersect these side streets bear a large part of the internal traffic, take up the majority of humans and goods that move about in them, and together with the traffic that flows to and from the business center, almost like the head of a comet at the southern tip, transport them all further northwards or southwards.

The most important of these thoroughfares and the main street of New York is Broadway, the great trough into which more than 180 side streets empty like little streams. This street runs in a straight line from the south tip for about 3 kilometers (1.86 statute miles) up to a point where the business section gradually becomes a residential area. Then with a slight turn to the northwest it goes along for about 4 kilometers (2.5 statute miles) to the entrance of Central Park, the present-day northern end of the densely inhabited part of the city, in such a way that it intersects five of the big longitudinal streets to the west of it. New York possesses the longest main street of any large city and many parts of this boulevard are equally beautiful. Already in 1730, when New York could not even boast of having ten thousand inhabitants, Broadway was beginning to develop into a major thoroughfare, and it has continued to grow with the city until it received the reputation of being one of the wonders with which our age has replaced the seven of the ancient world. The city is therefore making sure that in the future it will remain one of the most magnificent things in the world, for in the plan that is the basis for the expansion of the city, there is provision for its continuation as a splendid boulevard that will be miles long, the first part of which has already been completed.[9] The size and magnificence of the buildings that stand along the older parts of Broadway are still in the process of changing, and here there is much room for improvement, since the present architectural character of Broadway, at least to a European eye, has little that is pleasing about it. The pretty white and white-gray marble and granite that is amassed there arouses one's pity because of the clumsy forms into which they have forced this valuable material. In fact, the most sumptuous buildings, such as the New Post Office or the well-known establishment of the cloth merchant Stewart, are the most outstanding failures.[10] Wealth and magnificence do not compensate for the lack of taste, which is so frequently apparent here.

Noteworthy is the extraordinary amount of activity and bustle on Broadway and the many-sidedness of its character, which its great size has created. Innumerable elegant stagecoaches travel along its most popular stretches; horse-drawn trolley lines, which are excluded from this section of the avenue, at least run parallel with it in order to join it again later on. The number of conveyances with goods in them is so great that one often sees hundreds of them going by in a row, and the most complicated traffic tie-ups, which occur here and there almost hourly, are patiently waited out and cleared up as if they were a normal part of daily traffic. On the wide sidewalks on both sides of the street the people without exception go by in a hurry, frequently pushing their way through. They are on the whole rather quiet, and because of the predominance of men, usually businessmen, they all look alike in outward appearance. One cannot help notice a strong general disposition towards energetic activity and a youthful elasticity in the faces and movements of the people or fail to observe the absorbing results of this animated hustle and bustle. Very soon they will voluntarily give up the habit, which is enjoyed in Berlin or Vienna, of calmly strolling about. The people feel that the traffic flows by too quickly for them to be able to observe it quietly from the side, and so in the end they move along with the rest.

Striking sights, like everywhere else in this land, are less frequently to be seen along the main streets here than in other large cities of the world and are of a different type. People who arouse pity in others, idlers, either high or low class, are very rarely seen here. In this bustle where no one has a minute to spare they would hardly feel comfortable. On the other hand, the numerous wandering petty tradesmen or those sitting at the corners or in front of the buildings, the bootblacks with their stereotyped call, the men walking around like kiosks, festooned with advertisements in front, in back, and even on their heads, those who shove leaflets into the hands of the passerby or even throw them by the bushel into the coaches, the boys who deliver newspapers from house to house—all these groups are part of the permanent scene on this street. More immutable are the inanimate witnesses of the great traffic and activity on this street, which in the form of the most varied, gaudy, obtrusive announcements cry out their wares from every window, from every wall, and even from the rooftops. Since advertising flags, banners, and placards are not strung directly over this street as they are in nearby business streets of lesser importance, Broadway has less of the character of a market fair than do the others. Nevertheless, the abundance of ballyhoo still gives this impression, which with all its colorfulness and excitement allows no trace of the street's true greatness to come through. This atmosphere is even more in evidence in the side streets where the display of goods is placed under canvas awnings that extend out over the sidewalk so that one often has to walk entirely between booths.

One notices less care taken with regard to the arrangement of goods in the display window here than in Germany, and this only helps give Broadway more of a commercial character rather than one of beauty or magnificence and strengthens such an impression in the visitor. The reason for this attitude toward arranging goods is probably that New York is the principal outlet for the petty

1 THE HUSTLE AND BUSTLE OF LOWER BROADWAY, NEW YORK CITY, SHOWING THE WHITE STAGECOACHES OR "STAGES."

tradesmen of the country; the big bazaars on Broadway seem to be made just for them while individual retail business is crowded more into the side streets. In the booths of these bazaars, one no longer has to look at the goods through a window since the bazaars stand open to every visitor, so that a few, particularly large and prosperous businesses, such as those dealing in gold and jewelry, are frequented as much by those just looking as by those people who are purchasing something. Whoever goes along New York's streets still misses the nice arrangement of color and form of those numerous little things that rivet one's attention to attractive window displays, particularly the well-laid-out merchandise in the art and book shops. Not finding this, one finally prefers to turn again from these displays and look at the mass of humanity that moves along the edge of the buildings like noisy waves along the banks of the river.

That Broadway offers many different faces can be explained by its length. When people talk about the very busy traffic on it, they only mean the first one-third mile or so going northwards, for the rest of the way is surrounded by many smaller buildings, and the traffic gradually thins out into the parallel and intersecting streets. The area of transition between the two parts is a rather long stretch with an atmosphere of its own. Big stores, confectionary shops, restaurants, and saloons are all crowded together on it. At certain times of day you can see the well-to-do, particularly ladies, more frequently here than along any other part of Broadway, occupied with that wonderful pastime known as "shopping," i.e., wandering about from store to store. There are also two pretty, open squares in this area (Union Square and Madison Square) whose entire appearance would certainly be improved if their lawns, trees, and fountains were maintained better. These squares indeed offer very beneficial resting places from the hustle and bustle of the southern part of the city.

A remarkable contrast exists here when the business and residential areas intersect as you turn off Broadway into one of the side streets containing only homes on it. Running along in rows of hundreds, scarcely ever interspersed with a church or a school or some other more distinguished building, these homes are built according to a few constantly repeated models. The buildings are constructed of red-brown sandstone (known as brownstone here) or of red bricks and are narrow, so that houses with only a three-window front are quite frequent. Usually they are not especially high but almost always kept clean, at least on the outside. These streets are certainly uniform, but I have never found them to be as unbearably boring as some travelers have described them or as widely used geographical reference works have portrayed them. In neither big nor small cities are residential areas generally built just for pleasure or amusement, for the majority do not live in palaces, nor can everyone have trees and a garden on his property. If a house is not distinguished architecturally or by its surroundings, how can one get around the uniformity in building material, the straight rows, or the purpose for which these homes were built?

I feel that the better residential blocks in New York appeal to me more than those in either Berlin or Vienna. The style is simple and unassuming; thus I feel that the entire building conforms to the modest means with which small private homes are mostly built, and if the same house model is constantly copied, at least it is a pleasing one. And where would you find more tree-lined streets, more lawns in front of houses, or more airy gardens behind them? Generally the entrance is set back from the street so that a little plot of about a stone's throw in depth remains open before the house and is then usually planted with grass, sometimes with flowers, frequently with the red-white blooming hibiscus bushes. Many otherwise unpretentious houses have their fronts decorated with creepers, and a street without trees, even if sometimes only a few scattered along the edge of the sidewalk, is a rarity. The ailanthus is most prevalent among the trees along the streets, but the oak, sycamore, linden, white poplar, and the weeping willow, which is a very common tree over here, can also be seen. Unfortunately, it depends, so I hear, on the preference of the landowner whether or not trees will be allowed on his property, and since you see so few young, newly planted trees along the streets, it appears as if New York, at least in the older sections, is facing the loss of something that makes it so attractive and that cannot be replaced some day with parks and squares however beautiful they may be.

INNER CITY TRAFFIC. LAYOUT OF THE STREETS. TROLLEYS. CITY PLAN.

The coincidence and arbitrariness in the construction of our big cities and particularly in the layout of their very important transportation arteries or street plan do not seem strange to us. We regard them as so common that they appear to be part of the nature of every large conglomeration of human dwellings. We have become used in part to putting up with their detrimental aspects and in part to letting them be outweighed by the artistic attraction, the venerable age, and the large and small memories that to a degree spin a web around us. Here in America, where most cities developed during a period that was already energetically trying to free itself "from hovels and oppressive rooms, and ugly walls and garret glooms, from streets that stifle, crowds that crush,"[11] where houses are no longer put up alongside one another according to chance or whim, looking like a mass of rock crystals, but where they are arranged according to careful, fixed plans on the premise that air, light, and broad thoroughfares would become increasingly necessary the more they grew, one is all the more surprised then that the people here would ever build anything so meager and close together, and construct their cities with so little consideration for the needs of those coming afterwards. Even if the Americans someday were to recognize that there was a time in Europe when no city could exist without ramparts and a town wall, thus giving historical justification for a cramped and irregular city layout, this would still hardly help them understand why their own forefathers, the original settlers, the English and Dutch city founders of the seventeenth and eighteenth centuries, were so typically European with regard to narrow winding streets and appeared in this respect to have little feeling for their mission in the world, which they were very much aware of in other matters: i.e., to separate the new seed from the old weeds on this virgin soil. In his own way, Washington Irving appropriately expressed this characteristic of his fellow Americans when in his humorous history of New York City he wrote: since the wise city council did not feel in the position to decide on a building plan for the city, in a commendable burst of patriotism the cows took up the matter themselves and made paths through the brush that they used in order to go to and from the meadows. Along these paths the good people then built their houses, and this is one of the causes for the remarkable labyrinthine turns and bends that distinguish certain streets of New York until this very day.[12]

Along with the straight and wide streets, which for the last fifty years have become a necessary ingredient in the concept of an American city, there are also, as in our cities, some narrow and twisting streets. Once they exist and develop and fulfill needs, they become part of everyday life. With time, we get so used to them that the very reason for their existence and growth seems entirely natural and indispensable to us. New York could and would have without doubt also become a great city with less consistent planning; but inasmuch as it continued to be built according to the farsighted, grandiosely conceived plans of 1811, the building needs that have arisen since then come to be accepted as part of the character of the present city, and the majority of the people feel that New York is fine just the way it is and should remain that way. The truth is, however, that a New York built with cramped and winding streets, although never able to spread out like the present-day city, would have required different and expensive means of transportation, its sanitary conditions would have been less satisfactory, and its gas and water supply and sewer systems would have been much more difficult to maintain. Today they level the land on construction sites, but if New York had been as large sixty years ago as it is today, it would be full of more winding streets and more hills than Rome, and with its elongated shape and its traffic and business heavily concentrated at one end, that would scarcely be tolerable.

Because of the spacious layout of all newer cities in this country, one of the needs that has to be met is provision for a speedy and inexpensive passenger service. The great distances require this, and the breadth of the streets makes it possible to meet this demand without interfering with normal traffic. Thus, as time has passed, the use of horse-drawn trolleys has become a development that has added an entirely new aspect to the general picture of large American cities. Our large cities of the Old World have all but barely made do with little vehicles and stagecoaches for transportation within the city. But until a new underground transportation system is built, numerous trolley lines have been instituted in the downtown area of every American city so that even in New York, which in its older sections does not belong to the most well-laid-out of cities, one can and does use the "car" (the name given to the coaches of the horse-drawn trolley as well to those of the railroad) for any trip that as a rule takes more than four or five minutes. Nineteen lines, eighteen of which have been built within the last twenty years, now transect the city in all directions and primarily run along the main traffic arteries, the longitudinal streets or avenues, and only Fifth Avenue, which is reserved for the quiet enjoyment of the rich, lacks a trolley line. On Ninth Avenue the trolley is connected with the Elevated Railway, a railroad resting on iron supports high above the street level over which steamcars run.[13] Wherever the streets are too narrow to allow tracks for the trolley, a large number of the neat, white stagecoaches, the "stages," which used to be the dominant means of transportation within the city, still hold their own. Since the fare is so low (five cents in most "cars," six cents in a few, and generally ten cents for the stagecoaches), this trolley system is of obvious importance for the housing situation of the lower classes.

In Europe, people have suggested, among other things, an improved transportation system as a means of remedying the housing shortage. Here in New York you can see this in practice, for there should not be anyone capable of working who cannot easily afford to travel to and from his place of work in order to live more cheaply in the suburbs in a healthier environment. This is also beneficial for the school children, and in many streets during the afternoon you come across a trolley car filled with girls coming home from school. In general, one can say that just as the steam engine has made traveling from country to country and from city to city a common thing, thereby making mankind more mobile and more cosmopolitan, the trolley has improved communication within cities and between cities and their surrounding areas and has beneficially set the urban population in motion. Here is something that is the common property of all the workers, both upper and lower class, who after their exhausting day can leave the noise and fumes of the city and reach their homes in a short time no matter how far out of the city center they are. In Germany this is to a much greater degree the monopoly of the better classes. The fact that so many people in Europe do not have the advantage of rapid transportation can also be cited as one of the causes for the huge increase of social problems and dissent. In fact, traveling in a city where the distances easily require a trip of one or one and a half hours is no longer a luxury but a convenience that should be made accessible to many people. For many people it is even a necessity. The Americans are right when they say that appropriately broad streets in which a trolley line can be built are a fundamental prerequisite of a big city.

The trolleys here are simply furnished and have no class divisions, and since the exclusion or segregation of Negroes was forbidden a few years ago,[14] they now contain a very interesting cross section of the New York population. Virtually no one, even among the wealthy class in New York, even if he owns his own vehicle, does not now and then use the trolley. Many times the cars are packed with ladies who in Germany would scarcely condescend to be exposed to the danger of such a mixed society. I have heard complaints that masculine courtesy is on the wane and that today a lady runs the risk of having to stand in the "car" while a man makes himself comfortable without any qualm about occupying a seat. Indeed, I have often observed this myself, although the opposite, as far as I can tell, is still more prevalent, and I have seen old men get up to give Negro women seats. I believe personally that in such matters it will be hard to abide by the deferences paid to women as a general rule or as a social law, in part because men cannot see the reason for this preference and in addition because not all women and girls deserve this courtesy. It is very unpleasant to see a frail or elderly man standing while school girls are sitting all around him. In this respect they accuse the German immigrants of being partly responsible for the undermining of good old American manners, and I do not think this accusation is entirely unfounded if they expand the statement to include all immigrants. For better or worse, we like to be bound by rules less than the Americans. Moreover, the main source of the emigration to America does not come from the best bred classes of the population. In any event the two first mentioned reasons are the main ones.

The trolley cars each have a sign indicating their points of departure and their destination as well as the streets through which they go and are also labeled by particular colors indicating which line they belong to. The cars are drawn by two horses and inside usually have two upholstered benches running lengthwise along the car's sides, seldom with benches facing the front, and with neither individual seats nor places provided for standing. The size of the cars varies; the smaller ones traveling along the less frequented lines have no conductor, so that each passenger has to throw his five cents into a box that is so placed behind the driver that he can keep an eye on what is in it. Since the driver often must make change, this system is not a particularly good idea. The stagecoaches or "stages," which have a seating capacity of twelve and provide space only inside the coach, also have no conductor; the driver, whose attention is gained by ringing a little bell, receives his ten cents through an opening behind his seat. But with the little bell he also demands his money when someone has gotten on and waits a few minutes before paying, for a leather strap leading from the door to the coachman's seat lets him know every time the door opens. Together, the cars and stages service an average of 300,000 people every day.

Smaller vehicles are infrequently seen, are more expensive, and most often are used only by those really in a hurry to get to a certain place, are traveling with luggage, or else seeking to ride around to be seen or for pure pleasure. It is not customary to use such vehicles at all; one often sees private carriages only along the promenades. When it comes to driving, the Americans know what they are doing; they prefer the very light, supple carriages, the two and four wheelers, and sometimes have very attractive two-horse trotters. Canadian horses are supposed to be able to endure pulling carriages longer than the local breed and therefore are frequently imported.

While on the subject of transportation facilities, I want to say a word about what here takes the place of our porters. Anyone who wants to have a small parcel quickly carried to some point in the city will seldom find anyone who is willing to do it, and he will have to walk several blocks before he finds some teenager loitering about who will undertake the job. For larger objects, there are the express cars, which will transport something for half a dollar, and extra heavy objects for a dollar, but very often it takes a long time before they do the job. By such observations foreigners soon notice how expensive labor is in this country, and many things a porter does elsewhere for a few cents must be done by the person himself if he does not want to use the mail or telegram service or to dig very deeply into his pocket.

As much as New York's trolley network seems wonderful and very practical in comparison with the transportation systems of European capitals, it cannot be denied that it also has drawbacks too basic to the system for one to expect quick solutions. In winter, snowstorms create obstacles for traffic, in summer many horses frequently succumb to sunstroke, and conflicts between the streetcars and anything else that tries to push its way along the streets make such things as traffic jams frequent and inevitable. Besides, one of the busiest sections of the entire city, the area of old streets between the southern tip of the island and the city hall, which includes the stock market, post office, customs house, and numerous banks and similar buildings, can enjoy the benefits of this transportation system only to a very limited degree since the nature of the narrow, winding streets makes access to it via trolley possible only by round-about means. These disadvantages have become acute, especially within recent years, because, as noted earlier, an increase in population always causes an increase of traffic within the limited area of the business district; and since this district has to extend lengthwise due to the island's narrow width, the necessary inner cohesiveness of the northern and southern parts of the city becomes increasingly difficult to maintain. Thus, plans have been developed and published for a pneumatic line, an underground steam-powered railroad, an "arcade railroad," and a "viaduct railroad." The last of these is supposed to run high above the ground, the other three under the earth. The third one has provisions not just for a railway line but also a sidewalk for pedestrians. Some new kind of city rail line will undoubtedly in part replace the horse-drawn trolley, and this will probably occur in the not too distant future.[15] However, no definite plan has apparently been made to carry out the project, nor has any choice been made between these or other proposals.

Just as this amazing, well-considered city plan has helped make the construction of a great transportation network possible, it also is of great help in promoting the construction of a water supply and sewage system. Probably, people living in a more closely packed city would have deliberated longer before undertaking the original idea of using gas lighting than they did here where already in 1825 the first gas lights were burning on the streets. New York's historians rightly give credit to those who almost seventy years ago drew up the plan for most of the city as it now stands, at a time when the growth that has since come about could in no way have been foreseen. They tell us that it was Governeur Morris along with Simeon Dewitt and John Rutherford who from 1807 on began incorporating the area of the city up to what is today 154th Street and laid out the new straight longitudinal and intersecting streets.[16] Since then, all streets running east to west with the exception of every tenth one, which is 100 feet wide, have been laid out as 60 feet, and all avenues as 100 feet wide; and the streets as well as the avenues have been designated by numbers. The former run from east to west, the latter from south to north. The basic plan has been changed somewhat with regard to further expansion, to try to give still more consideration for light and air than has already been the case. Since 1869 a boulevard 150 feet wide has run from 59th Street to 150th Street.[17] The center strip has been planted with trees and shrubbery, and it has impressive roadways and sidewalks on both sides. The plots of land along the way are now being sold at very high prices, and this entire layout seems to be destined one day to become one of the most original and most magnificent in all New York.

The numbering of the buildings also goes from east to west[18] and from south to north, and because of the uniform size of the plots of land, it is on the whole so orderly that anyone who knows the area can tell exactly where most build-ings are situated if he knows the street and the number. This regularity is of more value to businessmen than one might at first think; with a little practice, one can have a mental picture of the particular parts of the city at any time so that one can get to know any locality without effort.

The paving of the streets has been carried out according to various methods and in many places is not in very good condition. Wooden paving and the various types of asphalt are not supposed to last as well as the paving with cobblestones, which are quarried in large quantities right in the vicinity of the city. With time, this last method of paving will probably become the generally accepted procedure.

HEALTH OFFICIALS OF NEW YORK

In the year 1866 the New York State Legislature passed a law establishing a board of health for the district of New York City.[19] This law specified that the governor, with the approval of the senate, is to name four residents of the district, of whom three should be medical doctors, to membership on the board, and that these men, together with the director of the harbor sanitary force and the four commissioners of the metropolitan police, are to make up this Board of Health. The members of the board hold office for four years, and every year they are to elect a president from amongst themselves; every member receives a salary of $2,500 and the four police commissioners $500 each, from which $10 is to be deducted every time a regular meeting is missed. Authority is given to this board to appoint an official, a doctor who will carry the title of Sanitary Superintendent, to carry out its instructions or to supervise their execution. It is also to appoint two assistants for this official, a specified number of health inspectors who generally should be doctors, and finally lower officials of the kind and number as should be found necessary. In particular, the jurisdiction of this board is to extend over building inspectors as far as the necessities of public health are concerned, over the regulations governing indoor and outdoor mar-kets with regard to cleanliness, ventilation, garbage disposal, and the exclu-sion of unwholesome foodstuffs, and over the removal from the streets and plazas of all injurious materials. It also has control over the cleaning and maintenance of public toilets and is responsible for the prevention of incidents that could become dangerous to life or health, and in general for the prevention of all things or events that would be detrimental to public health. For these purposes the board of health has been given the right to issue bylaws and ordinances, inspect buildings, streets, and plazas, have anything that seems injurious removed or altered, and summon the municipal police to carry out their ordinances. Originally no more than $100,000 per year was to be spent by the board on its activities, and its president is supposed to make detailed reports about its work and make sure that the public is informed about public health ordinances once a year via the newspapers.

In recent years this law has been altered and expanded by numerous amendments. The amount of money at its disposal, for example, has been increased to $150,000, detailed regulations have been enacted concerning the guaranteeing of individuals infected by contagious diseases and the rights of the board with regard to private property, and a law dealing with rented houses and rooming houses has been added. The task of keeping the statistics dealing with births and deaths has been assigned to the board, regulations regarding slaughterhouses and butcher shops also fall within its province, etc. We have gone over these details here in order to get an idea of the actual work of the board of health since this gives us a better idea of the nature and activities of this institution than merely counting up a list of laws passed. The aims and scope of this agency can be grasped from the numerous reports of various minor officials to the board and the board's own annual report to the governor.

If we take any year, for example 1867, we find that the following very significant things were accomplished: measures were instituted to prevent the transmission of pieces of clothing or the like from infected ships into the city as previously had happened so frequently, and a general inspection of rooming houses was undertaken and a long report submitted, which formed the basis of new ordinances for rooming houses. Similarly the public schools of New York and Brooklyn were subjected to a general inspection, and on the basis of the reports, the board of education moved to make sweeping reforms, the results of which today can be seen in such things as the upkeep of the interior and exterior of the schoolhouses, the number of students per class, and the furnishings in the classroom. The results of the investigation led to provisions for a biannual inspection of the public schools and their students; inquiries were made about the inoculation of children; a series of suggestions was made for setting up isolation hospitals at the approach of a cholera epidemic and some of them were immediately carried out; the slaughterhouses were inspected and twenty-five of them were closed; and the removal of all slaughterhouses from the thickly populated southern half to the northern edge of the city was begun. Where the board found it necessary, certain sections of the city were subjected to more frequent cleanings than others, swampy areas were drained, certain areas received regular disinfections. The board issued thousands of writs via the police to individual parties who through their failure to comply with the ordinance had become liable to the law. The board caused garbage to be taken away in 1,163 cases, had 877 cellars cleaned up, the plumbing in more than 500 cases repaired, about 20,000 lavatories cleaned out or disinfected, 679 lavatories closed, over 3,000 improvements made in the sewage system, 768 courtyards cleaned, et cetera.

Individual cases of contagious diseases, specific problems for society and the like have resulted in some interesting analytical studies. Thus the fact that twenty-eight ships arrived in New York harbor during that year (1867) with smallpox cases aboard and that relatively few cases of smallpox occurred prompted the board to compile the statistics of all deaths due to this disease. From 1804 to 1867, in a period when the population of New York increased twentyfold, the number of deaths due to smallpox as listed every decade were in 1804, 169; 1814, 2; 1824, 394; 1834, 233; 1844, 21; 1854, 611; 1864, 382; 1867, 19. Its decrease, which, as one sees, is very significant considering the population increase, is attributed in the board's report to the ever-increasing practice of inoculation, while the irregularity of the disease's recurrence is attributed to the immigrants who still frequently brought it with them. When cholera appeared in the same year, the board drew up parallel charts of the population density of individual parts of the city, the comparative degree of sickness present, the manner in which the cholera cases were distributed among the parts of town, et cetera. On the basis of the simple facts here, the theory was convincingly advanced that the more crowded the population, the more badly ventilated and dirty the dwellings, the more receptive was the breeding ground for this devastating disease. The typhoid cases support this theory even more strongly; the majority of them can definitely be traced to a certain faultiness in housing facilities, bad drinking water, and similar things. The typhoid statistics that were compiled indicate the interesting fact that from 1848 on the number of deaths due to typhoid fever and the cases of those sick with the disease decreased as follows: 1848, 943; 1853, 541; 1858, 302; 1863, 951; 1867, 603. When one thinks how enormously the population has increased in the meantime, while taking into consideration all the inevitable deficiencies of such statistics, then this is welcome proof that life in New York, at least with regard to this matter, has become a healthier one. Of course, this occurred exactly at the time when great urban expansion was taking place to the north, where along the very wide streets better ventilated houses were being built and greater care was being taken to keep the streets and houses clean and to expand the plumbing and sewage systems.

Special care is taken in collecting statistical data and interpreting it in the best possible manner. The American predilection for statistics, especially for the often very effective graphic presentation of the results, can find here a broad area in which to put them to use. Year after year we find in the reports careful statistics that seek to get to the bottom of the various causes of deaths, which moreover actually bring to light many remarkable facts. It was discovered that while in 1868 the mortality rate in New York rose to 25.45 per 1,000, in Brooklyn, the quiet residential city where there is more breathing space, it only amounted to 23 per 1,000. The child mortality rate, long recognized as a blot on the public health record of American cities, was noticed to be highest in the warm months and lowest in winter, and it was pointed out that in some parts of the city it amounted to 80 out of 100 deaths. Pertinent instructions were issued, which with time will reduce the causes of the child mortality rate insofar as they do not result from the unquestionably injurious climate of this part of America. It was demonstrated that of almost 20,000 deaths that occurred in nine months, more than 11,000 occurred in tenement houses containing more than three households. As a consequence of this, the board proceeded to enact strong controls over these buildings, which up until then had been completely left to themselves, and in 1868 alone, 3,756 complaints were brought against the owners or their agents. As a result of the statistics on child mortality, a more careful watch was also kept on the notorious homes of certain doctors and abortionists. Nevertheless, even though about fifty or even more of these practitioners fell under suspicion in the first year, it was only recently that a few of these were subjected to prosecution, and unfortunately the biggest of these houses, almost a palace, situated in the best street, still is one of the sights that one shows a stranger.

The accident statistics show that in New York someone loses his life by drowning almost every day. Since the board of health found that means for saving someone were often lacking in the most critical places, depots with lifesaving equipment were thus set up, and in places where they could be of help, instructions in lifesaving and resuscitation were given. In all the northeastern states of the Union tuberculosis is a prominent cause of death, and in New York it accounts for no less than fourteen or fifteen out of every one hundred deaths. Research done on the geographic distribution of the deaths among the various city boroughs revealed what European statisticians had already shown: that a great many of the tuberculosis cases resulted from the damp location of the houses. Great care was spent in the periodic testing of the city's water supply, and it was found to be as pure as water coming from a generally rocky, thinly populated area is supposed to be. The water of the Croton Reservoir,[20] which exclusively supplies New York, contains, according to frequent testing, 7.5 solid particles to every 100,000 parts liquid; Brooklyn's water supply contains a little over 5 to every 100,000. The board of health turned its attention even to less important matters, and it is to be especially thanked, for example, for the abundance of public drinking fountains, which are a true blessing for the inhabitants of every class during the hot summer. When the number of fires caused by petroleum, naptha, and the like rose in 1869 by 10 percent and in 1870 by 18 percent, the board stepped in against the uncontrolled sale of these fuels by bringing government action against the same.

The international organization of the board of health has undergone some changes in the last few years, which aim at strengthening and expediting its activities, whereas the aims and methods of the work it performs have hardly changed, as we can see from the last few annual reports. I assume that the following information will be of general interest:

Though New York's sewage system can be considered adequate, the board sees a serious defect, probably an important cause of disease, in the sewer emptying into the ocean right at the water's edge and resting high and dry at low tide. For the time being, it is making no suggestions for its rectification but rather raising the often discussed question of whether it is right to empty the sewage of large cities of a predominantly agricultural land such as America into the sea. The board believes such action to be wrong because agriculture can no longer do without the fertilizer that is being lost by the present system of sewage disposal. The board also definitely opposes all kinds of paving other than cobblestones since this is the only type that allows the city to keep the streets adequately clean. Wooden paving is completely condemned by the board.

The disposal of household garbage takes place in the following manner prescribed by the sanitary code: every houseowner or tenant must take care of putting the boxes or barrels with the ashes and other rubbish in front of the house, where trucks of the company responsible for keeping the streets clean will collect and empty them into their carts. The city tried to remedy the defects of this system by regulations concerning specifications for garbage receptacles, by having them picked up in the backyard, et cetera, but the dirt that lies around on so many streets sufficiently shows how hard it is to carry out such a comprehensive system without continual supervision. Since 1872 the supervision of this important business has been in the hands of the police, and since then, for example, an ordinance has been issued, which requires that the ashes be kept separate from other garbage, and this makes any salvage work all the easier.

The already mentioned tenement houses figure prominently in every report. They are usually described as old buildings, warehouses, or the like, which were once intended for purposes other than dwellings and in which every family is assigned a living room ten by twelve feet and a bedroom four by six feet in length. One such old building may sometimes contain over one hundred of these so-called apartments, and naturally scarcely any consideration is given to ventilation or cleanliness. Light and air can barely find their way in here. This bad situation, despite the rapid expansion of the city outwards, has probably increased in the last few years as the stores have taken over one residential area after another and have continually pushed out the inhabitants. Already in 1870 the poorer quarters of New York were more densely populated than those of London (here the highest number of people per square acre is 328, there 307) and half of the population living in the poorer quarters previously accounted for 85 percent of the deaths in that year—a figure that has since decreased to 66 percent. It is also unfortunate that recently the plots of land in the northern part of the city, i.e., where there is room to expand, have become so expensive that to abandon the tenement system in favor of smaller private homes cannot even be considered. People here are now therefore concerned with converting all possible unused space in the inner city into such economically built houses in order gradually to decrease the overcrowding. This problem will most assuredly keep the board of health quite busy for some time to come.*

---

*SOME BIG CITIES IN GERMANY ARE SUFFERING CONSIDERABLY MORE FROM THE PROBLEM OF OVERCROWDING AND PROVIDE IN EVERY RESPECT POORER HOUSING FOR THEIR LOWER CLASSES

In the year that ended with the last day of April 1872, the board of health spent over $206,000 on its work.

I am closing with the remark that I am well aware one cannot take everything these reports say as absolute truth; even in these reports there are attempts to flatter and to impress the sovereign people among whom so many thousand copies are distributed. But the New York Board of Health enjoys a good reputation, and I have put these bits of information together in order to show how such an agency works.

The annual reports at present are volumes of some four hundred pages with many maps, tables, et cetera, and are distributed in large quantities. Certainly a great deal of information about health affairs is disseminated through them to the public at large.

PUBLIC SCHOOLS IN NEW YORK. VISIT TO A PUBLIC SCHOOL. SCHOOL HOUSE. DAILY OPENING CEREMONIES BEFORE THE LESSONS. SOME COMMENT ABOUT TEACHERS AND CURRICULUM. NUMBER OF SCHOOLS IN NEW YORK. EXPENDITURES FOR THESE SCHOOLS. SALARIES. BOARD OF EDUCATION.

One morning I went to the public school on Twenty-seventh Street, which had been recommended to me by people who were familiar with city schools as a good example of such an institution; a friend from my university days, who is

---

THAN DOES NEW YORK, BUT ONE PAYS UNQUESTIONABLY MORE ATTENTION TO THIS HERE THAN ELSEWHERE. I THINK THAT EVEN A FEW DAYS CANNOT GO BY WITHOUT SOME NEW YORK NEWSPAPER RAISING THESE SORE POINTS. I CAN SEE FROM THE REPORTS THAT I HAVE IN FRONT OF ME HOW THE OFFICIALS ACTIVELY CONCERN THEMSELVES WITH THESE SOCIAL ILLS. THIS PROBLEM IS DISCUSSED SO FREQUENTLY IN EDUCATED CIRCLES THAT ALREADY IN THE FIRST FEW DAYS I HAVE BECOME THOROUGHLY INFORMED ABOUT THIS AND OTHER CONDITIONS INJURIOUS TO HEALTH. EVEN OUTSIDE NEW YORK I HEARD MANY RELEVANT MATTERS DISCUSSED KNOWLEDGEABLY AND WITH LIVELY INTEREST. IN BOSTON AND PHILADELPHIA, TOO, WHOEVER WANTED TO INFORM ME ABOUT THINGS THAT COULD BE CONSIDERED OF GENERAL INTEREST BEGAN FIRST BY TALKING ABOUT PUBLIC HEALTH CARE IN THAT PARTICULAR CITY, ESPECIALLY ABOUT THE LIVING CONDITIONS OF THE LOWER CLASS. WE WILL HAVE TO ADOPT A SIMILAR MODE OF THINKING IF WE DO NOT WANT TO ADMIT THAT IN SUCH A YOUNG DEMOCRACY THEY ARE MORE ZEALOUS IN LOOKING FOR AND POINTING OUT THE PROBLEMS THAT ARE OF PUBLIC CONCERN AND ABOVE ALL IN SHOWING MORE CONCERN FOR THE WELFARE OF THE LOWER CLASSES THAN ARE THOSE LIVING IN OLD, ACCOMPLISHED SOCIETIES ANCHORED IN TRADITION.

now a chemist and, like so many "self-made" men in this country, himself for many years a primary school teacher, accompanied me. The schoolhouse, maintained both inside and outside very simply without appearing shabby, is a somewhat projecting, tall central building with large windows and two narrow wings. Constructed of red brick, it appears to be rather new and so simple and distinctive in the midst of so many narrow, grime-coated houses whose windows are filled with curtains that it clearly gives the impression of having a worthy purpose.

As we entered and climbed the spacious stairway, we saw how the allocation of space conditioned the building's outer contour, for we found that on all three floors of the main building there were large, chapel-like halls, from which doors and hallways led into the classrooms, which were in the wings of the building. We asked for the principal, found him in the upper assembly hall and learned, when we had made our request, that we—it was shortly before nine—had come just at the right time to be present at the little opening exercises that begin every school day. We were offered seats on the platform where the principal and some of the teachers from this section of the school usually sit. One teacher pulled on a series of bell ropes to summon the boys from the classrooms, and the boys took their places in long rows before each of the doors, without any sign of talking or confusion. At the signal from the principal, a female teacher sitting at the piano in front of the platform began to play a march, whereupon the boys simultaneously came out of all the rooms in rapid military fashion, marched into the hall, and as they reached their benches sat down one row after the other. The whole affair seemed to have been very well rehearsed, there was not one sound out of the rows, I didn't see one muscle move on any of the faces, and every class knew very well how it should march and where it should go. When everyone was seated—they sit with their hands clasped behind their backs—the principal got up and read an excerpt from the Psalms, whereupon the entire assembly sang a few verses of a hymn. Then, in just as military and orderly a fashion as they entered, everyone left the hall again.

Going down to the assembly hall on the second floor, we found the girls in the midst of similar opening exercises; they sang a cheerful song. The same exemplary discipline prevailed here as with the boys.

An extraordinary show awaited us in the hall on the first floor, the place where the youngest boys and girls were assembled. This hall is larger than the other two we had visited and contains in the back part, closed off by a sliding wall, a long row of benches, which are elevated in step-like fashion one behind the other. In addition to the piano in front of the teachers' platform in this hall, there is another one in front of the benches. The principal of this section of the school, a middle-aged, short, heavyset lady, whose eyes, under short graying curly locks, appeared good natured but not without drive, was just about to ring and summon the children, and obligingly gave us in the meantime all sorts of information about her classes. We learned that together they contained on the average more than 900 pupils and that in 1871 in toto no less than 2,250 children had been taught here. Eighteen female teachers besides herself are in charge of instruction, which in principle avoids corporal punishment. But because of the irregular attendance of so many—compulsory attendance, as is well known, does not exist here[21]—and because of the little support that the school generally receives from the training at home, educating the pupils is made very difficult.

When the children had taken their places in rows in front of the doors, one of the teachers began to play a simple melody to which they marched in from all sides. They walked in very short steps, close behind one another, their little heads thrown back, their arms hanging down close to their sides, with a peculiarly gliding, varying step, and when they reached their places, they immediately put their arms behind their backs and sat down; from one side came the boys, from the other the girls. When everyone was seated, some boys pushed back the partition, which up until then had shut off the elevated part of the hall. There in very bright sunlight shining in from above sat a few hundred motionless children, mostly in bright clothing, with their hands clasped over their eyebrows, in one row after another. It was a remarkable sight, and a huge picture of the mountainous part of the Hudson valley, which occupied the rear wall of the hall, contributed toward making this a very original, although somewhat theatrical scene. The principal now stood up, gave a signal upon which hundreds of children clapped their hands, and then gave another one at which they patted their cheeks. Afterwards, she read a few short verses from the Bible and wished them good morning, to which the crowd loudly replied, and again it was done in a formal cadenced manner without screaming. Then a few easy songs were sung, a religious one and one about robin redbreast who always wants to fly away, and at the end, one little girl got up on one of the chairs on the platform and went through all sorts of motions, which were imitated in orderly fashion by the others. Whereupon they all streamed out again just as they had come and no one uttered a peep.

Afterwards, we walked up again to the boys' section to listen to the instruction where nothing impressed me as much as the facility with which the twelve- to fourteen-year olds could mentally add. I can understand why they emphasize this mental suppleness here, for arithmetic plays such an important role in the life of this country, but I do not think I ever remember having seen such quick calculation at that age. Speaking scarcely slower than usual, the teacher gave a problem that required the use of simple methods of reckoning and figuring with digital powers and square roots in order to solve them. The boys, however, were mentally right behind him, and a few gave the correct answer right after he had finished speaking. The instruction in penmanship also seemed to me to have produced good results and to be handled very practically. The pupils have lined notebooks in which the handwriting example to be copied is given at the top on the side; a letter or a word is often repeated; the individual letters are written almost exclusively with the upstroke or fine line while the downstroke or heavier line appears only in initial letters and in combinations like *mm* or *nn*, where without this differentiation everything would be too uniform. Since by writing quickly, one naturally develops his own writing style consisting of strokes not very different from one another in width, and moreover since there is an almost inevitable stumbling block to training students to write in an attractive and at the same time flowing style because of the incessant alteration of heavy and fine strokes common in German penmanship, it appears to me that this method of writing is very practical. I looked at many pupils' notebooks in various stages of development and found some excellent examples of fine penmanship in them. Using lead pencils, most of the children take down the teacher's dictation in an attractive handwriting. Part of these writing lessons is also devoted to practice in bookkeeping.

What I saw of the furnishings of the classroom was better than those we are generally used to having in the primary school. In the boys' classes, for example, every pupil sat on a little wooden chair with a back support that could swivel on an iron base and before which was placed a desk with a top that could be raised. Big blackboards covered all four walls of the room. There seems to be enough light and ventilation everywhere, and the cleanliness of the rooms and corridors, when one remembers that almost two thousand pupils attend this school, was astonishing. In the upper assembly hall an apparatus used for physics was displayed in a glass case.

The strict discipline that prevails everywhere in these schools, most especially in the morning exercises, as I previously mentioned, is not praised by everyone, and the German schools are said to use much less strict methods. For my part I am limiting myself to criticizing only the most important thing about this discipline, i.e., its effect. With regard to everything else, I just want to remind the reader of the careless upbringing at home or the complete lack of any upbringing of the poorer American children, and of the fact that they grow up very early and that the normal development of the mental and emotional qualities proper to childhood is not possible in these schools; this all helps to make the raw material with which the teacher has to work turn out very differently from German school children. In the lower grades, children of the most varied age levels are put together since it is only the degree of the parents' interest for their children's education that determines if, when, and how regularly they will permit them to go to school. The majority of children don't go to school long enough; many work a few months for their parents and then get some schooling again for awhile. In addition, the ease with which families here change their living quarters also helps to make school children an extremely variable factor in education, for it would be very difficult to maintain correct social discipline if some conventions and etiquette were not observed by each and every one of us and if these were not fully a part of school life. The almost military discipline that prevails at the general morning prayers and to a lesser degree is also maintained in the classroom helps mold the children's character every day so that it becomes inextricably identified with school in their minds. To remain silent, to obey, to conform to the rules, these are taught alongside reading, writing, and arithmetic and, in effect, even if they are harder than the latter, the children learn to put them to use.

This school, which is one of the largest among the fifty-eight municipal primary schools, was built in 1849 and enlarged in 1859, occupies a space 125 feet wide and 100 feet deep, and has a value, according to the estimation of the official reports, of $203,000 (property and building). In 1871, 4,254 children received an education here; the faculty consisted of 8 male and 45 female teachers. Of the latter, 10 are in the boys' school, 16 in the girls', and 19 in the primary school. Of the male teachers, one is the music teacher, one is the principal, while the other 6 teach in the boys' school.

The curriculum is briefly as follows: in the primary schools, which correspond to our basic elementary schools (*Volkschulen*), the course of instruction is divided into six half-year semesters. Mental arithmetic is begun as early as the third semester; in the sixth they are expected to know completely the four basic operations of arithmetic,[22] have begun geography, and are taught measures and weights and how to work with them. This method of education clearly is based on the idea of imprinting as many of the most important things on the students' minds as possible, as when, for example, during the last semester every pupil has to sign his name at the bottom of every page he fills up with his penmanship exercises, or when the curriculum of the last three semesters continually calls for the systematic practice of writing one's signature, the place, and the date. Teaching with visual aids plays a very important role in the curriculum. Indoor sports are required, and a class is not supposed to be larger than seventy-five students.

The separate schools for boys and for girls attended after this simple primary school are called grammar schools, have their course of instruction divided into eight semesters, and are, according to their purpose and course offerings, something between our advanced elementary schools (*Volkschulen*) and our lower-grade secondary schools (*höhere Bürgerschulen*). In the first two years, fractions, the geography of North America, and the rudiments of natural history are added to the basic subjects, so that by this time they are offering what is usually being taught in our better elementary schools. They go on to English grammar, the history of the United States, applied arithmetic, and physics; also touch on astronomy, chemistry, and physical geography in the last two semesters; teach the Constitution of the United States and acquaint the students with some facts about world history and the principles of accounting. In mathematics the pupils also begin to learn simple equations and the elements of plane geometry. In the girls' division sewing may also be taught. Foreign languages are not required, but the municipal board of education has at least announced a curriculum plan in its report for 1871 according to which German would be offered in those schools where it has already been introduced.

The primary and grammar schools are not always in the same building as in the schoolhouse I visited today; for although many people, indeed anyone who wants a reasonably good background in preparation for the business world, go through both of them, it is not absolutely necessary. This can be seen by the fact that of the 238 schools that are under the supervision of the board of education, 88 are grammar schools (42 for girls) and 94 are primary schools. After a recent increase, the annual salaries for male principals of a grammar school are now $3,000, for female principals up to $2,000, for principals of primary schools (almost all women) up to $1,800. Male teachers receive $1,400, while females receive $600 to $850. It should be noted here that a dollar in New York does not have as much purchasing power as a thaler in Berlin; when figured out, it is worth scarcely more than two marks.[23] In addition, since the weekly earnings of even the common workers has risen often enough to $20 and $25 (according to statistics for 1870), bright capable men will only apply for the better paying teaching positions. Therefore almost seven-eighths of all teaching positions in the city schools are held by women and of these 2,500 female teachers only one-fifth are teaching in exclusively girls' institutions. The males in the school system do not look on this female invasion with particular pleasure, but, considering the ease with which any industrious highly educated man can get a job in this country, without the women the schools would stand deserted. Let us hope that the improved methods of professional training, which are being offered of late to young female teachers and prospective teachers, will gradually enhance the natural female pedagogic gift for school teaching more than has previously been the case. This predominance of female teachers is moreover a situation that can be generally found all over in the United States.*

*I WOULD LIKE TO ADD HERE A BRIEF DESCRIPTION, BASED ON NOTES TAKEN LATER ON, OF A LITTLE RURAL SCHOOLHOUSE WE VISITED IN SEPTEMBER 1873. THE SCHOOL WAS LOCATED IN ONE OF THE MOST THINLY POPULATED AREAS OF THE ADIRONDACK MOUNTAINS, HAVING JUST BARELY EMERGED FROM THE WILDERNESS.

ON THE WAY TO LAKE PLACID, WE VISITED THE SCHOOLHOUSE OF NORTH ELBA, WHICH STANDS ALONE ON A SOMEWHAT RAISED SPOT VIRTUALLY IN THE MIDDLE OF THE WIDELY SCATTERED FARMHOUSES. IT IS A ONE-STORY BUILDING, THE INTERIOR OF WHICH IS COMPLETELY TAKEN UP BY THE CLASSROOM. THE TWO SIDE WALLS HAVE EACH THREE WINDOWS, WHILE THE WALL OPPOSITE THE DOOR HAS TWO. THE DOOR LEADS TO A LITTLE PORCH, ALSO POSSESSING A WINDOW, WHICH HAS PROVED TO BE VERY USEFUL IN WINTER OR IN STORMY WEATHER. THE TEACHER'S SIMPLE PODIUM STANDS IN THE RIGHT-HAND CORNER BY THE DOOR, THE BLACKBOARD HANGS TO THE OTHER SIDE OF THE DOOR, AND BENCHES FOR ABOUT THIRTY CHILDREN, FROM THE UPPER AND LOWER GRADES, STAND IN ROWS BEFORE IT. THIS IS THE PLAINEST, SIMPLEST SCHOOLHOUSE CONCEIVABLE, BUT AS SIMPLE AS IT IS, IT IS KEPT IN GOOD CONDITION AND IS SUFFICIENTLY BRIGHT AND AIRY. IT SERVES ITS PURPOSE. UNFORTUNATELY, SCHOOL WAS NOT IN SESSION AT THIS TIME AND WE MISSED AN INTERESTING EXPERIENCE, BUT WE ASKED AND WERE TOLD ALL ABOUT THIS SCHOOL. ONE OF THE PEOPLE MAKING THE TRIP WITH ME, WHO HAD ONCE BEEN A TEACHER HIMSELF, WAS ABLE TO ADD SOME GENERAL INFORMATION ABOUT THE ELEMEN-

I want to make a few comments here about what the city of New York does for education. In school taxes (which the state requires), it pays $1,269,156, i.e., over half of what the whole state pays, and receives back for its own education needs $507,602. In 1871 the municipal school expenditures ran to $2,460,296, of which $1,602,217 went for teachers' salaries, $99,855 for the

---

TARY SCHOOL SYSTEM OF THIS STATE AND PARTICULARLY OF THESE MOUNTAIN AREAS. THUS I LEARNED THAT IN THIS BUILDING SCHOOL WAS IN SESSION FOR SIX MONTHS OF THE YEAR, THREE IN SUMMER AND THREE IN WINTER, THAT CLASSES WERE HELD FOR FOUR TO FIVE HOURS EVERY DAY, THAT THE YOUNGER PUPILS GO TO SCHOOL DURING BOTH SESSIONS, WHILE THE OLDER ONES STAY AWAY IN SUMMER BECAUSE THEY HAVE TO HELP THEIR PARENTS IN THE FIELDS, AND THAT A FEMALE TEACHER IS IN CHARGE OF EDUCATION HERE. I ALSO HEARD THAT WHENEVER POSSIBLE THEY PREFER TO HAVE A MALE TEACHER FOR THE WINTER SESSION BE-CAUSE HE WOULD BE MORE CAPABLE OF CONTROLLING THE LARGER NUMBER OF PUPILS, ESPE-CIALLY THE OLDER ONES WHO COME THEN. NEEDY STUDENTS ARE GIVEN WINTER LEAVES OF ABSENCE FROM UNIVERSITIES AND COLLEGES EXPRESSLY FOR THIS PURPOSE, AND FOR THREE MONTHS' WORK THEY RECEIVED $60 TO $90, AS WELL AS ROOM AND BOARD. THE ARRANGE-MENT IS FREQUENTLY WORKED OUT SO THAT THE YOUNG TEACHER LIVES SUCCESSIVELY WITH EACH OF THE BETTER-OFF FAMILIES OF THE SCHOOL DISTRICT, STAYING A WEEK OR SO WITH EACH OF THEM. THE INSTRUCTION IS COMPLETELY FREE, SINCE THE COMMUNITY DEFRAYS ALL SCHOOL EXPENSES BY TAXES, AND FREQUENTLY THE STATE ALSO HAS A FUND FOR EDUCATIONAL PURPOSES FROM WHICH THE INDIVIDUAL DISTRICTS CAN RECEIVE SUPPORT FOR THEIR SCHOOLS. IT IS SAID THAT THE CITIZENS IN MORE PROSPEROUS DISTRICTS OFTEN VOLUNTARILY DECIDE TO EXTEND THE SCHOOL YEAR AND PAY FOR ITS COSTS BY A SPECIALLY ADDED TAX. THERE IS NO LACK OF SPECIAL PHILANTHROPIC FOUNDATIONS FOR EDUCATIONAL PURPOSES HERE, AND THE FINE FURNISHINGS IN MANY RURAL SCHOOLS CAN BE ATTRIBUTED TO THEM. THE TEACHERS ARE INTERVIEWED BY A TOWNSHIP COMMITTEE, AND EACH SCHOOL DISTRICT SELECTS ITS TEACHERS FROM AMONG THE CANDIDATES.

I ONLY WANT TO TOUCH HERE UPON WHAT HAS ALREADY BEEN MENTIONED EARLIER—(WITH REGARD TO THE NEW YORK SCHOOLS), UPON THE FLUCTUATING CHARACTER OF AMERICAN ELE-MENTARY SCHOOL TEACHERS AS A WHOLE, I.E., VIEWED AS PROFESSIONALS. THE AMERICANS WITH WHOM I SPOKE DO NOT DECEIVE THEMSELVES ABOUT THIS MATTER AND COMPLAINED ABOUT IT TOO. VERY SELDOM DOES A MAN STAY IN THIS PROFESSION. GENERALLY IT IS A TEMPORARY JOB FOR THOSE WHO WANT TO GET AHEAD, AND AS SUCH IT HAS PLAYED AN IMPOR-TANT PART IN THE LIVES OF MANY IMPORTANT MEN IN THIS COUNTRY. ONE WOULD HAVE TO ASSUME THAT THIS WOULD HAVE A BAD EFFECT ON THE QUALITY OF INSTRUCTION IF LIFE ITSELF HERE DID NOT SUPPLEMENT THE ELEMENTARY SCHOOL AS A MANY-SIDED EDUCATIONAL FORCE AND IF THE MEANS OF EDUCATION OFFERED OUTSIDE THE SCHOOL WERE NOT SO VERY GREAT NOR SO EASILY OBTAINABLE. SO IN SPITE OF THE LACK OF PROFESSIONALLY TRAINED TEACHERS AND THE GREAT QUANTITY OF IMMATURE AND NONSERIOUS ONES AMONG THE PRESENT-DAY ELEMEN-TARY SCHOOL TEACHERS, THE AVERAGE UNDERSTANDING AND DISCERNMENT OF THE POPULATION IS STILL CONSIDERABLY HIGHER THAN ANYWHERE IN EUROPE.

school custodians, $44,255 for the upkeep of the schools for colored children, $101,648 for books, maps, and blackboards—the children receive what they need in the way of books, writing materials, and the like. As mentioned above, the total number of municipal schools comes to 238, to which can be added 13 schools in charitable institutions supported by the city. Of this number, 3 are normal schools (for the training of teachers), one a model school, 89 grammar schools, 94 primary schools, 27 evening schools, one an advanced evening school, and 13 are schools for colored children. The total number of pupils in 1871 amounted to 213,709, of which 187,605 were in grammar and primary schools, 21,561 in evening schools, 2,185 in schools for the colored, and 2,358 in normal schools.[24] The average attendance for this year was 95,862. The number of teachers came to 2,564, of which 2,192 were women. Besides these schools, the city also supports a college, which in what it proposes to do goes partly beyond our high schools (*Gymnasien*); it is called the Free Academy.[25] In addition there are also about 400 private schools of various sorts, among which are some excellent institutions of higher learning founded and supported by different groups and organizations. In these schools, which do not fall under the jurisdiction of the board of education, there are in toto another 2,000 teachers, and their number seems to be growing more rapidly than that of the city school teachers.

The board of education, which I have frequently mentioned, has a history that to a degree is characteristic of the way and manner in which important things develop in this country. Up until 1795 all schools in New York State were run by private individuals or organizations, naturally most frequently by churches. During that year, the legislature for the first time approved $50,000 for educational purposes, and ten years later the proceeds from the gradual sale of 500,000 acres of state owned property were designated for the same purposes. At that time various societies arose in New York, which championed the cause of education for such groups as the poor and the colored, so that in 1787 a school for colored children was founded, and in 1802 a school for poor girls. Later on many schools were also established in this way. Among these groups, the Free School Society, later known as the Public School Society of New York City,[26] became so important because of its able leadership and intense activity that it soon became a kind of supreme school administrative board in whose hands the city and state placed the means with which it could then establish and maintain schools. Then in 1842, after this society had carried out its duties for thirty-seven years to the satisfaction of the citizens, an official board of education was instituted, which worked alongside the society for eleven years until both were finally combined. At the merger, the society brought $600,000 to add to the general funds. In the forty-nine years of its existence, it had helped instruct and educate well over half a million children. At present the board consists of twelve members who are appointed by the mayor of the city to five-year terms and who are simultaneously trustees of the Free Academy.

INSTITUTIONS OF HIGHER LEARNING IN NEW YORK. COLLEGE FOR FEMALE TEACHERS. FACULTY. POSITION OF FEMALE TEACHERS. FREE ACADEMY. BUILDINGS. CURRICULUM.

Because of the dominant role women occupy among the elementary school teachers in this country,[27] I was particularly interested in visiting at least a few of the institutions, corresponding to our teacher training schools (*Seminarien*), which are set up for the general education and professional training of female teachers, and I eagerly seized the first opportunity that was offered me here to get to know such an institution.

In 1869 the New York City Board of Education founded a college for women in order to help alleviate the great need for elementary school teachers. This Normal College, as it has since been named, began its first academic year three years ago, and last summer it moved out of an unsatisfactory, temporary building in which it had felt cramped and into a handsome and roomy one that had been built especially for the college. Brand new inside and out, this school more than any other promised to supply us with information about current practices concerning higher education for women and the objectives this educational program sets for itself, with particular regard to the future professional work of its students. When I visited it in October 1873, the classes were in session, and its director, Mr. Thomas Hunter,[28] one of the most distinguished of the city's educators, accompanied us from class to class explaining the origin and history of the institution, the teaching methods and their results, and telling us about many interesting experiences from his many years as a teacher. What I saw and heard, supplemented by some data from official school reports, I have now compiled and summarized in the following account.

The school building,[29] situated at what was then the north end of the city, occupies 26,000 square feet, has four floors, thirty classrooms and lecture halls, some of which can accommodate two hundred students, an assembly hall seating two thousand people, a gymnasium (*Kalisthenium*) of almost 4,000 square feet, and big, bright, excellently equipped rooms for a library, collections, and exhibits, a teachers' room, and the like. Very close to the main building there is an elementary school, smaller than what one is otherwise used to seeing here; in it prospective teachers are supposed to get practical teaching experience.

Admission to this institution is open to every girl who has passed the age of thirteen and who is able to prove by means of a test her knowledge of those subjects one studies in the upper grades of the elementary school (*Volkschule*). This test covers reading, writing, mathematics (from simple and decimal arithmetic to simple equations), the rudiments of geometry, English grammar, and ancient history. The curriculum of the Normal College itself is divided into six half-year semesters in which the following courses are taken: Latin, German,

and French in the first five semesters and German and French conversation in
the sixth; mathematics beyond quadratic equations, geometry, plane trigo-
nometry, and solid geometry in all six semesters; the history of Greece, Rome,
and England in the first three; rhetoric and literature in the fourth and fifth;
physiology in the first, physics in the second, astronomy and botany in the
third, astronomy, physics, and minerology in the sixth. In the last semester
they also get psychology, law, and education courses; music and drawing are
given throughout the first five semesters, while penmanship is taught in the
first two semesters, and accounting in the last semester.

The faculty consists of the president, four professors, and twenty-three female teachers; the number of pupils when the college opened was 1,068, and
the number of students in attendance during the last few years tends on the
average to be about 1,000.

In the rooms we visited, classes were being held in, among other subjects,
physics, Greek history, rhetoric, and zoology, and in the last three the teachers
were lecturing. The president seemed generally to expect more results from the
effectiveness of the professor who taught physics and from all capable male
teachers than he did from the female teachers. He felt that the budding chival-
rous attitude that teenage boys show to their female instructors often has a
beneficial effect on their attentiveness and diligence, and there is a similar
situation here with the girls who try to do their very best for their good male
teachers and who unfortunately often do not show this same enthusiasm in
classes with female teachers, although these may be equally competent. He
also does not believe that the predominance of women among elementary
school teachers will ever completely rule out the need for male teachers. Although from his own experience he can point to many excellent results that
women have had in educating children, he nevertheless is inclined to attribute
their success in part to the fact that in America so few excellently qualified
men commit themselves permanently to teaching.

It must also be remembered that before the Normal College was founded,
most of the girls went directly from the upper classes of the elementary school
into teaching and still had a great deal to learn even after they were already
teaching. Consequently, the difficulties these women encountered at the beginning of their careers were greater than those of the young men who went into
this profession. Only time will tell whether the Normal College will contribute
as much to the creation of a group of well-trained female teachers as one had
assumed it would at the time of its founding. Up until now it seems that the
majority of pupils have used the opportunity it provided for acquiring a good

2   WOMEN STUDENTS WORKING IN THE WELL-EQUIPPED
SCIENCE LABORATORY OF THE NORMAL COLLEGE, NEW YORK
CITY.

education more for their own advantage than for that of elementary education. Very few, after they leave the college, want to devote themselves to teaching; rather, they employ the knowledge they have gained in a way that is personally of use to them. An instructor in another school told me that this is neither an unexpected nor an undesirable result. A major hope of reasonable people has always been to see an institution of higher learning for women included in the program of public education. Given the opposition, which in many circles is always against any state or municipal support for anything but elementary education, this would not have been so easily achieved if the training of teachers had not been emphasized as the main purpose of the college.[30]

Of all the things that I saw and heard in the classes what pleased me most, since it was a rather new experience, was the easy and confident manner of the teachers as well as of the students, who were not disturbed by our entrance and presence but calmly continued to do what they were then busy doing. In the rhetoric class a girl was reciting a speech (if I am not mistaken, from Scott's *Ivanhoe*) with a very artificially modulated voice and a superabundance of pathos, such as you can frequently hear on the stage or on a lecture podium in this country. The only thing I liked about this performance was its brashness and the benevolent expression of the teacher who watched the enthusiastic orator without showing any sign of reproach, ridicule, or impatience. The zoology class was occupied with starfish and thoroughly went into the mysteries of a piece of coral and of the skeleton of an echinoderm. The pupils had several dried starfish in front of them, had already observed specimens in alcohol, and some of the students, when called upon, gave correct explanations about the subject. The teacher, a pupil of Agassiz,[31] who also taught Latin and plane geometry, appeared to be more adept at handling her subject than many university professors, and when I later had the opportunity to speak to her about the difficulties of teaching zoology, I found her a woman of good mind and much learning. She admitted that zoology was one of the less popular subjects among the girls but that the initial indifference to frogs and grasshoppers could be overcome and that the greater problem in any event was the lack of frequent and detailed study of real specimens, a lack that can not be completely met by literary aids, with illustrations and descriptions. She complained about the lack of good zoology textbooks, and I could at least assure her that, despite the great love with which this branch of natural science is studied in Germany, in this respect we are not much better off.*

---

*IN FACT IS IT NOT ASTONISHING THAT OUR AGE, WHICH HAS SHOWN SO MUCH SUCCESS IN THE STUDY OF NATURE, HAS MADE SO LITTLE PROGRESS IN DEVELOPING THE MEANS AND METHODS OF DISSEMINATING WHAT WE ALREADY KNOW? WE NEED GOOD TEXTS AND ABOVE ALL SCHOOL BOOKS FOR NATURAL HISTORY. HOW NICE IT WOULD BE TO HAVE SOME PUBLISHED, FOR THEY CERTAINLY COULD BE USED! THERE IS NO LACK OF MEANS OR PEOPLE TO ACCOMPLISH THIS, BUT

There was more done in the Normal College to furnish the classrooms with educational equipment than in any other school or college I have seen, even in any of our new *Polytechniken* (technical colleges). They clearly did not skimp in spending here, and many rooms gave an unusually good impression of being comfortably equipped. In most rooms the seats and tables were made of walnut; the former were able to swivel and turn in various directions, having both comfortable seats and back rests designed so as to allow the students to sit upright. Some of the desks are built with hinged tops that can be pushed up, some with pull-out drawers for books and writing materials. There were no desks in one room where the rows of seats were mounted up towards the back of the room, but attached to the back of each seat, at the left side, was a movable piece of wood on which, when notes were to be taken, the pupils could hold their notebooks in a comfortable position. On the ground floor was a room through which ran a large number of heating pipes on which the pupils could quickly dry their overgarments in inclement weather.

If the library and the teaching materials are as good as the equipment in the classroom, then this institution will hardly leave anything for the pupils still to desire, and then the only big problem remaining will be building and retaining a competent faculty. Being accustomed to a specific course of instruction, state examinations, and permanent teaching positions, we may find it hard to believe that it is possible to obtain a good faculty on the basis of competition alone, but it is so. They value a person here for what he does and not because of the way in which he got his skills. By looking at things in this manner, they reduce, much more than we are able to, the burden of incompetent or half-competent civil servants and officials who first laboriously squeeze through the examinations and then plod through their work with even more difficulty. However, the assumption of the educational system—that there will be a generally uniform quality of education, completion in all cases of the uniform course requirements, and the availability of a faculty equal in size and quality—also has to be abandoned, for many teachers go on from employment in the school, as from

---

THE DESIRE TO DISCOVER NEW THINGS STILL HAS A GRIP ON PEOPLE; THE SEARCH FOR NEW DISCLOSURES AND FOR THE LITTLE FAME THAT GOES WITH IT GIVES THEM NO PEACE. THAT IS WHY OUR MEN OF LEARNING TOO OFTEN RESEMBLE THE MISERLY WHO ONLY THINK ABOUT AMASSING AND COLLECTING, NEVER ABOUT THE VALUE OF GIVING AND DISSEMINATING SOMETHING. IN FACT, I BELIEVE THAT IF ONE WANTED TO COMPARE IN IMPORTANCE THE VARIOUS CONTRIBUTIONS MADE IN THE REALM OF INTELLECTUAL ACHIEVEMENT, THEN THE PRODUCTION OF GOOD TEXTBOOKS AND POPULAR EDITIONS OF SCHOLARLY SUBJECTS WOULD CERTAINLY RANK HIGH. AMERICANS IN PARTICULAR COMPLAIN THAT THE FREQUENT CHANGING OF SCHOOLBOOKS, WHICH CAN OFTEN BE ATTRIBUTED TO THE SHADY DEALINGS OF THE BOOK DEALERS AND AUTHORS INVOLVED, AFFECTS THE USEFULNESS OF THE FEW GOOD BOOKS THEY HAVE.

many other jobs, to better positions in life. While many faculty members are still uneasy about teaching because they have still to learn how to teach, others soon begin to lose interest because they have set their professional goals far beyond the walls of a schoolroom. Institutions of higher learning naturally suffer less from this problem since, because of the higher salaries they offer, they are in the position to be more careful in their selection and are able to attract and hold on to the more competent candidates. But they are not left entirely untouched by the influence of the system of free competition either, and above all they will come to perceive a lack of an esprit de corps among their faculty members and of a homogeneous class of teachers with its own set traditions and goals. Even if, as the results show, the American system can accomplish a great deal, nevertheless, it still seems that at least in this regard America cannot evolve independently, because whenever it needed the benefits of the long and hard work that the Old World has produced, it was able to draw upon these mature accomplishments. Could education similar to that produced in the calm of our more stable European environment have ever evolved from nothing and been brought to such a state of development here with such a disparate and transient body of teachers lacking uniform educational training? Would the teaching profession here have been able to carry out the necessary duties if Europe had not placed the means in its hands and shown the way?

Nevertheless, it must also be remembered that such a practical and fast-living people as the Americans have taken to heart more deeply than we have the true meaning of one of our good old sayings, "Mit vielem kommt man aus, mit wenig hält man Haus."[32] It strikes one that the basis of so many enterprises in America is the urge to extract what is necessary from all the nonessential, customary things that have enveloped it, always undertaking to do only that which is necessary and to do it well and quickly, and one suspects that most probably this way of thinking has also affected the way in which schools are run here. They actually require no other knowledge from the teacher than what he has to teach. Whether he can explain the a-b-c's and that $1 + 1 = 2$ is for them a more important question in selecting the teacher than where and how he learned it and what else he knows besides these things.

On another day I visited the municipal college for young men, the Free Academy of the City of New York as it is officially called, and observed something there that may be worth relating.[33] This institution is considerably older than the Normal College, which is clearly indicated by the grey, dark, ugly Gothic building it occupies and even more so by its interior design—a style that fortunately seems to have gone out of fashion. The halls, stairways, and rooms are all smaller, the furnishings much poorer than in newer schools, and naturally to some degree worn out. Nevertheless, this is like an outgrown piece of clothing, which only seems to indicate that the body it covers grew stronger and more robust than thought possible by the careful planners who fitted it a little too exactly.

Upon entering the somber first floor, I noticed a few bulletin boards near the door on which written notices were tacked up, and when I looked more closely, I found that they gave the time and place for meetings of a rowing club and for a Clionian Society.[34] The latter was debating the question of the economic consequences of war, for which speakers for and against were already listed. This Clionian Society is regularly found as one of several but generally as one of two such organizations at colleges here. They speak and write about questions on a wide variety of topics and are influenced by the faculty only insofar as it provides a room in the building for their meetings, offers an annual prize and, if necessary, lends a helping hand with advice and information. Most of these societies have assembled little libraries. I also noticed a horseshoe, which was nailed over one of the doors, and since I am well acquainted from my own country with the significance that the superstitious ascribe to this object, I asked what the meaning of this symbol was, especially here in this place. I was told that this was the door of the school custodian's apartment and that the custodian was Irish and, like most Irish, was very superstitious. I was really surprised by this situation, which seems to be another example of the lack of bias that allows the most varied opinions and points of view to exist here peacefully and unhindered side by side.

On the second floor I found the president of the college in his office.[35] He is no educator in our sense of the word but assumed this position after having come straight out of the army, where he served with distinction as a general during the Civil War. I found him to be a man of fine engaging manners, but behind these manners seemed to be a distinctly determined character with something of the military exactness coming through here that is just right for such a position. Entering a room on the opposite side of the hallway, I found myself in the library, which at present contains some twenty-two thousand volumes. The room is big and bright, and the furnishings are quite attractive. On the other side of the hall was an impressive collection of physics and chemistry equipment. As we came nearer, we saw a small laboratory on the right in which an instructor, the professor's assistant, was working, while on the left the professor himself was lecturing in the amphitheater-like auditorium to an audience of more than one hundred. On the same floor there are additional classrooms, and the second floor consists entirely of such rooms. On the third floor is a room, something between an assembly hall and school chapel, where the students assemble before the beginning of classes to hear the president read a psalm or a chapter of the Bible. The size of some of these rooms in the school seems to bear no relation to the number of students they hold.

In a separate building nearby is the preparatory school, which has a college preparatory and a commercial division; the former prepares young people for the first of the four years of college, the latter for going into business. In 1871 both sections together had an enrollment of 538 pupils, while the college had only 370. The faculty of the entire institution consists of 14 professors and 19 assistants; the former receive a salary of $3,750, without any differentiation, the latter either $2,500 or $1,200, which even by New York standards can be considered quite good.

Upon entering the college preparatory school, the student is given a test in English, mathematics, geography, and the history of the United States. The first-year college class, the freshman class, as it is called according to the old division of university students into the four classes of freshmen, sophomores, juniors, and seniors, is taught the rudiments of descriptive and analytic geometry, surveying and navigation, anatomy and physiology, world history, and English and American literature. The students read either Sallust and Cicero, Lucian and Aesop, or begin the study of either French, German, or Spanish. In the last year of the college preparatory curriculum the senior class reads selections from Plato, Thucydides, and Sophocles, studies German, French, and Spanish, and attends lectures about astronomy, solid geometry, chemistry, engineering, aesthetics, the general history of literature, metaphysics, economics, the constitutional history of the United States, and law, while the commercial students in the last year are just beginning to read Caesar and Sallust. As the wealth of courses offered during one year in schools of this high quality shows, it is certain that students can find something to appeal to them with regard to their future careers, further study, or just their plain interest in one subject or another.

Every college requires some kind of elective or optional studies for its upper classmen, and I found, for example, in the curriculum plan for Harvard College in Cambridge, which is the oldest and most respected institution of its kind in the country, the following pertinent requirement: besides the required courses, every sophomore must select four courses that meet at least two times per week, every junior three three-hour courses, and every senior four three-hour courses. In selecting his electives, the student must also prove to the teacher that his previous studies enable him to follow the course he has chosen. With this one limitation the student is allowed to take any course or lecture offered in the college, although he is seriously advised to make his selection with great care and after thorough consultation with his adviser so that his elective courses from beginning to end can form a fitting, cohesive whole.

It should be noted, however, that Harvard is one of the institutions of higher learning whose faculty and educational facilities are among the best in the country, and therefore it is able to offer more electives and optional courses than other schools with similar objectives. But it is always introductory survey courses that are incorporated into the curriculum in this way. Even if a college here is wealthy enough to hire more teachers for instruction in the liberal arts curriculum than a German university can, by omitting more specialized and technical courses, it retains the character of a liberal arts undergraduate school and does not go beyond a specific level of study, which we could think of as something ranging between that of a German high school (*Gymnasium*) and the philosophical faculty[36] of a German university. This system creates the need for technical or graduate schools, and these are founded independently of the college, although they may be placed under the same administrative authority or might even be housed under the same roof. These are clearly regarded as supplemental to the basic college, but due to the nature of the system will one day most probably merge with the college to form a university in our sense of the word. At the present time, however, they are considered as separate from and additional to the colleges. We have an example of this type in the oldest New York college, Columbia College, which is affiliated with the Episcopal Church.[37] Here the students in the most advanced or senior class are taught the fundamentals of natural and revealed religion, modern history, economics, philosophy, the history of classical literature, astronomy, physics, chemistry, geology and minerology, and, if they want it, differential calculus after they have already finished Latin and Greek in the junior class, studied the history of modern literature, logic, literary criticism, modern history, physics, chemistry, philosophy and the history of mathematics, and sampled one of the modern languages. The same president, however, administers not only the college but also a law school and an engineering school. Besides these schools, the same funds also support a medical school, without anyone from any of the schools being able to have a say or word in the running of the others.

This system has developed even further in the above mentioned Harvard College, which with its affiliated institutions is clearly evolving into a university. The college itself has a complete liberal arts faculty and has gradually seen schools for theology, law, medicine, dentistry, mining, engineering, chemistry, natural sciences, agriculture, gardening, as well as an observatory and a unique, wonderfully equipped zoological school grow up around it. But here at Columbia, as far as I can determine, it is pretty well recognized that soon a more organic interrelation has to replace the uncoordinated way in which the schools exist in relation to one another. Some knowledgeable people were of the opinion that in a few years the college would probably combine with the specialized schools to form a university.[38]

CHAPTER TWO

The Hudson

SIGNIFICANCE FOR NEW YORK. SCENIC BEAUTY. ACTIVITY IN THE
AREA. WEST POINT. CORNWALL.

The Hudson River offers the city of New York, situated at its mouth, not only
one of the most excellent harbors of the world and a mighty, valuable artery
running deep into a most fertile region, but also brings the rolling country and
mountains along its banks much nearer and facilitates access to a large and
beautiful natural area so close to the deafening hustle and bustle of the big city
that, with regard to this advantage, New York leaves European cities far behind. Below the estuary island of Manhattan on which New York has spread
out, the main branch of the river expands into the splendid bay; a branch, the
East River, runs in an easterly direction into Long Island Sound with all its
little islands; while a trip upstream toward the north would bring one in a half-
hour into the middle of a thickly wooded, rocky and hilly area filled with lakes
and streams. This is a fabulous region whose significance as a resort for the
mental and physical recuperation of the huge, growing population of the urban
complex on the lower Hudson (New York, Brooklyn, Jersey City, Hoboken, et
cetera) increases in proportion to the population, which continues to expand
around the center of the metropolis.

The people here love to compare their Hudson with the Rhine, but when one
takes a closer look, the similarity seems mostly to be in the physical characteristics of both rivers and in their importance for the society and culture of their
respective countries. Even here, however, the similarity is slight. The Rhine is
narrower, but its banks, because of their natural formation and their cultivation, are more important. Like all the other North American rivers, the Hudson
is impressive especially because of its width, but this mighty body of water is
more fortunate than the others because of its gentle, wooded, hilly surroundings. As far as we Germans are concerned, we have absolutely no river that can
be compared to the Hudson. Whoever wants to get an idea of what it is like will

have to see it for himself, and the best opportunity to do this is to take a trip upstream, similar to our Rhine trips. Such a trip is on the agenda of every vacationer and is taken by many thousands.

The steamer leaves the west side of New York from Twenty-third Street at a place on the river which is a little too far north to be part of the amazing activity further south in the area closer to the bay. Nevertheless, it is filled with enough shipping traffic for us to realize that we are on the periphery of a very important center of world trade. Along the landings on both sides of the river, surrounded with pilings and raft-like piers, the mast and rigging structures of docked ships, which are loading or unloading, stir in almost unbroken rows above the warehouse roofs; bit and little steamships, serving as ferries and tugboats, advance here and there, and a crowd of sailboats glides upstream. On the New York side a few impressive buildings arise further on in various places out of the mass of commercial wooden and brick warehouses along the river edge—a hospital, an insane asylum, an institution for the deaf-mute, which seek some sun and fresh air here for their patients; and some of the towers of the city can also still be seen from here. In contrast, the opposite side of the river is already steep here with forest, even if frequently interrupted by houses that run down to the water's edge, while here and there the crests of the bank's rock structure stick out from its green covering. As we travel on and approach the northern tip of the island, the Manhattan side also gradually takes on a less urban character. The flat ridge of hills in which it ends, although already laid out in streets, avenues, and boulevards, begins to have country houses with spacious parks, and here and there, between fields and wooded areas some cultivated plots and gardens have been squeezed in, and finally on the right is the entrance to the river or branch of the river that separates Manhattan from the mainland. If you look back from here, only the haze due to smoke, the towers, and the forest of ships' masts give evidence of the existence of a city on this island, which rises before your eyes out of the river here with its north point so thickly wooded that it could scarcely have seemed more solitary and undisturbed to its discoverer when in September 1609 he sailed for the first time up the river that has been named after him than it does to anyone viewing it at this moment.

The city has passed out of sight and only here and there still sends out signals from the land indicating that we are still quite near New York. Several large buildings used for educational or charitable purposes and several country houses, which try to look elegant with their turrets and oriels (among which is one that seems to be a real imitation of a castle ruin), all attract attention on the east bank. On the west bank perpendicular rocks arranged in long row-like columns (the Palisades) appear out of the green covering of trees and bushes, which now only grow in two thin strips below, squeezed in between the wall of stone and the water, and above, crowning the ridge itself. This wall is seldom broken except for a talus slope or a strip of bushes, which grow here because of a favorable location, and it extends for almost five German (about twenty-three statute) miles along the west bank, rising in some places to a height of over four hundred feet. It is formed out of igneous rock, which because of its tendency to form regularly shaped fissures has developed into one long wall that is all the more imposing when compared with the less craggy rock formations thereabouts, especially across the river. But this body of water is wide enough not to be overshadowed by its rocky border-frame. Measuring in some places, in a direct line from shore to shore, about a quarter of a geographical mile in width (1.15 statute miles), it still remains dominant in the whole picture. The river, with its mighty brown currents, which flow by very imperceptibly, could easily be compared to a branch of a sea if a ridge of hills were not placed crossways in front of us to the north or if Manhattan were not pushed forward into the middle of the river to the south. Moreover, the tides are noticeable 30 German (140 statute) miles upstream (approximately up to Albany), and the water here is still salty enough, while the river gradient from Albany to New York is extraordinarily small. Although today the Hudson is no longer more closely connected to the ocean than any other body of water that flows into it, judging by its deeply grooved rocky bed, it probably was different in earlier geological periods. Most likely, it once played a role similar to that played by the St. Lawrence River for the great North American lake region.[1]

Since one bank remains almost inaccessible for miles because of its rocky inflexibility, the land under use became all the more compressed in a narrow space on the other side, which has low hills, is wooded, is furnished with two railroads (the Hudson River and the New York-Boston Line), and one canal. It can especially boast of Yonkers, the flourishing little city of suburban villas, three German (about fourteen statute) miles away from New York, one of the most charming places in the state. This place lies at an indentation at the mouth of the Neperhan or Saw Mill River; it is a favorite summer resort for New Yorkers, and the hilly slopes all around are covered with many country houses and gardens irregularly set in an almost completely wooded landscape more thickly forested than in the parks. In this area, which is not the widest part of the Hudson, Henry Hudson[2] cast anchor on his first voyage of discovery and, because of the strong tides and the breadth and depth of the river, became more thoroughly convinced that after two failures he had finally found the northwest passage to India—an opinion he only gave up when, near Albany, he saw that the river bed was narrowing and its gradient rapidly increasing. Disappointed, he turned back and the same thing that happened in the West Indies one hundred years before was repeated: here, as there, the vain search occurred for the countries of the Indies, rich in gold and spices; here, as there, the new territory was not at first highly regarded but soon very clearly proved its unsought and unexpected value. Columbus discovered the continent, but Hudson opened the door through which one day the valuable trade of the region, upon which its metropolis was to be built, would flow in and out.

Exactly at this historically important spot a steamboat filled with hundreds of passengers coming from Albany and a group of eighteen barges carrying stones and wood into the valley met us—both living witnesses of the civilization and society that have developed in this area in the 264 years since its discovery. America does not have many such spots as this, for it is young and its history is not filled with world-shaking events, but the associations that are attached to it are very frequently of a welcome and very promising kind. Some 60 years ago did not a certain Fulton,[3] whom his contemporaries considered crazy, travel up this very river with the first serviceable steamboat the world had seen? That was certainly a historical moment and by no means an unimportant one. The Hudson will one day be as famous as the Nile, the Ganges, the Tiber, or the Thames.

The wall of sheer rock, which forms the Palisades, falls off rather sharply to the north above Yonkers, and lower hills now come into view, which gently reach down to the water's edge on the west side as well. This bank is covered by a forest that is only infrequently broken by clearings. In spite of the almost uniform brownish-green color of the foliage, as characteristic of trees here in high summer just as it is in Europe, the diverse contours of the treetops and the varying density and height of the trees present a more diversified pictorial composition than do our deciduous forests. Seldom do fir or pine trees stand out here against a group of deciduous trees. Only the cypress-like juniper tree (*juniperus virginiana*) springs out of the earth in every clearing like an opaque flame, and clusters, as is its way, frequently in narrowly circumscribed, bare, stony spots, so that one believes he sees a deserted graveyard. The coloring of the juniper, however, is lighter than that of the cypress.

As we approached West Point, one of the most beautifully situated places on the lower Hudson, both sides look alike here. On one side as on the other, long extended ridges mostly with flattened, seldom-pointed contours seem to predominate, and the countryside, which in the distance appears to be perpendicular to the direction of the river, is made up of one row after another of flat hills. Whenever the land rises to any particular height, it is a broad, rounded ridge, a sharply truncated peak with perhaps at best a terraced slope running down to the river. The height of the hills does not exceed the fifteen hundred feet of Storm King, the broad crest that lies before us between West Point and Cornwall. These hills would look uniformly bleak if they were not covered everywhere by a deciduous forest and if the mighty river framed by the hills and far exceeding the Rhine in width even here did not lend them meaning. Even the sky enhances them, for it is an impressive picture to see a thin streak of red evening sky shining through thick round, grey-blue cloud formations, with a dark, hazy-blue row of hills rising on the horizon and the last bit of sunshine rising out of the valleys and up to the hilltops.

The river contains many curves here, although on the whole it flows very definitely from north to south, often cutting off the view on all sides so that it looks like a long lake. Were it not for the missing snowcaps of the Alps, here and there along the way I would have found it very similar to Lake Zurich; the width of both bodies of water and their surrounding terrain are really very much alike, only here the water, more brown than green, is different.

3   WEST POINT CADETS AND
THEIR FEMALE VISITORS, WEST
POINT.

We disembarked at a spot where a stream filled with clear water rushed into the river over smooth, rounded cascade rocks. We followed the street, which leads to the little plateau of West Point on which the United States Military Academy with its numerous buildings, structures, parade grounds, and fortifications is located.[4] The site is magnificent and dominates the area. To the north the view extends far upstream; to the east it roams over the rolling countryside where here and there a cluster of homes, a church, or a large country house can be seen in the midst of forest foliage and orchards. In the west there are some more wooded hills, particularly the Storm King with its very broad base, and at the rear, on the little plateau on whose edge we are standing, there is a low hill on which the ruins of Fort Putnam are found surrounded by a forest of oak, chestnut, maple, and walnut trees. This place is, at least in summer, sort of an extension of New York, a municipal summer colony, and it is not merely the natural beauty that is the attraction here. The little war games, which the cadets put on so well, always draw a crowd of excited spectators, and the Sunday afternoon parades are supposed to be one of the highlights of fashionable life at West Point. I was told to go to such a parade because it would be an excellent opportunity to observe a typical display of expensive clothing, which the occasion offered to the female half of the New York moneyed aristocracy. But on weekdays I had already seen so many dressed-up people on the sunny parade grounds that I had enough of this and could very well picture what it looked like on Sunday. So I decided to skip West Point for that day and turned to Cornwall, a less resplendent but scarcely less charming summer resort situated directly on the Hudson, where the valley widens, on the same side as West Point and opposite Storm King.

Now here at last was a genuinely rural place even if by no means a village in our sense of the word. Little, neat houses, mostly surrounded by trees and gardens, seldom built right next to one another in a street but more frequently separated by orchards and fields, are scattered about by the hundreds over the rolling terrain, which lies between the foot of the row of hills and the river. Many of these homes are the summer residences of New Yorkers, but even the homes of the permanent local inhabitants have nothing of the farmhouse about them. Most of them are covered by wooden boards painted white or yellow, with large windows and a veranda at the entrance covered by a roof supported by wooden beams. Many houses are surrounded by a gallery-porch that runs around the entire house, and few have the red bricks of their masonry exposed. Of course, Cornwall is dependent on large-scale agriculture, for the proximity of the city makes the cultivation of garden fruits and vegetables very profitable and a chief source of income, while the fact that so many thousands of vacationers stay here creates of itself a demand for more urban facilities and accommodations. Nevertheless, the general impression one gets is a strangely mixed one when you remember that here you are only twelve German (about fifty-six statute) miles from New York and by no means in a predominantly business or industrial area. I will shortly be taking the reader to villages that, because of their geographic position and income, are much more truly villages than this one. This will then give us an opportunity to see the slight difference that separates town and country and to observe in detail the high level of prosperity that predominates among all segments of society in this state as in most of the northeastern states. One must become familiar with this situation, not simply because it indicates the living conditions of a large and influential section of the American public, but more importantly because of its economic and political significance; it is a mainstay of democratic institutions in a republic, and these in turn are the lifeblood of the republic itself.

While I was passing a day with friends in Cornwall, I was especially attracted by the surrounding hills to the west and south where there was a forest that, although neither tall nor dense, was nevertheless still a forest—the first in the New World into whose shade I was able to enter. I was naturally quite curious as to what it looked like. We see this and that American tree in our gardens and parks in Germany, but how they look next to one another in a forest, what kind of general picture they form there, which bushes and plants grow next to them—such things we can only with difficulty imagine with the aid of pictures and descriptions, and we never know if the artistic conception comes near nature or not. It is an unhappy, makeshift solution. When you are so close to the real thing and get the feeling that in an hour you will be able to experience so many new things, so many unexpected things, and when you think back on the enjoyment you have already had from all the walks you took in the fields and forests at home, then it is as if one were to say, "in an hour someone is going to give you something valuable." Thinking about it increases the expectation. The trees of this section of North America for the most part belong to species that are also well represented in our forests, and thus frequently have recognizable characteristics, for few of them are purely native American. Pine, fir, larch, and yew among the conifers and oak, elm, maple, beech, birch, poplar, alder, and willow are the main species the German forest has in common with the American. The varieties, however, are different, and even if the differences are seemingly small, they can nevertheless be very important in providing an impression of the landscape. Moreover, the undergrowth can also contribute considerably to the overall picture; creeping plants, which in our country do not play a very important role, are quite significant here. Various sorts of plants growing in close proximity to one another, singularly striking leaf formations, or beautiful flowers can introduce new lines or colors to the scene. In addition, the similar yet at the same time different animal kingdom here should also be mentioned. Thus, all the elements in the overall picture here are generally the same as ours, yet in many respects, the way they interact produces very different results.

AUTUMNAL LANDSCAPE. LITTLE TOWNS ALONG THE MIDDLE HUDSON. TRAFFIC ON THE RIVER. THE CATSKILLS. LANDSCAPE ALONG THE RIVERBANK. ALBANY.

Once more I stood on the deck of a Hudson steamer that was going upstream. This time the next stop was Albany, further objectives were Lake George and Lake Champlain, but the final goal was the Adirondack Mountains, the source of the river. The last few days have brought frost and heat in quick succession as well as a lot of rain and thunderstorms. Today does not look like the summer day of a little while ago but rather like one of those bright clear days that frequently occur here at the beginning of autumn. The forests have also gone a shade more from green to brown, so that the treetops already stand out from the more protected low-lying foliage, and the evergreens, dark, single-toned pine and fir trees, are brought more sharply into relief against the deciduous trees. Here and there at the edge of the forest or on a slope stood a sumac bush that had turned red very early, with its long, scarlet feather-like leaves looking more like a piece of coral than a plant. These were all signs that the vegetation here is beginning to go into dormancy or to die, but the sun was still strong, and what it lacked in warmth it now poured forth in light and made the area both near and far so clear that everything seemed to be nearby. These meteorological conditions—this clarity of the autumn air and the preponderantly warm temperatures—are naturally more pronounced and last longer than in Germany, for the area here is located below the latitude of Rome. Nevertheless, they make the period coming after summer a time of easy transition that contains more elements of summer than of winter. Moreover, since the plants that are the most common here remain for weeks dressed in bright reds and yellows before they finally die out, they too contribute in differentiating autumn more sharply from winter than from summer.

Beyond Cornwall, the goal of my first Hudson excursion, which I have already described, the banks become flatter and allow the built-up land to come closer to the river itself, while the hills along with the forest recede from the river. The rock base, which is covered here with only a very thin layer of soil, emerges from its sheath and is exposed to daylight for long stretches, especially along the right bank where those bright groves of juniper trees, reminiscent of cemeteries, tell us immediately that the soil is very acidic. Now one town after the other comes right up to the river. The area running inland from the river on both the eastern and western banks is very fertile and tries to bring its produce to the road leading to New York. This territory is also traversed by the railroads, which connect the rich coal and iron deposits of Pennsylvania with this part of the country and with the New England states to the northeast, the industrial center of North America. Thus, above Cornwall came Fishkill and Newburgh, terminals for trains running to Connecticut and Pennsylvania. Poughkeepsie and Hudson, which lay further on, have sizable blast furnaces close to the river, draw their ore from the neighboring area, and are also terminal points of the more important railroad lines. By Rondout,[5] which lies between the two towns just mentioned, the Hudson-Delaware Canal, the connecting link between the major rivers of New York and Pennsylvania, empties into the river. All these places are attractive little cities with populations of between ten thousand and twenty-five thousand and are, as far as I can see, prosperous, bustling, and strikingly full of life. There is always a street that looks like New York's Broadway in miniature, another lined with elegant villas, and on some elevated spot, however slight, stands the city hall surrounded by trees and lawns.

On the whole, the various signs of human productivity and activity are just as much a permanent part of the scenery as the hills that surround them both near and far, or the rocks and woods. Flotillas of barges tied together in twenties and thirties and attached to a tugboat, which in addition hauls a half-dozen heavily laden vessels on its flanks, rafts of several hundred feet in width and breadth also pulled by steamboats, passenger ships, and steam ferries all enliven the broad surface of the water in a very impressive manner. Sometimes you can see a characteristic scene, such as when a few ships at anchor in a bay where, except for trees and stones, only a few wooden shacks and a landing place are seen but which indicate the presence of a village or small town beyond the heights along the bank, or when a clearing suddenly appears on a hill or a slope on which stands a country house with columned front, or when the dense woods in close proximity look down upon the rows of warehouses and industrial buildings. In general, two types of buildings all along the river seem to crowd in where there is space free between the water and its banks: icehouses, tall, wooden buildings painted white, from which sloping landing bridges or steps lead to the water, and long, low sheds and drying stands of the brick factories, which in some places run along the banks for a quarter of an hour. The icehouses choose the site close to the river because they take their ice out of the river or from many lakes, which are found everywhere in the heights especially above the west bank, and because they can ship their ice so easily from here. The brick factories similarly have an excellent raw material in the nearby environs and produce almost exclusively for New York and the neighboring cities. Thus they too can best ship their product directly to their destinations from here.

The area far up along the banks of the Hudson is in many respects dependent upon the city at the mouth of the river, and places that have an independent life begin only from Newburgh on. My companion explained to me the concept of a dependent city with the example of the Federal capital Washington, the only city that was artificially created. I then silently thought about the hundreds of big and small cities that lack an independent life of their own in Europe—of creations of senseless aristocratic whims, which have to make an effort to live, of once flourishing cities that were deprived of the sustenance so necessary for life by some light shift in trade routes, of the countless places that live on the fame of a long-gone past. What a difference all this is from the enterprising life style one finds here, where modern civilization grows right out of nature like seeds in virgin soil, where it does not have to force itself with difficulty through the residue of earlier stages of development, and, restrained in a thousand ways, be satisfied with a compromised situation, with a mixture of the old and the new! In view of the facts, the words "Old World" and "New World" take on a much deeper meaning than people in the Old World associate with them when they use them lightly like an everyday expression.

Soon nature dramatically comes into the picture again. The Catskill Mountains, which already appeared above Cornwall in the form of long, slowly rising heights behind the hills on the riverbanks, now come closer to the river. As one passes them on the left, they divide into two ridges separated by a deep valley and then soon appear in the south, just as they did shortly before in the north, looking like rising clouds. Their shape is subdued, flattened out in width and breadth, and rounded off; real peaks are not to be found and only seldom does a flat elevation extend up from one of the ridges. The Indians, who, during their time, conferred the name Onti Ora or "Mountains of the Sky" on this chain of hills, showed here that they were better able to "read" the general characteristics of nature and knew how to express them better than did the stronger and more clever race that came after them. The similarity of this mountain range to clouds, with each of its hills towering closely one behind the other, with their dark, uniform forest covering and the bluish haze that surrounds them, was what struck me both times I saw them, and now I have learned from reading that this similarity is what that name really means.

The Catskills, like the entire countryside along the Hudson, are a summer resort for New Yorkers and other city-weary people from near and far and are more popular than closer-lying places because they have the attractions that mountains offer while still not being much farther away. Their highest point measures over three thousand feet;[6] they are more than amply covered with forests, do not lack little lakes and rivers along with a few waterfalls, and also have some of the large hotels that spring up so quickly in such places in this country—I see in the brochure from one of these hotels that it has a piazza, i.e., a veranda-like porch, which is 370 feet long and 16 feet wide. All this is there for the many people for whom this natural environment, despite all its charm and size, is still no substitute for the attractions of urban society and living together with several hundred fashionable people. They also call this area the "Switzerland of America." I have not really visited it myself, but the view it offers from various points and what I have read and heard about particular things give me the impression that it is more like our Thuringian Forest or Odin Forest (Odenwald),[7] although in places here it is more impressive and thickly wooded and filled with more lakes and streams. More so than other parts of this young country, this area is noted for the legends and stories that have grown up around particular places during the time of the first settlers. Here is the place where Rip van Winkle drank and played with Henry Hudson and his crew, ghosts who were placed under a spell in these mountains and who only awoke every few decades to bowl and drink whiskey. Here van Winkle was to sink into a deep sleep like his comrades, only to awaken when he was an old man. Washington Irving's tale in the *Sketch Book* has made this legend well known. The story, in a slightly altered form, is current in the Old World, from whence it has surely been brought over.[8]

Cultivated acres, fields, and bright farmhouses are spread out along the shore, and sometimes one even sees vineyards on the steep slopes. For us who are used to the German landscape, the only thing lacking is the decoration of orchards and fruit trees around the houses, which at home would never be missing from such a scene. A great deal of fruit, and excellent fruit at that, is grown more to the south in New Jersey and Pennsylvania, and northern New York State towards the Great Lakes is famous for its apple orchards. But here, so it appears, planting trees in front of the houses is not customary as in Germany; where one does plant them, then the big shade trees like the elms, maples, and oaks are preferred. Nevertheless the sight is a cheerful one, particularly because of the white color with which the people in this country like to paint the homes, ships, stagecoaches, and many other things that catch the eye. Moveover, the farmhouses, because they are constructed of wood, are easy to build in attractive styles and shapes, and if they are damaged, they can easily be replaced or repaired. The houses appear quite pretty from the outside and generally look like summer houses in the middle of fields of corn or oats.

Since the Catskills recede toward the north and west, the long ridges look packed together, and when you view a ridge from the side, along its entire length, you get the impression that there are more hills than there really are. Such a mountain range has the appearance from afar of greater height and massiveness than it actually has, particularly when it quickly gets covered with the blue haze in which we usually see things that are in the distance and when the range exists without a gap as does this one. The uniform brown-green color of the woods heightens the contrast of the highlands from the cleared, cultivated lowlands. Rolling hills, which at home are covered with a patch-work of brown, yellow, and green fields and meadows and which hardly stand out any more than the flattest countryside, are free from human cultivation here, remaining in the genuine natural garb in which we can see nature unadulterated and unfettered, as we picture it in the mountains or at the seashore. In this respect the extensive forestation is actually of advantage to the scenery of the eastern states and Canada, for the contours of the land are generally not significant enough nor are waters fast moving or clear enough to prevent the area from being called monotonously uniform. The celebrated beauty of the hills and mountain ranges in this part of America stems to a large degree from the beauty of its magnificent forests. This is a transitory beauty, but the owners of the forests and the people who use the wood seem to take this into consideration just as little as they do the susceptibility of the sources of the entire river system in this area. Anyone, however, who looks at the thin layer of topsoil, which for the most part covers the rocky earth of this region, will easily understand that the destruction of the forests will prove to be particularly harmful in a very short time. The hope still is, nevertheless, that after many repeated warnings from specialists, the proposed legislation for the protection of the forests, which has been mentioned in the last few years, will finally be put into law,[9] although many powerful interest groups would like to oppose it. The law naturally has first to become popular, and this is always difficult when one can only appeal to rational judgment for precautionary measures.

North of the Catskills not only does the chain of hills recede from the river banks but the rocky extrusion recedes inland as well, and a flat alluvial area comes into view along both sides of the river, protruding above the water in the form of long narrow islands, of which for long stretches nothing but the tops of the reed bank can be seen, not even their bed. They say that Henry Hudson, on his first voyage in these waters, near the little town of Hudson, first recognized the nature of this river and only at this point did he finally give up the idea of seeking a northwest passage. Even though this far up the tides still make the water saline and to a lesser extent cause a rise and fall in the water level, the existence of flat islands in the river prevents anyone from retaining the idea of this being a canal or throughway. The story about Hudson does not sound too unlikely if we remember that this seaman was a Dutchman, and that this entire region must have reminded him of the region around the rivers in his homeland, which along their lower course flow slowly down to the sea between flat banks, having long beforehand mixed their waters with salt upstream.

Because of the many shallows, navigation is quite dangerous here. There-fore, very frequently one comes across little lighthouses, which show up here and there on one of the islands or on the bank, and for long stretches one also sees man-made embankments extending on both sides where the river had widened too much at the expense of its depth. All this construction was built and maintained by the Federal Government, for it has the responsibility for all waterways whether they are tidewater bodies, which according to the legal definition are navigable high roads, or simply ocean inlets. As previously men-tioned, on the Hudson the traffic goes upstream 32 geographical (155 statute) miles or 250 kilometers, while in other parts of the country it goes even further inland and opens up to trade the interior parts of the south as well as the north.

Already heralded for some time now by heavy clouds of smoke, Albany, the capital of the state and the most important city on the upper Hudson, finally comes into view. The city, filled with steeples and houses, rises on the gentle slopes of the west bank behind rows of ships and warehouses. And right in front of an imposing iron and stone bridge, which spans the river and which takes a quarter of an hour to cross on foot, our boat puts us ashore.

CHAPTER THREE

Saratoga

ARRIVAL TOWARDS EVENING. A GIANT HOTEL. FOOD. DRINK. SO-
CIAL LIFE. INDIAN CAMP. SARATOGA WATERS. AREA AND PEOPLE.

The early September evening on which we arrived in Saratoga[1] was clear and as
warm as summer, the streets were bright with the light from illuminated windows, a profusion of bright light poured out of the open hallways of the hotels,
along with the sounds of well-known dance music intermingling in the distance with all sorts of dissonances, which then faded away. In this village, tree
tops towered over houses, fluttering shadows of trees and bushes covered all the
places the light could not reach, and a cool, crisp breeze, like the one that
usually emerges from forests and fields at sunset, pervaded the whole place.
Gigantic elms lowered their branches before windows in which the most varied
types of golden jewelry, precious stones, and pearls were displayed, and a grove
of trees, which seemed to lead into a dark valley, stood on one side while the
other side was filled with rows of shops stacked with the requirements and
needs of a large city. It was a remarkable combination of unspoiled nature with
traces of overrefined culture combined according to the recipe we know from
Baden-Baden and Interlaken,[2] yet altered by new ingredients, which this restless people's keen sense of taste requires.

The coach stopped in front of a long veranda, or piazza, whose roof rested on
tall, thin pillars, while decorated rounded arches connected the pillars and
numerous torches illuminated the surroundings. Many people were sitting in
rocking chairs, smoking; others were walking around engaged in lively discussion; and still others were gazing out into the night. We went up the broad
steps, crossed the piazza, and entered a room that was illuminated from above
and again supported by pillars that went up to the height of several floors.
Several men were standing here behind a long table. One of them pushed a
large book towards us in which we signed our names and where we came from,
whereupon another man gave each of us a numbered key. Then several colored

men picked up our baggage to take it up to the floor where our assigned rooms were to be found. We entered a little room, paneled in dark wood, whose walls were lined with padded seating and sat down in the midst of a very quiet group of people who were obviously waiting for something. After a few minutes, the entire room together with its ten or twelve occupants rose gently upwards, gliding from floor to floor, letting some people out and taking others in, finally letting us off on the floor with numbers 703 and 705—the highest room numbers I have ever had. The rooms were small and simply furnished; for us unpampered hikers, they were fine enough. My companion, an American familiar with the customs of his countrymen, told me to put on my very best clothes, whereupon we again went down to the ground floor and entered the dining room where once again a colored man respectfully opened the doors for us.

Here were numerous serving and dining tables set up for several hundred guests. Since it was already late, only a few were occupied, and several dozen waiters, colored, as in all the best places, were standing around in the large room in a bored fashion. They say here that the Negro is a born waiter, but those at this hotel had nothing of the grace, nothing of the disposition, nothing of the hidden virtues and capabilities that make the European waiter such an interesting phenomenon for the observer of human nature. Here they work like machines. They scarcely finish what was required of them before falling back into a leaden inertia in which they remain until a new command galvanizes them into new efforts. As they stood there, staring ahead with all their limbs hanging loose, they looked so limp and tired that one almost hesitated to disturb them. At our entrance, one of these men, who rose from his meditative position with a jolt, offered us the menu, which had everything on it that hungry stomachs or a spoiled palate could demand, from oysters to roast beef. Across the way from us sat a man who had tea, oysters, roast salmon, a beef-steak, and six varieties of bread in front of him, and whoever wanted ten times that amount could have had it. Most people are less demanding and allow the proprietor to make a good profit in return for the pleasure of knowing that they have the possibility of enjoying a splendid meal every day.

From the dining room we went towards the large common room, where at any time of the day one finds people playing music and dancing and where in the evening fashionable society meets to see and be seen. The dressed-up ladies and gentlemen, amongst whom there were quite a few children moving about, the vacuity and dreariness one notices in so much of the conversation and movement, and the incessant poor piano playing all make this room a very unpleasant spot, although for the majority of the guests it is really the center of activity in such a place. In a luxury-class establishment such a scene in the common room does not seem out of place, but rooms providing such activities are found in every hotel of any importance, even in the lonely areas around Lake George and Lake Champlain where they do not fit in with the surroundings at all. It is very difficult to live alone here for very long, since the rule of sociability completely dominates. This rule, upon which the very popular boarding-house style of life is based, permits many families to give up for years the comfort of private family dwellings to live in inns and hotels. The individual seeks his relaxation and enjoyment by doing something with or at least being in the company of a group. The bedrooms in such an establishment are seldom such that one enjoys spending time in them. On the other hand, it is rare that the common rooms are not equipped with all the comforts in keeping with the circumstances. It is very possible that in reasonably large company, subgroups are naturally formed within the confines of this general meeting area, groups that with a certain degree of necessity seek to separate from the larger group. One can easily imagine, however, what kind of pastimes and conversations take place in such casually formed circles. The amazing thing is that one puts up with the constraints of such artificial conditions.

But why do people sacrifice their individuality so easily? The reason is not a simple one, but the democratic form of government and the role that women play here appear to me to be an important part of the answer. The political party system strongly emphasizes and teaches quite early the subordination of the individual to the thoughts and leadership of others; this political equality introduces among the entire populace a desire for social equality, which in turn favors the unique development of the individual less than is the case in European states with their varied, sharply differentiated societal and governmental structures. The women, for their part, who give evidence of strong social inclinations and talents, who are easily stirred, and who often like to dress up—they remind one in many ways more of French than English or German women—see a real advantage for their purposes in these general conversation rooms to which they tenaciously cling.

This room was the only place in the entire hotel where I saw no spitoons standing about, where, in other words, no smoking was permitted. In all other areas, one could find these symbols of a more relaxed sociability in ample abundance, and I often had the opportunity to admire the dexterity with which the men, without taking much time to aim, hit the mark, or how as they were sitting they stretched out a leg in order to bring these "inseparable companions" over towards them. This household article is a glazed earthen vessel with a crater-like opening inclining towards the center, similar to what one finds on ocean liners.

The reading room, smoking room, and barroom are the meeting places of the male guests of such hotels, and all three are heavily frequented. In the last of these they stand or sit before the bar, behind which the barkeeper mixes up all kinds of little drinks that are imbibed in this country—some to cool off with, some to warm up with. They are sometimes very strange concoctions but generally not bad tasting. On this evening my friend tasted and then presented me with a milk punch that was made out of milk, brandy, ice, and herbs. Later I got to know still other nice mixtures of this type like iced claret (red wine, ice, slices of lemon and pineapple), sherry cobbler (sherry, ice, lemon slices), various types of grog, and similar drinks. The iced drinks are sipped through straws.

Most people who come to the bar for a drink take their drinks standing up and do not stay very long, so that the stranger gets the impression that not very much is generally drunk here because he never sees the tavern as full as in other countries. My own experience and everything I have heard from others soon corrected that impression. The Americans, however, do not drink for show, since it is perfectly proper for respectable people to take little or no spirits, but in private quite a bit is consumed and what is drunk is then mostly brandy. But the peculiar custom of reciprocal treating does its best to prevent temperance from becoming all that widespread. One is frequently introduced, makes numerous acquaintances, and if the time and opportunity are right and someone (and there always seems to be someone there) starts inviting the group to a drink, it can easily happen that every few minutes another drink is placed in front of you, for no one wants to appear lacking in generosity. At first this custom seemed to me to be both artificial and coarse, but one gets used to it and soon finds that it is rooted deep in the character of the people. It surprised me very much when one evening in New York I went with two German-American acquaintances to one of the Thomas symphony concerts and met a man and a lady with whom I had just become acquainted.[3] One of my companions, who had just been introduced to these two people a few minutes before, asked during the intermission what everyone at the table wanted to drink and without contradiction from anyone ordered and paid for everyone, the lady included. Later I was informed that this was completely acceptable, and I have had similar experiences dozens of times since. The nature of the Americans, which contains little pettiness, least of all stinginess, and their peculiar desire to stand out and to give the appearance of being at all times more than generous with material goods, contribute to this practice.

Nevertheless, I still believe that more people here completely abstain from the pleasure of alcoholic drinks than in Germany, and I have heard some men say that the climate here does not allow them to drink what they would have drunk in England or Germany. A very robust man among my acquaintances who lived for a long time in Stuttgart could no longer, once he returned to Boston, take a bottle of beer as he had been used to having in the evening. A Frenchman, a man of learning who lived here for many years, told me that frequently when he enjoyed wine in quantities to which he was accustomed in the old country, he became very drunk, until the experience taught him that different climates require different modes of living. I saw tables in hotels where among twenty seated guests not one touched an alcoholic drink, and even I, who am

---

4   "A FEW PALE, MELANCHOLIC SPECIMENS, THEIR
DRINKING GLASSES IN THEIR HANDS AND A FEW PINTS OF
WATER FROM THE COLUMBIAN SPRING IN THEIR STOMACHS,
ARE ALREADY WANDERING ABOUT." SARATOGA SPRINGS.

transplanted here from the city of Munich, where great quantities of alcohol are consumed, feel little desire to drink beer or wine for weeks. The climate is of itself so exhilarating and invigorating that it probably makes alcoholic stimulants up to a certain degree unnecessary, and the desire for "respectable," not loud yet still jovial conduct, as well as the high cost of good drinks, all add to this. Another factor is that even in such a thoroughly democratic society the upper class, through tradition and education, tries to prevent themselves from unnecessarily mingling with the lower classes, above all from the type of *Gemütlichkeit* that exists among the patrons of all classes in our beer halls.

The next morning we took care of the few things worth seeing in Saratoga. Congress Park, a grove full of beautiful trees in which the most famous of the Saratoga springs, the Congress Spring, originates, provided us with shade, and we walked along its winding paths northwards to a so-called Indian settlement where Indians and half-breeds who come down from Canada in the summer offer braided and hand-carved trinkets for sale and demonstrate their skill at archery. The settlement looked exactly like a section of one of the gypsy camps of Hungary. Though apparently often racially mixed, the inhabitants showed by their deep golden or bronze facial color, their little black eyes, their pitch black bristly hair, and their broad cheekbones (the last trait also appeared to be very pronounced in the half-breeds, who had the most European blood) that they belonged to the original inhabitants of this land. On Lake George we later found an opportunity to visit a similar settlement and to speak with several Indians, one of whom, as serious and monosyllabic as one would picture him à la Cooper,[4] was carving away on his wooden arrows, while another, who had an exceptionally good-natured, broad-smiling and yet still not quite ingenuous facial expression, enjoyed showing and telling us, but in short and phlegmatic words, how the little baskets are woven out of ash wood and the arrows carved out of oak and hickory. In one hut some young girls were singing and laughing while busy with some sewing, and in spite of their broad faces, they did not look at all unattractive. These people are dressed like we are, but they do as they wish with articles of clothing. The preference for loud colors and, in part, the awkwardness in adapting to our clothing, which we notice among the gypsies, can also be seen here among these people. The Canadian Indians speak mostly a French patois; the men in addition also speak English. They looked well nourished and happy, and even today they do not appear in any way to envy the race that overcame and displaced them in this land, a few pale, melancholic specimens of which, their drinking glasses in their hands and a few pints of water from the Congress or Columbian Spring in their stomachs, are already wandering about—a feeling I completely sympathize with in the red men.

We went from spring to spring but found them everywhere pretty much all the same, the water having the same salty, prickly taste (kitchen salt, bicarbonate of lime, magnesia, natrium, iron, and lithium and not insignificant quantities of carbon dioxide in various proportions to other components are found in most of these springs). The people went to and fro, letting the boys who were dispensing the water fill their glasses, looking generally drowsy and intent on taking the cure. However, the cure routine was apparently not taken very seriously, for in comparison to the large number who are always there, only a few were taking their morning drink.

The springs of Saratoga are supposed to have been recognized quite early by the Indians for their healing powers but began to be used by the settlers only after the end of the border wars, which violently raged in this very region between the English, French, and Indians during the 1750s and 1760s of the previous century.[5] The earliest to be discovered was High Rock Spring. Here, it is said, in 1767 some Indians brought the sick Sir W. Johnson[6] on a stretcher through the wilderness, which at that time took in the site of the present-day Saratoga. The waters worked so well for the sick man that he was able to go home without assistance after he had drunk from them for several weeks. At least so it is said.

Since then more springs have been discovered or drilled for, and the exploitation by companies, one of which commands a capital of one million dollars and owns the three most important springs, is being carried out on a large scale. From one of these, Empire Spring, at present over 400,000 bottles are shipped per year to other places, and the number of visitors on many a summer day is supposed to reach 18,000. The village of Saratoga itself has a population of about 8,000.

Except for the springs, nature did not endow this place with anything outstanding: Saratoga is in an unattractive, low hilly area, and many larger cities in this country are quieter and have fresher air and more attractive, greener, shadier streets than this well-frequented spot. But there is something intriguing about the temporary transplantation of big-city life to the confines and tranquility of the village. Saratoga in summer is a little New York; the high society from the big cities of the Atlantic seaboard, particularly from New York, which at home feels itself scattered and spread out among the general populace, for a few weeks comes together here, along with everything else that goes with its life style. Every individual is pleased to see his own personality flatteringly reflected in the mirror of the resplendent high society. The many people who do not come here with an ailment are looking for this part of Saratoga life. One can probably assume that a visit to such a place is seen more as a necessity, much in the same way that close, lasting social contacts among the better circles are viewed as usually more difficult in this country due to the many fewer sharp class distinctions existing here than in Europe.

To conclude, it is not to be forgotten that Saratoga also has its impressive aspects. To live at a hotel that has 1,364 feet of frontage, one mile of piazzas, 2 miles of halls, 13 acres of carpets and marble floors, 824 rooms, 1,474 doors, and 1,891 windows is certainly a great pleasure; $2.50 a day is not too much to pay for the feeling of living in the biggest of hotels, especially if it is in America and one is an American.

CHAPTER FOUR

Boston

HARBORS OF THE NORTHEAST COAST. ADVANTAGES OF BOSTON'S
SITE. NEW ENGLANDERS' TALENT FOR COLONIZATION. FOUNDING
OF BOSTON AND ITS EARLY DEVELOPMENT. BOOM AFTER THE WAR
OF INDEPENDENCE AND BECAUSE OF THE RAILROADS. PRESENT-
DAY IMPORTANCE OF COMMERCE. ICE TRADE.

Since the coast of North America, running from south to north, increasingly
projects out towards the east, the further north the harbors are situated, the
shorter the distance to Europe. With the exception of Greenland, which is
almost uninhabited, Cape Race on Newfoundland is America's closest point to
Europe, and from here on we see the coastline receding southwestward more or
less in three large intervals marked off by Cape Breton in Nova Scotia, Cape
Cod on the New England coast, and Cape Hatteras on the North Carolina
coast. South of Cape Hatteras the sea carves out a slight curve from the coast,
but even though the coast again extends eastward with the peninsula of Florida, this area still does not project out as far as the northern part of the coast.
Thus, if one observes this contour line, it becomes easily understandable why
all attempts directly emanating from Europe that sought to discover America
always first sighted the continent at those northern promontories—above all at
Newfoundland, Labrador, and Nova Scotia—and all the more so since the route
that runs somewhat more northerly than a direct line between the two continents has always proved the shortest route. Even today, seamen traveling from
English or French ports to New York talk of a sailing route that looks like an
ascending arc that crests at 50° latitude, with New York at the other end
situated on 40°. If they were to take a more southerly course, the Gulf Stream,
flowing in an easterly direction, would give them problems.

But since America developed as a European colony and still has Europe for
its most important trading partner, it is important for every commercial city on

the East Coast to find the shortest way to our part of the world. Today, when unrestricted travel has already made a voyage of ten to twelve days seem unbearable to us and one or two days less appear as a big bonus, a city situated a few degrees more to the east can have a very great advantage. Among the prominent commercial cities on the Atlantic coast of North America, Boston is the one located farthest east, and this important and very basic advantage is something no city of comparable stature disputes. Located farther north, it would find its hinterland more thinly populated and less fertile; placed farther south, it would be farther from Europe.

However, Boston, to be sure, does not enjoy this location alone but shares it with a great number of seaport towns situated on a relatively short stretch of the coast north and south of Cape Cod. The reader will probably remember from the map the peculiar form (similar to a beckoning arm or an arm carrying a pilgrim's staff) of this projection extending far out into the sea. This shape, together with the no less peculiar-looking islands that lie south of the Cape, indicate a broken coastline, for as little as it reminds us of the gentle line of a chain of hills suddenly broken by an alpine fissure, the idea of that contour, broadly conceived, would nonetheless be something like the uniform shape of this straight or lightly undulating shoreline full of dunes. This section of the New England coast is uncommonly rich in bays under whose protection numerous harbor cities began to spring up soon after the colonization began. From Portland down to New Haven, one can cite an impressive list of them, among which, in addition to the former two, Portsmouth, Salem, Bristol, Providence, and New London can be mentioned, some of them already important and some now on the upswing. They all could probably contest the position of preeminence with Boston except that the latter already from earliest colonial times was the seat of the government of Massachusetts and thereby was naturally raised to the position of a leading city for the other less powerful New England states as well. Boston owes the precedence given it to its centrally located and protected site and to its early colonization in which we can find a second and perhaps most important reason for its rapid rise to prominence.

The character and general outlook of the population have had by no means an insignificant influence on the development of the leading city of New England as well as on the general development of this entire section of the United States. Nevertheless, the oft-praised attributes of the people of this region, and about whose character (despite its obvious negative traits) so much has been written, are perhaps a synthesis of the best qualities needed for fulfilling a very difficult task: the forming of a state on strange new territory and the winning of a bleak and wild land for agrarian cultivation and civilized purposes. Their love of liberty, their enterprising spirit and industriousness, their level of education far above the average of all other immigrants, their seriousness, their moderation, their generally peaceable disposition are all clearly evident in the history of the numerous colonies they founded one after the other in America. In addition, Boston has certainly gained because of its inhabitants' attributes.

One can probably assume that in the first century after the founding of the city, when the original ethnic components were present in virtually an undiluted form, the beneficial and cohesive effects of these attributes were at their peak exactly at that time when they were most needed. Later, when the city had reached a level of importance that inevitably had brought it into increasingly closer contact with broader segments of the globe—when, in other words it began to be transformed from a large colonial city into a world metropolis— then the same attributes, under different circumstances, however, were able to exert a constricting and restraining influence. Everywhere we see the shadows they cast, how they outlast their profitable effectiveness by virtue of their strength and importance.

A quick survey of Boston's development will best show how the factors mentioned here, together with numerous other varying circumstances and events, make the city what it is today.

The first settlers, who came to New England in 1620, landed in the bay behind the curved arm of Cape Cod and founded Plymouth Colony there. They only discovered the nearby mouth of the Charles River, on which Boston is now situated, during trips along the coast, which they undertook in the next few years for the purpose of exploring the land along Massachusetts Bay. Another group of settlers, which set out in 1623 from Dorchester, England, and whose object was to provide a place of refuge and above all a church for the fishermen who sailed every year to the New England coast, dropped anchor at Cape Ann, to the north of the place where Boston now stands. Only later did these colonists move south to found Salem. This city soon became a harbor of no little importance, but today, in spite of its communal independence, it has in many ways come under the sway of Boston. After 1629 the stream of immigration primarily flowed towards this new colony, and from here more settlements were then founded, all of which now enjoy positions facing that island-studded bay into which the Charles River runs. By this time Charlestown had already been established, and Boston, Dorchester, Roxbury, and Watertown were founded in 1630, so that soon five communities, separated only by narrow inlets, were situated close to one another. They all flourished, but Boston, distinguished by its central and almost insular position, the proximity of a well-protected harbor, and its good drinking water, grew faster than the others. In 1630, when it was declared the meeting place of the council of the Massachusetts Bay Colony, it was precisely the proximity of the other settlements in the Charles River Bay area (whose number had already risen to fourteen by 1644) that gave a solid foundation to its position as the major city of this region.[1] The Charles River Bay area was soon the most thickly populated part of New England, and Boston, its major city and center, grew in importance as a commercial city at the same rate as its population increased in size and wealth. Therefore, only later in the first decades after the colonization could other cities in mid-New England, especially Salem, think about rivaling Boston, and the second-generation settlers already saw Boston as the uncontested natural capital of the region.

The historians fix September 7, 1630, as the city's birthday—the day on which the council of Massachusetts Bay Colony gave the name Boston to the new settlement on the peninsula, which up until then had been called Trimountain. Many years went by before the immediate needs of the colonists—housing, food, clothes, religious services—were so far fulfilled that surplus energy could be expended on something more than the most necessary work, such as trade, industry, and maritime commerce. The history of these years is not known in detail, although the major events have been handed down to us, and we can surmise what this period was like in general. We only know that the first ship was launched in 1634, and that wharves were already in use before 1639. We also have, in the report of Hutchinson, one of the early chroniclers of the city, a short, not uninteresting description of how commerce gradually developed here. Hutchinson says: "Straits and difficulties, at the beginning of the colony, had produced industry and good husbandry, and then they soon raised provisions enough for their support, and an overplus for exportation."[2] With the exception of barter with tools, trinkets, and articles of clothing for skins and furs, which the Indians brought, we hear little about trade in the first seven years. The people directed their attention primarily towards furnishing more comfortable living quarters and towards the cultivation of as many acres as they needed for maintenance, and with this they were kept busy enough. With hard work on the part of the colonists, after a few years the land yielded more than the settlers consumed, and the surplus was sent to the West Indies and to other places. In return, the products of these regions as well as money began to flow into the colony, though this money and the hides produced by the local population were mostly used to pay for manufactured goods, which came from England and were always needed. Since it was no longer necessary for everyone to engage in agricultural and domestic pursuits, many turned to converting wood into boards, beams, hoops, and the like, others to fishing, and still others to shipbuilding. So the people here gradually and imperceptibly, without having followed a plan or developed any grand designs, seem to have gone into types of business and commerce that were the most natural for this part of the country and best fit in with its local conditions.

The main purpose of their emigration had been the desire for civil and religious liberty. Merchants and other people, enticed by the prospect of gain, came over only later, joined the original colonists, brought commerce to a flourishing level, and influenced the lawgivers to take action in favor of further commercial development. Another chronicler wrote that already in 1644: "Boston, which of a poor country village, in twice seven years is become like unto a mainly small city and is . . . chiefly increased by trade by sea. . . ."[3] In the same year a fur trading company was founded. Boston's population at that time can only be approximated, since exact censuses were not taken, but we learn, for example, that in the year 1674, when all New England had 120,000 inhabitants, the capital contained around 1,500 families. We then get reliable information again only towards the middle of the eighteenth century, when we learn that between 1742 and 1765 the population fluctuated between 15,000 and 16,000 inhabitants and that in 1748, 540 ships left from Boston harbor.

It should not be forgotten that the man-made restrictions, which the jealous mother country never tired of placing on the trade and industry of its colonies, were more of a burden to Boston's development and to that of all commercial centers in the English colonies than any natural ones. Even Cromwell,[4] otherwise so favorably inclined towards his coreligionists and fellow political partisans in New England, did not reject the idea of compelling them to pay an indirect tax to the mother country by means of the Navigation Acts of 1651.[5] If at the beginning the colonists did not grasp the full severity of these regulations—that non-European goods were only to be brought into England in ships built in England, belonging to Englishmen, commanded by Englishmen, and manned by a crew consisting of three-quarters Englishmen—then they soon understood the injuriousness of another decree according to which only Englishmen could become merchants in the colonies and a whole series of goods could only be exported to other countries via England.[6] Even more than these restrictions, New England and particularly Boston felt the limitations on colonial industry, for as the population grew, the naturally poor soil encouraged the people to take up more industrial pursuits. For example, because New England's shipping, which because of the area's large coastline, abundance of wood, and the seaworthy population, threatened to become strong competition for England, all kinds of restrictions were placed in the way of the colonies' trade, and the big and small, in part very picayune, duties and impositions did not stop until, precisely because of them, the Revolution broke out. The fact that in Boston, after a long period of agitation, the first step towards open rebellion to the government's oppression was taken, when in December 1773 the tea of the East India Company was thrown into the harbor because of the high import duty on it, is an important factor for the material development of the city when first of all it is considered, like Boston's general deportment during the Revolutionary War, as evidence of the energetic, independent, self-reliant attitude of its citizens. With this step the colonies shook off the burdens that threatened to restrict the city's natural development, and the period of prosperity, which began after the War of Independence, clearly indicated how many sources of power had lain fallow and how the revolt and casting off of the foreign yoke had been, so to speak, a natural development.

In the hundred years that preceded the War of Independence, Boston's population grew more slowly than that of the territory of which it was the capital. In comparison with Philadelphia, which took precedence over Boston because of its location and the size of its population and in the eighteenth century was considered the true capital of the English North American colonies, Boston in those days of sailing ships only had the not unimportant advantages of being located in the midst of the most seaworthy people in the country and of being inhabited by highly alert, enterprising true Yankee stock.

Immediately after the end of the war, like all older parts of North America, New England began to experience an entirely different rate of growth in trade and industry than it had previously known. In the last decade of the century Boston alone grew as much as it had in the preceding seventy years, a growth of 7,000. Even if its growth was not as rapid as that of New York or Philadelphia, it proceeded rapidly enough for it to expand from 25,000 in 1800 to 43,000 in 1820, to 93,000 in 1840, to 136,000 in 1850, to 177,000 in 1860, and approximately 250,000 in 1869 (including incorporated suburbs). The number of ships docking in Boston in 1791 amounted to 399; in 1806, 1,083; in 1870 over 3,500; and today Boston stands behind only New York and New Orleans in foreign trade. The most significant stimulus for its development, however, was given by the construction of the railroads, whose number and expansion in the 1830s and 1840s were more rapid here in New England than in any other part of the Union. The importance of the railroads for Boston was no less than the importance of the great canal construction to the Great Lakes was for New York, for apart from its coastal navigation, the railroads are Boston's only link with its hinterland. Today no less than eight railroad lines come into Boston.

Within the last twenty-five years, Boston's trade has undergone significant fluctuations. Exports to other parts of the country and abroad, whose worth in 1846 amounted to around $9,000,000, rose in 1851 to $10,500,000, in 1855 to almost $27,000,000, around 1860 had fallen to $15,000,000, in 1865 once again had risen to $21,000,000, and in 1869 amounted to $14,381,078. If we deduct the value of precious metal exports, then the approximate value of exports, based on an interval of every five years, can be placed at $9,000,000 (1850), $14,000,000 (1855), $13,000,000 (1860), $21,000,000 (1865), and $14,000,000 (1869). Imports from foreign countries followed a similar pattern, for from a value of $29,000,000 in 1850 they rose to $43,000,000 (1855), sank to $39,000,000 (1860), down to $25,000,000 (1865), and in 1869 stood at the level of $44,628,395.[7] The tonnage of the foreign ships that came into Boston harbor amounted to 218,295 tons in 1850 as compared to 525,125 in 1869; the tonnage of native ships stood at 260,540 in 1850, 252,035 in 1869; the number of foreign ships during this period rose from 1,908 to 2,905, while native ships coming into the harbor declined from 1,028 to 644.

Comparison of the most important harbors of the Union for the year ending June 30, 1873, placed Boston in fifth place in the value of its exports. At that time, New York was exporting goods valued at $313,000,000, New Orleans $104,000,000, San Francisco $39,000,000, Savannah $32,000,000, Boston $27,000,000, and Philadelphia $24,000,000. As regards imports, with $68,000,000 worth of incoming goods, it stood ahead of San Francisco with $39,000,000, Baltimore with $29,000,000, and Philadelphia with $25,000,000, but was far surpassed by New York, which boasted of imports amounting to $426,000,000.

As the capital of industrial New England, Boston regards the products of her

many factories as her most important export commodity. Especially typical for Boston is the shoe and boot business, for which this city is America's center. Some towns in Massachusetts occupy themselves almost exclusively with shoe production on a large scale. Already by 1856 the yearly sale of shoes and boots was estimated at about $50,000,000, and more than two hundred Boston firms were occupied in this branch of trade. Since then this business has grown considerably in importance and is said to have doubled its sales in the last ten years. The West and the South are the main markets for these as for all New England products. The hides that are used in this industry at present come in almost equal quantities from the South (Rio Grande, Buenos Aires, New Orleans) and from the West, with about one-fifth the required amount imported from Africa. The import of hides has also doubled in the last ten years; in 1869 their worth amounted to about $1,000,000. I have no statistics, however, concerning the output or produce of the tanning industry. The import of cotton, which in 1860 amounted to around 400,000 bales, was only up to 249,299 in 1869, coming in for the most part from New Orleans, New York, and Norfolk. Woolen imports from abroad have risen insignificantly in the last ten years, the largest quantities arriving from South America, England, Turkey, the East Indies, and South Africa; of almost 200,000 centner (11,023.1 tons) that were imported in 1869, half of this came from South America and one-fifth from England. The supply of wool coming from the West is very important and constantly growing. The products of the cotton and woolen industries in this state were estimated in 1870 to be worth about $200,000,000, and Boston is the market for the greatest part of these goods. Their export to foreign countries is small, the major consumer being the United States itself.

A more important article among Boston's exports, whose history is not uninteresting, is ice. In 1806 a ship was sent for the first time with this commodity from Boston to Martinique; in 1807 a second one with a double cargo went to Havana, and although during the first years the profits were slight because of imperfect techniques and other difficulties the new enterprise confronted, the industry grew in time and was encouraged by the Spanish Government, which granted monopoly rights and licenses. As compared to the one shipment of 130 tons sent in 1806, in 1816 there were 6 shipments (1,200 tons), 1826 15 (4,000 tons), 1836 45 (12,000 tons), 1846 175 (65,000 tons), 1856 363 (146,000 tons). In 1869 11,376 tons of ice were sent to Bombay, 8,685 to Havana, 6,237 to Calcutta, 3,405 to Batavia, 3,542 to Aspinwall, 3,020 to Demerara,[8] 2,000 to Rio de Janeiro, et cetera. More than 40,000 tons went to various places along the East Coast. Quite a few thousand people are given employment in winter in and around Boston by this business, and even insignificant things like sawdust, bran, and the like have risen in value because of this industry.

5   THE HARBOR AREA, BOSTON.

In the development of Boston's East India Trade, ice played a by no means insignificant role; cargo returning from these regions consists principally of flax and hides whose value and consumption have risen very notably in the United States during the last twenty years. Moreover, saltpeter, jute, and several drugs are also major imports. Ten years ago the returns from this trade amounted to over $10,000,000, and since then they have risen considerably. In 1869 around 3,000,000 pounds of tea were imported to Boston directly from East Asia.

The grain and flour trade, so important in New York, was never able to develop to any degree in Boston because of the expensive freight charges incurred in transporting the grain from the Western growing areas, although sufficient attempts have been made to capture a part of this important trade. Actually Massachusetts imports grain for its own use via New York, and it is questionable whether Boston's more favorable location vis-à-vis Europe and its railroad connections with the West, which are to be completed as soon as possible, will ever be able to outweigh the advantage that New York possesses with its waterways to the Great Lakes region and its already firmly established dominant position in world trade.

The timber trade, which was formerly so important to Boston when there was still a thickly wooded hinterland available, has moved northwards along with the shipbuilding industry and now occupies a low place amidst the overall commercial activity of Boston. The harbors of Maine and Canada have surpassed it here.

No less significant is the importation of fruit from the South, for in 1869 over 200,000 crates of grapes and around 250,000 crates of oranges and the like came in. A small Portuguese colony mostly controls this business. Oranges are brought in from Florida and the West Indies but compare as little as do the lemons with those arriving from southern Europe. Considerable quantities of grapes and dessert fruits are imported from California.

OVERALL VIEW. LAYOUT. SURROUNDING AREA. PROSAIC CHARACTER OF THE OLD PARTS OF THE CITY. STORES. RESIDENTIAL BUILDINGS.

One has to view Boston and its environs from an elevated spot, for in no other way is one able to form a clear picture of the whole area out of the confusion of inlets, peninsulas, islands, riverbanks, and seashores. Here there is no middle point and no main transportation artery, no firm plan and no decisive course of growth. Insignificant settlements developed on the promontories and in the bays of a very rugged section of the seacoast; some grew up quickly, others slowly, and then one of them surpassed all the others, incorporated some of them, gave them its name, and now stands before us as Boston, a city of 250,000 inhabitants. All these settlements started along the rugged seacoast and extended inland and now exist side by side in a broad semicircle, though partitioned off and very different from one another, having on the surface nothing in common but their position along the seacoast. This entire conglomeration has had a remarkable amount of "chance" in its development, giving very little impression of being constructed or "newly born" as do other big cities in this country; it appears more to have evolved than to have been made. They call it the most European city of North America, and in view of its narrow, winding streets the comparison is not inapposite. But the land formations on which it is built really prove to be the most significant factor in determining the city's outward appearance.

If you take a look around on a bright day from the highest point of the Blue Hills, the mountain chain not far from the sea, which rises out of the flat land south of Boston like a petrified flood tide, you can get a very good idea of the site of Boston and the surrounding area. You have the city to the north there in front of you. You see the entire broad tongue of land on which the old and original Boston is built, covered with houses, which stretch here onto the mainland and on up the flat heights over the once narrow isthmus that has now become quite wide through landfill. You see South Boston, a similarly house-covered peninsula, which from the south stretches like a mushroom with one side of its umbrella-like expanse extending towards Old Boston and with the other side extending out into the ocean. A little further on you can see Charlestown, a peninsular suburb recently linked with Boston by new transportation arteries, that is expanding in like fashion from the west, and finally there is East Boston, a three-pronged island full of houses and landings, which completes the semicircle to the northeast. You can also sight other places quite near—such as Cambridge and Chelsea, which are on the mainland and connected by bridges to the various sections of Boston; Brookline and Roxbury, which are now incorporated suburbs; and Dorchester[9] and Somerville further to the north. All of these villages, in conformity with the contour of the shoreline, form a semicircle bending inland towards the west, while far out in the water big and small islands form an arc that stretches out to the east. Together both sides of this circle enclose the harbor, where right in the center little Governors Island with its bright fort stands out clearly. All around you can see the landscape covered with not quite low hills, rising out of the plains that extend down to the ocean. Where there is no sea, there are high and low hills on the horizon, and still in my range of sight, far in the distance, are two New Hampshire mountains, Monadnock and Wachusett, formations lazily stretched out like giant crouching sphinxes.

An odd picture—this dovetailing of land and water, these slender yellow dunes, these silver-grey surfaces of the water, which sometimes reflect like a mirror and at other times look worn out from the beating of the waves, and finally the vast number of houses on the shore and on the peninsulas! The distant city looks like nothing more than an eroded granite base with the sharp-edged profile of crystals in tightly compressed form appearing on its surface. In the foreground are woods and meadows and numerous little bodies of water, ponds as well as streams; and the forests, even if not tall nor dense, are much more extensive than they would be around a comparably large city in Europe, particularly a seaport. This is a characteristic trait of the American landscape, which you continually find at least everywhere here in the East—a proof of the youthful civilization of this country.

When one looks over this whole area, then only the sea appears significant, as it always does everywhere. Boston's land environs by no means look very impressive. It is the usual low hilly area, which contains many individually beautiful things in its streams and in its woods to recommend it, but the overall picture appears dull. We have a similar landscape along the Baltic seacoast in the area around the Trave River.[10]

The city of Boston itself can be surveyed very well from the cupola of the State House, which occupies the highest point in the city. Here from the center of Old Boston you can see all the suburbs on the other side of the waterways, the harbor with its surrounding chain of islands, the waterways within the city, and the forest of shipmasts. Another very pretty view is from the heights above Charlestown, where you have before you Old Boston with all its breadth stretching out to the northeast. Here you see the houses stacked up on the hill, the gilded cupola of the State House towering above all. You see how the city and its suburbs are washed on all sides and in all kinds of ways by the sea; you see the particularly flat, evenly laid out portions of the city, which were built on filled-in sections of the sea floor because the peninsula provided too little space even then. These areas are so close to the water and rise so little above it that if they did not stand there so uniformly, so entirely prosaic, lacking any storybook atmosphere, they would appear to be a mirage, especially at sunset when the sun hits their red walls and casts a glow on their windows.

Boston has not had the space nor the rapid development of New York or Philadelphia and therefore is more crowded and haphazard in its entire layout. Broad residential streets with proud, silent buildings were not built directly adjacent to the business sections but had to be located far out if they were to be spared the noisy bustle. In time, business activities encroached upon all parts of the city situated near the harbor. But with all the train lines running into Boston, it was considered no great sacrifice to live a few miles away from the center of town. Then gradually the peninsulas and islands began to fill up with businesses, and the better families preferred to move inland, especially toward the higher areas. This gives the city a split personality, for all the traffic moves about the narrow streets of the town's dark old business sections, while with few exceptions the broad, bright, new residential streets are unpleasantly dead and deserted. This is the very opposite of what is needed in order to bring some harmony to the matter. The narrow streets could be much quieter and the broad ones show a bit more life—both would profit by this change. Now as it is, everything—fine and coarse, rich and poor—surges through the narrow, circuitous path in Washington Street or Tremont Street, pushing and shoving, leaving no place for comfort. Thus there is no street in this entire metropolis where city life in the more aesthetically pleasing sense of the word can evolve, where people can go without hurrying to observe and be observed, where they can experience the pleasant realization that there are places to relax amid all the bustle. A city of Boston's stature should not be without this harmonious interaction of these two aspects of urban development, otherwise it looks too much like an anthill.[11] Just as we are not exactly happy with a person who is always bent on the correct utilization of time, on work and profit, who doesn't relax now and then, let himself go, and show that he and not his one-sided work is master, we have a similar attitude about cities: they should offer pleasant locations for leisure hours where their best and most beautiful can be seen. In their own way, they should actually bring some beauty into the world and allow it to flourish.

Since Boston does not have this, it cannot really look old, for noble tranquility is also really part of old age. The word "old," however, has many meanings for inanimate objects. An old barracks has an entirely different meaning of old than does an old house stemming from "the good old days," some kind of building of quality and distinction on which the most bold volutes, narrow wndows, or high gable all seem to fit in with its general appearance no less than white hair and the old-fashioned dress coat fit the grandfather. The latter examples have the venerable beauty of old age, the former one only decay and the passage of years; the latter have the spirit, the former only the outer manifestation of it. A number of things are old that cannot be called old in an aesthetic sense, since every trace of that ideal value of old age is gone.

On the other hand, you can say that Boston was never really young. The worries and cares of existence never weighed more heavily on New England than in the first decades after its founding. Work and prayer were the core of its life, and no other mental attitude was perceptible here than that which stirred out of the "stuffy Puritan meeting places." Religion was life's only pleasure, yet this religion was more opposed to beauty and aesthetics than any religion that had ever been preached before, a religion of iconoclasts, which in this area under the influence of hard life was bleaker and more monotonous and which kept all expressions of life more firmly under its control than anywhere in Europe. An externally unattractive way of life does not try to beautify the residential areas, and although plenty of space and every sort of building material were at hand and enough wealth had been gradually acquired, still no one tried to construct beautiful or more permanent buildings. Whatever pictures are still preserved of the better old houses show very simple, mostly wooden structures, which only have a second story extending outward above the ground level and upward to a pointed gable. Franklin's birthplace, which used to stand here in Boston but was destroyed by fire in 1811, was a simple house of this type as engravings that have not been lost indicate. The slightly larger houses in Boston, which have been preserved without much alteration or change from the period of 100 to 120 years ago, are completely insignificant, not simply ordinary in design but also poor in execution. What a different era this was from the period when the Hansa cities[12] or the Flemish and Italian commercial cities, which in some ways were not so important as this, the most outstanding city of the North American colonies of its times, built churches and city halls that still remain for the admiration and enjoyment of later generations! The spirit of the Old World culture has been successfully transplanted to America and has quickly succeeded in making a significant contribution on the new soil, but it has not been as rapidly successful with beauty. It would appear as if the stimulating inspiration from overseas, which arouses one to similar accomplishments and is found in abundant measure in the works of the philosophers and poets, has been withheld from the great works of the artists here. At any rate, everywhere you turn you see how art is a very tender plant, how in many ways it depends upon the conditions of the soil in which it is transplanted, and how it is even capable of being so stunted that no ripe fruit will be produced.

In the last decades, however, a great deal of construction, which is quite different than before, has been going on. Since 1830, not only has the population quadrupled and their wealth increased eightfold, but with the growth in trade and the influx of numerous foreign elements, new incentives have been offered and higher demands placed on life. Puritanical austerity gradually began to wane, and a reasonable enjoyment of the wealth that the inhabitants' forefathers had gained with so much work and privation appeared less condemnable. As time went on, a very splendid and ornate style modeled after that of New York and other fast-growing "mushroom cities," came into vogue especially for the commercial buildings, and many of the residential buildings also sought to make their exteriors look beautiful and elegant. Recently the great fire of November 10, 1872, which destroyed what stood on forty acres in the heart of Boston, has given this endeavor a special stimulus and a great opportunity to make it a reality. In the space of one year they have erected rows of commercial buildings and stores with a splendor the likes of which may not be found in any other city. But only the ostentatious magnificence makes these buildings noteworthy, and when one sees them standing there, festooned and besmeared from top to bottom with cheap advertisements, in the end one is not sorry that this defacement hides no more noble architectural styles.

As regards the homes, their façades are decidedly inferior compared to those of New York. It is the custom here, precisely in the best sections strangely enough, and virtually without exception, to construct an almost semicircular protrusion, like an extended oriel, from the ground up to the roof. And if one of these baroque-looking objects did not already give each individual house an unattractive padded look, the unrestricted view that the straight, broad residential streets provide, where one sees forty to sixty house fronts in a row, makes a simply devastating overall impression. This looks like a company of Falstaffs.[13] The ovens that project out of the walls of the south German farmhouses like ugly swellings are in their way no less artless than these protuberances. The rest of these buildings are dominated by an agreeable stylistic simplicity, and they seldom lack the little garden near the door and are often covered with climbing plants. The preferred construction material is the same red-brown sandstone (brownstone) they use everywhere in New York. It is only fastened onto the brick walls in thin slabs, but in this area where it must be brought in from great distances it is still more a privilege of the well-to-do. In the dreams of the young men here who haven't made their fortune yet, the brownstone front takes the place of a marble palace in Europe. Moreover, it is not insignificant that the homes in general differ markedly from the commercial buildings by their unpretentiousness. The overblown nature of the latter thereby takes on the character of something used for business competition, of a building furnished more in the interests of business than personal taste. This fact then can be added to the many others, which seem to indicate that the businessman within each American still cannot take over the individual so completely that the flaws that frequently mar his personality are able to affect his basic character in every instance.

The number of trees along Boston's streets do not, as a matter of course, approach that of other American cities, for the older streets are too narrow for such adornment. But whenever a street is laid out anew it has two, even four rows of trees, and the especially elegant ones like Commonwealth Avenue enjoy a well-cared for, not too narrow, fenced in strip of grass in the middle. Here I see that particularly the elm tree is used for the purpose of beautification.

BURNED-OUT PART OF THE CITY AND RECONSTRUCTION. FREQUENCY OF FIRES. BUILDINGS OF HISTORIC INTEREST. FANEUIL HALL. OLD SOUTH CHURCH. STATE HOUSE. PARK AND GARDEN. INTELLECTUAL IMPORTANCE OF BOSTON.

No part of the city is at present so interesting as that which was affected by the great fire of 1872. In one night (from November 9 to 10) the best constructed sections, where most of the commercial buildings were located in an area of forty acres, were burned to ashes; around four hundred houses with a value approximated at $70,000,000 were destroyed. But already the entire district stands there almost all finished, with broader streets and more elegant houses than ever. Already the streams of traffic pack the expanded thoroughfares; business after business is springing up in the iron and granite palaces, which have been constructed within the space of a year. Except for some disputed plots, which therefore still remain vacant, by January 1, 1874, every trace of the fire has supposedly been effaced. This fact is excellent proof of the enterprising spirit of the populace here, and the Bostonian is right when he proudly calls his newly built district the most noteworthy thing to be seen. Whoever visits this area will not disagree with the speaker who says, of course in the effusive manner that unfortunately is unavoidable in this country, that the best of Boston cannot be demolished by fire. The assets this city has in education and character, knowledge and capability, humaneness and religion cannot be destroyed by any flame. Let the houses, schools, churches be destroyed but let the population remain with its history, customs, and practices; it will always form one of the richest and most significant communities on earth.

On November 10, the fire was extinguished, on the eleventh, permits to rebuild had already been applied for, and although the city withheld issuing them for the time being in order to carry out the long-desired rational planning and expansion program, preparations for new construction were made when the debris was still so hot it could not be touched by hand. In April 1873 the first new building on the huge burned-out space was completed and occupied in the same month. I have been told remarkable stories of the sangfroid with which the people took their large and generally irreplaceable losses—on this occasion twenty-six insurance companies in Massachusetts alone had to make payments—and of the tirelessness and dauntlessness with which they went about replacing and rebuilding. There must have been very little crying and moping about to be seen here.

Everything standing today is entirely devoted to commercial pursuits. Shopping arcades, department stores, and factories occupy these palaces, sometimes seven stories high from the ground floor up to the garrets. After one has gazed in wonder at the outside of these huge edifices made of fine granite or marble or at the cast-iron girders and frames that serve as ornaments that go right up to the roof, it is always such a contrast to enter through narrow corridors and up precarious stairways into a stocking or pocketbook factory. As to why they overload these buildings with decorations, one can only say that it is also connected with the attempt to show the public a striking, grand exterior. The columns, medallions, and whatever else is put up as decoration are to help in their way to sell the products. Thus we can characterize this entire method of building as simply an advertising style and will make no further demands on it.

There are no attics for storage areas under the roof in these buildings, for the roofs are flat and, almost without exception, designed like the so-called French mansard garrets, whose frames in the burned-out buildings were completely made of wood and in part covered with tarboard and the like. This, together with the excessive height of the majority of buildings in this district, their thin walls, and the narrowness of the streets, is supposed to have been the main cause for the rapidity with which that great fire spread. Granted, the new streets have been designed to be broader, but the houses are still relatively tall and more than a few are again topped with wooden mansards. Thus the danger of fire stemming from this cause really does not seem to have decreased appreciably. On the other hand, according to general opinion, after its reorganization the fire department is better than before, and if the fire alarm be promptly given in the future, extensive fires will not easily be able to make headway. There certainly is not a lack of little fires, since scarcely a day goes by without the fire alarms ringing at least once. Barely six months after the big fire, in what was left of the district it had devasted, a few dozen more stately mansions were burned down. The worst of it is that so many of these fires without doubt are set, mostly by people with a great deal of insurance, who in this way, particularly if they are having no luck in business, attempt to get money to start new enterprises. Some people say that the great fire was also started through this kind of incendiary work, and I have many times heard the assertion that more than half of all fires are planned.

Toward the northern edge of this large, burned-out area are some of the most prominent monuments of Boston's early history. There is Faneuil Hall,[14] a building with many windows and topped with a tower, which was built in the 1760s from the bequest of a Huguenot gentleman as a covered market or commercial center but which during the events that prepared and preceded the American Revolution was most frequently used for political meetings. It bears the proud name of "Cradle of Liberty." Not far away stands Old South Church,[15] an unassuming church building with a long nave and slender spire. It became famous at the same time as Faneuil Hall, for the meetings of the protesters were held in it since the space in Faneuil was too small. Here the violent measures against the enforced import of English goods were planned, and on the evening of December 16, 1773, a daring band marched out from this church down to the harbor where they captured English ships and organized that "Tea Party" from which one usually dates the beginning of the Revolution.[16] Since the fire, the church has been used as a provisional post office, and it has a clock in its tower about which the latest travel guide for New England proudly comments: "More eyes are upturned to its clock daily . . . than to any other timekeeper in New England."[17]

More peaceful, however, are the memories associated with the Old State House, which still remains standing in this quarter of the city.[18] This is also a simple two-storied, elongated building with three windows in the front, eleven on each side, and a small spire placed at the back of the building. Originally, as long as it served its purpose, the building was even plainer than at present, but since being turned into a commercial building it has been spruced up. From 1748 until around the end of the century, it housed the seat of the government of Massachusetts, and every year the legislature or General Court met here. On the first day before the beginning of the session, the entire assembly went in solemn procession to Old South Church where a clergyman appointed by the preceding legislature had to hold the so-called election sermon. Because of the close interrelation of politics and religion, which characterized New England's history up to the Revolution, this established custom was more than a mere ceremony, and what the eloquent ministers said from the pulpit to the representatives of the people sometimes has had significant practical effects. Today the election sermon is held in the State House itself and is merely a formality.

Across from this old seat of the government, which in its almost humble unpretentiousness does not give a bad picture of the simple conditions of the "good old colonial days," a building proudly stands in the shape of a Greek cross surrounded by a decorative wreath of heavy pillars and crowned in the middle with a flat cupola. This is the Custom House,[19] which was built forty-six years ago, a very massive building that shares the style of its monumental steps and Doric columns with a vast number of public buildings constructed during that and the preceding period. At one time Boston must have scarcely had a prominent building without columned halls, for even today one sees a few hotels with temple-like entrances, private homes whose elegant roofs float more than they rest on powerful columns, and even churches that have wrapped themselves in classic dress. The new State House[20] also belongs partly to this period and style. In any case, it stands imposingly on its hill, the highest point in the city, even if some of its component parts do not appear as impressive as the whole. It is a building with a cupola whose entrance one reaches by crossing a grass-covered plaza, past fountains and two very poor statues of New England statesmen, and ascending a broad stairway. Seven entranceways lead into a hall where once again you see statues, busts (Washington, Governor Andrew, Lincoln, Sumner),[21] and flags that were carried by the Massachusetts regiments in the last war. The assembly rooms are, as far as I could observe, very simply maintained. The main decorations here are portraits of prominent statesmen who during their lifetime played an active role within these halls. They are actually poor pictures but nevertheless show us some interesting, vigorous-looking people.

In front of the State House lies Boston's park and garden, the Common and Public Garden—the former is an undulating plot of land complete with lawns and shady walks, the latter a well-tended garden, with a pond in the middle, left over from one of the arms of the sea, which were filled in to provide the space for the garden. Compared to the large parks or city gardens of newer American cities, the grounds here seem very small, but they have the advantage of being so close to the center of the city that they can be reached with ease. Thus they are as readily accessible and as familiar to that large family, Boston's inhabitants, as the little arbored garden that one plants behind the house, while the others, although much larger, can only be reached by means of transportation through noisy, dusty streets. One should remember that Boston, together with its pleasant environs of both seashore and hills, can very well content itself with these recreation areas, since anyone who is looking for a nice view or unrestricted space in which to move about can find them in a hundred places within the vicinity of the city. But the rivalry among the leading cities of the East and West has not left Boston, which is progressing more cautiously than the others, unaffected either, and the civic-minded citizen is decidedly made unhappy by the thoughts that his city can only point to seventy-five acres of garden space compared to the two thousand that are set aside for that purpose in cities like New York, Philadelphia, and Chicago. So now the citizens are endeavoring to establish a new park, even if it is several hours away from the city. In this regard they seem to consider the city as a business: they have to match what the others are doing if they don't want to be put in the shade; they have to go to some unnecessary lengths in order to show that they can afford anything. Just as the individual who even in the smallest details seeks to live, to act, and even to dress like everyone else, the small and large communities do the same. This competitive spirit promotes many good things, but it also creates much that is monotonously uniform.

Boston has enough individual qualities of which to be proud and which, if developed, would assure Boston its own high place among its sister cities. New England, that section of America that matured politically earlier than the others, has given the greatest part of the United States its political institutions, has been the cradle and nerve center of the Revolution and the Anti-Slavery movement, has had right up until today the most and best institutions of learning of every kind, and has seen the most important movements in literature and religion begin in its capital, in Boston. Even today the leading figures of modern North American literature: R. W. Emerson, Longfellow, J. R. Lowell the poet and critic, and Holmes the humorist, live in Cambridge, the suburb of Boston; Thoreau, the highly original author of books on nature, as well as Hawthorne, America's best novelist, and the historians Prescott, Motley, Palfrey, and Bancroft have all lived in and near Boston; and Agassiz, who gave such an important impetus to the study of natural history in this country, has died here only recently.[22] The best journals originate here, and some of the most important publishing firms are located here. Boston is probably comparatively more richly endowed with charitable institutions than any other city in the Union, and it certainly doesn't take second place to any other city with regard to the number of churches and houses of worship, even if it doesn't contest the name "city of churches" with Brooklyn, preferring to be satisfied with the often used honorary title, "the modern Athens."*

New Yorkers, as well as the citizens of Philadelphia and of the ambitious,

---

*AS EARLY AS 1821, AN AMERICAN TRAVELER WROTE ABOUT BOSTON: "THIS TOWN . . . IS, PERHAPS, THE MOST PERFECT, AND CERTAINLY THE BEST REGULATED DEMOCRACY THAT EVER EXISTED. THERE IS SOMETHING SO IMPOSING IN THE IMMORTAL FAME OF ATHENS, THAT THE VERY NAME MAKES EVERYTHING MODERN SHRINK FROM COMPARISON; BUT SINCE THE DAYS OF THAT GLORIOUS CITY, I KNOW OF NONE THAT HAS APPROACHED SO NEAR IN SOME POINTS, DISTANT AS IT MAY STILL BE FROM THAT ILLUSTRIOUS MODEL." W. TUDOR, *LETTERS ON THE EASTERN STATES*. [ED. NOTE: THE FULL CITATION IS WILLIAM TUDOR, *LETTERS ON THE EASTERN STATES* (BOSTON, 1821), P. 364. ALTHOUGH RATZEL STATES THAT TUDOR WROTE IN 1821, IT IS THE BOOK THAT WAS PUBLISHED THAT YEAR, THE MATERIAL BEING WRITTEN IN 1819.]

aspiring, fast growing cities of the West, have to concede to Boston the honor of being the "most American" of the big cities of the United States.[23] For its character has been altered less than any other city's through immigrants from Europe, and the New England spirit, which has made North America what it is, can still be found in its purest form in its pace-setting social, political, and religious circles. The New England climate also seems to be a most important influence on the populace and to exhibit most strongly those characteristics of North America's climate to which we attribute the development of that new variety of humans, the Yankee. This observation should not be considered lightly in evaluating the importance of Boston. The New Englander is the proper Yankee, for in this country this is the nickname that sets him apart. The lean, intense, physical features, the restlessness and hyperactivity, the spirit of invention and initiative, and also the sense of liberty and justice and the tendency to go to the limits of the possible to reform something are found nowhere else so readily. Just as on one hand a sense for business and enterprise can most tellingly be seen both within and emanating out of New England, on the other hand the most radical and also the most absurd beliefs and movements cannot find a soil anywhere as fertile as here. Nowhere else is the Women's Suffrage Movement as active or the belief in the miracles of Spiritism so devotedly practiced.[24] In the future, New England will surely occupy a prominent place in the history of bizarre sects. All these things merge together in Boston, as at a focal point, and endow this city with a significance for America, which larger, richer cities do not approach. This significance is still important and not yet simply a matter of historical interest, no matter how quickly the rest of America is being transformed by the important, growing impact of the huge number and varied types of immigrants. One hears people who are serious observers of this country say that "there in Boston is the head and heart of the country."

Thus, up to a certain point, one can probably consider Boston as the intellectual center of North American life, and one will scarcely deny that until now no place in America can incorporate in a similarly small area so much learning and desire for learning and so many educational facilities. Nowhere is there more teaching and learning, and it is said that classical music has found enthusiastic support and understanding in America most particularly here. The question, however, is whether Boston can ever free itself sufficiently from a certain provincial narrow-mindedness in order to remain the leader of the intellectual life of such a large nation with so many varied interests. The atmosphere, in any case, is somewhat depressing for the arts and sciences, since sabbath and temperance laws still blithely flourish, since despite all the political freedom complete academic freedom for research is still only attained by the very few, and since *pro forma* church attendance is part of the rule of life of the great majority of "respectable people." Such truly cosmopolitan cities as New York and Chicago represent the current overall American way of life better than does Boston, which in its own right is nevertheless important but at the same time to a great extent one-sided. Boston could only remain the intellectual capital of North America as long as the New England element set the pace for the entire Union. A type of American way of life that is less one-sided than in the old New England states is now developing in the mid-Atlantic and western states and shows the influences of the large immigration of the last forty years, the influence of growing international contacts, and the increase in wealth and knowledge. Because of this trend, Boston will lose a great deal of its importance for this country in the next decades.

CHAPTER FIVE

Cambridge

SURVEY OF THE HISTORY OF ITS UNIVERSITY

Like the kernel in a seed, the best school in the New England colonies developed in and along with them. One of the most splendid aspects of their history is how the settlers, even during the first hard years of the young colony, did not forget to provide for popular education, how, considering time and place, the wonderful sense of charity of the citizens quite early supported the founding and upkeep of primary and secondary schools, and how, despite numerous problems both within and outside the colony, above all their school at Cambridge, Massachusetts, uninterruptedly continued to prosper visibly, to grow in importance as a place for independent scholarship, and to increase in overall importance for the country as a whole. This story does not need elaborate words of praise; it has had more than enough of these already as if it didn't speak sufficiently for itself, but a simple enumeration of the facts at this time would not be unprofitable. Whenever one speaks about America's cities, it is really imperative that this, one of the brightest pages in its history, should not be turned over silently.

In the year 1636, sixteen years after the founding of the first Puritan colony on New England soil, the council of the colony decided to allocate the sum of £400 for the founding of an institution of higher learning, a college. At that time only basic needs were being provided for. Roads, bridges, and walls had not yet been constructed, an Indian war had just broken out, the mother country was threatening infractions of the colonies' rights, and here within this colony, as in the others, dissension, like a worm in fast-ripening fruit, was present, affecting all of them. But the goal these immigrants had carried with them across the ocean to this rugged, deserted area taught them not only to bear the hardships of the present but also to fix their sights on the future. The goal had been freedom of religion, and in order to preserve this for the coming generations, it was necessary to have a clergy that would be filled with the spirit of the first settlers and would pass it on undiluted to those coming afterwards. This was the motivation for founding the school. A chronicler from the time of the first colonies expressed it clearly: "After God had carried us safe to New England, and we had builded our houses, provided necessaries for our livelihood, reared convenient places for God's worship, . . . one of the next things we longed for and looked after, was to advance learning, and perpetuate it to posterity; dreading to leave an illiterate ministry to the churches, when our present ministers shall lie in the dust."[1]

In the year after this decision, a council of twelve was appointed and given the task of founding the school. At the same time, it was also decided that its location should be in Newtown, a place near Boston. Perhaps it would have been impossible during those troubled times to have carried out the plan as desired immediately had not John Harvard,[2] a minister just recently arrived from England, left in his will half of his sizable fortune and his entire library to the then as yet unborn institution. This was a gift twice the amount the council had in mind to set aside for this purpose, and the 260 volumes of the book collection—among which were to be found, in addition to theological writings, works by Bacon and by Robinson, the Pilgrim father,[3] and many old classics—were a real treasure for the poor colony. The good example also inspired imitation, and when the bequest was made known, another £200 was soon designated for the library of the school then being set up. They have preserved the contribution lists, and you can see how the people donated sheep, clothing, and all kinds of utensils. With such help the work thrived, and when the school building was finished, they named the section of Newtown in which they had built it, Cambridge, in memory of the English university where some of the colonists had studied.

Since a system of primary education, in true Protestant tradition, had already been provided for by the settlers, they could require a certain degree of knowledge, which even included a fair amount of Latin and Greek, as a prerequisite for admission to this institution of higher learning. Bible reading and prayer were the most important parts of instruction and took place twice a day. During the three years that constituted the course of study, logic, physics, etymology, syntax, and grammar were taught in the first year; ethics, politics, dialectics, poetry, and Chaldean in the second; arithmetic, geometry, diction, Hebrew and Syriac in the third; while rhetoric, history, and botany were added at certain times to the curriculum. In the first decades after its founding, the school gave half of its students to the ministry, but the curriculum shows that it was already more than a theological seminary and everything leads one to believe that the directors of the college were not narrow-minded in the selection of the instructors. The first two presidents themselves did not agree to all the teachings of the "purified Christianity" of the old New Englanders but were, for those times, very learned men—one had been a professor of Greek and Hebrew at Trinity College in Cambridge, England—and they seemed to have administered the school well.

Thus, when enough had been done to take care of the school's basic needs, the enthusiasm for the institution seemed to have waned for a time due to such matters as the attention given to the Indian wars, the internal dogmatic disputes, the upheavals in the mother country, and the still rather tentative development that normally occurs in an institution's formative years. In 1655 its wealth consisted of not much more than £1,000, and one history of the school speaks a great deal about shortages, fruitless appeals for help, and neglect during this period. But then the general public helped out again. In 1669 the community of Portsmouth, New Hampshire, sent a message to the General Court (council) of the Massachusetts Colony in which its inhabitants expressed their thanks for the assistance given during the Indian war and in conclusion pointed out that even if they had arranged with the council to make no financial remuneration, they would still not be satisfied before God and their own consciences with the way they were expressing their thanks. While they had been considering how they should show their gratitude, the great difficulties that the school was experiencing had come to their attention. Now, in the hopes that their action would encourage others in the colonies to aid piously in such a good cause and also to strengthen the council to take strong action to avert the danger threatening all New England should the school close, they had taken up a collection and were prepared to contribute annually £60 for seven years to be used by the directors for the support of good scholarship.

Since this time, which concluded what was surely the hardest and most trying period of the colonies' history, the period in which their very existence appeared several times to come into question, the school no longer has had to fight with external poverty. As their development and progress became more secure, the colonies became more willing and capable of providing help of every kind; time and again the school received bequests from people. Many considered it, as one donor expressed in his will, "a lack of gratitude to the Lord for wealthy people to leave everything to their wives, children, and relatives and nothing to the community or the poor." During the seventeenth century the school received around £8,000 in currency, 2,000 acres of land, in addition to books with a value of about £1,000.

Having taken care of its external problems, the school turned its attention to internal improvement. The excellent position it occupied as a training center for ministers and teachers in this commonwealth founded on religious principles but already shaken for some time by religious controversy made it a main showplace for the battles that the orthodox adherents fought against the more liberal minded who sought to extend the old formulas to fit a new age and new circumstances. The faith and deeds of the Pilgrim fathers had been so influential that for over a century many people regarded these as the only things from the past worth maintaining or imitating. But the times and the people were changing. After two generations, just as the secular character of the state had already replaced the religious, in time its leading educational institution also was made to serve the purposes of a state that was unconcerned with sectarian squabbles and that served all the citizens equally and not just the interests of a particular cast or sect. There were many champions of the old doctrines who, when the clear minds of youth could no longer be clouded or forced to submit, still sought to plant their opinions in the unguarded thought patterns of young people and to cultivate and nurture the seeds there with all the patience that comes with conviction. Forced out of public life little by little, the old believers now held on with twice as much tenacity to the school they had controlled for so long. The fact that one of their most important exponents, Increase Mather,[4] had become president of the college in Cambridge only strengthened their efforts towards this goal. In the early years of the eighteenth century, however, after a long struggle, this party was finally forced out of the administration of the school, but only after it was able to drag the school into the witch-hunt controversy (which had so deeply aroused New England at the end of the previous century), which, however, soon worked much to the disadvantage of those who had started the controversy. Just as quickly as excitement had spread because of insane accusations did the populace also recoil from their own deeds once the first victims had perished. In the long run the old Puritan sense of freedom and justice showed itself stronger than those of fantasy and fanaticism. The misguided turned away and the guilt rested upon the instigators, the leaders of the old believers whose image was considerably tarnished as a consequence of this dark episode.

At the same time, the liberal elements within the colony won a powerful ally in the Anglican Church, whose importance continued to increase along with England's growing influence after the revolutions of 1640 and 1688. Living in most bitter enmity with the Puritans for a hundred years, it did not hesitate to make common cause with their enemies wherever it appeared possible to reduce their power. But this produced some real good, for both sides became more tolerant, more peaceable. On the other hand, it was only natural that the college in Cambridge became a focal point in this struggle.

It was the school's good luck to have won rather than lost because of the struggle. That its presidency (what we would call *Rektorat*), despite all the party conflicts, never came into the hands of incapable people gives excellent proof of the intelligence possessed by this nation's governing classes. With the single exception of Increase Mather, none of the presidents of the college were zealots, and some were influential enlightened men who also made other contributions to the public good. As has happened at many other points in American history, living and working in a free country seem to inspire the man of learning to better deeds. The knowledge of the history of other times and other peoples, and the realization of how hard it is to find truth, enable him not to take notice of party antagonisms to any great degree and prevent him from searching for the common good along just one path. Participation in public life, which he does not seek to shun, teaches him to know reality and what it demands and gives in return. Finally, this sense of moderation, which allows him to make fair and right decisions, and which is developed and nourished by a basis of broad general knowledge, finds thousands of opportunities in the duties the state and the community place upon its citizens to refine its objectives and renew its vigor with practical activities. Cambridge has experienced this blessing many times.[5]

The participation of individual citizens, moreover, has prevented factions from using the school to serve their one-sided purposes. For instance, when in 1719 Thomas Hollis,[6] a Baptist, i.e., an apostate in the eyes of the Puritans as well as the Anglicans, established a chair of divinity and a few years later one for mathematics, and within a few more years also gave the college gifts amounting to £5,000, these were events of great significance. The donations were presented to the school because it was the most liberally run college of that time. These contributions then made Harvard even more independent than it had been and prompted it to keep clear of sectarianism if only to fulfill Hollis's sole condition for granting the bequest, that no one should be denied entrance into the school because of religious beliefs. Every donation increased the school's ability to become an institution that stood above factions, dedicated to the pursuit of knowledge. The only requirement still to be fulfilled if its growth was to stay healthy and unhindered was always to find men who were capable of administering and teaching. Fortunately these were not lacking.

Another event that worked to the advantage of the liberal development of the Cambridge school was that the theological conservatives founded their own school of higher learning in New Haven, Connecticut, which was named Yale College in honor of its generous donor.[7] This occurred in the early years of the eighteenth century and made the more liberal, enlightened tendencies at Harvard soon seem less annoying to the orthodox, less worth fighting over. The struggle for spiritual supremacy thus came to an end here in a way similar to many other struggles of this kind in this country. If one party does not quarrel over its beliefs, then the other has to step aside and look for other ways to reach its goals. In the end then, having been spared violent quarrels, the public at large only gains and has many avenues of approach now open to it. In time, next to Harvard, Yale College became the most important institution of higher learning in North America, but in the decades after its founding, it perceived its main task as propagating the extreme one-sided teachings of the strictest Calvinist-Puritan sort. In 1753, just as Harvard College had successfully asserted its more liberal position against various theological attacks, Yale College took the opportunity to demonstrate clearly anew and to good advantage the orthodoxy of its teachers and its course of instruction. Its directors announced that the school recognized the basic writings of Calvinism as the only valid precepts of theological instruction, demanded from every teacher a public acknowledgment of the doctrines contained within these writings and a rejection of those that digressed from them, and declared that they wanted, at their discretion, to test every teacher's knowledge of these dogmas.

Meanwhile, Harvard College continued to grow steadily. In 1764, through a bequest, a chair for oriental languages was established, in 1770 one for physics and anatomy, and in 1771 one for elocution. Small gifts came into the library or the school itself annually, and when the library went up in flames, help came from all sides so that it soon stood in better condition than it had before. The War of Independence interrupted this expansion for several years, but the successful ending of the war and the resulting stimulus to the nation's intellectual and material development, which then occurred, also brought brighter prospects for the future of the school than had been the case in the prerevolutionary days when it was surrounded by a more narrow, limited, provincial atmosphere. By establishing three professorships for medicine in 1782, the college increasingly began to assume the character of a university. In 1780 instruction in French was introduced; in 1805 a chair for natural history was established by a contribution of $30,000 voluntarily subscribed to by the citizens of Boston; and in the same year the would-be demands of the theological conservatives were rejected with the appointment of a non-Calvinist as professor of divinity. In 1810 a chair for critical theology was established, and 1817 the Board of Overseers of the school, which according to the regulations of 1642 consisted of officers of the colony and clergymen, was transformed into a council on which fifteen Calvinist ministers and fifteen laymen were to sit in addition to the highest officials of the government. The number of professorships in the medical school was increased in the period up to 1820 so that gradually a real medical school developed. Professorships of divinity were also added and incorporated into a separate school. During the same time, donations provided chairs for Greek, law, technology, philosophy, and modern languages, and a natural history collection and a botanical garden were opened. The library, which in 1764 owned five thousand volumes, in 1840 contained around fifty thousand. That part of Harvard's wealth that stems primarily from gifts and earns interest amounted in the last few years to $646,000.

The sources from which this support comes have not ceased aiding the institution and encouraging its growth in a manner for which no example can be found in the recent history of European educational institutions. Whatever money and good will can do has been accomplished in a magnificent manner. But what is more important is that the results are such that the entire country must be thankful to little Cambridge, for the center of a most vigorous, creative intellectual life is located here. Emerson was a member of the Board of Overseers; Longfellow, J. R. Lowell, and Holmes were professors at Harvard University; the historians Palfrey, Bancroft, Motley, and Prescott were students and some of them instructors here. Two of the most original figures of American literature, Thoreau and Hawthorne,[8] studied at this school, and one need not say anything about the number of important statesmen and clergymen who have come out of Harvard. One thing is sure: in all America, intellectual and cultural life have nowhere struck root so strongly or borne fruit so consistently as here.

Cambridge has also become the model for numerous newer universities throughout the country and the "mother-school" of their teachers, and is therefore truly of no less importance in the diffusion of knowledge, especially for the West.

WELL-TO-DO APPEARANCE OF THE CITY. UNIVERSITY BUILD-
INGS. GERMAN INFLUENCE IN THE EDUCATIONAL SYSTEM.
LAW SCHOOL. LIBRARY; ACCESS TO IT. SCIENTIFIC SCHOOL.
L. AGASSIZ. COMPONENT PARTS OF THE UNIVERSITY. PERSONNEL.

Cambridge is no less unique as a college town than perhaps New York or Philadelphia are as centers of commerce or than Washington is as the capital. I know of no European city with which to compare it, especially no German one. The city itself is purely American, and that part of it that belongs to or is connected with the university stands apart, at least architecturally, from the rest of the city.

Only a shallow arm of the sea transversed by two bridges separates Cambridge from Boston, so that one can almost speak in terms of city and suburb, although Cambridge has a population of thirty thousand and is an independent community almost as old as Boston itself. There is a lovely walk over the bridges from which one can see many ships riding at anchor by the shore or slowly moving toward the harbor mouth where Boston has grown up around its broad hill, rising right up to the golden cupola of the State House, which glistens above the roofs like the crowning ornament on a step pyramid. In this contrast between the two cities one gets the impression of Cambridge's rusticity when one sets foot in its streets, where at first quite a few little wooden frame houses, workshops, storage areas, stables, and the like are to be seen. But these streets, which all lead into Boston, are to some extent part of Boston's business and commercial complex, and only when one goes away from the metropolitan area does the true character of Cambridge reveal itself. Here its neat houses stand in quiet, pleasant, many times even beautiful surroundings, in gardens and behind magnificent rows of trees. Now and then the view becomes really splendid. There are long rows of homes, each of which is situated on a grass-covered incline, surrounded by all sorts of statues and ornaments made of zinc or stucco. Each house with its large windows exudes such a feeling of self-containment and self-satisfaction that one gets the impression there is a substantial bit of wealth in this city.

At the end of one such street of villas are a gray stone church and right behind it, surrounded by lawns, trees, and all sorts of intertwining paths, a large number of uniform-looking buildings, which can be recognized as some kind of school by small entrances, numerous windows, unpretentious architectural embellishment, and the many juvenile decorations to be seen. The buildings are on a huge enough piece of land so that none of them blocks the intake of light or fresh air for the others. A few are new, others a little older, but none of them appears to be more than a generation old. Some are simple in appearance, others more highly embellished, but fortunately none of them suffers from that pervasive evil of American architecture—overstatement and excessive ornateness. In return, behind these buildings they have now erected a church out of lovely brownstone, which exemplifies only all the more this American tendency, a tendency, one hopes, that has gone out of fashion again for a time.

Since I inquired after an acquaintance of mine who taught at this school and who had graciously offered to be my guide, I was directed to another group of buildings, apartment houses, with broad fronts, which are located on the main street directly across from the university buildings. These apartments also belong to the university and are occupied by younger faculty members, teaching assistants, and many students, who have to pay a relatively small sum for their use. Here apartments are available for $44 to $300 a year, and those I saw are very roomy and bright, generally furnished with a separate bedroom and very often even a private bath. I should say that the American student in general lives considerably better than his counterpart in Germany. In any event, from viewing the rooms one sees that they put more emphasis on externals, on luxury, and the life of the dandy appears to be regarded less negatively here than it is in our country. If one wears anything one wants, one runs the risk of not being regarded as a gentleman. Since no one voluntarily desires to put himself in this position, the fashion journal plays a more important role here than one might rationally desire.

I entered the building and was astonished by the almost palatial size of the hall and the staircase; correspondingly, the rooms, as already mentioned, are bright and have high ceilings. Nowhere in the homes of my acquaintances, who for the most part have only come back from Germany within the last few years, did I find any lack of memories of Germany. In this house I saw portraits of Mittermaier, Gneist, Bluntschli, and the well-known copperplate engraving "Heidelberg" (seen from the Wolf Fountain side with a flock of sheep in the foreground) made me feel right at home.[9] I also saw a great number of German books and heard such good German spoken out of an American mouth that I could almost have forgotten where I was. Certainly Cambridge is,[10] so to speak, the most German of the American universities. Moreover, although only a few German-born instructors teach here, nevertheless the German approach both in the type and method of academic research and instruction is all the more pronounced. One can say that from here the door to the understanding of our literature, particularly Goethe, has been opened for the Americans. Agassiz, although French-Swiss, never made a secret of his great esteem for German learning within the large circles of people that he has influenced. In fact, there are few important instructors here who in their day did not sit in the lecture halls of Berlin, Göttingen, or Heidelberg.

First we visited the law school, which is housed in a new building of its own. This includes a lecture hall, library, and reading room as well as faculty offices under its spacious roof. The lecture hall is roomy and very bright, has seats for around one hundred students, and has portraits of famous teachers and former students who have since become famous. The seats are not mere benches but chairs, each with a little writing desk in front of it; only along the walls of the room are there benches with cane seats. A young assistant was at that moment busy explaining to his listeners about some aspect of law and was doing this not merely by making a speech or lecturing but by presenting questions and then discussing the answers with members of the class—a method that particularly pleased me for the study of law. I thought for a moment about the pedagogic method of our law faculty (or for that matter the lecture method predominant in all our university curriculums), which in terms of its logic and purpose I have never understood, and I have seldom seen the results that are expected from the listeners. Here in Cambridge every student has a textbook in front of him where, in case of need, he can look up facts. Many take written notes, and the attention of the students leaves nothing to be desired. The instructor is still a young man and, considering his position, still somewhat hesitant. I am acquainted with him and have seldom seen a more perfect example of what I might call the charming, modest youth; one who in character and disposition is sensitive and introspective. I am glad to see him in this type of career. Such natures almost always remain unspoiled and good human beings, and if they seldom attain great influence, it is still a pleasure for us in evaluating a nation as a whole to find them, because we can say to ourselves that wherever they are we can also find many favorable variations and combinations of their traits in people ranging from individuals such as these right down to the average man.

The law school contains very good academic facilities including a library of fifteen thousand books, said to be the best collection of works concerning English law in America. The library is connected to a large, well-furnished reading room and is open from 9:00 A.M. until 9:00 P.M. By this arrangement poor students can entirely do without purchasing their own books, especially since the most frequently used books are available in numerous copies. The main library of the university is also open daily from morning until dusk, and its facilities are also made very accessible, which shows that the principle of the theory that books should above all be made serviceable, that is, useful, is being carried out. Unfortunately, the value of this theory has as yet not become completely evident to the administrators of many libraries and other types of collections in Europe. I have never heard Americans who have studied at German universities complain of anything more frequently than about the restrictions we frequently impose on the use of such study aids.

The main library is housed in a special building built in gothic style out of granite. It contains 120,000 volumes and whoever loves books per se will, so they say, find more noteworthy and rare books here than in any other American library. Some of the first editions of American presses, manuscripts of famous writers and poets, handwritten examples of prominent statesmen, and also old woodcuts and similar things are displayed in showcases. The entire edifice is built in the shape of a great hall in whose side aisles the books are located in niche-like compartments. Busts of famous men ornament the walls and the pillars. The book catalog is located in two large cabinets, which contain a clearly written card for every book, filed alphabetically and according to subject in the subdivisions of numerous drawers. I found this system in all the libraries I have visited in this country, and it appears to be a practical one.

In one simply constructed red brick building with many windows, there were student accommodations and several large rooms used for meetings by one of the student societies—the Hasty Pudding Club[11]—which holds meetings and actually serves pudding, milk, and water at its sessions. Here there is a fine library, a little stage, humorous yearbooks and similar things, and on anniversary days when the alumni show up, it is supposed to become very lively and interesting here.

In other buildings used for university purposes I saw various sorts of lecture halls, some were small with very spotted and carved-up benches as in Germany, but most were big and bright with real chairs and little writing tables. There were also committee rooms, faculty offices, and the like, things that on the whole did not offer anything special about which to report.

Most often, however, I turned my steps towards the zoological and pale-ontological collections of the Scientific School,[12] where the elderly Agassiz[13] was always to be found, ready by word and deed to meet every request of a scientific nature. Now that this active, amiable man is dead, much will be missing around here, for the diligence, prudence, knowledge, the ability to utilize various skills in the right place, and whatever else they credited him with were not the only attributes he brought to this place. The constant goodness that without need of words shone in his face, the childlike joy in communicating with others with which he "ruled" amongst his treasures brought a bit of light and warmth—of a type that not the eye but the soul quickly senses—into these halls filled with old bones and shells. All these good qualities he possessed and utilized at Harvard will not be easily replaced, for people with such radiant personalities are not plentiful in such a profession; instead one finds most frequently stuffy and calcified people among scholars of such dry subjects. This institution is obviously well-off, rich as few others are, already organized into individual divisions, and set up with consideration given to its use by even the less than most interested student, something that is to be commended. The labels, catalogs, and explanatory pictures around the walls make a visit to these collections interesting for every person with reason and understanding, and, if he is looking for it, useful. Of all the collections I have seen, none is

arranged in such a splendid manner. Whoever knows how widespread interest is, especially for natural science collections, and how these collections can work as a stimulant in expanding the knowledge and love of nature among large groups of the population would like to see this example imitated many times over. In Germany we have many good collections, but none of the more important ones completely correspond, as regards the arrangement and accessibility of their holdings, to the purpose for which they were founded.

On Fridays, Agassiz was in the habit of giving a lecture, which was attended by many students, among whom were quite a few women. He showed himself on these occasions to be an extraordinarily captivating and stimulating teacher. During the summer he worked with his students on the nearby island of Penikese,[14] which a Boston merchant had presented as a gift to the institution and which in time, if the appropriate personnel are brought in, will become, because of its resources and location, an outstanding zoological school, for the museum founded by Agassiz has already given the entire university a name and significance, especially in Europe, which it would not yet otherwise possess. Agassiz employed a number of young women as librarians, secretaries, et cetera, and expressed his satisfaction with their work. One also sees girls and women in their quiet manner working in the university library and in the administrative offices, and everyone whom I asked praised their work.[15]

If we now turn back from the more external conditions in individual institutions within the university and take a look at the inner structure of the school as a whole, we find that the organization and curriculums of Harvard University are briefly as follows: besides Harvard College, the university also contains specialized schools for theology, law, medicine, dentistry, natural science and natural history, and engineering. In addition, it has more-or-less close ties with the astronomical observatory, the Peabody Museum of American Ethnology and Archeology, and the Museum of Comparative Zoology founded by Agassiz.[16] All of these schools and institutions are under the general supervision of the president, five fellows, and a Board of Overseers, which consists of thirty members. Formerly only the leading officials of the State of Massachusetts as well as several pastors of specific Congregational churches belonged to the Board of Overseers. With the approval of the board in 1810, it was reorganized along more liberal lines, whereby besides the fifteen pastors, fifteen laymen were added to the board as elected members. In 1834 the restriction that only Congregational ministers could be elected to the board was dropped. In 1851 the numerical specifications about clergymen were dropped. Finally in 1865 the most important of these reforms, upon which the present government of the university is based, was instituted. By this reform the election to the

6   LOUIS AGASSIZ LECTURING ON NATURAL HISTORY,
APPROXIMATELY ONE YEAR BEFORE HIS DEATH IN 1873.

Board of Overseers was placed in the hands of the graduates, that is, of all those who have received any sort of degree conferred by the university. These graduates now elect the members of that board from their own numbers so that the school in the broadest sense is self-governing. Despite the university's broad basis, there is nevertheless a strong ecclesiastical element still represented among the officials of the university, so that a decidedly Unitarian influence can be seen here at Harvard[17] similar to the Presbyterian influence at Yale College in New Haven, the second big university of this country.

Forty-four full professors and 36 instructors on various levels, together with a varying number of assistants, constitute the faculty. Of this number, 33 (19 professors and 14 instructors) teach at the college, which in 1872 had 635 students, while the Law School has 9 teachers and 113 students, the Scientific School 14 teachers and 37 students, the School of Engineering 10 teachers and 3 students, the Medical School 27 teachers and 171 students, and the Divinity School 4 teachers and 10 students.

The connection between the various divisions within the university is only superficial, and many of the students of the various professional schools have not taken one course in the college. In the Law School, for example, anyone is accepted without proof of academic preparation, which naturally assures an unfortunately uneven basis of knowledge on the part of the students, upon which the teacher is supposed to build. They informed me that they hoped this abuse will be remedied, since in the last few years there has been a strong tendency to institute something similar to the requirements of German institutions of higher learning, which in many ways are more liberal but in many important matters more demanding than those of American universities.

STUDENT LIFE. VARIOUS SOCIETIES. PHYSICAL TRAINING. ACA-
DEMIC NEWSPAPERS. STUDENT HABITS. STUDIES. CURRICULUM.
PURPOSE AND OBJECTIVE OF THE STUDIES.

The nucleus of such a university naturally always remains the college, and the students of the college, the undergraduates, consider themselves the real students as opposed to those of the professional or graduate schools. The colleges are also the preserves of real student life, whereas the mixture of so many more youthful elements as well as the peculiarities of the general form and outlook on life of the Americans give a definitely different character to college life than in Germany or even in England. On the other hand, there are also similar basic traits in American and English student life, since the universities of this country at first strictly adhered to the English pattern and have only recently begun to develop their own individual characteristics or to follow the example of German universities.[18]

We have already sketched in the general character of such a university and, in part, the course of study, and would now like to consider the leading features of student life outside the classroom.

The boy who comes to the university will not simply be subjected by his teachers to a hard test of his academic qualifications, but he will also be put through a series of trials by older fellow students, which are intended to prepare him for a rougher life than that to which he had been used to at home. The methods with which they try to draw him into one of the literary fraternities are the same as those used by German fraternities to get pledges. Here, as in Germany, it is not a question of the quality but of the number of members. The fraternities send recruiters to the schools that have already sent some students to the college, place a member of the fraternity on the trains coming in or post one to keep a lookout for new students at the railway station. At times these eager partisans literally fight for the people they want. Even if the fellow has been accepted into "Linonia" or the "Brothers in Unity,"[19] he still cannot really be called a true American if he does not also try to get into one of the numerous so-called secret societies that exist among the university students as they do among all groups and age levels of society. Here membership is more selective, but in the end everyone seems to get into one group or the other. After all sorts of practical jokes, sometimes even rough ones, have been played on the new initiate, and after he has been relieved of a tidy sum of his pocket money, he may then wear one of the golden breast pins that are the characteristic trademarks of secret society members.

Until just recently the secret societies in New Haven initiated their pledges as a group at night, renting the large ground floor of the State House[20] building for this purpose, where they gave the poor initiates a taste of some refined torture. First the pledges are blindfolded and led around the city, through ditches and ponds and over all sorts of obstacles, and introduced to the art of heavy drinking. Then someone brings them before a skeleton with which they have to shake hands; next someone guillotines them with a wooden axe and leaves them down in the cellar with a coffin. Naturally, funeral orations and incidental blows and bruises come with this, and before the symbolic resurrection takes place there is also talk of lynch justice and the fires of purgatory. But the tortures are not ended here, for as long as someone is a freshman (that is, one who is in his first year of college), there always exists the danger that he will be dragged out of bed by a wild bunch and forced to dance and sing, or be smoked out by heavy tobacco smoke, or one fine day discover his door broken in and some of his most essential furniture carried off or destroyed. The more difficult this initiation period, the greater the happiness of the freshmen when they finally become sophomores (second-year students), and they cannot refrain from symbolically announcing their admission into this more manly, more esteemed class by wearing ridiculous high hats, long tailcoats, and massive collars when they go to church for the first time as sophomores.

Only now for the first time can they really enjoy their youth and freedom, taking part more eagerly than ever in ball games, rowing, and even boxing. The hard New England winter offers the students ample opportunity for ice skating, and therefore, this sport plays a bigger role here than it does in Europe. Since Cambridge and New Haven are both so close to the ocean, sailing is also a popular activity. In addition, the universities have a so-called gymnasium where within an enclosed area all sorts of apparatus are found for any of the usual games and exercises. Competitive games and races are the order of the day, and certain groups in this country get no less excited about the crew racing between Yale College and Harvard College than the English do about the competition in this sport between Oxford and Cambridge.

The literary societies occupy much less of the students' time than do these sports, and their meetings, at which previously announced questions are generally debated, are well attended only on special occasions—when a skit is being performed (which happens frequently during the year), or when an important person of the academic community is speaking. I have already talked about the rooms occupied by one such society, which housed a considerable library and no mean sized stage. Most of the academic newspapers, which appear monthly and semimonthly, are published by these societies. Besides the inevitable doggerel poetry, without which no newspaper in New England seems to believe it can appear, these papers mostly carry articles of general and local interest to the academicians. Of course, one finds a lot of gossip and foolishness in these journals (Cambridge and New Haven each have two), but on the whole I was surprised by the maturity rather than the immaturity of their contents and must say, at least about those appearing in Cambridge, that compared with German academic newspapers with which I am familiar, these papers are much more clearly and objectively written than ours. This is not astonishing, however, when one considers at what an early age the American enters into the "school of politics" or rather how early his entire milieu pushes him into it. Even in the formation of student fraternities, political motives are frequently manifestly present.

Concerning the secret societies, I have not been able to learn much more except that they exist partly for social recreation, partly for promoting the studies of their members, and partly for religious and political purposes and that they are widespread here. The members do not wear any uniform or specific colors but, as already mentioned, let their fraternity pins serve as their insignia. By chance I learned that the drinking customs of German fraternities have been introduced here by students who have been to Germany, but certainly this is the case in only a very limited degree. One of my friends asked a young doctor in N. whom we had met, how he was thinking of spending Christmas Eve and learned (naturally under the seal of secrecy) that along with his friends who had been to German universities he had formed a secret drinking club where they drank, smoked, and sang; there this fellow, having studied at Würzburg, spent his Christmas Eve, which pleased me very much. In general there is not much drinking on American campuses. By nature the American is not built for German drinking. He gets agitated too easily and always has to think about his weak stomach. He throws down a good deal of brandy or grog in order to reduce himself as quickly as possible to the appropriate level of intoxication, but he seldom finds any pleasure in our long-lasting, merry drinking sessions.

In general, a trademark of the American student is that he wants to be, and is, less isolated from society than his European counterpart. This has good and bad consequences. Since the entire educational system here is based on the idea of turning the child as quickly as possible into an average human being who is prepared to face life's problems, and since they put girls and boys not yet fully mature into society and into the adult world and completely deny the existence of a beneficial intermediate period, which we have specifically designated the "awkward age" (*Flegeljahre*), we clearly find little of real student customs and traditions here. The student wants to be counted, for better or for worse, as a member of society and that naturally takes a lot of the poetry out of life. To want to prolong youth would be looked upon as an impropriety in a land where everyone strives for a self-sufficient place in society, where young men of twenty-two and twenty-four years of age assume prominent positions, where in general they get married much younger than we do. The simple joy of youth, living for the present in unrestricted abandon, is not to be found. Quite early in life the American begins to strive for specific goals. The bud, so to speak, wants to become fruit before it is ready, and even if in so doing only a few do not make it, still only a few really mature properly, and the average remains standing at the level of mediocrity—but which for a republic, however, will be the most useful measure for its talents.

This desire to be part of society probably makes the average cost of student life here relatively more expensive than in Europe. Six hundred dollars would not go very far here; the great majority of students need three times that much and more. For the poorer ones, who cannot even afford that sum, apparently everything is splendidly taken care of. A large number of so-called scholarships are available at Harvard and Yale primarily to help the poor students with regard to housing, and under certain circumstances they receive completely free housing, and by no means the worst. If they do well academically, then they can acquire prizes that go as high as $100. For the industrious ones there is the opportunity to tutor, for which they are also well paid. We were told that such students formerly also earned their meals in an interesting way. They provided the meals for a number of fellow students who had formed a sort of a cooperative society, supervised the purchases, and took care of the bills in return for which they ate free with the others. This much I saw here: without a fortune but with some application and talent, one can confidently get a college education. In Germany, as is well known, that is a dangerous venture, which seldom comes out to the person's advantage.

Something has already been said concerning the work of the American universities,[21] but I only want to add that many indications seem to point out that—although the teaching methods and the greater earnestness of American young men produce an impressive number of hard-working and industrious students—more things are learned mechanically and less thoroughly than in Europe. I got the impression that the knowledge and learning of students here are certainly more varied and practical, but the system does not provide for as much independent development or individual assimilation as in our schools.

Some teachers whom I asked about this matter complained about the small amount of classroom time required of the students of the college and explained that it was impossible within the allotted time even to reach approximately similar results as those of the German high schools. In the Harvard College catalog for 1872–1873 I found that the weekly number of hours of instruction for the first year was fifteen and one-half; for the second year it was four required classes and six to eight electives; for the third year, six required and six to nine electives; and for the fourth year, nine to twelve electives. At the beginning of the school year, if the student demonstrates by a test that he has the necessary knowledge in one of the required courses for that year, then he will be excused from attending classes in that course. The required courses in the first year are Greek and Latin (three and one-half hours), mathematics (four hours), German (two hours), ethics (three hours) in the first semester and chemistry (three hours) in the second semester. In the second year comes physics for two hours, rhetoric and history with two hours together; the third year finishes the requirements with two hours of philosophy, two hours for both economics and rhetoric together, and two hours for physics. Earlier, while discussing the New York Academy,[22] I mentioned the most essential things about the role in the curriculum of the so-called electives from which the students under certain conditions can select a certain number of courses, and I only want to repeat that by being included in the curriculum, in many ways they are causing the college to expand and become transformed into a true arts and science faculty. For example, the natural science electives alone have fourteen instructors offering courses in Harvard College.

I spoke earlier about the great seriousness of the American students, but would like this only to be taken together with what I previously said about their general outlook and way of life. It is an earnestness of people who have definite goals in mind, but the objectives for the most part are not directed towards learning and understanding per se, but above all towards a good job and a secure position and towards the means to obtain these ends: money. One of my friends, who is an instructor in the natural sciences at a university in one of the Midwestern states, told me that this widely accepted dominant tendency to utilize learning from the very beginning to produce tangible gains as quickly as possible has completely spoiled teaching for him, for wherever knowledge is esteemed only to the degree that it is useful in making money, then the entire teaching profession is debased to an ignoble, thankless task. It is rare, he said, that students learn because of the joy of learning, simply because of a desire to know, or because of a desire for self-improvement or self-enrichment; they want to know something specific with which they can earn some money. Agassiz once stated something similar to me, although not as strongly expressed, when he said that he would feel more than compensated for all his efforts if the pursuit of knowledge, as he taught and encouraged it in his school, took away some of the exaggerated value, which many people had, that money and work are to be used only to make more money. Such a belief, he said, was held to the exclusion of all nobler values and standards.

As noted previously, the early suppression of all aspects of youthful conduct is basically connected with these aspirations, but since nature has made the period of growing up, both mentally and physically, a part of our existence, we have to remain young for a certain length of time and should not try to become adults before the proper time, as this will court danger. But I fear that the curtailment of the growing-up period in this country is not merely a custom but lies deeper in what appears to be its unhealthy, intense, fast-pulsating, many times almost crippling, way of life.

CHAPTER SIX

Philadelphia

SITE. FOUNDING AND GROWTH. CITY PLAN. LARGE NUMBER OF HOUSES. TYPICAL RESIDENTIAL HOUSE. WHITE MARBLE. CHURCHES. TROLLEYS.

Philadelphia lies at the far end of Delaware Bay, the most northerly of the bays between Cape May and Cape Lookout, which cut opening upon opening in the low-lying Atlantic coast. Its latitude is 39.5°. It is 23 geographical (106 statute) miles from the entrance to the bay, but the tides in both rivers, on or between which the city actually lies, go upstream considerably beyond Philadelphia, and no matter how deep their draft, ships come up the Delaware and anchor at the edge of the city. Only a broad projection of land belonging to New Jersey separates Philadelphia from New York, and the railroad covers the 19-geographical (87.6 statute)-mile route between the two cities in three hours. For this reason both cities in part complement each other in trade and industry, for presently almost an eighth of Philadelphia's imports come in via New York; in return Philadelphia supplies New York's industry with iron, coal, and oil. Nevertheless, Philadelphia is primarily important because of industrial activities. Although it competes, not without some success, with the other Atlantic ports (Boston, New York, Baltimore) in overseas trade, in this regard it is still surpassed not only by them but also by New Orleans, San Francisco, and Savannah.

Philadelphia's main advantage is its location at the natural gateway to the richest coal and iron areas that have as yet been developed in the United States, and also its almost central position between the northern and southern sections of the eastern half of North America and its densely populated industrial hinterland. Despite all this, it has many fewer natural advantages than does New York. First of all, the Delaware is much more restricted in navigation than is the Hudson and, in general, communications with the West are much more difficult. The harbor of Philadelphia has to contend with more ice than does New York. Even Baltimore is more important for trade with the West than Philadelphia. In the last century Philadelphia benefited from the peace that Pennsylvania enjoyed in the midst of the French and Indian wars of the North and West,[1] and in those days of meager traffic its centrally located position was more significant than today. The city was not simply the political capital but was also the largest city of the Union up into the 1820s, when it was superseded by New York. Its population growth, measured by decades, went from 45,250 in 1790 to 70,287; 96,287; 119,325; 167,325; 258,037; 408,762; 568,034. In 1870 there were 674,022 inhabitants, and in 1873 an estimated 740,000. Philadelphia, as founded in 1682 by Penn, was laid out on a tract two miles long and a mile wide between the Delaware and Schuylkill rivers, according to a street plan that carefully avoided all curves or bends and adhered as much as possible to rectangles and squares.[2] According to this plan, a wide piece of land running the length of the city, on the banks of both the Delaware and the Schuylkill, would not be built upon, and many areas would be reserved for parks. Two main thoroughfares one hundred feet in width, one running from east to west, the other from north to south, were to intersect in the center of the city, and the side streets were to be laid out parallel to these, of which the more important were to be sixty feet wide. In the older sections of the city the plan has been faithfully carried out insofar as direction and width of the streets are concerned. Thus, the portion of Philadelphia that lies between the Delaware and the Schuylkill is a large collection of rectangles of all different sizes. Conforming to this regularity, the north-south streets are merely numbered, and the house numbers have also been so systematized that finding the location of a house can be done at a glance. The even numbers are on the south, the odd numbers on the north side. Between First and Second Streets the houses are numbered from 100, between Second and Third streets from 200, and so forth. If a house number is 836 one knows that it is between Eighth and Ninth Streets. On the east-west streets, which are named rather than numbered, the houses are numbered from 100 to the next 100, from street to street.

Philadelphia, therefore, is probably the most exactly and evenly laid out of any city of comparable size or larger, unless some day one arises among the rapidly growing cities of the West to compete with this city for the title.[3] It is remarkable how, over the years, the Philadelphians have adhered to the rectangular system of intersecting streets and how few exceptions have been allowed. This regularity notwithstanding, the city has accommodated itself under all circumstances to its position between the two rivers that at one time formed its outer limits on the east and west. Nevertheless, it is apparent that this external regularity, advantageous as it may seem, particularly as compared to the haphazard, crammed methods of construction in our old cities, is not really appropriate for big cities in such an extreme form. Only one of the two streets designated in the plan as main streets has become a commercial thoroughfare filled with storehouses, offices, signboards, vehicles, as well as a lot of dirt and dangerous pavements, with few people there for other than business purposes.[4]

The other street remains empty and deserted and without being distinguished looking, or only so in an appealingly lonely way.[5] It runs through the business area, partakes of some of its noise and refuse but does not share its life and activity. The elegant traffic is concentrated on Chestnut Street, which runs south of Market Street from river to river, and on this street there is no lack of grand, at times attractive, buildings, for here among others are to be found the State House,[6] the post office, the banks, and the big hotels, but on the other hand, it is too narrow to represent worthily the main street of a really important city such as this. The situation is the same on Walnut and Pine Streets, the next two parallel streets north of Chestnut,[7] where quite a few plain but elegant brownstone and marble homes have been built. These streets are also much too narrow to give any appearance of importance.

What Philadelphia lacks is a main artery and this can only be a diagonal street, which would take the traffic from the rectangular streets of a large part of the city and carry it farther on, a street such as Broadway.[8] In the newly layed out sections of town they were wise enough not to shun diagonal streets and once in a while even a winding one.[9] In its early days this Quaker sense of regularity was responsible for the beauty that characterized the center of the new, large, rich, and well-situated city—the true Philadelphia. Now, because of the regularity of the city layout, traffic seems uncoordinated and is even hindered by the omnipresent right angles, and the whole idea of a grid for Philadelphia looks somewhat like a botched job as does any project that does not coincide with its intended purpose. Traffic simply did not want to go the way the "rational city" founders wanted it to. These Philadelphian superrationalists of the eighteenth century had more important things to do than just plan the city. Nevertheless, it is well that they did not live to see how their plan worked out, or else in the end they would have had to recognize that things take their natural course and do not always obey reason.

The old city plan, however, is unfortunately not being adhered to precisely in that area in which its creators really were striving for something permanently useful, that is, in reserving certain places that should be maintained as parks or open squares. Thus, instead of having open space along the attractive sloping banks of the Delaware, this area is so crammed with ugly storehouses and offices that the view of the other bank or of the islands in the river can nowhere be really enjoyed. Girard,[10] a Philadelphia benefactor, sought by means of bequests to renew interest in Penn's idea of leaving these banks vacant and laying them out as parks, but it is not an easy matter to clear the area of buildings again. Likewise, the original plan with the large central square in the middle of the city was abandoned in favor of a number of little squares, which do not appear to me to be very well maintained.

In local phraseology, Philadelphia is called the "Quaker City" and "the city of homes," the latter implying that Philadelphia (in proportion to the number of inhabitants) has more homes than any other big city in the United States. It deserves this reputation, and probably of all the big cities of the civilized world it suffers least from overcrowding. The area of the city encompasses 6 geographical square miles (127.5 statute square miles) and contains 134,740 buildings, of which 124,302 are home dwellings; thus no more than six people reside on the average in one house. How the number of houses in other important cities compares to that in Philadelphia today cannot be ascertained, but the census of 1870 definitely shows that Philadelphia, in absolute terms, has more houses than any other metropolis. As of that date there were 112,336 home dwellings in Philadelphia, whereas New York, in spite of its appreciably larger population, had only 64,044. This fact can be explained only by tradition, which tenaciously holds on to a type of living accommodation that is recognized to be beneficial in spite of the many apparent advantages the row-house system offers. Moreover, it must also be noted that Philadelphia's life style in general is not so complicated and is less expensive, work is taken more seriously and is more conscientiously performed here than in New York. One hears complaints of the difficulty in obtaining liquid capital here, although the city is very wealthy. When one inquires as to the reason for this, one is told: the money Philadelphians possess has been earned through work, while in New York speculation is paramount; New York can easily throw around the millions of dollars that are always passing from hand to hand in transactions. I am told that the middle class, self supporting, well-off yet not indulging in luxury living, is much larger here in Philadelphia than in New York and might also help account then for the favorable ratio of homes to inhabitants here.

The typical Philadelphia home dwelling, the model for about four-fifths of all the homes here, is a building constructed of exposed brick with the steps, sills, and door and window frames made out of some kind of cut stone, which in the better and middle-class houses is actually white marble. The ground plots are generally long and rectangular, the house taking up the entire depth of the land except for one of the two rear corners, which is used as a courtyard. The interior of the homes seemed to me to be narrower and plainer than those I have otherwise seen in America; the arrangement of space is different here in that no basement has been added to the home, and while the parlor, dining room, and kitchen are found on the first floor, all other rooms are on the second. Most houses, even better ones, have only two stories, with a very small minority having more than three. I got to know some very nice little homes in the suburb of West Philadelphia—long rows of small villas with verandas, considerably higher than the street and set back from it. One of my acquaintances lived here with his wife and child in half of such a small villa where there were two rooms and a kitchen on the ground floor, with two more rooms upstairs. It was an inexpensive and very pleasant dwelling, simple and homey.

A curious practice is the already-mentioned use of marble in all homes that are in any way semirespectable looking. Marble is not found in this region, is not cheap, and does not go particularly well with the dull red of the brick. But the people appear to be so proud of having something of white marble on their houses that sometimes the door and window frames are painted white in an attempt to imitate it (not very convincingly), with only the thresholds made of marble, even if of a multiveined, gray variety. Generally they have hidden their marble steps so well under a wooden covering that one would think they are trying not to look at them! I really think that it is the neatness of such a marble-trimmed little brick house, the red and the white together, that makes them attractive to the Philadelphians. The owners diligently clean and wash these buildings, and on Saturdays they create veritable floods on the sidewalks, actually scrubbing the marble with soap. Thus, Philadelphia could be a really clean city if so many of its streets were not so dirty. This is a fault it shares with all the large cities I have seen in America. Perhaps conditions are better in summer than in the damp winter of 1873–1874 when I observed them!

In the few cases in the city where an expensive house has been built, the people prefer to use brownstone in the New York style. In West Philadelphia there is a magnificent block of three-story dwellings that are very simply built and covered from top to bottom with the most beautiful white marble slabs. The simple design and the excellent shingling material perfectly complement each other. The reader who is coming over for the Exposition[11] should take a look at some of the marble houses on Chestnut Street, especially one located between Fourteenth and Fifteenth Streets, which is constructed from a stone with grey veins and cloud-like configurations in it—I was impressed with its very stately, fine appearance.

Although the churches and other public buildings are by no means as elegant as in New York, they nonetheless definitely stand out from the mass of predominantly uniform, plain, small houses, which certainly do nothing to give this city a metropolitan atmosphere. I have actually heard it called "an overgrown village" by someonw who was born here and still lives here. The majority of public buildings in the older part of the city dates from the period when everywhere in America people built in Greek style.[12] You can hardly find a street in which a Doric or Ionic temple, be it a church, lodge hall, mint, or post office, does not appear together with its colonnade. There is also no lack of curious-looking churches and richly decorated, mammoth commercial buildings. Just recently a Masonic temple[13] was erected on Broad Street (the Leipzig *Illustrirte Zeitung* featured a picture of this in 1873),[14] which was admired very much because it was constructed out of a beautiful granite, richly decorated with ornaments, and lavished with towers and turrets. At the moment some large buildings are under construction in the area, some of which should be finished for the Exposition, and if nothing else they should have an imposing appearance. Philadelphians have high hopes especially for the new City Hall now under construction.[15] One gets a really strange impression from the big prison near the park entrance, the Eastern Penitentiary;[16] enclosed by massive walls and towers, the entrance heavily bolted, it looks almost like a citadel and appears to fit better in one of our medieval cities than in this one.

The spacious layout in Philadelphia has naturally caused the streetcar network to be extensively developed. There are at present 45 geographical (207.5

statute) miles of streetcar tracks on which 794 cars, with 4,860 horses run daily. In 1872, according to the statements of the fifteen companies, around sixty-seven million people traveled on these lines. Oddly enough the price here is two cents higher than on the New York streetcar, and it seems, as in so many cases, that a coalition of companies is withholding the fruits of competition from the Philadelphians. I noticed here a device, which I had also seen in Boston, for preventing the conductor from embezzling; it is a ticket punch that rings. Every time he receives a payment, right in front of the eyes and ears of the passengers, he has to punch a hole in the strip of paper he carries in his button-hole. Thus passengers can keep a check on him, for they soon get used to hearing every payment answered by the shrill ring of the punch. In the cars large placards give detailed information about the purpose and use of this device.

Philadelphia has so little hilly ground in the entire extensive area it occupies that the water and gas conduits encounter fewer difficulties than in other cities, especially since its soil consists of fine gravel. In 1872, 120,516 homes received 13 billion gallons of water from the five waterworks, and there were about 35,000 bathrooms in the city with running water. In the same year 1.5 billion cubic feet of gas were used in something over a million gas burners, the number of private consumers totaled around 80,000, and the price was $2.25 for 1,000 cubic feet of gas. In the streets, whose aggregate length amounts to 195 geographical (899 statute) miles and of which more than half are paved, there are 9,000 gas lights.

FAIRMOUNT PARK. WATER SUPPLY OF THE CITY. SITE OF THE EXPOSITION OF 1876. FRANKLIN INSTITUTE. UNIVERSITY. GIRARD COLLEGE. PUBLIC LIBRARIES.

Philadelphia's city park, Fairmount Park, is certainly the most interesting attraction Philadelphia has to offer. It is to be the site in 1876 of the projected International Exposition in celebration of the hundredth anniversary of the Declaration of Independence. This makes the park doubly interesting, since it is also an instructive example in land-use planning for all those who take an interest in the good health of urban populations. This park encompasses some three thousand acres of land, running for more than a geographical mile (4.6 statute miles) on both sides of the Schuylkill River and includes a stretch of 1.33 (6.14 statute) miles along the banks of the Wissahickon, a tributary of the Schuylkill. The reason for this vast spread, of which the Philadelphians are so proud, is found in more than just a rivalry with other cities that had good parks before Philadelphia did; the old, rather small park, which lies at the south end of Fairmount Park, actually also runs so far upstream along both rivers because of a concern for the city's water supply. With the growth of industry, the upper part of the Schuylkill, from which Philadelphia gets its drinking water, became so polluted from all kinds of waste as to prompt serious concern about the state of the city's health. The transformation of both banks into a park not only has stopped all that kind of pollution but has also provided the city with a charmingly landscaped recreation area without too much effort or cost. For non-Americans there is little point in arguing whether this park is three or four times larger than New York's Central Park or whether there are many in Europe that cover a still greater area. Similarly we do not ask whether it is correct when the *Pocket Guide of Philadelphia* states that there are "not many streams in this country and few in Europe like the Wissahickon."[17] The park is big and beautiful enough to be sufficiently enjoyed without all these exaggerations. The Schuylkill in this area is approximately as wide as the Neckar[18] near Heidelberg but makes a greater impression because it contains considerably more water. Six railroads cross over it near the city via several imposing bridges, a seventh is just being built at the entrance to the park, and at the same place a wooden bridge still serves pedestrians and vehicles. Right below the park on the left side Philadelphia comes into view, on the right, close by, one comes upon the busy commercial suburb of West Philadelphia with buildings used for business purposes and all the accompanying noise. In the park itself the banks are mostly rocky and steep and remain covered with wooded and grassy areas down to the water's edge. The tributary stream, the Wissahickon, flows almost down to its very estuary among wooded hills, and plenty of picturesque views can be seen from its right bank on the street running up the hill.

Because of both these rivers and a landscape filled with numerous hills and rock formations, Fairmount Park needed to deviate from nature only to the extent of removing an occasional rough spot in order to be utilized to its maximum as a recreation area. Except for its size, it resembles one of those areas that one sees laid out around a spa in the mountains: they have graded a few paths, placed a few benches along the way, perhaps also encased a spring. Now, almost effortlessly, an entire mountain slope has become the most beautiful garden that one could imagine. As mentioned already, here are the two rivers, mighty, unadulterated natural phenomena, which make you forget everything in the entire park that has been designed or laid out by man. In contrast, an area like New York's park, for example, will never be able to bring such complete satisfaction as here despite its abundance of trees and pools.

In this park they are going to build the next International Exposition.* The site has already been decided upon, and a white flag edged with stars with the

*WRITTEN IN JANUARY 1874.

words "1776 Centennial 1876" on it as well as a few national flags fluttering here and there from tall poles announce far and wide where the location is to be. The spot seems to be well chosen—the best in the entire district (as far as I can judge from my small knowledge of the area around Philadelphia).[19] One travels from the city through the old park, over one of the three bridges, which run right next to each other over the river, going about sixty feet along the right bank of the Schuylkill through a very pretty area, until one comes to a level spot stretching out towards the west on which the large field for the International Exposition has been staked out. It is a slightly rolling terrain, predominantly meadowland with occasional clumps of trees. If one walks about a quarter of an hour farther, one comes to a thirty-foot elevation, which rises like a step, from which one can obtain the most beautiful view over the whole park and sections of Philadelphia. This park dominates the entire Exposition area, and it certainly will make a magnificent picture once the colorful activities start to unfold here within the confines of this beautiful landscape. From the Exposition area itself there is also a broad view up the Schuylkill towards Philadelphia, which offers some interesting sights. I hope the smell of kerosene here will not be as overwhelming during the jubilee festivities as it was both times I visited the place! Philadelphia has very humid summers, and this smell could make people with sensitive natures rather uneasy.

On the average, a person could go by foot from the center of town to the Exposition grounds in a good hour, but there are also horse-pulled and steam-powered trains aplenty on this route and no lack of steamboats on the Schuylkill. A Centennial Restaurant is already being advertised prominently, although at present one can see only a big stable behind the huge sign.

At the moment there is little to be said about the preparations for the Exposition. Some building plans for the art gallery, for example, have already been agreed upon, and when Congress has approved its appropriation, then the State of Pennsylvania will see what it and its major city, Philadelphia, are in a position to contribute. At present the newspapers are urging on the work with all their might, and in most states and territories, Exposition commissions have been appointed. No one among the competent people to whom I have spoken about the matter doubts, however, that the task to set up and run the Exposition properly will be an extraordinarily difficult, if not impossible, job, considering the number of men and minds that will, or will want to, bring their influence to bear and the fraud that without doubt will creep in here in many places. A *Journal of the Exposition*[20] has been out for a few months already but really does not say anything yet about the Exposition itself.

In this center of large and small industry and manufacturing, the capital of coal and iron, an institution like the Franklin Institute[21] could not have been more appropriately situated. In Europe we know this institute from its monthly bulletins in which valuable specialized information as well as reports of scientific experiments in chemistry and physics are published. Here in this country it enjoys a high reputation, deriving in part from the great practical value its

7   AN AERIAL VIEW OF THE
CENTENNIAL EXPOSITION
GROUNDS, PHILADELPHIA,
1876.

contributions have produced. The exterior of the institute contrasts sharply with the local university and college buildings (as well known, the hardest-working daughter contents herself with Cinderella-like old clothes). In an unassuming building on Seventh Street, on the first floor, there are the large lecture hall and rooms for an art school; on the second and third floors the library and collection of models are housed. Every member, and there are now thirteen hundred of them, has the right to use this collection, to hear lectures, which are given weekly during the winter by eminent professors. He also receives the publications of the institute and can ask the staff, who are available at any time all day long, for advice on all sorts of technical or scientific matters. For this service a very small fee is charged, which, together with several endowments, sustain the institute. Correspondence with scientific societies and institutions across the country and in Europe brings with it a wealth of magazines, which are laid out in the nicely furnished reading room for everyone's use.

An extremely valuable facility is, it seems to me, the committee of eminent members, which was voluntarily formed and to whom discoveries or improvements on things can be submitted before they go to the Patent Office. Here one can receive advice or perhaps support or can be protected early enough from the waste of money and effort, which ruins so many "inventors." For years, the journal of the Franklin Institute was the official organ of the Patent Office, and since the archives of the latter were destroyed by fire,[22] its early volumes have remained the only records of old patents issued in the United States.

The Franklin Institute has also engaged in major research in steam-generated combustion, water wheels and the like, partly on behalf of the government and partly on its own initiative. What I found especially interesting in its history was the fact that it fostered the nuclei of a number of public welfare institutions that, when fully developed, were taken over by the state or municipal authorities. In the 1820s, shortly after its founding, the institute established a kind of nonclassical secondary school (*Realschule*), which continued up until the time the city itself provided for the needs for which this school had been founded. Later a similar thing occurred with the founding of evening continuation classes, and in 1850 it established the first school of drawing and wood engraving for women, which is now likewise independent. There is a good sort of self-government operating here, which provides for the things that are lacking. Now it runs a drawing and design school for young men, which has 250 students, and thirty to forty lectures are held annually at the institute.

The University of Pennsylvania,[23] like other institutions of higher learning in this country, has gradually developed out of the high school and the college and is still in the process of growing. The buildings are magnificently laid out, and the one for the department of arts and sciences (which could be described as something a little less rigorous than a European philosophical faculty (*philosophische Fakultät*)[24] is already occupied and looks, both inside and out, like a building on which they spared no money, out of which they want to make something both useful and imposing. The foundation is a dark gray stone, its walls are genuine green serpentine stone, brown granite columns stand at the entrance, the window casings and the bays are light sandstone, the woodwork is painted yellow, and all the mortar is red as are the roofs of the large number of towers and turrets, which rise above the roof level, some to an appreciable height. There are square and lancet windows, protruding pillars, real towers with clocks, and chimneys disguised as turrets, and whoever takes a closer look, noting even the flooring of the hallway, will see that an architect has been working here who was striving after a striking effect. The building, with its bright green basic material for the colored trimmings, stands out and really pleases the public very much; thus, seen from this perspective, it serves its purpose. As I have found almost everywhere in America, the inside of the building is really as finely furnished, spacious, serviceable, and as good as, even in many ways better than, that of our newer polytechnical schools. The library is in the process of being developed, as are the scientific collections, of which I saw some good beginnings: soon the duplicates of the famous Hall collection of North American fossils,[25] which were purchased for $10,000, will be on display, and an excellent collection of minerals has been acquired with the aid of Professor Genth, the chemist.[26]

This university is organized similarly to Harvard University, except that its offerings are less comprehensive. Its faculty consists of thirty-six professors and three assistants, and the school is administered by a Board of Trustees whose president, as prescribed by law, is the Governor of Pennsylvania. In the department of arts the students study primarily the humanistic subjects in the traditional annual class divisions of freshmen, sophomores, juniors, and seniors. The department of science serves to train chemists, mining experts, metallurgists, architects, mechanical engineers, and civil engineers, and has a four-year course, of which the first two are preparatory. The school year is divided into three sections of three months each; just like the department of arts, the department of science requires a $150 annual tuition fee. Each of these departments, however, keeps fifteen places open for needy students. The medical and law schools, however, are purely professional schools.

Not to be forgotten, of course, is the chapel, the most beautiful room in the building, though it is so full of stained glass windows and carved seats that it looks morbidly medieval. Here a little religious service is held daily for the students, but, if I am not mistaken, the students of the department of science are no longer required to attend.

The older college of Philadelphia, named Girard College[27] after its beneficent donor, is at present more famous than the university. Girard, whom Philadelphia has to thank for a great many institutions serving the public, gave $2,000,000 and forty-five acres to the college, which at present has over 500 students, who are exclusively orphans, so that it possesses substantial wealth in spite of the fact that funds were clearly not spared in the construction of the buildings. Externally Girard College is one of the thousand and one buildings rated as "the purest example of Grecian style architecture on the entire continent." In addition, it is considered an excellent school.

There are 396 public elementary schools in the city with 1,630 teachers and 84,387 pupils; in 1873 their budget amounted to $1,381,460.

The two major libraries, the Mercantile and the Philadelphia Library,[28] do not compare with similar institutions in New York or Boston. The Mercantile Library is a former market building, a spacious bright place that offers a very favorable impression until one sees how the public unrestrictedly wanders around through the bookstacks, and how anyone who wants can take and replace books on the shelf, so that no one can find what he is looking for. This library is primarily filled with light reading material, but because of the confusion created in the stacks by the somewhat too idealistic application of the "help yourself" idea, it is not as useful as could be desired. A more scholarly atmosphere prevails in the Philadelphia Library, yet even here every Philadelphian can look at any book he wants, and when I boldly went in and asked for two books, I got them immediately without having to show the recommendation I had brought. There is also a German library here in Philadelphia,[29] which is said to contain about ten thousand books in German.

DAILY NEWSPAPERS. THE *PUBLIC LEDGER*. SOME BOASTING. ITS HISTORY AND THE HISTORY OF ITS FOUNDER. PHILADELPHIA'S BUSINESS AND COMMERCIAL ACTIVITY.

Philadelphia has a large number of circulating daily newspapers, of which two have circulations of 85,000 each, three circulations of 20,000 (at times 23,000) each, and five with circulations of over 10,000 each; even a cheap weekly, *Saturday Night*,[30] has a sale of 200,000. In addition, four German dailies appear here. There is nothing outstanding in what is contained in any of these newspapers, but to become familiar with the history and inner workings of one of these is still not uninteresting for the cheap popular newspaper has greater significance here than we in Germany are inclined to give to any newspaper.

Through its circulation and the considerable trust it enjoys among the public, the *Public Ledger*,[31] a two-cent newspaper, is probably Philadelphia's most influential paper. It is inexpensive enough to make it accessible to almost everyone and not as cheap as the one-cent papers, which are seldom seen in the hands of the better class. It appears in the format of the *Kölnische Zeitung*,[32] four to six mornings a week and has on every side eight columns, of which over half are filled with advertisements. It does not represent the views of any particular party but attempts to diffuse, as they tell me, sound opinions be they independent or those of a particular party. On the whole it is respected on account of its moderate, decent tone, although unfortunately like almost all papers here, it goes much further in praising itself and exaggerating its importance than any respectable paper of ours would dare do. But in this regard the Americans are thick-skinned, and since such shameless lying and boasting only bring the desired results, it is considered "smart," deserves respect, and if possible imitation.

One day I visited an impressive building in which this daily was written and printed, and through the kindness of its owner and especially that of one of its staff, Col. Muckle,[33] an extremely capable and amiable American, I was able to become acquainted with this entire operation in detail and to hear about everything that could be of interest to me in this line. The present reader will not be very interested in the technical aspects of the newspaper's preparation or in the way the rooms are furnished, one of which, by the way is heralded in an information pamphlet with the statement that "no business apartment anything like it has ever been constructed in America, and with the exception of a few old baronial castles and one or two libraries, but little of the kind is to be seen even in Europe."[34] The whole place is a large establishment worth seeing, and the Publication Office (what we would call *Expedition*) is really gorgeously equipped for the benefit of the public. Like everywhere in similar cases, the wealth of the beautiful kinds of wood that this country possesses comes into its own, and various types of walnut and butternut, oak, maple, and other sorts of wood are used in paneling and furniture in the most diverse and attractive way. The editorial rooms, since they are supposed to be work rooms, seem to me somewhat too comfortably furnished, painted, and upholstered. It must be difficult to remain really hardworking here.

The visitor to these offices is handed a booklet—a description of the building and the dedication ceremonies, which offers little interest to an outsider but for the observer of the American way of life it is by no means uninteresting. The entire thing is a big advertisement, which both shouts the praises of the newspaper's owner and at the same time attracts the public to something to which they are very susceptible, admiration of a successful, bold enterprise. Here Mr. Childs[35] is called "prince of princes," "noble man," et cetera; in one breath the goodness of his heart, his charitableness, spirit of enterprise, generosity, and justice are praised; and in a speech by the employees he is thanked for having built a palace for them to work in, a place of employment that finds no parallel in the world, and is the most spacious, most comfortable, healthiest in all America. Sixty pages of speeches, addresses, menus, and the like are presented, and at the end there is yet an adulatory biography of Mr. Childs, which begins, "Our portrait represents a manly man. He stands 5 feet 7 inches, and weighs 165 pounds. His hair is brown, eyes blue, skin fresh and florid; he is a fine specimen of real temperance and sound health. His features are regular, and as nicely chiseled as any piece of sculpture. As is the mind, soul, spirit, and temper, so the features and the character become. The brain, in size and quality, is in perfect keeping with the body; it is between extremes, and the quality of the whole is the best. . . . His mind is never idle. The only perfect repose enjoyed by him is when in sleep; and so long as he sleeps well, he can, like the original Napoleon—whom he resembles in body—work almost incessantly. . . . Then what *are* his faults? . . . His desire to do good will cost him many an agonizing hour, will overwork his overactive brain, he will assume burdens greater than he can long stand under. . . . He is not low, sensual, cruel, deceitful, mercenary, gluttonous, dishonest, neglectful, nor forgetful of his obligations. . . . He is now living the life of a regenerated Christian citizen."[36]

The history of this newspaper and its owner was for me an interesting piece of American local history, almost in every aspect instructive. It was the first successful penny paper, the pioneer here in Philadelphia, appearing for the first time on March 25, 1836, a Friday, which caused quite a stir because of the well-known superstition attached to this day of the week, but it was nothing more than a "smart" and cheap way to make itself known—a good advertisement. The paper was small then but clearly printed and certainly better written than the majority of penny papers of that time. It contained an article about Robert

Burns,[37] the inevitable sentimental poem, numerous bits of political and local news, and a considerable number of the usual advertisements that appear in the sample issues of a new paper. An excellent journalist, Jarvis,[38] a New Englander by origin, was the city editor and understood how to make the paper grow in public favor without resorting to that disgusting flattery of the general public, which unfortunately all inexpensive papers in this country seem to do. Of course, suitable reasons to "sound the alarm" were not passed by; a few months later the publisher involved himself in a libel suit but was acquitted and came out of it as a martyr to the public welfare. After half a year of existence, the continuance of the new enterprise was assured, and its coverage grew to such a degree that after the first year it was at times first on the spot with the latest news before the larger papers, which at the beginning had heaped scorn on this unsightly competitor. At the end of the 1830s, when the mob began riots against the Negroes in Philadelphia, the *Ledger* immediately placed itself on a higher plane than the other inexpensive newspapers by defending those who had been attacked. Soon thereafter, when it opposed the malice against new immigrants, it demonstrated that it took its promise seriously to serve no party but the public welfare, and from then on its respectability was beyond all doubt.[39] But the dislike for the general tone of the tiny paper was so great that, as the publisher explained, at the beginning even his friends did not display it in their office as they did other publications.

In 1840 the format was enlarged after it had already added a weekly edition costing six cents to the daily one, which cost one cent. Only in 1864 was the price of the paper, now enlarged to four and often seven times its original format, raised to ten cents per week, the price at which it presently sells about eighty-five thousand daily copies (in May 1870 of the seventy-two thousand copies printed daily, sixty thousand went to the city itself, while the rest went by mail to all the important towns in Pennsylvania and neighboring states). At the same time, the price for advertisements was raised considerably, and the very praiseworthy system of excluding duplicitous ads was introduced. After a short decline brought on by these measures, a more rapid growth in sales and advertisements than ever before soon followed. By and large unaltered, the paper still seems to have kept something of the high-principled character it had at its inception and is now without question Philadelphia's best written, most respected paper, one of the best in the entire country and one of the most widely circulating.

The life of its present owner, G. W. Childs, who brought the *Ledger* to this successful level, is also worth taking a look at as a model for a true American success story. Born the son of poor parents in Baltimore, at age ten he was already working as an assistant in bookstores during his school vacations in order to earn necessary money. At thirteen he went to sea, and after one and a half years of service, he switched from the United States Navy to a position as shop boy in a bookstore. He worked and learned very diligently and was so able that the owner of the business sent him, sixteen years old, as his representative to the book auctions in Boston and New York. When he was eighteen he left his job with a few hundred dollars in savings, rented a little space in the present *Ledger* building and opened a small book shop, which did so well that after only three years he was able to become a partner in a prominent publishing house. From then on, after varying but generally very successful ventures, he took over the management of the *Public Ledger* at the critical moment when the paper's one-penny price was barely able to cover its expenses and weekly losses often amounted to $3,000, and successfully brought it through the feared changeover to its present-day secure position. Childs, who in his youth came to Philadelphia without friends, is now one of the most popular men in the city, prominent because of his material wealth and mental powers, a man moreover who knows generally how to give with an open hand just as much as to get.

As I was taken on a tour through the rooms of the *Ledger* building by a very worthy official who has been working for the paper for more than thirty years, I was reminded of the best things I had seen here and there in the large business offices in Germany. Everything was so well arranged, and the faces of the workers were so engaging, so confident, friendly, and contented in their manner. I asked whether or not difficulties arose now and then between management and labor, and my guide said that this would hardly be possible since the leading employees who have been working here for so many years, some for twenty or more, regarded themselves as part of the firm and were happy in their secure positions. For the most part they trusted the owner and even stood on a friendly footing with him. Acquaintances then informed me that Mr. Childs had a reputation for being very generous to his employees; for example, he has given them life insurance policies as a gift, donated considerable sums to the typographers association, et cetera. I now understand why I was struck by the pleasant atmosphere in the work areas, which I really had not expected to find so easily especially in America. But the manner in which all these good things were then unfortunately used for advertising purposes has been mentioned in the above paragraphs.

I was interested in the way in which the *Public Ledger* is put out and distributed throughout the city. The entire city has been laid out in "routes," which have been given to reliable men, none of whom are allowed to sell one copy in another territory. Each one pays for the number of copies he takes with him before he leaves the dispatch office. Now, since the *Ledger's* circulation has become so significant, these routes have become increasingly profitable and are at present very much sought after. One hour after these distributors have gone out, the paper is then sold to the newspaper boys and other carriers. People wishing to take a subscription do so from the distributors. Through this system the number of subscriptions is a little less variable than if the paper's distribution were less regulated, more haphazard, as is the case with most other American papers.

Concerning the present situation of Philadelphia's trade, perhaps the following figures, which we have taken partly from the report of the city's board of trade and partly from the report of the trade exchange (both for 1872), would be of interest: in 1870 exports from the harbor of Philadelphia amounted to about $17,000,000, in 1872 to over $20,000,000; imports during these years came to $19,000,000 and $26,000,000 respectively. Goods worth $3,570,642 went to Germany, $3,409,764 to Belgium, $4,754,572 to Great Britain, $1,698,011 to the Netherlands, $1,540,472 to Spanish America, and $1,087,959 to France. The most significant imports came from Great Britain with a value of $8,113,112 and from Spanish America; Italy shipped goods worth $928,080 to the United States, Venezuela $682,005, Sweden and Norway $608,360, Belgium $589,373, France $559,909, and Germany $465,270.

The exports were (listed according to importance): for Great Britain corn, kerosene, wheat, molasses; for Germany kerosene, tallow; for Belgium kerosene; for the Netherlands kerosene, tallow; for Latin America materials for making barrels, iron products, coal; for France kerosene and tallow. Imported from Great Britain were primarily iron, tin, chemicals; from Latin America sugar, molasses, cigars; from Italy raw materials for paper, sulphur, marble; from Venezuela coffee, sugar; from Sweden and Norway iron; from Belgium iron, lead; from France iron, wine; and from Germany lead, iron.

In 1872 the number of ships docking in the harbor were 480 American, 346 British, 73 Swedish-Norwegian, 49 German, 26 Italian, 15 Russian, 14 Portuguese, 10 Austrian, and 13 other ships of various nationalities (including 2 French). In the same year, 371 British, 306 American, 87 Swedish-Norwegian, 62 German, 25 Italian, 13 Portuguese, 12 Russian, and 25 ships of various nationalities (including 3 French) sailed from Philadelphia.

Of the approximately 42 million tons of hard coal mined in the United States in 1872, 1.25 million tons were brought to Philadelphia and over 400,000 tons were exported. Over two-thirds of this coal comes from Pennsylvania.

Of the 2,046,123 tons of pig iron produced in the United States in 1870, more than half came from Pennsylvania and is a significant part of the amount needed for industry in and around Philadelphia. It is probably not well known yet that Philadelphia and the two manufacturing towns of Chester and Wilmington, further downstream along the Delaware, have been busy of late constructing iron seafaring vessels on a large scale. Steamers for Atlantic and Pacific lines are for the most part built in Chester; river steamers, some intended for South America and China, and coastal vessels usually come out of the Wilmington shipyards. Here a great deal of hope is attached to everything dealing with the iron industry. "The Delaware is becoming our Clyde, and in ten years in addition to Philadelphia you will see a half dozen imposing-looking manufacturing towns between here and Cape May." A Philadelphian, a man who knows, told me this, but the next minute he complained about the difficulty of converting the capital, which is unquestionably here, into liquid funds: "In New York you can get $10 in ready cash in the same time it takes to squeeze out $1.00 here, and what that means is that we still have a lot of work to do before our International Exposition is ready for viewing."

The rapid development of the North American and particularly of the Pennsylvania iron industry has not had such an impact on any other city as it has had on Philadelphia. I only want to give the major outline here. Thriving during the Revolutionary War, falling off again after the end of war because of English iron imports, this industry in 1810 had 153 blast furnaces and 316 ironworks and produced 78,449 tons of iron; in 1830 production had risen to 236,007 tons; in 1840 there were 804 blast furnaces producing 484,136 tons of pig iron; in 1850 only 377 blast furnaces with a production of 842,799 tons were listed. In 1860, 574 blast furnaces were listed with production figures that, although not quite clearly specified, certainly went over the one-million mark, and finally in 1870 the same number of furnaces reported a production of 3.5 million tons with the number of people engaged in this work at around 75,000. Iron production for 1872 is projected at 4 million tons. Iron consumption is rising even faster, and it is estimated that in 1872 the railroads alone will take more than half of domestic production, that in the same year around 50,000 tons will be used in New York, Newark, and Brooklyn for building houses, and that overall consumption will amount to around 5 million tons.

Kerosene, which occupies such a dominant place in Philadelphia's export trade, is primarily a Pennsylvanian product. In 1861 the first ship carrying kerosene left the harbor; in 1872, 334 vessels loaded 1,314,439 barrels aboard in Philadelphia—somewhat more than one-third of the entire kerosene exports of the United States.

Concerning Philadelphia's manufacturing industry we have the following figures: in 1871 there were around 9,000 factories and shops, and an estimated $205,000,000 had been invested in these businesses, while the value of the goods produced amounted to $362,000,000; 15,550 persons (100,661 men, 40,760 women, and 11,129 children) were employed here; steam-powered machines with a total capacity of 57,304 horsepower were in use; 590 factories made textile goods, 549 iron and steel products; presses and book binderies operated in 254 shops; the manufacturing of clothes and shoes, two particularly important branches of industry, employed 12,000 and 8,000 workers respectively. The number of people employed in the various industrial plants is said to have grown in the last ten years to 50,000 employees. One thing is absolutely certain and that is that the value of the products had practically doubled in the period from 1860 to 1870.

CHAPTER SEVEN

Washington

GENERAL IMPRESSION. SITE. PLAN OF THE CITY. CAPITOL. SEN-
ATE AND HOUSE OF REPRESENTATIVES.

It seems an odd twist of fate that the United States, where the greatest, most
vigorous, most varied urban growth of our times has occurred, has its capital in
a place that seems more than perhaps any other site in the country to be
artificial and empty. Washington is not a pleasant sight for those who have
seen New York or Boston, and it will be even much less so for those who are
familiar with the cities of the Middle and Far West. In official newspaper
phraseology, I have heard it called "the city of magnificent distances," which
seems to sound almost ironic. However, those who coined this phrase have
actually hit upon and highlighted the best one really can say about Washington: it does have a magnificent design. If the expectations of those who
planned it have not as yet been fulfilled and the city has been able only slowly
and imperfectly to realize their plans, honor is still no less due its founders,
even if they overestimated their countrymen and their development in one
small aspect. I imagine they assumed that as the nation grew and matured, the
people would increasingly see the need of having a capital worthy of them. The
Athenians had Athens, the Romans Rome, the Americans as the world's new
nation had to present something novel. Thus they selected a very beautiful and
imposing site, one suitable for shipping. They created a city out of nothing on a
spot where hitherto not even a village had stood, where there were no old
streets or houses to hamper the grand design, and laid out streets and squares
onto which only palaces rather than farmhouses had to look out. Soon Greek
temples were raised, whether as the repository for the government's funds, as offices or archives, as a post office, or as some other institution, which today is
considered worthy enough to occupy buildings of as noble design as those the
ancients built for their gods.

If these beautiful buildings stood spread out on small elevations surrounded only by tree groves and lawns, they would offer an attractive and even magnificent picture. But instead the buildings are separated by rows of dissimilar, low, and frequently poorly kept up houses. Even the best parts of town are shabby by contrast with the larger cities of the country. People of prominence, of wealth and education, do not live here as one would in a true capital; the only people who live here are employees of the government and those who make their living from these civil servants. During some of the winter months, of course, the political life of the entire country is concentrated in Washington, and then many leading people congregate here; but this has been going on now for almost eighty years and so far has not left any significant mark on the life of the city. Washington does not have much life except for what the government employees give it and, as we well know from the little capitals that serve as seats of the court and administration in the German states, that tends to be rather limited, even meager and, because of its dependence on these employees, very often unwholesome. For several years now a change seems to be on the way, for, as someone told me, since the close of the war more and more families have been moving permanently to Washington and this has already given a great deal more life to the city and made it more attractive.

Washington was declared the seat of the government by an act of Congress on July 16, 1790. An area of several miles was appropriated and, under the name of the District of Columbia, converted into the territory of the capital. On a commanding site they began the construction of the Capitol Building, and the inhabitants of the new city began to settle on all sides around it.[1] The major streets radiate in all directions of the compass from three central points, the principal ones from the Capitol,[2] others from the presidential mansion, and still others from a square in the east end.[3] These three points are then connected by main thoroughfares. The side streets, which are relatively wide, all run either north-south or east-west and intersect at right angles; together with the large radial streets they form all sorts of angles, acute and obtuse in all gradations. The Capitol is in the middle of this complex, to the extent that one can speak of there being a middle in the irregular, peninsular-like site of a city washed on three sides by the Potomac and one of its tributaries.

The radial streets are called avenues and have been given the names of the older states of the Union. They are 130 to 160 feet wide. Among them, Pennsylvania Avenue is the only one that has a great deal of activity on it. The parallel and intersecting streets, some named by letters of the alphabet and others by number, are 90 to 110 feet wide. The paving, lighting, sanitary maintenance, et cetera, of these streets was understandably a heavy burden for the city, especially in the beginning, which is cited as one of the reasons for its slow growth. Even today all the avenues are not yet paved, although Pennsylvania Avenue has the best wooden-block paving I have yet seen.

The Capitol Building, which is the seat of the legislature, is in every way the most impressive structure in Washington. It becomes this country fittingly. It stands on a small, gently rising elevation and is visible from many places in the city. From the grounds one has a wonderful view of the city and its surroundings, and from its upper balconies above the Potomac valley the area from the mountains to the seashore is spread out to view. The neighboring countryside is made up of gently rolling hills with wooded areas here and there but largely covered with cultivated fields and houses. These gentle and pleasant configurations form a peaceful picture into which the broad, almost imperceptively moving river wonderfully fits in. If one views Washington from any point in the vicinity of the city, the picture is always one of fitting significance, for the marble Capitol Building is like a beacon shining in all directions. On many clear January days I saw it from the west, just as the sun was setting, and its white walls then appeared much brighter than anything else around, so much so that in the twilight they looked as if they were really emitting light. In sunlight, the marble seems to glow with a warm, yellowish glimmer, yet at night the building stands out coldly like a tower of snow against the nocturnal sky.

The Capitol, in its present form, was built at different times by different builders, but there is no noticeable lack of unity. On close observation, one recognizes evidences of age in the middle section to which the two wings were first added in the 1850s. It is said that the uniformity among the three sections, which prevents none of them from significantly predominating, would probably have provided for a more effective structural arrangement had the entire building been constructed all at one time. If the imposing dome did not stand out prominently atop the central section, the building would look like a series of links in a chain, but because of the combination of three equal parts and because of its enormous length—almost eight hundred feet—it would definitely suffer from the lack of distinguishing features. Once one has become accustomed to the overall impressiveness, one feels the lack of variety all the more, and this is further underscored by the much more lively architectural composition of the wings in comparison to the central section. Although similar in basic construction to the central section, on comparable surfaces they exhibit more contours, actually more attractive ones, by means of more closely spaced and more strongly relieved columns, pilasters, and windows. Despite all this, it is the grandeur of the overall view that dominates everything else.

The edifice stands on an artificial incline that rises from the natural elevation at right angles like a platform, which one approaches by a series of broad steps. The main stairway on the west side has a beautiful oval pool in front of it. The flights of stairs on the east side, the main façade, are equally long and broad for both the central section and the wings, thus giving the building beautifully designed projections, which boldly and spaciously spread out on the green lawn like the paws of a resting lion. To begin with, the designers constructed a good foundation of pillars. Every pillar is divided by deep cross lines and each one is connected to its neighbor by rather small rounded arches. Behind the pillars there are galleries, which almost circle the entire building. On this massive yet elegant ground floor the walls of the main floor rise among innumerable columns and pilasters, which run up to the height of the roof in a circular open gallery. I have already mentioned that the features of the three sections of the building on this level are considerably different. The wings are without any doubt more beautiful than the central portion, and anyone who has seen the best in Europe will admit that there is a beautiful, agreeable simplicity pervading their proportions.

The dome, built in three tiers resting on pillars, rises 396 feet above the ground on which the building rests. If one enters through the East Portal into the middle section, one comes into a large rotunda whose ceiling consists of the inside of the vault of the dome. This vaulting is covered with allegorical figures painted by Signor Brumidi.[4] You see Washington seated in the middle, surrounded by thirteen feminine figures who represent the oldest states of the Union; at his side are Freedom and Glory. In a circle around this middle group all sorts of personifications are seen, among them the goddess of Liberty with the phrygian cap and the star spangled banner standing out. Just as she has vanquished greybearded Tyranny, she sees below her feet an armed warrior, holding an ermine mantle, fall in a pitiable position behind the clouds. Revenge and Hate are also brought into the picture; the only thing missing here is the Golden Age, which is surely yet to come. Further on, groups representing agriculture, commerce, trade, navigation, learning, and art try to attract attention in their own way but without much success. On the walls of this hall there are six large painted scenes from the history of North America. The natural likeness of one of them—depicting the Kentucky pioneer Daniel Boone fighting the Indians—is said to have so impressed a group of Indians visiting Washington a few years ago that they let out their war cry here in the middle of the hall. Then suddenly, as if frightened by the sound of their own voices, they took flight and ran outside. At least that's what the guide says, and he admits to no doubt about the subject.

We turn then from these artistic endeavors, which after all are only ornamentation, to the heart of the matter, the legislative chambers. The House of Representatives as well as the Senate convene in large rectangular rooms containing skylights. When we entered, neither was engaged in significant business, only unimportant matters were being passed upon. Nevertheless, the proceedings were lively, and in the Senate there was scarcely an empty seat to be seen. They were speaking here about the Louisiana question,[5] and in barely more than one hour I heard, among the five speakers who took part in the discussion, three superb orators, the likes of which I have seldom heard in German *Landtagen*.[6] They speak here much more animatedly, with more gesticulations, than is customary in Germany, sometimes making motions that were entirely new to me. One legislator vigorously clapped his hands when he ended a sentence emphatically; and arms outstretched in front of a speaker seems to indicate a desire to draw the listeners deeper into the matter. One senator who is familiar with European parliaments claims that there are more good orators to be found in this Senate with its small membership than in the

English Parliament. The good impression the speeches make is even further underlined by the sight the assembled group itself offers. There are mostly older men here, and among them there are many whose entire appearance is impressive. In their faces one sees predominantly energy, keen understanding, constant awareness, and together with their white hair and well-built, generally trim figures all this adds up to making a good combination. Needless to say, the members of the Senate are recruited from the best segments of the population.

In the House of Representatives, on the other hand, the atmosphere was less placid. In relation to the number of members in the House, the chamber is not as spacious as the Senate's, while the House's composition is much more varied and is, as it seems, most of the time in a more-or-less tumultuous state. No dignified atmosphere prevails here. On lounging seats, which are placed around the sides, several dozen representatives have stretched out in all possible restful positions; within the semicircular area of the seats there is a continual coming and going; similarly dressed boys, who serve as pages, run back and forth as if possessed, and one really doesn't see then why the orator takes so much trouble about speaking. Perhaps he only makes the speech to see it in print the next day or to be able to send it to his constituents. Here younger men are strongly in evidence, and the assembly as a whole gives a good idea of the cross-sectional character of the American people. From the real Yankee of New Hampshire or Massachusetts to the Negro and the cattle breeder from the Southwest, who from his looks could have been imported straight out of Mexico, all elements are represented except for Indians and Chinese. In Philadelphia I saw the congressman from one of the Southwestern states appear in a sensational stage play, where as hero of the wild frontier he fought with desperados and Indians; his colleagues here, however, seemed to be more sedentary. Among the members of the House, a few unmistakable, pure Teutonic types can also be seen. The galleries, whose spaciousness as in the Senate strikes the viewer—the one in the House holds fifteen hundred people—are predominantly filled with people from the lower classes, and especially blacks.

The Senate is somewhat more richly furnished than the House, although a dignified simplicity prevails in both chambers. The House, however, does not seem to me to have very good acoustics. A park runs around the entire Capitol Building, is beautifully cared for, and contains some very beautiful trees from the North American forests. There are also some evergreen trees, which herald the proximity of the South.

THE SMITHSONIAN INSTITUTE

The Smithsonian Institute,[7] which can be seen from a great distance, stands in a garden with park-like surroundings on the large empty space extending westward from the Capitol towards the Potomac. It is an odd-looking structure, of

8 "IF ONE LOOKS OUT FROM THE STEPS OF THE CAPITOL AT THIS COMPLEX, ONE WOULD BELIEVE HE WAS VIEWING ONE OF THOSE ODD-LOOKING MONASTERIES." THE SMITHSONIAN INSTITUTION, WASHINGTON, D.C., EXTERIOR VIEW.

which they proudly say that "although it is symmetrical—a main building with wings—still no section is similar to any other. No façade and no tower looks like any other, and it is exactly this interesting characteristic of the building that because of its variety is so pleasing." Eight towers of various sizes and shapes are seen here; there is no lack of chapel-like additions, odd-looking oriels and pillars, church-like entrances; the windows are high, relatively narrow, and quite round-arched. If one looks out from the steps of the Capitol at this complex, which alone stands out from all its surroundings because of the rather bright brownstone used in its construction, one would believe he was viewing one of those odd-looking monasteries; one could scarcely think otherwise.[8] The incomprehensible drive in this country for exact imitation of a structure consisting of forms and styles long since empty has caused a lot of thought and effort to be wasted on such buildings, more than one would think.

But if you open the door, the interior makes you forget the puzzle about the exterior, for one of the finest natural history collections, richly furnished and superbly organized, is displayed there in a large, well-lit hall. One does not have to make a thorough study of the objects, which are exhibited here in elegant display cases, to discover that one has before him a serious collection and not merely a simple exhibition for public show. Dozens of polar bear skulls; skulls of that animal recently said to be the ancestor of the house dog, the so-called *canis latrans*, which we seldom see in European collections but which here can be seen in more than one hundred specimens; choice rare examples of wapiti[9] and elk antlers in addition to long rows of specimens of every American bird species demonstrate that this collection is one predominantly intended for the serious student. Whoever is able to get a look at the storage areas where, in an unpretentious way, two and three times as much material is piled up as in the exhibition rooms, where case upon case full of mammal hides, stuffed birds, skeletons, bird nests and eggs, and the like stand about, or whoever visits the library or the magazine room would surely note that this is an unusual scientific institution. It is an institution that on one hand certainly has gaps—one misses completely the insect and annelid kingdom and the invertebrates; one sees the clothes, ornaments, and weapons of primitive man but nothing of the skulls of the various races, which are usually the last thing lacking in such institutions—but on the other hand, it is more richly endowed than any other comparable institution. Indeed, it seems to be so richly supplied that one can barely figure out where all the specimens should be stored or what should be done with them all.

Truly this is an extraordinary institute, the likes of which can be found neither here nor on the other side of the ocean. Above all, it corresponds to the particular needs of American scholarship, which flourishes here far from the old centers of learning, having previously been more isolated and dependent on itself than was good for it. But at the same time, the Smithsonian, by its founding principles and day-to-day activities, so wonderfully represents the ideal of free, international exchange of intellectual materials, serving altruistically as a clearing house, assisting and providing for the most various interests and needs of people concerned with knowledge—be they students, teachers, or researchers—that one truly feels he is on free ground, elevated above the inevitable national differences in our modern civilization. There have been many international things that have been planned or talked about in the world since the railroad and telegraph came into use, and almost everyone has at one time or other felt his heart swell with joy over the wonderful prospect of eternal peace, world brotherhood, et cetera. Generally nothing was needed, not even a storm, only a good restful night's sleep, nothing more than the natural sequence of tomorrow following today to make us realize that these beautiful visions were a kind of mirage, a reflection of our wishes, nothing more than air. But something international has been realized here on a large scale, which has been operating for forty years, has not been deceived in its purpose, and now with greater security views only a steadily growing range of activities before it. This is something wonderful that one likes to see.

I will relate the most essential things about the Smithsonian's history and founding. The purpose of the institute, as its Secretary, Professor Spencer F. Baird[10] (a distinguished researcher in the field of America's vertebrates) aptly indicated to me, was to perform the functions of an academy of learning, having no members other than its staff. Its material existence comes basically from the grant of a scientifically minded Englishman, James Smithson,[11] who died in Genoa in 1828. He bequeathed his estate, under certain conditions, to

9 "THE INTERIOR MAKES
YOU FORGET THE EXTERIOR,
FOR ONE OF THE FINEST
NATURAL HISTORY
COLLECTIONS IS DISPLAYED
THERE IN A LARGE, WELL-LIT
HALL." THE SMITHSONIAN
INSTITUTION, WASHINGTON,
D.C., INTERIOR VIEW.

the United States "to found at Washington, under the name of the Smithsonian Institution, an Establishment for the increase and diffusion of knowledge." As a consequence, in 1838 more than $500,000 came into the Federal Treasury, where the sum remained until in 1846 Congress passed a law that created the institute as it now exists and functions. Through a board of directors, which meets once a year, the government keeps in touch, assigning the institute this or that project (for example, surveying land in the western states or territories, undertaking expeditions of a purely or partially scientific nature, distributing some of the government's own publications, et cetera), but otherwise leaving it so completely independent that it actually gains many advantages with scarcely a disadvantage in its role as a state institution. The institute deals directly with all its correspondents, the various academies, associations, and public officials, but should it have need of official channels, which run via the Department of State, or should it have some business with the governments of the individual states of the Union, then naturally its official position stands it in good stead.

The main task of the Smithsonian Institute is to exchange scientific publications and educational research materials and to publish valuable scientific works. Most importantly it is, so to speak, a clearing house for scientific societies, government agencies, and private individuals in Europe who send their publications to societies, government agencies, and private individuals in America and vice versa. For this purpose it has its representatives in the most important European cities. Thus, for example, the Leipzig representative will receive, let's say, all the publications of the Museum of Comparative Zoology in Cambridge[12] that are to go to German scholars, societies, et cetera. He will also receive the works of any professor or printed matter of a useful nature from any other individual who wants to send it to colleagues, societies, agencies, or the like in Germany, and this agent will do the same for all German publications that are to go to America.

The expenses for the most part are borne by the institute, which, however, enjoys considerable advantages—for example, it pays no freight charges on all trans-Atlantic steamship lines. People who would otherwise have been too lazy and cost conscious are now sending their material to Leipzig, and in turn America, which for the largest and most important part of its scholarly sustenance still remains dependent upon Europe, quickly receives everything of any importance that has appeared in Germany. At present, fifty copies of all United States Government agency publications, which are known to contain as a rule a great deal of material—at times very important material—are designated for distribution in Europe, and the institute takes care of sending them off. Many publications arrive at the Smithsonian to be distributed but without any addressee. Then, according to the knowledge and experience that it is gradually acquiring in such matters, the institute sends the literature on to those people in Europe whom it assumes most competent to make use of the material. In this way the Smithsonian makes contact for exchange programs between the newly formed learned societies and the older sister societies in Europe. I heard, for example, that the new California Academy of Sciences[13] already has received a library of three thousand volumes with the help of the Smithsonian Institute. Just like altruistic, obliging people, the institute has earned many friends for itself in all corners of the world, and these people gladly assist it with this kind of work. Thus its very existence serves a good purpose: it awakens the desire to help, shows the donor where help is wanted, preserves things valuable for learning and science from the dust of neglect, and distributes all unused material to places where it can be of benefit.

An interesting register has been compiled at the institute, where every person and group with which an exchange program exists have been listed. Mr. Baird showed this register to me and explained the meaning of the ciphers and references. The number of correspondents, selected from each country with such impartiality and discretion, is a good indication of scholarly activity in that country. It was not unexpected but nontheless pleasant for me to see Germany, together with Austria, represented by almost three times the number of correspondents as France boasts of.[14] The total number of correspondents consists of 2,145 names, of which 587 come from Germany and Austria, 412 from Great Britain, 257 from France, 167 from Italy, 157 from Russia, 127 from Belgium, 68 from Switzerland, 77 from the Scandinavian countries, and so on.

Every correspondent, be he a private individual or an organization, has a certain code mark before his or its name. One to four x's means, for example, the degree of exchange activity this person is engaged in with the institute. I found the German Emperor[15] and the King of Saxony[16] noted with four x's, the Berlin Academy of Science with three. Before the name of some by no means insignificant learned societies I found a zero, which means that nothing has been heard from that particular group for some time, and therefore communication with it has ceased for the time being.

This then is the main field of activity of this excellent institution, but the publication of its reports and its brochures is also of special importance for America. Every year it brings out a report in which several monographic works are included together, works for the most part for which the author lacks a publisher or for which he would not have found one who would have published it in such an attractive form, at such a reasonable price, and with so large a printing as the Smithsonian would. Wherever someone demonstrates need, the institute also pays honoraria, thereby becoming very helpful to many aspiring scholars. Among its publications are some of the best monographic works about American natural history and ethnology. Every work receives a printing of 1,250 copies, for the most part given away, to a lesser extent sold at a low price. One Smithsonian project, which will be very important for understanding America's natural history, is a series of short, systematically arranged monographs about the classes of animals.[17] Information for the weather observer, the collector of natural history specimens, et cetera, is also published by the institute. In cases where the government needs information of some kind for its scientific expeditions, it simply asks this institution to prepare it.

Some very capable natural scientists are employed at this institute and together with the scientific staff of goverment researchers—the officials of the hydrographical, meteorological, geographical, and other institutions here in Washington—they form a finer and more diverse community of scientists than any other city of the United States can offer. Should the much discussed plan of founding a "National University" in Washington ever be realized, then with the help of what already exists here, the intellectual life of the United States would make Washington its center, the resources here being many. The collections of the Smithsonian Institute and the Library of Congress would abundantly offer teachers and students what they need. Here then, one thing above all would not be missing, the lack of which is generally regarded, and rightly so, as a main deficiency of American institutions of higher learning—the stimulus of experienced great minds. Would it not also be important for the intellectual life of a people to have its political capital also serve as the scholarly and especially as the intellectual capital of the country? Would it not be good to have the best minds of the nation working at research and promoting knowledge in this city from which so much influence radiates and upon which so many people have fixed their gaze? These are questions that I would only like to propose. Certainly, despite all the fears of centralization, there is still much to be said for it.

WEATHER BUREAU AND ITS PREDICTIONS. PRESIDENTIAL MANSION.

In a side street near the War Department there stands a building with curious insignias on it. All sorts of variously shaped weather vanes (strange-looking machines!) are on the roof, busily but quietly turning here and there, and behind the window thermometers and barometers are visible. This is the Signal Service and Weather Bureau,[18] where every day weather reports from all over the United States arrive and from whence the "probabilities," or weather predictions are sent out, which during these raw winter days the newspaper readers look for more rapidly and eagerly than they do for any other bit of important news. I visited this institution because all over the country people talk quite a bit about its activities and usually with a great deal of respect. This respect is underscored because the bureau has taken up the problem of weather forecasting with obvious success, something that several European countries have also tried to do but because of various reasons have not been able to deal with anywhere near the success they have had here in America. Only lately have daily weather forecasts been published by several official bureaus in Europe, while here the system is fully developed and in time will probably produce even better results, worked out in greater detail, extending over larger geographical areas.

One of the staff explained to me how the work is done here, and I saw and heard the following: three times a day, readings from fifty-five observation stations are taken and telegraphed immediately to the bureau. At 7:35 A.M., 4:35 P.M., and 11:35 P.M. (Washington time), the readings are taken at all these places and published in Washington through the Weather Bureau as the morning, afternoon, and evening weather report. The observations consist of the current barometer readings, changes since the last reading, the temperature reading, changes in the last twenty-four hours, humidity, wind direction and velocity, degree of cloudiness, precipitation since the last report, and the overall weather situation. This information is immediately entered on a map, where places with equal barometric and temperature readings are connected by lines, that is, isobars and isothermal lines; these maps are published and distributed in more than three hundred copies. On these maps there is printed as well a so-called synopsis, that is, a general weather report with the latest changes, the prevailing tendencies in the various parts of the country, and also the "probabilities." Thus, three times a day a general weather report, predictions, and a compilation of weather statistics are published together with a weather map. I would like to give here the synopsis and probabilities for the afternoon of November 2, 1873.[19]

Synopsis: The air pressure during the day has decreased in Virginia and North Carolina and generally along the seacoast. The storm center over Lake Superior this morning has slowly moved eastward. Decreasing temperatures, northwesterly and southwesterly winds, and overcast but increasingly clearing skies will prevail in the northwest along the Great Lakes and in Illinois. Southeasterly winds, falling barometer, warmer weather with increasing cloudiness in the Southern states. Fresh, southwesterly winds, cloudy, rainy weather along the Gulf Coast. Southerly and southwesterly winds, clear weather and decreased air pressure in the Eastern and Midwestern states. The water level of the rivers has fallen considerably near Marietta and Oil City, less so by Nashville and Pittsburgh, and has risen slightly near La Crosse and Evansville.

Probabilities: For the Gulf Coast, southwesterly, at times brisk winds, overcast with slight rain, with lower temperatures, and clearing skies on Monday. For the Northwest and the Great Lakes, a sharply rising barometer, fresh northwesterly wind, very cool, clear weather. For the area from the Ohio valley to Tennessee, southwest and westerly winds, falling temperatures, overcast sky, rain, becoming clear on Monday. For the Gulf states, falling barometer, southeast wind, increasing cloudiness and rain in the western parts. For the Southern Atlantic states, southeast wind, high temperatures, cloudy. For the Middle Atlantic states, southwest wind, increasing cloudiness and light rain in the northern and western sections. For New England, southwesterly and southeasterly winds, cloudy weather, light rain. There are as yet still no reports from the Southwest, the Northwest, and the Pacific Ocean.

In the monthly report from which I am taking this information there are the readings from the following morning, which are compiled in such a way as to show to what degree many of the predictions have proved true, and then from this data the following general conclusions as to their reliability are drawn: the above-mentioned predictions were realized with the following exceptions—for New England "light rain" was only partly true; for the Northwest the "sharply rising barometer . . . very cool . . . weather," for the Gulf states the "falling barometer," and for New England the "southeasterly wind" did not prove true.

This was an average day, for on other days all the predictions are borne out, while on most days a few are incorrect, and on few days are there many more mistakes to record. Last year the lowest number of accurate predictions was seventy-one out of one hundred (this was in the Southwest), eighty-four out of one hundred were realized in New England, and the other sections of the country fall between these two points. The number of correct predictions has annually continued to rise, and in the three years since the system has been in use, they have learned a great deal. One of the primary ways by which they have been able to accomplish this was by the comparison of data such as that given in the example above and made by a staff member other than the one making the predictions.

The systematic, careful comparison of the weather observations with the predictions naturally soon uncovers some of the wrong methods the forecaster preferred to use—in the first few years, for example, it was always the same official who made the predictions. The rapid increase of statistics brought to light a series of up until then unknown and therefore nonevaluated factors, which have now been taken into account, thus gradually making the "probabilities" appreciably more accurate than they had been. One big advantage was the exclusion of the Pacific Coast and the Far West, approximately all the states and territories beyond the Missouri, from the area for which forecasts were made. This was done partly because the distance from Washington was too great, communications too uncertain, and above all because the chief determinant for the weather in these areas, the Pacific Ocean, was not yet during that period covered by an adequate series of observation stations. In time this will change; but in the meantime there is enough to do here in the East to perfect the system and to extend it, especially southwards where at present the most distant observation station is located in Cuba and to stations on the edge of the meteorologically very important Gulf of Mexico.

It hardly needs mentioning, however, that in these endeavors the Washington meteorologists have a much more favorable situation to work with than do their European colleagues. The size of the territory they cover with their observation network and the relatively simple surface conditions make their task easier than anywhere in Europe, with perhaps the exception of Russia. The weather conditions are simpler here. Also, since the entire area with the exception of the unimportant border areas in Canada and the West Indies belongs to the same country, all stations can operate within its frontiers according to the same system, under the same administration, and with the same objectives. This is also an advantage that we in Europe have to do without.

Another important scientific agency well known even in Europe by way of excerpts from the Hayden reports is the Geological and Geographical Survey of the Territories.[20] The commission's activities are spread out across the country, and although because of the nature of its work it really does not have any real home base, it nonetheless has its main office in Washington, where it significantly contributes to the promotion of scientific activity there.

Shall I trouble the reader with a description of some "sights," monuments, public buildings, et cetera? I think that it makes no sense to describe things in which the writer is really not interested himself. One only enjoys doing this when other people desire it or when this information can be of especial use to them, and I assume that in neither case is this so. Nevertheless, in order not to seem too arbitrary, I would like to explain very briefly what the residence of the president looks like.[21] It is a rather unadorned dwelling, 170 feet long, 86 feet wide, made out of sandstone painted white. Simple porticoes have been placed before the entrances on the north and south side. The walls are completely plain, the windows without awning or enclosure, and the building stands in a beautiful garden almost in the center of the city.

Part II

CHAPTER EIGHT

Southern Cities

NORTH AND SOUTH IN THE UNITED STATES. TRANSFORMATION OF THE SOUTH BY MEANS OF THE CITIES. CHARACTER OF THE SOUTHERN CITIES. THEIR NEGRO PROLETARIAT. CENTERS OF MARITIME TRADE. CITIES OF THE INTERIOR. EDUCATION.

If someone were to travel on foot from Canada to Florida avoiding the cities, the transition from north to south, to an almost subtropical south, would seem to be a very gradual one, for there are no natural barriers here such as the Alps or the Carpathian Mountains in Europe. Moreover, the same ethnic group that lives in the North also inhabits the South. Even if mountain barriers did exist, the distinctive climatic conditions of this continent would not allow the southern sections to be very different from the northern ones as they do in Europe. Here the winter, even in Georgia or Alabama, is much more severe than in southern Italy or Spain, so that only in Florida can the citrus crop become as important a branch of agriculture as it is in the corresponding areas of Europe.

The cities, however, affect the situation so as to make the difference between the South and the North in America a very great one. They present a sample of the area's population in such a concentrated form that its distinguishing features become more pronounced; even in appearance they already display a Southern trait, that is, certain problems that concern city dwellers are less completely solved almost everywhere in the South than in the North; finally, these cities bring Southern flora, whose varieties people especially like to use in adorning their home gardens, genrally much farther north than they could come if they were growing wild with no protective walls surrounding them. The hills around Lyons, France, for example, tell us little about the warm south, but for someone from the North, the perennially green parks in the inner city convey the friendly atmosphere of the South just like the laurel bushes and palm trees do in Cannes and Nice and in other neighboring sheltered places. This is the case in Richmond and all cities further south. The snowstorm can rage as it may, yet one sees magnificent magnolia trees, almost as big as lindens, standing before the houses in parks and gardens; one sees them forming pretty groves with the ilex (the same species as our holly bushes), spreading its branches like birch trees, and the leafy, dark green live oaks. One cannot doubt when one sees all this that one is standing at the threshold of the South.

In the South, as in the North, there are old and new, deserted and busy, stagnant and progressive cities. In the young state of Florida and many parts of the older slave states, particularly in Georgia and Alabama, large areas are only now in the process of being settled and could be compared in the level of their culture and the character of their urban settlement with the western states in the North, which find themselves in a similar stage of development. On the other hand, there is St. Augustine, the oldest city this side of the Mississippi, and in Richmond one finds one of the historically most important cities of the Union. In addition, the South is not lacking in commercial cities worthy to take their place beside a Boston, Philadelphia, or a Baltimore. But what is completely missing here are the typical types of Northern cities: the big cities that grew up over night, the important industrial centers, the large educational centers. The lack of such things helps characterize the South's true nature. It marks the South as the center of large-scale agricultural production, which felt itself too comfortable with the lucrative proceeds of slave labor even to try competing with the industrious, ambitious, educated North.

After the Civil War, with the end of that "unique" economic system, which could do nothing else than promote inactivity and impede the diligence and enterprise of the majority of people for the benefit of a few, an economic revolution began whereby the border states like Maryland, Virginia, and Kentucky started in large degree to assimilate the conditions and outlook of the North. Even the Gulf states and Florida have not remained unaffected. But the cities show fewer signs of improvement than the countryside. They have suffered more from the Civil War itself and from the circumstances that accompany war than the rural area has, and if some of the newer ones have made gains with the new railroad lines and the beginning industry, the older ones without exception show strong traces of decline. The majority of the Negro proletariat, who since the abolition of slavery have shown a strong inclination to move to the cities, also bears a certain responsibility for allowing these features to become prominent, and with their poverty and inactivity they cling like a lead weight to the more productive classes of the population. Wherever these Negroes are strongly represented, the agitation, discord, and hostility that their political demands arouse, and the corruption that accompanies the racial conflict, have hindered such important cities as New Orleans and Charleston from taking part in the revitalization they seemed destined for at the end of the Civil War. This colored proletariat is also quite large in the Northern cities on the coast, especially in Boston, New York, and Philadelphia, and now an influx of Negroes is beginning to be seen as a definite major trend in Baltimore and Washington. Instead of being surrounded by factories on its outskirts like Northern cities, Richmond is surrounded by Negro villages, which far surpass in dirt, idleness, and demoralization as well as in a picturesque disorder and lack of civilizatory amenities, the gypsy camps on the outskirts of Hungarian and Romanian cities. In many of the cities further south, the Negro and the mulatto determine the character of street life more than the white person does.

Nevertheless, even without the Negro population, the general character of Southern cities would still be very different from their Northern and Western counterparts. Those that are located on the seacoast and possess good harbors have, as is well known, a considerable commercial importance based primarily on the export of the South's main products: cotton, wood, tobacco, and rice. This importance is, however, one-sided, since imports by sea run far behind exports, and because for many necessities these cities are dependent on the big Northern commercial centers. Although in the last decade many indications have shown that healthy, independent economic activity was beginning to develop, the commerce of this area is still not connected to any industrial activity to speak of. For that reason, besides the big merchants here there are no big industrialists, no skilled workers, nor a vigorous white working class of any size worth mentioning. The shopkeepers and handworkers cannot make up for the lack of these hearty classes that create civilization and wealth. Therefore, after the middle-class society of these cities lost its main support—the rich landowners, who used to spend their income in the cities, having all but disappeared—this society has an incomplete, half-developed profile like that which one tends to associate with the industry-less large cities of predominantly agricultural countries. In this regard, New Orleans, Mobile, Savannah, and Charleston look more like Havana and Veracruz than, say, Boston or Portland. Just as in these Latin American cities, wholesale trade here is predominantly in the hands of foreigners, primarily Germans, who are less assimilated with the rest of the population than the foreign merchants in such cities as New York or even Baltimore. While foreigners in the North integrate their diverse interests with the life of a many-sided city, which carries on its "independent life" in a proud, influential, and cultivated manner, those in the South do not feel themselves any more at home in their cotton emporiums than in any real tropical colony where one stays only as long as is necessary to make the desired fortune. In addition, although the economic and social conditions existing in these cities are essentially the reasons for the colonial character of their business communities, it is only further reinforced by the unhealthy climate of most Southern harbor cities, which are situated on mostly low-lying ground in swampy surroundings.

If you can imagine a city without the wholesale trade, then you can picture most of the cities of the interior as looking like the seaport towns. Only here there is still more inactivity and misery amongst the Negro population, and there is less constructive activity, less independent gain, less prosperity amongst the whites. On the other hand, it cannot be denied that through the transformation of the entire economy, that is, through the abolition of slavery, many of these cities have decidedly gained and now have a bright future before them. The excellent sites, which a whole string of these cities have on the east ridge of the Alleghenies, exactly where powerful rivers and streams emerge out of the interior of this mountain range, create favorable conditions for industry through the accessibility of water power and plentiful wood. Other cities have become important transportation centers because of the rapid extension of old railroad lines and the building of new ones that took place during the war, while still others are on the way to becoming American Nice's and Menton's[1] for the thousands of sick people and vacationers who annually travel south, especially to Florida, to spend the winter and spring there.

The number of cities of the interior with a future, and in some cases a great future, before them as industrial locations, transportation centers, or health spas is not small, and some of them like Augusta and Atlanta in Georgia and Lynchburg in Virginia have already attained considerable importance in this regard. The coal and iron deposits of Alabama, the most important in the United States next to Pennsylvania's, present some Southern states with advantages for industrial development available to few other states of the Union, so that we can certainly expect large future urban growth on the south and southwest slope of the Alleghenies. But the white working population, which is absolutely necessary for the utilization of these resources, develops slowly in a state where for years the specter of Negro revolts and the outrages perpetrated by the whites were rampant, and as in all other matters concerning the progress of civilization, one must accustom oneself to a significantly slower tempo here than in the North. But one should not let one's hopes sink too quickly, even if the racial conflict, which has already been frivolously bantered around as an inevitability for years, should postpone the budding development of the area for a few more years.

The intellectual life of the Southern cities cannot even be remotely compared with the breadth or depth of those in the North or West. A general look at cultural conditions in America makes this apparent. Even in the new cities of the West, which have barely existed for a generation, there is more stimulating, creative interest in knowledge, more is read, taught, written, and published, and above all more money is spent for higher and primary education than even in New Orleans or Charleston. Not one Southern city can boast of such well-organized, rich, and accessible public libraries and reading rooms as, for example, Cincinnati or St. Louis, or even the new city of San Francisco. Formerly, in better days, the large sums allocated in some Southern states for educational purposes were more of a luxury when one considers the small number of people who needed an education or who were capable of receiving it, and when one remembers the ban on freedom of speech that existed during the rule of the slave owners; actually, few lasting effects of these expenditures remain. Much has been done in the last ten years for the primary schools, especially for those that are supposed to educate Negro children, but the time has been too short to evaluate the worth of the hundreds of these schools that have so suddenly been set up or to judge the practical results of the education given to the Negro youngsters. Thus in general one can only say that the new path onto which the people of the South, once so indolent and self-satisfied, have been thrown, has made them realize the necessity for knowledge more than would have ever been possible during the era of slavery.

CHAPTER NINE

Richmond

SOUTHERN CLIMATE. NEGRO QUARTERS. BEAUTY OF THE SITE.
PLACES OF INTEREST. GROWTH. CONVERSATIONS WITH SOME CITI-
ZENS OF RICHMOND.

A snowstorm was raging in Baltimore and Washington when I saw these cities
for the first time two weeks ago. After it stopped, icy winds blew across the
snow, which lay so thick and deep that its whiteness put the marble of the
Capitol to shame. Eight days later the wind switched to the south and southeast; overnight the snow and ice disappeared, and in the middle of January it
felt like spring. I thought this would be the best time to take a look at Virginia,
for it is a good idea to see this young country in a light that corresponds to its
character and not under the exceptional circumstances of bitterly cold days,
which now and then make themselves felt with their icy blasts even down to
the Gulf of Mexico.

I was glad I made this decision for it could not have been better here. From
morning until evening the sky was clear, and the days were warm like the most
beautiful April days of the German spring. The air is so invigorating and yet so
mild that you think you could never become tired or listless again. But you
don't feel any incentive to do much except lie in the sun, peacefully enjoying
its radiance and warmth and forget all the cares of the world. We don't have
many days like this, but here with the exception of summer they occur frequently. Our clear days are cold in winter, hot in summer, and during spring
and fall are reduced in number by wind and rain. This kind of day here gives
people a cheerful, carefree disposition and helps them maintain it. If the few
dozen Negroes whom I see lounging about in front of the hotel were a little less
brown and a bit more civilized, they would really look like the beggars or street
idlers in Palermo,[1] for what they have completely in common with their European counterparts is that they enjoy life, are satisfied with their existence,
don't need work, good clothes, or fancy food, and do not have to employ either

their mind or hands, since their contentment does not induce a feeling of emptiness or uneasiness, which would require some effort or work to satisfy.

Clear skies and idle people are probably the best trademarks of the South, but Richmond has still more to show in this connection. Its streets are not really narrow or winding, for it is an American city. When it comes to filth, however, then many of them do not take a second place to Naples' worst *vicolo*,[2] and the majority of the houses are in a state of neglect that indicates an indolent population. There is also very little activity on the street, and the shops, although numerous, are not as well stocked as one might expect of a wealthy city of this size—the population of Richmond is now between fifty thousand and sixty thousand. On the other hand, it is more picturesque than any city in the Northern states would be, even with a comparable wonderful site. There are no factories or working-class areas here, no uniform rows of houses, nothing of the excessive exactitude or pretentiousness that insults the eye in the North. One can scarcely go a few steps into any street, the three or four best ones excepted, without coming upon a group of shacks—dwellings of all sorts of shapes, with stables and sheds standing there all together. Frequently they are found behind trees, and the cows and goats graze along the street in front of them or in the space in between them. Not very far from the main streets one finds large areas where only isolated cabins and gardens are seen. Moreover, since so much work is done outdoors, so many children are to be found in the Negro quarters, and with so much cattle and poultry milling around, there is really more activity here than in the heart of the city. This activity is neither elegant nor clean, but it is vigorous, ample, and varied. To us it looks like a piece of unadulterated nature, and one that would like to be considered as such.

The site of Richmond, moreover, is of such beauty that few cities in the United States can compete with it. Situated in a valley whose floor consists of a chain of tiny hills, it is built upon and between these hills, so that no street is completely level, the main street, in fact, having two very significant inclines. On the highest hill stands the State House (Capitol),[3] a majestic building that looks like a Greek temple and can be seen from afar. Right near Richmond the James River changes from a rapidly flowing river into a bay-like expanse, and although it rushes down to the town like a mountain stream, near Richmond it is already affected by the tides. In the vicinity of the city it is filled with a great number of islands, big and small, most of which are thickly covered with trees. In summer when these islands and the river banks are green, this must be a wonderful river scene.

Almost every road in the city itself brings us to some kind of higher elevation from where we can look down on its lower parts, on the river, or over to the hills that surround Richmond on all sides. There one sees all types of houses and cottages built upon a hill, and behind it, the spire of a church situated at a lower elevation peeks out. If you go across the river to the suburb of Manchester, you can see almost all of Richmond rising on different levels before you, and if you go upstream a few hundred paces from the Petersburg bridge, you are in the midst of the noise and smoke of a large iron foundry. Every step brings with it something interesting to look at. Because of the hilly position of the city, the irregularity of its buildings, its river, and the dominant position of its imposing capitol building with the tall steeples of three churches right near by, the views are always new, rich, and varied.

There is not much to say about specific things to see here. The Americans, Northerners and Southerners alike, naturally find many things of interest, even from the most recent past, in this former capital of the Confederacy. But for us who are less concerned with the internal history of the country these things are only of slight interest. The former arms factories, which are now converted into ironworks, the former treasury building, which now houses the post office, the notorious Libby Prison,[4] now a tobacco factory, the houses where Lee, Davis, Jackson and, in former happier days, Monroe[5] lived—these and similar historic monuments do not arouse in us the lively memories they do in the minds of the population here. We can only people these places with something less than shadows of the past, with only some notions we have formed through our fragmentary knowledge about the people and things of that time. But for us this is not sufficient for places that are not important enough in themselves to have a greater significance for history. Nevertheless, even for foreigners there is a venerable air hovering over this former capital of the Confederacy. Think what one may about the South's cause, one has to respect the heroism of its leaders and of its army. Even an enemy can have sympathy for the energy and staying power to which Richmond's history from 1861 to 1865 bears magnificent witness. There is no doubt that the leadership of the rebellion, as well as many individuals in all segments of the free population, exhibited a strength and perseverance that many other people in similar times of trial have scarcely shown.[6] Regardless of what the goals of these efforts were—we now see wonderful forces starting to work here as soon as circumstances had roused them from their sleep. I am pleased to see a people like the Americans, who had for such a long time busied themselves with the most leisurely everyday matters, now beginning to bestir themselves.

Today, it is true, Richmond is increasingly becoming an industrial and commercial city and is thus more like Northern cities, for with the exception of perhaps Missouri, Virginia has adapted to the new situation more quickly than all the other slave states, since it fortunately does not have an immoderately large colored population nor a climate as arduous to work in. As far as I could learn in the short time here, the most important branches of industry are presently the manufacture of locally grown tobacco, then the iron industry and the mining and cutting of the beautiful granite, which is quarried in the nearby area; the workers employed for the menial type of work in these industries are exclusively blacks. In one of the granite quarries about three hundred black convicts were employed.

Richmond's history, like that of the entire South, which from the beginning has had such an extensive slave economy, shows a very slow growth: first a little settlement, then a fort, then an independent community (since 1742), and only becoming the capital of Virginia in 1779 because of Williamsburg's exposed geographical position. It has grown more slowly than most German cities of its size. In 1800 it had over 5,500 inhabitants, in 1830 16,000, in 1860 40,000, and in 1870 51,000. Growth in the last decade came in the period after the war and indicates by all appearances the beginning of a rapid increase.

In Richmond I had some interesting encounters with fellow Germans, and I want to mention one of these because it shows the conditions in America as seen by a simple Hessian tradesman. One day on Broad Street, the main street, I entered a small shop where walking sticks, fishing and hunting equipment, and a few stuffed wild geese were displayed in the window. I had not read the name of the owner but immediately recognized a German when he came toward me. He had a better selection of walking sticks made out of native types of wood standing in a corner than I had seen in the largest emporiums in New York. I selected one and then looked in on the workshop, where a good handle would be attached. While he was engaged in this work, he told me many things about his life, and when the work was finished, he had so much to show me that I remained for quite some time. On another day I went back there to buy powder and shot, but also mainly just to chat some more. Immediately he offered me the tripod chair near his workbench and began to talk and to ask questions.

We got to speaking about the situation in Germany, how it was resolved by the wars in 1866 and 1870.[7] Like so many people, he thought that it would have almost been better if he had remained in Germany, for here life has not been very good. "Anyhow, you never known." In 1854 he had saved more than $1,000 and went over to Europe; he could have stayed there then but quarreled with his uncle who was not happy to see that the "American" was a big spender; later the uncle married again and that put an end to any hopes of an inheritance there. "So I remained sitting here in Richmond; now have a wife and children myself, live comfortably all right but have trouble saving anything. The Confederacy has set us all back. Wait a minute. I have to give you something from my savings."

He went to a closet, took out an old pocketbook, and showed me a bundle of Confederate paper money, which of course had lost all value at the end of the war. He presented me with a dollar bill from the collection.

"It was good," he continued, "that we middle-class people were already so impoverished, that we had no large amounts of this money in the cash box. But you have no idea of the poverty that prevailed after the end of the war. We are still suffering from its effects; Richmond is a poor city, and only after all sorts of trouble and effort are you able to get just the bare necessities. And what we didn't have to see! For a while I worked in the armory, the most beautiful armory I have ever seen, but later we were recruited as sentry guards, and I belonged to a company that had four people who had to go about on crutches. They slung their weapons around their shoulders and hobbled about on their

10 "I'LL NEVER FORGET
WHAT WENT ON IN LIBBY
PRISON." LIBBY PRISON,
RICHMOND.

crutches. I'll never forget what went on in Libby Prison[8] where we stood guard. No nation has ever treated its prisoners of war so inhumanely. They did not give their own people enough to eat, much less the prisoners whom they would have rather killed immediately. Some of them tunneled a passage under one of the streets, and sixteen, if I am not mistaken, escaped that way. And when the war ended, the slaves were freed, and they made the suffering only worse, not working, and living just like cattle. I have lost all faith in them since I see how they use their freedom. I tell you, when I came here I had a lot of compassion for their lot and tried to do them a good turn wherever I could. But I believe there are very few of them with whom one can deal any other way than domineeringly. Give one an inch and he will take a foot; the rougher you treat him, the better he behaves. That's the way it is. Yes, one gets to experience a lot of things here of which the outside world knows nothing at all."

We got to talking about arms, and he showed me a number of various sorts of weapons, which were hanging side by side in the workshop. There was an Austrian infantry gun, an English hunting gun, a Belgian gun—all weapons that the Confederates had smuggled in during the war. Then he took a heavy rifle down from the wall, of good workmanship and old-fashioned styling like the Tiroleans used for target practice. "This is the best gun," he said, "that I have ever had in my hands, and I am only sorry that I myself can't use it. It comes from the Tirolean colony that we had here. This story you have to hear too. At that time a certain nobleman X from the Tirol had a wayward son for whom he bought a large farm in the neighborhood of Richmond, outfitted it, brought good workers over from the Tirol, and put his son in charge of the property. The father was a great nature lover—I have stuffed many birds for him—and when he returned to Europe, he took back trunks full of all sorts of natural specimens. He often sat here in the workshop and talked about the mountains of the Tirol. As long as the father was here, everything went well, but scarcely had he turned his back when the son began a loose life. When his brother, who was not much better, came over, between the two of them they went through everything in no time. Who knows where they are now. We really had a problem with the Tirolean families and lost a lot of time until they were able to get on their feet. Some of them returned home poorer than they had come, others are sticking it out here and just about making it. They are industrious, honest people. Some strike it rich and others work hard and never make it."

"A few years ago two Germans from Rhenish Prussia also came here and wanted to build a mill on the river. The mills usually draw water out of the canal for which a fee is paid; these two wanted to take it from the river where they would not have to pay anything. They had a Russian as builder who in no time used up $100,000 on them; then one of their ships went adrift down the river and had to be brought back up again at great cost. In the end it became clear that the enterprise could not be completed and these people had spent both their money and effort for nothing. Unfortunately, it happens that way to many Germans; they often get taken up with the American spirit of enterprise before they really know the country, and in no time the money is gone. Skilled labor really pays the best here, and in the North, where there is enough money and work, the trades are as good as a gold mine, just as they are in Europe or perhaps even better. A man should have really learned several kinds of work before he comes over." Taking a small elegant saber out of a drawer, he said, "Look here, I made this in 1849 in Frankfurt. At that time I was an armorer but had also learned other things; here I have had to shoe horses and rim carriages with metal fittings. I have worked as a metal fitter, made weapons, and stood at the lathe, and now in my spare time I carve these canes and pipe bowls and hope to find a ready market for these carvings and make a pile of money. Yes, one has to be versed in many things in a country where everything happens so fast."

His carvings were admirably made, mostly humorous-looking heads; then I also had to look at his collection of stuffed birds, his white mice, and all the other things he was fond of. I noticed that he did not simply have a tender affection for nature but also an unusual gift of observation. He explained how on Sundays he took long walks with his son, how he would go looking for snakes, lizards, and salamanders, and how he had gradually gained a good idea of the animal life around Richmond.

"What I really miss here," he continued, "is that there is no one with whom you can talk things over. There is no socializing, no place where you can get together with other people to relax and to talk about this and that. That alone makes me want to go back to Germany. In the end you have to do everything alone and for yourself and look for relaxation in the woods amongst the animals and trees."

This able, kindly man said much more, since he noticed that I enjoyed listening to him. It was a great pleasure for me in the midst of a strange country to find a human being, without being aware of it himself, whose thinking and life style were so typically German. In the future his children will have very little of a German look about them, but I'll bet that some good German traits will be instilled in them that are not as easily forgotten as our mother tongue.

Other people whom I met by chance in Richmond also seemed to be remarkably talkative. It may be a Southern trait, like the candor and amiability for which the Virginian is generally praised. There was a tobacco dealer across the way from the hotel, a book dealer, and a man who approached me as I stood on one of the heights above Richmond, who all apparently enjoyed telling me this and that as soon as they knew I was a foreigner. The tobacco dealer was pleasantly garrulous like a barber, the book dealer was a choleric fellow, and the man on the heights was at the talkative age. What they all had in common was that they had nothing good to say about the North; the book dealer was so fanatically pro-Confederate that it seemed as if the last fourteen years had passed him by without a trace. I don't attach any importance to their statements, which only seem to show that the kind of politician whom we call a "beer-hall politician" (*Bierhauspolitiker*) has either not yet made his peace with the North here or does not want to admit he has. They praised their section of the country like the inhabitants of such mild fertile regions usually do. As I expressed my admiration for the beauty of Richmond's site to the old man on the heights, he said, "There is no place in the world where you can live as well as in Richmond, and I am only surprised that more Northerners don't come and stay here. We can manage without them, but we could really use their money." The tobacco dealer explained that Virginia had a phenomenal climate but did not want to admit that this winter was unusually mild, that in summer it is oppressively hot, or that the style of houses is not adapted to the climate as it is in Europe. "I don't want to wish," he said jokingly, "that you're going to die, but when you see it coming, perhaps you'll think, in Richmond I would certainly still have had a few years left to live."

CHAPTER TEN

Charleston

SITE. GENERAL IMPRESSION. GARDENS. STYLE OF THE HOUSES. SCENIC CHARACTER OF THE SURROUNDING AREA. SANITARY CONDITIONS. TRADE. GERMAN COLONY.

Charleston's site can be compared with New York's in that it is built on a narrow piece of land bordered on both the left and right by a wide river and whose tip extends out towards the sea. Although spacious and protected, its harbor, which the two rivers, the Ashley and Cooper, shape as they together empty into the very flat, swampy coastal area, is much smaller than New York's. As regards the city itself, its character is so decidedly Southern and so provincial that looking at it would hardly make you think of the exciting, bustling, half-European and more cosmopolitan New York. Only when you view it from a tower, when the individual details recede into the general contours, does the similarity of the site strike you. Only then, when many ships are at anchor in the harbor and there is brisk activity on the landings as at this time of year, can you from such a height possibly feel yourself reminded of New York.

A walk along the streets, however, offers views that definitely show the Southern character of the city. The better homes are surrounded by gardens or have species of evergreen trees and bushes in the yards, which stretch along the side of every house up to the street and are separated from one another by walls or fences. The most common trees to be seen are the tall, large-leaved magnolia, and the small mock or wild orange (*prunus caroliniana*),[1] a tree that frequently only grows to the size of a bush with very thick, luscious evergreen foliage. Now in February the buds are already appearing in thick clusters on the stems of the three-to-four-inch-long, broad lance-like leaves, while numerous black berries as big as cherries are still on the trees. The live oak is also seen frequently on the public grounds but seldom in the gardens; it gets covered too quickly with long grey beards of Spanish moss, thereby acquiring a grotesque, gloomy, unkempt appearance that the people rightly do not like in their well-cared-for gardens. Of all the bushes, one sees the youpon most frequently. It is a type of holly, which they also call Christmas berry bush. Woody and rigid right up to the very tips of its stiff branches, it is thickly covered with little ivy-like leaves, and at the point where these leaves join the stem it has plenty of shiny scarlet-red berries, which make it look almost as cheery as a currant bush at harvest time. The people like to use the bush to form hedges because the berries remain on it during the entire winter, the leaves always stay green, and the bush can easily be trimmed. Then there is another bush with slender hanging branches, which belongs to the spirea family. It is entirely covered for some time before the leaves emerge with little snow-white, rose-like flowers no larger than a nickel. I saw it blooming in many gardens.

Camellias, cultivated as bushes and little trees, are now full of red and white flowers and are frequently found in the gardens, for they do not require much care in this climate, which is similar to their land of origin.[2] Orange trees with beautiful reddish fruit, palm trees and woodbine growing wild, palm ferns, and others are common here, where they seldom suffer from the cold.

The style of houses is much different than in the North. In addition, more attention is paid to the pure pleasure of enjoying light and air than in the thick-walled, enclosed houses of the cities and even the villages of southern Europe. Lengthwise the homes take up half of a rectangular piece of property, with their shorter sides bordering on the street. The other half of the property contains a yard, which frequently takes up the entire width of the plot in the rear and is usually made into a garden. The house faces this yard with a frontage of thirty to fifty feet before which extends a veranda one or two stories high. They call them piazzas here. Most rooms lead with doors and windows onto this veranda, and only one room on each floor faces onto the street, which by the way is also lined with trees whenever there is enough room. There are two entrances: a yard gate and a door that leads to the veranda of the ground floor. Thus the houses are very narrow on the street side and generally also very plain, but on the yard side they are spacious and cheery; the verandas, which whenever possible face southward, are the favorite place in the house throughout most of the year.

Houses like this occupy entire streets, especially in the southern end of the city, and give them a secluded and very pleasant tranquility that is rarely pierced by the noise of the harbor streets and the dirt from the Negro shanty quarters. One description of Charleston really captures this feeling by calling it "retiring respectability."

Nevertheless, the shattering impact of the last thirteen years also manifests itself here in the frequent traces of decay and devastation. Many of these homes have changed owners since the war and are inhabited by chance tenants instead of the families of rich plantation owners in whose hands they passed from generation to generation. Some stand empty, others bear signs of fire and gun shots, and still others give evidence that the time is past when a large merchant class possessed enough money and human resources to make a comfortable living. Almost all of these beautiful houses have something weather-beaten and neglected about them, which nonetheless frequently makes them picturesque in these pleasant surroundings full of trees and bushes. Under this sun and under such proud, massive trees many things are made more attractive, and the homes and even the people themselves can afford to "let go" a little here. We can easily understand how, with this kind of daylight and under this type of shade, one would not want to make life more difficult nor just be satisfied with working constantly.

Charleston, on the whole, has been systematically laid out, with straight streets that intersect one another exactly at right angles, but curiously enough, they are, like those in our old European cities, so narrow that in those streets that run along the harbor the carriage traffic is very congested. The reason for this compact style of construction may lie in the problems the surrounding swampy soil presents for an expanded network of streets. Charleston lies entirely in the lowlands, surrounded by swamps that stretch far inland from the banks of both principal rivers, the Ashley and the Cooper. But this low-lying site gives the city and its surroundings, if viewed from the sea, a particular charm. As far as the eye can scan, no land rises above the shining edge of the water, and trees, houses, steeples, and everything on the shore appear to swim on the water or to grow up out of it. Between water and sky there runs only a thin chain of varied objects all crowded together, whose forms are sharply outlined against the blue and really stand out because of their contrast to the two uniform and unicolored surfaces between which they have been inserted. Everything is reduced to one line. The forests on the shore are not a thick multitude but a thin row of trees. The city is no mass of houses but a row behind which only church steeples and some taller buildings indicate the further expanse of land. Nothing is telescoped; everything looks as if it were reduced to the simplest components. The only thing visible is that for which there is room on the thin line between water and sky; nothing towers in the background casting shadows. What one sees contrasts with the heavens, thus forming a very simple, peaceful, impressive view. That the Americans call Charleston the "American Venice" has, of course, no more reason than that both are built on low-lying areas, for Charleston, because of its modern bustling life, its semivirgin wooded environs, and architecturally unassuming character, is an entirely different city from Venice.

Because Charleston is situated on such low ground, it is one of the least healthy places in the South. As is well known, frequent outbreaks of yellow fever occur here, and whoever does get an attack of this disease is bothered until he becomes acclimatized by some kind of intermittent or broken-bone fever.[3] The latter is seldom fatal but has, as its name indicates, symptoms similar to those with which yellow fever begins, namely pains in the back and limbs, and is considered by many people as a milder, substitute form of yellow

11 "THE STYLE OF HOUSES IS MUCH DIFFERENT THAN IN THE NORTH. THE HOUSES ARE VERY NARROW ON THE STREET SIDE, BUT ON THE YARD SIDE THEY ARE SPACIOUS AND CHEERY." THE EAST BATTERY, CHARLESTON.

fever. Like all epidemic diseases, these also have a whole group of beliefs surrounding them. Everyone can give some other causes, some other means of prevention, some other cure. Nevertheless, one thing is sure: the best remedy is a change of air, which fortunately is to be found at the somewhat higher elevation starting only a few miles inland from Charleston and extending towards the mountains. Here the air is the healthy sort one is looking for.

Charleston is the import and export harbor for only South Carolina and a small part of North Carolina and Georgia, since trade with the West is at the moment still hampered by the lack of direct railway connections. The city has a more fertile hinterland than any of the other Atlantic port cities of the South and is linked with it by a comparatively complete railroad complex. Its chief export articles are cotton, rice, and the products of the pine forest, which are just now beginning to be utilized. In the year ending August 31, 1872, its exports totaled $37,257,000 and have been growing since the end of the war. Its population is over forty thousand.

During the last war, Charleston was the center of conversation. The seizure of Fort Sumter, which guards the entrance to Charleston's harbor, was the first military act of the Southern states (April 13, 1861), and they continued to hold it against several attacks right up until the end of the war. Today the fort still lies partly in ruins. In 1862 a fire consumed hundreds of houses on one stormy night, and the desolate condition, out of which the city has only slowly been able to free itself, has from the war up until today hindered the city's complete reconstruction.

In the good old days—which are not old in number of years but in degrees of maturity—Charleston once boasted a very active, very generously supported intellectual life. Our compatriot, Bachmann,[4] a New York German, minister of the German church, and one who published important works with Audubon about the animal life of North America, once formed along with Agassiz and Lieber[5] among others a scholarly circle that provided a great deal of good intellectual stimulation. Now the men are gone; and if one asks what happened to the books and collections, the answer is burned, stolen, sold to someone in the North ! The institutions of higher learning have had a sharp drop in the number of instructors and students, but hopefully not permanently.

The German community in Charleston, as opposed to many other groups, is noted for the harmony that exists within it and the excellent accomplishments for which its cohesiveness has for years qualified it. It consists of about three thousand people, forming one-fourteenth of the population, although its taxes amount to more than one-sixth of the city's total tax income. One can say that our countrymen are generally pretty well off here. This naturally contributes to promoting a closer cohesiveness within the community than is possible particularly in places, like in the Northeastern states, where the lower-class Germans overlap with the proletariat, while the upper classes belong to a rather cosmopolitan moneyed aristocracy. Here we have predominantly middle-class people, who have already succeeded or who are on the way to making their "mark in life"; a few very rich, who "represent" the German community to the outside world; and very few one could call poor.

This community has developed differently from the more important ones in the North and the West, since until recently there was no steady immigration to the Southern states. With few exceptions, the foreigners came drop by drop, so to speak, generally intending to settle in or near the city and to start a trade or business. But in the Northern and Western cities a lot of "foam and sediment" from the stream of immigrants have been left behind and burdens the German community with a sorry group of unfit and base types, as if they were just washed up and spit out over here. But there is little of this to be perceived in Charleston. In fact, the South really seems to offer an especially favorable soil for the industry and thriftiness of our countrymen, and in "antebellum times," as they say, the way to riches seemed to be easy. I have many times heard the Germans praised for being the first ones after the war to get to work energetically and in a short time to become economically established again. Here they do not have to compete with the cunning, restless Yankees but with a populace that through slavery has become somewhat indolent and one-sided, that through its abolition has become disorganized, and that probably because of the enervating effects of the mild Southern climate has less energy than our immigrant countrymen freshly arrived from northern regions.*

*IT WOULD BE UNFAIR NOT TO MENTION HERE THE NAME OF A MAN WHOM THE GERMANS IN SOUTH CAROLINA HAVE TO THANK FOR A GOOD PART OF THE RESPECTED POSITION THEY OCCUPY HERE IN COMPARISON TO OTHER SOUTHERN STATES. FOR ALMOST SIXTY YEARS, JOHANNES BACH-

Like foreigners everywhere, our countrymen also enjoy the advantage here of being farther removed from the internal entanglements and problems within the state in which they live than are the native inhabitants, thereby being able to pursue their business activities with less disruption. During the war against the North, they fought with a dedication that has assured them the lasting thanks of their fellow citizens. After the war, although having lost almost everything, they still had not lost as much as the indigenous inhabitants whom the war and its aftermath had separated in earthquake fashion from the entire past by a deep rift, while at the same time leaving the foundations of their lives and earnings in ruins for a long time to come. It was natural that the Germans bestirred themselves sooner and more vigorously than the Americans, for basically their sorrows had been caused only by material losses and by sympathy for their fellow citizens.

Fairly early in its history Charleston already had quite a few Germans among its inhabitants, for in 1775 a company of "German Fusiliers" was established here. But the steady and frequent number of immigrants began only in the 1840s, and these later immigrants have become Anmericanized less quickly than their predecessors. They have a nice church, a superb minister, one of the most attractive club houses in the city, and now with gratifying success are in the midst of raising funds to found a German school. It is certain that even more immigrants will be coming, and what will probably ultimately happen here in this beautiful section of America is that our countrymen will found a permanent and prosperous community.[6]

MANN LABORED AS A LUTHERAN CLERGYMAN WITH MUCH SUCCESS FOR THE ENTIRE COMMON-WEALTH AS WELL AS FOR HIS COUNTRYMEN. GERMAN-AMERICANS HONOR HIM AS ONE OF THEIR FOREMOST REPRESENTATIVES, WHILE SOUTH CAROLINA RECOGNIZES HIM AS A TRUE FRIEND AND BENEFACTOR OF THE STATE, AND THE SCHOLARLY WORLD, NOT SIMPLY NORTH AMERICA, ACKNOWLEDGES HIM AS A DISTINGUISHED NATURAL SCIENTIST. HIS LIFE AND WORK ARE INSTRUCTIVE. HE WAS BORN ON FEBRUARY 4, 1790, OF SWISS PARENTS IN RHINEBECK, THE OLD GERMAN-DUTCH SETTLEMENT IN NEW YORK STATE, RECEIVED HIS EDUCATION AT WILLIAMS COLLEGE (MASSACHUSETTS), AND AT TWENTY-THREE YEARS OF AGE WAS ORDAINED A MINISTER OF THE NEW YORK LUTHERAN SYNOD. IN 1815 HE WAS CHOSEN PASTOR BY THE LUTHERAN COMMUNITY OF CHARLESTON. HE OCCUPIED THIS POSITION UNTIL SHORTLY BEFORE HIS DEATH. HIS PUBLIC LIFE WOULD THUS HAVE BEEN A VERY UNEVENTFUL ONE IF HIS GREAT INTELLECTUAL AND WARMHEARTED PERSONALITY AND ENERGETIC CHARACTER HAD NOT LED HIM TO A MUCH MORE COMPREHENSIVE WORK THAN THAT OF A PASTOR OF A SMALL COMMUNITY, ESPECIALLY IN THIS VERY PLURALISTIC SOCIETY.

SCARCELY SETTLED IN CHARLESTON, HE VIGOROUSLY TOOK CHARGE OF THE SCATTERED LUTHERAN PARISHES IN GEORGIA, NORTH CAROLINA, AND OTHER SOUTHERN STATES, WHICH HAD FOR THE MOST PART BEEN DISBANDED OR WERE ON THE VERGE OF BEING DISBANDED, PROVIDED FOR CLOSER CONTACT AMONG THE CLERGYMEN AND FOR THE SCHOOLS, ET CETERA, SO THAT

TODAY HE IS HONORED BY THOSE WHO ARE CLOSE TO THOSE THINGS AS THE FOUNDER OF THE LUTHERAN CHURCH IN THE SOUTH. IN HIS OWN PARISH HIS ACTIVITIES WERE SO VARIED AND SUCCESSFUL THAT, DESPITE THE CHILDLIKE SIMPLICITY OF HIS NATURE, IN A SHORT TIME HE BECAME THE MOST INFLUENTIAL AND POPULAR CLERGYMAN IN ALL CHARLESTON. IN THE BEGINNING HE PREACHED IN GERMAN, BUT AS THE OLDER GENERATION, WHICH WAS BORN IN GERMANY, GRADUALLY DIED OUT, HE HAD TO ALTERNATE WITH ENGLISH—HE HIMSELF HAD ONLY LEARNED GERMAN IN COLLEGE. THE AMERICANS LIKED HIS PREACHING SO MUCH THAT EVENTUALLY WHEN NEW IMMIGRANTS ESTABLISHED A NEW GERMAN LUTHERAN CONGREGATION, HE FOUND HIMSELF PREACHING BEFORE A PREDOMINANTLY ANGLO-AMERICAN AUDIENCE COMPOSED OF THE BEST SEGMENTS OF SOCIETY. WHAT MADE HIS SERMONS SO APPEALING WAS THAT THEY WERE BASED ON TRUTH, FACTUAL SOLIDITY, AND SIMPLICITY—ATTRIBUTES ONE CERTAINLY CANNOT LOOK FOR IN THE OVERWHELMING MAJORITY OF AMERICAN PULPIT ORATORS. ONE OF HIS CLOSEST FRIENDS AND COLLEAGUES WROTE TO ME: "FOR FIFTY YEARS BACHMANN WAS THE MOST POPULAR MAN IN CHARLESTON AS WELL AS IN THE STATE, AND IN MANY CASES THE FINAL AUTHORITY. AND IT IS A FACT THAT HE WAS REGARDED AS HIGHLY BY UNEDUCATED PEOPLE AS BY EDUCATED ONES. HIS ERUDITION IMPRESSED THE LATTER; ON THE OTHER HAND, IN ADDITION TO HIS LEARNING, IT WAS HIS PRACTICAL KNOWLEDGE AND HIS UNDERSTANDING OF PEOPLE THAT IMPRESSED THE FORMER. HIS GOOD NATURE WON FOR HIM THE AFFECTION OF ALL HEARTS; A CHILDLIKE CHRISTIAN FAITH AND AN UPRIGHT WAY OF LIVING WON FOR HIM THE HIGHEST RESPECT."

FROM MY OWN EXPERIENCE I CAN ATTEST THAT THE CHARACTER AND DEEDS OF THIS SINGULAR INDIVIDUAL HAVE BEEN VERY BENEFICIAL TO THE WAY IN WHICH GERMANS ARE REGARDED IN THIS AREA. ON THE FIRST DAY OF MY STAY IN CHARLESTON, I WAS GREETED WITH UNRESTRAINED PRAISE FOR HIM FROM SOMEONE WHOSE JUDGMENT I HIGHLY REGARD. IT WAS WITH SINCERE PERSONAL PLEASURE THAT I LATER HEARD EDUCATED AMERICANS EXPRESSING THEMSELVES IN A SIMILAR WAY.

NO LESS GRATIFYING THAN HIS EFFICACY AS A CLERGYMAN AND SOMETHING THAT WAS BENEFICIAL TO A GREAT MANY PEOPLE WERE HIS EFFORTS IN THE FIELD OF NATURAL HISTORY, THAT IS, HIS FIRST-RATE WORK ON THE NATURAL HISTORY OF NORTH AMERICAN MAMMALS. WITH AUDUBON, THE "AMERICAN LINNAEUS," HE PUBLISHED THE *NATURAL HISTORY OF NORTH AMERICAN MAMMALS* (1845) FOR WHICH HE PROVIDED THE TEXT AND AUDUBON THE PICTURES. [ED. NOTE: CARL VON LINNÉ (LATIN, LINNAEUS) (1707–1778), SWEDISH BOTANIST, HELPED ESTABLISH MODERN SYSTEMATIC BOTANY AND DEVELOPED A SYSTEM OF BOTANICAL NOMENCLATURE.] THIS IS ONE OF THE BEST STUDIES OF ITS KIND AND WAS PARTICULARLY EPOCH-MAKING FOR AMERICA, WHOSE ANIMAL WORLD WITH FEW EXCEPTIONS IS EVEN TODAY ONLY SUPERFICIALLY KNOWN. IT HAS REMAINED UP UNTIL THE PRESENT BY FAR THE BEST ORIGINAL BOOK ON THIS SUBJECT. MONOGRAPHS ABOUT AMERICAN RABBITS AND SQUIRRELS, THE CHANGE OF FUR COATS AND MOULTING, AND VULTURES AMONG OTHERS, PRECEDED THIS MAJOR WORK, AND A SERIES OF LARGER AND SMALLER STUDIES FOLLOWED IT. TREATISES FOR THE UNITY OF THE HUMAN RACE HOLD AN IMPORTANT PLACE AMONG HIS LATER WRITINGS. THIS CONTROVERSIAL ANTHROPOLOGICAL QUESTION, AS EVERYONE KNOWS, HAD BEEN RESOLVED BY SOME IN THE INTEREST OF THE SLAVE OWNER, IN FAVOR OF RACIAL DIFFERENCES BETWEEN CAUCASIAN AND NEGRO, BUT AGAINST WHICH BACHMANN RESOLUTELY PLACED HIMSELF IN OPPOSITION. [ED. NOTE: THIS INFORMATION WOULD BE OF SPECIAL INTEREST TO RATZEL IN VIEW OF HIS GROWING ATTENTION TO HUMAN GEOGRAPHY AND HIS FURTHER WORK IN THAT FIELD. SEE THE INTRODUCTION.] IN PRACTICAL TERMS, HOWEVER, BEFORE AND DURING THE WAR HE SPOKE OUT IN FAVOR OF THE RIGHTS OF THE CONFEDERACY, THEREBY AGAINST THE ABRUPT ABOLITION OF SLAVERY. AN INCONSPICUOUS ASPECT OF HIS SCHOLARLY ACTIVITY WAS THE POPULAR-STYLE ARTICLES ON

NATURAL HISTORY FOR CHILDREN WHICH HAVE APPEARED IN VARIOUS MAGAZINES AND BELONG TO THE BEST THAT CAN BE PRODUCED IN THIS TYPE OF WRITING.

THIS OUTLINE OF A VERY RICH LIFE CANNOT DO JUSTICE TO THE MAGNIFICENT ACCOMPLISHMENTS THIS MAN INSPIRED AND CARRIED OUT, BUT IT SUFFICES TO SHOW HOW THE GERMAN CHARACTER QUIETLY, ALMOST UNKNOWN AND UNPERCEIVED, HAS INFLUENCED THE AMERICAN ONE IN NONPOLITICAL WAYS, DOING GOOD AND EVEN WINNING THANKS AND GENERAL RECOGNITION.

CHAPTER ELEVEN

Columbia

SITE. GENERAL REMARKS ABOUT THE SITES OF THE MAJOR CITIES OF THE SOUTH. DESTRUCTION DURING THE LAST WAR. PRESENT-DAY APPEARANCE. BLACK LEGISLATURE. BLACK AND WHITE SPEAKERS.

Columbia, the capital of South Carolina, lies on a promontory on the left bank of the Congaree River at the beginning of the gentle rolling country that marks the transition from the lowlands along the coast to the highlands of the southern Alleghenies. Already here the river winds lazily between its banks of low, rounded sand and gravel hills. A few miles further upstream it comes rushing out of the uplands via mighty waterfalls. In this area one can find granite, the basic stone of the Allegheny range down to the most southerly mountain spur, being quarried. It is a beautiful, light grey granite of fine grain from which people would like to build many stately homes once they again become rich and proud enough in this region to want to put a little beauty into their lives.

In 1786 Columbia was laid out according to plans similar to those of the neighboring cities of Savannah and Augusta, a spacious city with broad streets, full of parks, gardens, shade trees, and villas. Up until then the seat of the state government had been the seaport of Charleston, but the inhabitants of the interior of the state, who during the Revolutionary War had fought and suffered just as much as the rich rice and cotton planters on the coast, demanded that the legislature meet in a more centrally situated place. Thus in 1786, after the successful completion of negotiations between the inhabitants of the highlands and lowlands, a commission was empowered to find a suitable spot for the new capital. The selection was made strictly, as Ramsay the historian expressly notes, "according to health and philosophical principles without any influence from commercial interests or land speculators."[1] In this instance we can well believe the historian, no matter how suspiciously rosy this South Carolinian patriot otherwise loves to paint the picture of the era of planter hegemony. Here we see that he has not just written a lot of nice words but has told the truth. Columbia is really a well-situated, healthy place, which in the last few years has even been visited by Northerners because of its advantages for health, and is praised by everyone who lives there or who knows the city. In addition, the Congaree River brings the city water power in the form of a continuous supply of the muddy yellow water emerging out of the neighboring mountains where it rains frequently. The potential development of this water power is something that the local inhabitants very strongly believe in.*

One sees from a look at the map that Columbia is one of the cities that lies at the point where streams or rivers issue out of the watergaps of the eastern Alleghenies. From Georgia up to Maine these places are centers of commercial and industrial activity; whereas in the North, industrial cities established themselves from the very beginning along the line where the land slopes down, causing the water to flow more swiftly, in the South it has been only by chance that the cities were located there. In the future, because of the abundance of

---

*SINCE INITIALLY THE POPULATION OF THE SOUTHERN STATES WAS A PURELY AGRICULTURAL ONE, THEIR TERRITORY LARGE BUT WITH POOR TRANSPORTATION FACILITIES, MOST OFTEN THEY SELECTED FOR THEIR CAPITALS SITES THAT WERE DISTINGUISHED MORE BY THEIR CENTRAL OR PERHAPS STRATEGICALLY FAVORABLE LOCATIONS THAN BY ADVANTAGES THAT OTHERWISE USUALLY MADE CITIES LARGE IN THIS COUNTRY. THE POLITICAL CAPITALS ARE THEREFORE ALL UNIMPORTANT IN COMPARISON WITH THE COMMERCIAL AND BUSINESS CENTERS THAT HAVE SUBSEQUENTLY DEVELOPED HERE. IN NORTH CAROLINA, WILMINGTON IS LARGER THAN THE CAPITAL RALEIGH; LIKEWISE IN SOUTH CAROLINA, CHARLESTON, AND IN GEORGIA, SAVANNAH AND AUGUSTA, ARE LARGER THAN THE CAPITALS COLUMBIA AND ATLANTA. IN GEORGIA BEFORE THE WAR, MILLEDGEVILLE, A LITTLE TOWN OF THREE THOUSAND INHABITANTS, WAS THE CAPITAL. THE POLITICAL CAPITAL OF FLORIDA, TALLAHASSEE, IS FIVE TIMES SMALLER THAN THE COMMERCIAL CAPITAL, JACKSONVILLE. IN ALABAMA THE SEAT OF THE GOVERNMENT USED TO BE TUSCALOOSA AND IS NOW MONTGOMERY, WHILE THE MOST POPULOUS CITY IS MOBILE. IN MISSISSIPPI, VICKSBURG AND NATCHEZ ARE MORE IMPORTANT THAN THE CAPITAL JACKSON. THE SAME SITUATION IS REPEATED IN THE WEST AND IS WITHOUT DOUBT A SIGNIFICANT FACTOR IN THE BALANCE BETWEEN THE AGRICULTURAL AND COMMERCIAL INTERESTS, WHICH ARE FREQUENTLY SO OPPOSED TO ONE ANOTHER: INDIVIDUALS INVOLVED IN COMMERCIAL PURSUITS BECOME INORDINATELY INFLUENTIAL BECAUSE OF THEIR CAPABILITIES AND MOVABLE WEALTH, AND THE PLANTERS DO NOT WANT TO BECOME POLITICALLY SUBORDINATE TO THEM JUST AS THEY HAVE BEEN ECONOMICALLY SUBORDINATE FOR SO LONG. NATURALLY, THE INDUSTRIAL UPSWING OF THE SOUTH ALSO BRINGS NEW ELEMENTS INTO THIS SIMPLE ANTITHESIS. IN SOUTH CAROLINA, FOR EXAMPLE, COLUMBIA, BECAUSE OF ITS LOCATION AS A TRANSPORTATION CENTER AND BECAUSE OF THE WATER POWER IT CAN DRAW FROM THE RIVER, IS ALREADY CONSIDERED A PREDESTINED INDUSTRIAL CENTER. EVEN IN VIRGINIA THEY ARE PRESENTLY TRYING TO TRANSFER THE SEAT OF GOVERNMENT FROM OLD RICHMOND, WHICH BECAUSE OF ITS GREAT BUT TRAGIC DESTINY SHOULD HAVE BECOME SACROSANCT, TO A PLACE MORE CENTRALLY SITUATED IN THE STATE.

water, the American Southern states will have many an advantage over southern Europe, although both have a similar climate.

At present, however, Columbia, like the beautiful state whose capital it is, is more occupied with rebuilding than with new developments, for there is scarcely a place in the South where the war has left more traces behind than here. In February 1865, when Sherman again turned north from Savannah, Georgia, which he had taken, his route lead him by way of Columbia, and in the night after he had taken possession of the city, two-thirds of its houses, 84 out of 124 blocks, were burned down.[2] As always in such cases, there are very differing reports about the reason for and the course of these events. They originate from various groups and probably cannot be reconciled. Southerners say the fire was started by Sherman's soldiers at his express command, and credible private citizens told me how these men went ahead and plundered without in the least being stopped by their officers; how in the evening they came into the houses with full kerosene cans, drove out the occupants, and started the fires. A rocket is said to have gone up from Sherman's headquarters, and upon this signal the arson was to have begun. On the other hand, it appears to be confirmed that as they departed, the Confederates set the cotton, which was stored at the railroad station, and the station itself ablaze, since their commander, W. Hampton,[3] admits that he gave the order for this. Furthermore, it is known that the same general, while retreating, bombarded Sherman's troops in their camp when such action no longer had any purpose, because the city had already surrendered. Thus Northern troops entered the city embittered; their military discipline had never been what it should have been, and the march through Georgia had brought them down to a level that, according to all descriptions, was not much above the mobs that fought each other during the Thirty Years' War in our country.

The greatest part of the burned-out area has been rebuilt, but for the time being the buildings standing there are mostly temporary structures; the contrast between the few old streets that have remained intact and the rebuilt ones is very great. In the former, there are attractive villas, one after the other, and the gardens in their spring dress extend out to the streets and produce a colorful, cheerful picture. In the latter, there are bare, simple brick houses, separated here and there by burned-out places, by building sites, by half-burned-out or half-reconstructed houses, and along the main streets of this city once famous for its wealth you don't see one single house now that even has a pleasing appearance. Moreover, the broad streets are in a very neglected state, full of dirt and rubbish, with sparse activity, and at the end of these streets is one of the Negro sections, which like everywhere else are to be found on the edge of the city.

I came to Columbia at the time when the taxpayers and the members of the Grange (the Grangers) were meeting here, and I soon found some acquaintances, new and old.[4] The first words after the greetings were always "Have you seen our menagerie? Have you already been to our pigpen? You have to see our monkey theater." I did not have to ask what these words meant, for I knew already what kind of expressions the embittered whites of South Carolina used in speaking about their black legislature. I went to visit it on the first day here and many more times thereafter and found myself disappointed, since I did not see much of the scandal and absurdities that now and then are supposed to occur, and because I had to admit the slaves at least knew how to ape their masters pretty well. It was only a bit louder and livelier here than in the House of Representatives in Washington; otherwise there wasn't a big difference. Everywhere you look, and in America perhaps more so than elsewhere, practice in rhetorical speaking is, more than one thinks, very important particularly in the political arena. Who could blame the blacks, since they have not had any time yet to learn better, when for the time being they resort to imitating the phrases and gestures of their former masters and when they thereby now and then overstep the line somewhat?* In the few days I spent in Columbia, I heard more political speeches than I had in years, speeches by whites and by blacks, some by good white orators, others by famous blacks. If I had to make a comparison, I have to say that on both sides nine-tenths of all the words were

---

*I HAVE NOT BEEN ABLE TO OBTAIN SUFFICIENTLY ACCURATE REPORTS CONCERNING THE STATE OF EDUCATION IN SOUTH CAROLINA. SINCE, HOWEVER, IT DEVELOPED IN SIMILAR FASHION IN ALL SOUTHERN SLAVEHOLDING STATES AND HAS A SIMILAR SIGNIFICANCE FOR THEM, I AM ADDING HERE SOME DATA ABOUT THE PRIMARY SCHOOLS IN FLORIDA, WHICH ALSO HAS A LARGE NEGRO POPULATION.

ONE-THIRD OF THE POPULATION OF THIS STATE IS WITHOUT A SCHOOL EDUCATION AND THREE-QUARTERS OF THIS THIRD—ABOUT FIFTY THOUSAND—ARE NEGRO, MOSTLY FREED SLAVES. THUS THE EDUCATION QUESTION IS ONE OF THE MOST IMPORTANT FOR FLORIDA TOO. FORTUNATELY, WHEN A DECISION WAS MADE ON THIS QUESTION AT THE END OF THE LAST WAR, THE MEANS WERE NOT ENTIRELY LACKING TO FOUND THE NEW SCHOOLS THAT WERE BEING DEMANDED EVERYWHERE, PARTICULARLY BY THE NEGROES. THE LEGISLATURE HAD EARLIER ALLOCATED 85,000 ACRES OF LAND FOR THE ESTABLISHMENT AND ENDOWMENT OF TWO TRAINING SCHOOLS FOR TEACHERS AND OVER 700,000 ACRES FOR GENERAL EDUCATIONAL PURPOSES, AND BECAUSE THE PRICE OF LAND HAS RISEN CONSIDERABLY SINCE THEN, THIS PROPERTY HAS BEEN ABLE TO YIELD A GREAT DEAL OF PROFIT. TO THIS CAPITAL THE NEW CONSTITUTION OF 1868 ADDED THE INTEREST ON ALL PROPERTY THAT REVERTS TO THE STATE, A QUARTER OF THE YIELD FROM THE SALE OF ALL STATE PROPERTIES, AND A SCHOOL TAX OF ONE-TENTH OF ONE PERCENT ON ALL REAL ESTATE IN THE STATE. FURTHERMORE, IT HAS ASSIGNED ALL MONETARY FINES TO THE SCHOOL FUNDS AND DECLARED THAT EVERY COUNTY HAS TO MATCH FROM ITS OWN SOURCES THE MONEY THAT IS ASSIGNED TO IT FROM THE SCHOOL FUNDS BY AT LEAST HALF. IN 1870, AS A CONSEQUENCE, FLORIDA HAD 400 SCHOOLS WITH AN AVERAGE OF 45 PUPILS IN EACH CLASS, WHILE TEN YEARS EARLIER THERE WERE IN TOTO ONLY 5,500 CHILDREN IN ITS SCHOOLS. THIS INCREASE IS PRIMARILY SEEN AMONG THE NEGROES, WHO ALREADY HAVE BEGUN TO FOUND THEIR OWN

empty ones, and that the speeches of the Hon. Elliott,[5] who is as black as coal and whom a South Carolina electoral district has sent to Congress, amply attested to having as much good sense as the average speaker from among the white taxpayers or Grangers.

The scene really had an African flavor about it one evening as this Mr. Elliott spoke in the legislative chamber before an open meeting of white and black citizens. The blacks were naturally more numerous in attendance, since this fellow member of their race really wanted to speak to them, and the whites scarcely formed one-fifth of those gathered there. Elliott spoke about the necessity for an honest government in South Carolina, going without all too great a flood of oratory to the heart of the matter. He sought to make it clear to his fellow citizens what dangers there would be if through their support governments that compromised themselves and the voters by corruption came to power or remained in office. He was supported by his colleague Hayne,[6] a dark mulatto, who spoke to the citizens not without humor and a quick repartee and who *lege artis* disposed of a taxpayer who had interrupted him with some powerful oratorical blows. He had as much oratorical ability as one can ask for from any representative of the people but was inclined in speech and gesture a little too much towards burlesquing, which is a dangerous inclination for someone in front of a Negro public, which enjoys and can easily be brought to laughter. I stood in the midst of a group of shabbily dressed fellows who during the entire half-hour speech scarcely recovered for a second from the general merriment in which Mr. Hayne's allusions and highly animated gestures had put them, and that was the mood of the entire audience. Just as soon as one speaker had finished, the band in the gallery immediately began a racket with drums and shrill trumpets, and the people in the auditorium went into stitches

---

SCHOOLS FOR THE EDUCATION OF CLERGYMEN; THE BLACK BAPTISTS AND METHODISTS WILL SOON HAVE THEIR OWN SEMINARIES.

I HAVE THE REPORT OF THE DIRECTOR OF PUBLIC PRIMARY SCHOOLS IN FLORIDA FOR 1873 IN FRONT OF ME AND GATHER FROM IT THAT THE NUMBER OF PUBLIC PRIMARY SCHOOLS HAS RISEN TO 500 WITH 18,000 PUPILS, THAT DURING THIS YEAR ABOUT $10,000 HAS BEEN DONATED TO SCHOOLS, AND THAT ABOUT $107,000 HAS BEEN SPENT FOR PUBLIC SCHOOLS. FROM THIS REPORT AND NEWSPAPER ARTICLES THAT I HAVE BEEN ABLE TO SEE, I GATHER THAT SOME INTELLIGENT PEOPLE HERE ARE ALSO IN FAVOR OF INTRODUCING COMPULSORY EDUCATION. BUT, HERE AS IN OTHER STATES, INSURMOUNTABLE DIFFICULTIES WILL STAND IN THE WAY OF THIS REFORM FOR A WHILE YET. THE LOUDMOUTHS CALL IT UNDEMOCRATIC. THE SCATTERED PATTERN OF SETTLE-MENT ALONE MAKES ITS INTRODUCTION IMPOSSIBLE IN MANY DISTRICTS, AND THOSE PERSONS ANXIOUS TO LEARN WILL SOMETIMES HAVE TO GO BACK TO USING THE OLD SYSTEM OF ITINERANT TEACHERS WHO HOLD SCHOOL ONE MONTH HERE AND ONE MONTH THERE AND WHO, IN THE PLACE WHERE THEY ARE TEACHING, GENERALLY GO FROM HOUSE TO HOUSE IN A ROTATING FASHION AND RECEIVE ROOM AND BOARD. [ED. NOTE: SEE ALSO NEW YORK, NOTE 21.]

laughing over this joke, rhythmically hooted and howled, and kicked with their legs.

The morose American masters really lose their tempers over the levity with which their former slaves conduct government business. But here I could not entirely share their feelings when I reflected on how much mean hypocrisy and stupidity lies behind the earnestness with which their political parties and lawmaking bodies like to surround their own activities—which have not always been exactly clean—how they seriously have to assert this in order to outdo the by no means significantly large black majority, and finally how short the joy of these poor devils, the ex-slaves, will be, how bitter their disenchantment when the exmasters once again become the effective rulers in the state. The droll misgovernment of the blacks is certainly only a short intermezzo, a couple of carnival weeks before and after the bleak times of complete debasement and privation. Observing these abnormal circumstances, I constantly had one wish, which appears unworkable but which seems to me would be best for both conflicting groups, the whites and blacks: before they are removed from office, the black administrators should decree that they, together with all their people, intend to look for a new home in the West Indies, in Central or in the warmer part of South America, or even in Africa again, a homeland that will feed them more readily, a homeland where less work would be required of them than here. It would help both parties and would be less inhumane than if they remain. The indefatigable whites, like millstones, will take up this slow-moving, happy-go-lucky folk between them and in a few decades the Negroes of this country will be reduced to gypsies, and only a few of them will have saved themselves by climbing up to the "protective" cultural heights of the whites.[7]

CHAPTER TWELVE

Savannah

CITY OF TREES

Savannah, the major port town of the wealthy state of Georgia, is a unique city, the likes of which one finds only here in this new land. Its site in the flat, swampy lowlands almost four geographical (about eighteen statute) miles above the mouth of the Savannah River is of no importance, although the view over the broad river, filled with islands, and over its flat wooded banks will certainly attract the nature lover, who isn't looking for something special. Inside the city, however, Savannah is outstanding because of the abundance of trees, which lends a distinctive beauty to it. It has predominantly broad, straight streets that intersect at right angles, being without exception lined with perennially green oak trees (live oak and possum oak), magnolias, and some other perennially green trees. They are actually so thickly lined and with such healthy, broad-limbed specimens that from most angles the houses completely recede from view, and when you look down the streets you sometimes think you're looking at a very well-cared-for park avenue. Along some of the streets the trees stand in two rows on a grass strip that runs along the middle of the road; but in most, however, there is one row at the edge of the sidewalk, which the trees amply shade. As if this weren't enough, every second one of the streets running north-south opens out into a tree-lined green or square, so that the little city numbers no less than twenty-four open squares within its limits. Some of these squares are laid out with flower beds, some contain monuments, some fountains, but their main attraction remains the magnificent old trees. The lawns, on the other hand, do not do well here anymore.

A few years ago, at the end of the widest and most bustling of these shady streets, a city park was also laid out, which under the care of a German gardener-naturalist has rapidly become an attractive and interesting park. When I visited it in the last week of February, the camellia trees (some really good specimens can be found here) and the peach and almond trees were in bloom, and the delightful rosebuds (a type of robinia, similar in size and shape to our so-called acacia) were beginning to be covered with pale rose-colored buds that look like peach buds in color and like them, come out before the leaves. Both trees, peach and rosebud, are frequently seen in gardens and public grounds. The profusion of the two types of pale rose blossoms, which are hardly distinguishable from one another, on the still leafless branches offers an abundance of spring color all along Savannah's promenade streets. It is the large number and delicate color of these blossoms that help brighten up the green of the other trees, especially the oaks, which at this time of year are still somewhat yellow-green, and announce spring itself during these summery-sultry days with which we have been amply blessed this February.

Aside from the streets in the harbor area, Savannah's streets are not filled with much activity and because of their breadth would actually look rather deserted if the colored people, idling about, did not do something here to put a little life into the scene. But the wealth of trees does not allow any of these streets to have a boring look about them, and many a drab city in Germany and elsewhere could learn from Savannah how their dullness could be eliminated without a significant increase of traffic or population.

Since the city is situated on a hill that drops steeply down to the river and since ships anchor directly at the edge of the city, the view of the harbor is almost lost, for the ships, the landing places, and warehouses are in the low area on the bank of the river. In addition, the Savannah River is not very wide near the city and is further restricted by flat, reed-covered islands, so that the viewer looking over the broad, singularly busy surface of water sees no river channel, which makes so many less significant harbor towns really more attractive. Of course, the cotton shipping brings with it enough noise—cotton is the main item of this city's trade—even in the streets of the inner city, for the bales are carried in very squarely built wagons to the warehouses, and it goes without saying that the Negroes, who as masters in this instance have monopolized the whip and reins here, never neglect to produce snaps, cries, and as much clatter as possible. As long as the Negroes are on foot, they do not want to hear anything about their masters' axiom that time is money, but whenever they get behind the reins, they have to drive at least at a trot. With their carts full of cotton, they make such a clatter over the uneven pavement that a person would like to shut his ears. Without exception they stand up straight while driving, knowing how to balance themselves adroitly while wearing expressions of importance and pleasure on their faces. It is a task they enjoy—one of the few about which one can say that.

Savannah's exports more than tripled between 1860 and 1870, and their worth for 1872 was estimated at $70,000,000. In 1860 they amounted to around $18,000,000. Besides the increased production of Georgia and the neighboring cotton states, the primary reason for this upswing can be attributed to the expansion of the railroad.

CHAPTER THIRTEEN

Settlements and Spas in Florida

CLIMATE. WINTER SPAS. SETTLERS AND SETTLEMENTS. ECO-
NOMIC ROLE OF THE RURAL MERCHANTS.

Florida's greatest asset at present is its mild climate. North America has large
areas where summer and fall temperatures are higher than anywhere in southern Europe; but only in Florida are winter and spring as mild as in the regions
along the Mediterranean and elsewhere where our sick usually go to avoid the
rigors of the harsh climate. South Carolina and the other Southern states also
have winter resorts, but they still suffer from the sharp northwest winds, which
are not blocked and tempered as they are in southern Europe by high mountains
and a large inland body of water. Possibly someday little places in protected
spots here and there along the edge of the southern Alleghenies will be found,
which can serve as winter shelters for consumptives, but for the present only
Florida offers the most advantageous conditions, and for several years now it has
become so accessible by steamboat and train that in the winter and spring of
1872–1873, according to an unexaggerated estimate, more than forty thousand
visitors spent the entire winter or several winter months there. Today you can
travel in the same sleeping coach from Boston to Jacksonville in about three
days, while steamers leave several times a week from New York for Florida.
Large hotels have been built, and in the major resorts like Jacksonville and St.
Augustine, they say that you can find good doctors. In addition, the wealth of
rivers and lakes on the peninsula facilitates transportation to such a degree that
steamboats can go into even the deepest wilderness, thereby allowing settle-

12 "DESPITE THE MANY
UNSOPHISTICATED FEATURES
CONDITIONED BY THE
NEWNESS OF THESE PLACES,
[THEY] STILL MAKE AN
IMPRESSION SIMILAR TO THAT
OF THE EUROPEAN WINTER
RESORTS." A WINTER RESORT,
GREEN COVE SPRINGS,
FLORIDA.

ments, orange groves, and sugar cane plantations to flourish there. All this naturally fosters the tourist trade. Major resorts for the winter guests, like St. Augustine, Jacksonville, Palatka, and the like, despite the many unsophisticated features conditioned by the newness of these places, still make, on the whole, an impression similar to that of the European winter resorts. In each of these localities there are a few large hotels, a great many pensions called boarding houses, and souvenir shops in which beautiful stuffed birds, seashells, Indian relics, palmetto wicker items, alligator teeth made into ornaments, and many other similar objects, including some fraudulent articles, are offered for sale.* In

---

*I FOUND AT EVERY STEAMBOAT LANDING PIER, IN THE VESTIBULES OF THE HOTELS, AND ON THE STEAMSHIPS THEMSELVES, A LARGE ADVERTISEMENT PLACARD THAT SAID: "COMING TO JACKSON-VILLE? THEN GO TO THE JAPANESE SHOP AND SEE THE MERMAID." I FOLLOWED THIS INVITATION BECAUSE I THOUGHT THEY WOULD PERHAPS HAVE ON DISPLAY A SEA COW OF THE *MANATUS* VARIETY, ALSO KNOWN AS MERMAID, WHICH USED TO LIVE IN THE WATERS OFF THE FLORIDA COAST AND STILL CAN BE SEEN NOW AND THEN. BUT WHAT WAS IT? A FIGURE MADE OUT OF BLACK WAX, WHICH ENDED IN A REAL FISH TAIL AT THE BOTTOM AND TO WHICH A PAINTED MONKEY'S SKULL WITH HAIR PASTED ON IT AND A MONKEY'S TWO FOREFEET HAD BEEN AT-TACHED. I SAW ALSO OTHER THINGS LIKE THIS AND BELIEVE THAT THE WHOLE SHOP WAS FULL OF FAKE RELICS AND NATURAL CURIOSITIES.

addition, there are a large number of elegant carriages and horse and mule teams on the streets, Northern newspapers, travel guides, and poor maps to be had everywhere, and some excellent pharmacies and tobacco shops; there is a doctor living on every street corner, and one also sees strangers, sick people, and bored types, as well as sometimes the sunburned face of the sportsman made up to look rugged and courageous. One is certainly aware that several thousand rich people are here to while away their time.

From what I have read, heard, and experienced myself, it seems to be true that the climate of the northern half of Florida is the most pleasant of all North America, with the exception perhaps of southern California. It doesn't have exceptionally hot summers but does have milder winters than the other Gulf states. Because of the still almost undisturbed forestation, the high moisture content of the soil throughout the area, and its position between two bodies of water, the summer heat is mitigated, and above all the nights are said to be seldom sultry. From people who are or were ill, I heard enthusiastic statements about the salutary effect of this climate on their illness. Many of the business-men and farmers living here are afflicted with consumption, having come to Florida from the North and the West. After a stay of some length, they feel healthier than they ever thought still possible. Much of the reason for this may have to do with the absence of all city life in these remote settlements, the necessity of simple living and outdoor work. Of course, no one who makes a new home for himself here escapes the fevers,[1] which settlers on newly cleared land everywhere are subject to, but this is a temporary complaint and does not seem to affect people very much in areas of higher elevation.

Besides those who are here for health reasons, the coming and going of people to the area also bring unique types into the basically fluctuating popula-tion who then stand out twice as much from the semitropical environment of the virgin forest. There is practically always a family or group of this kind on the steamers on the St. Johns River. Sometimes they are true backwoodsmen, unruly fellows with rough manners who in time have become more comfort-able in the wilds than in human society; at times—and as it appears, very frequently—they are people whose concern for their health more than a love or ability to work the land has prompted them to make a home in this wilderness, while at other times they are foreigners coming from various countries who first want to see the country or who are traveling to the area where they have acquired some property.

Among these "movers" there are many well-to-do and educated people who give the influx of people coming to Florida a significantly different character than, for example, that of the American West or Southwest. Ever since Florida became part of the United States, thousands of people from the North and West who believed themselves to be in poor health have been drawn here, and only a very few of them have been poor. These immigrants devote themselves to the more fashionable types of agriculture, mainly the cultivation of oranges and subtropical fruits (bananas, guavas, persimmons, and the like), which can always be shipped easily to the North where they find a good market. Since growing these fruits proved to be both pleasant and profitable work, since Florida's reputation for having a wonderful climate had soon spread far and wide, and since communications with the various coastal centers and the interior had been facilitated by steamship lines from Charleston, Savannah, and New Orleans as well as by a whole flotilla of river steamboats, little by little other people, not just those seeking to regain health or to make money but also individuals who desired to live in a pleasant climate came to Florida, purchased land and slaves, and set up orange and banana groves. Often this new type of immigrant indicates nothing more than people's desire for simple, independent, country life—a desire that arises when people become aware of the contrast between the pursuit of money, and the overcivilized, unsatisfying way of life on one hand, and the large, rich, and beautiful nature of America, in many ways still untouched, on the other. It also indicates that the desire to return to nature, which poets are almost always talking about, can also be found among other people as well.

In America culture is too new, too superficial, and its negative side too much in evidence for it to be able entirely to satisfy people of lofty natures. All those things the European people derive from the riches of their culture, and especially from the history of their own country and from their intense intellectual life, have to be sought here in nature, which fortunately is found everywhere in this country. Thus you can see that when a country contains an area within its borders, which, like Florida, combines many of the advantages of the temperate zones with those that everyone finds so attractive in the tropics (a region that still retains something of the paradisical aura with which our childish imagination invested it when we first began to read picture Bible and Robinson Crusoe stories),[2] then many people will make that area their dream wish, just as in Germany many people in the north cannot think of anything better than to live in the sunny south.[3]

By chance I met many such people who were just on the point of settling in Florida. Along the way I met a German who owned a large business in the North, which he wanted to sell in order to grow oranges by Lake Harney and "to sketch and paint everything that is noteworthy in Florida," and in Jacksonville I got to know a young doctor who was thinking of moving further south in order to start a large tropical fruit farm in the neighborhood of Key West. Neither he nor his wife was in the least concerned about the lonely existence that awaited them there; instead they painted the future in the rosiest colors. On one of my outings I met a German-Russian,[4] a man of considerable education and experience, who had seen much of the world and now had finally decided to settle down together with many of his countrymen in southern Florida; he was just in the process of buying a rather large piece of land south of Lake George. There was nothing about this man that indicated any idyllic sentimentality, still less any trace of exaggerated love for America, but it seemed to him worth all the sacrifices that he had made and the still greater ones he would have to make in order to live as a free man in a beautiful, fertile region. Here and there one sees a plantation, a country house, or a cultivated area with something of the quaint elegance of an amateur's work about it; they are evidently the somewhat imperfect realization of the model the owner built years ago in the cloudy, overcast North. Near Tocoi,[5] the country home of the well-known author of *Uncle Tom's Cabin*, Mrs. Beecher-Stowe, looks exactly that way: standing under tall shade trees, very tiny, affecting country architecture—as we see in novels where a couple comes to a place like this after much suffering and waiting, finally having been united in a presumably exceptionally happy marriage.

The influx of inhabitants who devote themselves to agriculture and the ease of travel through the navigable rivers and lakes have caused a large number of little settlements to spring up in Florida, while at the same time city growth is continuing. For that reason no other region of the United States can offer as favorable an opportunity for comparative studies of the initial growth of settlements as does Florida. The single log cabin, which forms the beginning of a colony on a favorably situated spot along a river or the seacoast, is soon joined by several more dwellings, forming a row along the river where the soil is always more fertile and communication and trade facilities more accessible. Wherever there are six houses grouped together, one of them is surely a "store," a shop for everything—a tavern, a meeting place for everyone who has business to conduct or who just wants to chat, a bureau for all kinds of agencies and brokers, and an office for shipping goods, for steamboat tickets, and many other things. Such a store is so much more than one of our rural shops (*Kramläden*), just as a little American country town is much more than its German counterpart, the rural market town (*Marktflecken*). The "storekeeper" not only carries the usual provisions for his neighbors, the farmers, but here one finds everything these new communities require in the way of necessities and luxury items. Agricultural tools and machines, ready-made clothing, all sorts of spare parts for wagons, every kind of horse harness, weapons, jewelry, newspapers, books, liquor, and medicines are all to be had here. Moreover, the storekeeper is the purchaser of their products, which he either takes in exchange for his wares or for money, in the latter case mostly acting as agent for a wholesale company. In quite a few instances he really is, so to speak, the catalyst, the flywheel of these new settlements. To the degree that he introduces people to and supplies them with the necessities of civilized society and stimulates work and turns it to a profit, he protects these settlements from returning to a wild and stagnant situation. He keeps things steadily in motion and forms the indispensable and beneficial link between the most remote backwoods cabin and large and small centers of civilization in this immense, sparsely populated region. This unique institution, the rural general store, can be found throughout the entire Union. I remember that F. Römer's description of those in Texas is similar to what I saw here in Florida and later in California.* The role they play in the economic and social history of the settlement of North America is therefore especially significant, because by their versatility they have almost completely shut out industry, which at this stage would normally appear as handicraft work, and have made trade the second most important factor after agriculture in settling the area. Like the farmers, the basic pioneers of civilization, the storekeepers are the pioneers of trade, whose rapid and expanding development is the basis for that wonderfully quick and entirely healthy growth of larger commercial and industrial centers in the newly populated areas. In the formation of large cities and in the spread of urban life throughout the land, no element within the North American population has played a greater role than the storekeepers.

The growing value of real estate along the rivers and seacoasts is causing the latest arrivals to settle further inland, and it isn't long before that land strip where the first few log cabins stood becomes the business section of the new town, which as a rule consists of a street parallel to the waterfront and one perpendicular to it running inland. In a short time, wherever there is a nearby knoll, a church will be erected; numerous scattered Negro cottages, carelessly built and almost tropically thin in construction, will be put up around the farmhouses; a boarding house for the winter guests, who never fail to appear in any settlement, will be added; and after eight to ten years, when the little orange trees have grown to become smart-looking groves, a Floridian town is then complete. Of course, when steamboats begin to stop here, a new component is incorporated into the powerful, active organism of this country's vast economic life, which in turn continues the civilizing process.

*IN HIS BOOK *TEXAS* (BONN, 1849), AFTER A THOROUGH DESCRIPTION OF THE STORE IN THE TOWN OF NEW BRAUNFELS, WHICH AT THAT TIME WAS JUST BEGINNING TO GROW, HE HAD THIS TO SAY ABOUT STORES IN GENERAL: "THESE STORES ARE REALLY TYPICAL OF AMERICAN SETTLEMENTS, WHICH ALONG WITH THE GENERAL ADVANCE OF CIVILIZATION AND PARTLY BECAUSE OF THE NEEDS OF A MORE REFINED LIFE STYLE, ADVANCE INTO THE WILDERNESS, TAKING IT, SO TO SPEAK, BY SURPRISE AND BY STORM. AT THE SAME TIME, THESE STORES OFTEN DISPLAY A MIXTURE OF REMARKABLE CONTRASTS BETWEEN RAW PRIMITIVENESS AND THE TRACES OF A THOUSAND-YEAR-OLD-CULTURE, WHICH EUROPEANS ARE SURPRISED TO FIND IN THE FORESTS OF WESTERN AMERICA." (PAGE 122.) [ED. NOTE: NEW BRAUNFELS, FOUNDED IN 1845 BY THE QUIXOTIC PRINCE CARL ZU SOLMS-BRAUNFELS, WAS OVERWHELMINGLY A GERMAN TOWN THAT RETAINED A GERMAN ATMOSPHERE IN LANGUAGE AND CUSTOMS ON INTO THE TWENTIETH CENTURY.]

CHAPTER FOURTEEN

Through Georgia and Alabama

SPARSELY POPULATED AREA. A RAILROAD JUNCTION. OVERLAY-
ING. SOUTHERN RAILROADS. MACON IN THE RAIN. MONTGOMERY.
A WORKERS' BOARDING HOUSE. SOME OBSERVATIONS ABOUT SO-
CIAL CONDITIONS. ALABAMA RIVER. DOWNSTREAM TO MOBILE.

From Jacksonville, the commercial capital of Florida, which lies at the mouth
of the St. Johns River, there start two railroad lines, one running westward and
one northwest. The western one runs to the little port town of Cedar Key,
where once a week the steamers of the New Orleans-Havana line stop, while
the northwestern one forms the connecting link between central Florida's commercial artery, the St. Johns River, and the great rail lines that run from the
North and East to the metropolis of the South, New Orleans. At first it had been
my intention to travel west from Jacksonville to the county seat of Gainesville
and from there on to Cedar Key and New Orleans. When I heard, however, that
I could not travel directly to Gainesville, which is only about eighteen hours
away, but would have to stay the night in a whistle-stop town in order to catch
another train, that furthermore I couldn't go to Cedar Key from Gainesville
any day I desired if I did not want to take what in this country is the rather

13   ON THE RAILROAD THROUGH FLORIDA AND GEORGIA.

usual but uncertain expedient of going by freight train, and finally that the connections are even more uncertain via the Havana steamers, which stay out at sea in stormy weather or when there are too few passengers, I decided to take the northern route to the Macon-Brunswick Railroad and over this line westwards to Alabama. The train left Jacksonville Saturday afternoon, and since it averaged about 2 geographical (about 9.25 statute) miles per hour, it arrived the next morning at the Godforsaken junction of Jesup, where we got the unhappy news that since it was Sunday no train was running on our line and we would therefore have to wait until Monday morning. Jesup lies between Savannah and Brunswick in the midst of a pine forest and consists of some twenty wooden houses scattered about, a little wooden church, and an unattractive-looking courthouse, whose only distinction is being the junction of the Savannah-Florida and Macon lines, whose trains stop here for a while so that the travelers can get a scanty supper. The day was exceptionally rainy and windy so that we couldn't take a side trip into the nearby woods to make our involuntary stop here more interesting, and this small inconvenience had to be accepted just as it was.

But as soon as I had taken care of my luggage and entered the bare dining room of the Rail Road Eating House, I found that I was not as isolated as I had believed. Who should be sitting before the fire, smoking, surrounded by smoke like the pine boughs in the fireplace, but my fellow countryman S., the sawmill manager from Jacksonville. He looked rather depressed, out of sorts, and drowsy, but the moment he saw me his weather-beaten countenance lit up. We greeted each other as happily as if a shipwreck we both had experienced had cast us up here on a desert island where we were going to live for years like Robinson Crusoe and Friday. Jack, the black waiter, made some coffee, and instead of sleeping away the couple of hours until morning, to the annoyance of some people sitting around in the corners who wanted to sleep, we merrily chattered away into the early hours and went into the common area behind a wooden partition, which had been designated as the sleeping quarters, only when it had become light. As S., who knows this area, was complaining about these poor lodgings, we learned that two families had also been shipwrecked in this place before us on that evening and also been forced to "overlay the Sunday."

An elderly gentleman appeared at breakfast with a very sickly looking wife and daughter who were traveling to Florida for health reasons, and after we had already gotten up, a young corpse-like man appeared leaning on the arm of a very healthy and enterprising-looking woman who was scarcely more than a girl. She later brought in their lovely, cheerful baby whose joyful young life seemed to be of more concern to her than the hopelessly disintegrating one of her husband. The excusable cruelty of nature seemed to dominate their thoughts. These two people were coming from Florida, where the poor man had not found improvement, and was therefore hurriedly returning home to the circle of his family to await a demise that was clearly not far off. Among this company, who talked of their pains, expectations, and disappointments, we healthy people had little to say and therefore stayed out of the group. In addition, there were some local shopkeepers, railroad and telegraph officials having their special Sunday breakfast treat, commonplace American business-men who were occupied in that awful "conversation in English about money matters," which Lenau heard in a similar place,[1] and finally there were three ladies in their Sunday best who together ran this modest hotel. One was the wife of a railroad conductor, another the wife of a telegraph operator, and the third a housekeeper; the first two were enjoying the attentions of two young men of Jesup, while the latter was primly reserved, for she was an ugly-looking scarecrow and also devout.

The Americans were lucky; today they had to go to church. Perhaps here in this place in the woods this was more pleasant than anywhere else where they would have been able to fulfill this requirement of respectability. The ladies came carrying arms full of both song books and prayer books, and at ten o'clock they went to sit for a full two hours in the tiny little wooden building. The old gentleman confidentially told us afterwards that he had been terribly bored, asking aloud whether we had experienced anything of the Sunday laws here. I could truthfully answer that the barkeeper had told the waiter he could not even serve a little mug of ale without a doctor's prescription. Nevertheless, they faithfully went to church again in the afternoon and then whiled away the remaining time, with the housewives taking turns at abusing the public piano and with the men gloomily sulking around trying to start a wearying conversation about the weather or about business.

For the two of us, even without going to church, the day was not bad; we had enough to talk about, went to see an unbelievably bad section of track about whose rundown condition even their own officials made jokes, wan-dered around the entire settlement, saw a lot of beautiful trees, and met a few people with whom one could exchange a sensible word. There was a waiter as black as coal, who during the period of slavery had been the servant of a man in South Carolina who came from Bielefeld and who had traveled about a great deal in the United States. He could still speak a little German. In his conduct, with all its natural good-naturedness, he showed a certain dignity, which caused people to treat him with somewhat more respect than was usually extended to the Negroes. This natural dignity, a quiet, straightfor-ward, open personality—the unmistakable sign of sterling character—is al-most always lacking in the Negroes even if they are splendidly endowed in other ways. I have seen it in none of their leading politicians. This fellow was also a very intelligent man who with an astonishing clarity, perceived the sad, almost hopeless conditions under which his race existed here in North America. In the evening he went to preach at the Methodist chapel for blacks. In addition, there were also lumbermen in Jesup who came out of the woods on Sundays, who looked worn out and generally yellow as if plagued by fever, but who like all men in such work appeared to be frank and bold.

The Sunday repose was a real trial for these men. They barely spoke, slept a lot, and now and then made trips to the bar in vain, as the barkeeper could in no way be diverted from his adherence to the temperance laws.

The day, having been spent in smoking, sleeping, and waiting for time to pass, was over, and before five the next morning my long-awaited train came struggling along. Before we most cordially took leave of one another, S., who still had to wait the whole day until late evening for deliverance, filled all my pockets from his inexhaustible supply of Havana cigars and, on the basis of his knowledge of the area, gave me many recommendations and good advice about hotels. This did not take place without exchanging the often given and seldom kept promise to keep each other informed of the more important happenings and events and certainly to get together again upon our return to Germany.

The train rumbled along towards Macon. Why it rattled, groaned, lurched, and even swayed quite a bit now and then was no longer a puzzle to me, because yesterday we had walked along the tracks and learned something about the condition of the rails. They are made of so soft an iron that the pressure and traction of the weight that moves along on them peel off large pieces of iron, and in many cases only a thin, rough strip is left, which you would really have difficulty in recognizing as a railroad track if it were not found there, placed with all the others to form one line. Since there is little traffic on these lines as yet and they are more a matter for future speculation, for the present the owners do only what is absolutely necessary to maintain their upkeep, and although for safety's sake these trains travel as slowly as the freight trains do in Germany, accidents are so frequent that people talk about them as much as they do about any other matters dealing with rail traffic. My traveling companion jokingly asked a telegraph operator in Jesup: "What happened? No train has had an accident for over four weeks." Whereupon the latter answered: "You're misinformed; just the day before yesterday they overturned the sleeping car on the night train, and with regard to some other little matters you only have to ask the station master, who knows a little more."

Our route went through the state of Georgia, to be exact, actually through the middle of it. It was the same old low, rolling pine lands in which, like the few flowers embroidered on a piece of dull homespun cloth, the luxuriant growth and colorful splendor of the evergreen and blossoming vegetation lay scattered about here and there in the moist lowland. The settlements were widely separated, still very new and underdeveloped.* Logging and the lumber

---

*THE SIGNS ONE READS HERE AND THERE ON THE LOG CABINS IN THE SETTLEMENTS ARE NOT QUITE AS PLEASANT AS THOSE ONE FINDS IN OUR COUNTRY IN BACKWARD AREAS, PRIMARILY IN THE MOUNTAINS. "NO CREDIT" IS SEEN FREQUENTLY, AND AT THE STATION IN COCHRAN, ONE'S EYES WERE ATTRACTED BY THE REMINDER: "COME UP AND PAY YOUR DEBTS." THE OTHER INSCRIPTIONS DEAL WITH SECRET REMEDIES, ADVICE INTO WHERE ONE CAN BUY INEXPENSIVE

trade appear to be the main industries for the population, while agriculture seems to be just beginning to thrive. Many times we passed big steam saws— the only vigorous sign of life. However, all this was seen in a state of partial flooding and through a veil of rain, both conditions giving the landscape a much more desolate, rugged, uncultivated look then would normally be the case.

In Macon, Georgia, we were only supposed to have a short stopover, but the conductor let us get out for a time and announced that it did not look safe on the western and southern routes, since a large part of the area was said to be flooded, the Mississippi and Alabama rivers having overflowed their banks. In any case, we would not arrive in Montgomery on schedule, much less so in Mobile, because they were awaiting news about what was happening, and we would have to travel with the greatest caution. And so we went into the city. I won't go into details about how Macon looked in the rain. What I saw consisted of enormously broad, unpaved streets whose plankboard walks on the sides were full of holes, of waterfalls that came from the roofs and rivers that came out of the side streets, of totally empty streets, of many cabins and few real houses, of damp, cold air and a gray haze of rain and fog. I got the impression that these disproportionately built fragmentary cities of the South, for the most part dirty and poor, need a great deal of sunshine to make them look at all pleasant. Moreover, this impression also applies to many middle-sized and small cities all over America. They are too full of poorly built, defective houses and poorly kept streets, too insignificant to count as cities, possessing too much the character of large villages, which really need the aid of the light and color of a clear sky if they are going to make any kind of favorable impression.

Since the tiny waiting room was reserved only for ladies and those accompanying them and since they filled it completely, I spent the night in the station's public area. The train finally arrived, and we now saw that the delay had an advantage, for the boredom of waiting and the stop in the damp, cold weather had made us very receptive to the pleasures of a slow night trip. Whoever climbed aboard went right to sleep, and in as much as the mood against anyone disturbing the peace this time' was quite strong, soon dead silence reigned,

CLOTHES AND FOOTWEAR AND THE LIKE IN MACON, AND ON ONE HOUSE IN ONE OF THE POOREST SETTLEMENTS, "TIMES OFFICE" COULD BE READ AS EVIDENCE THAT EVEN IN THIS STILL VERY SPARSELY POPULATED AREA THEY HAVE A LOCAL NEWSPAPER. I WAS NOT ABLE TO GET A COPY, BUT A FELLOW TRAVELER WHO KNOWS THE AREA AND WHOM I ASKED ABOUT THE PAPER CONSOLED ME WITH THE COMMENT: "DON'T BOTHER LOOKING AT IT; IT IS A VERY STUPID, REPUBLICAN NIGGER PAPER." APPARENTLY THIS FELLOW BELIEVED THAT ONE MUST ASSUME EVERY RESPECTABLE HUMAN BEING NATURALLY BELONGS TO THE DEMOCRATIC PARTY. INDEED, THAT'S THE WAY IT USED TO BE IN THIS PART OF THE COUNTRY.

broken only by the nonprohibited snoring of a huge man who had curled up into an unbelievably small shape in his seat. When day broke we were still far from Montgomery, where the train was due at eight o'clock. I went out to catch a little fresh air and found the big man washing himself with the water coming off the eaves of a car; as I next did the same, we got into a lively discussion, and in two hours I had heard a pile of very original stories and gotten to know an interesting man. The easygoing inclination to talk, so typical of Americans, is a major factor in making traveling in America so attractive. This open talkativeness usually reveals a wealth of experiences and helps one to make many acquaintances.

A few stations before Montgomery an agent of the express company came into the car and asked each one about luggage that would have to be sent to an inn, boarding house, or the like. He wrote the destination on his blackboard, gave the person a coupon or a token and for a very small remuneration undertook the responsibility for the belongings. He also came to me, and I told him I would be traveling immediately on to Mobile and thus would not require his services. Whereupon he answered: "The line to Mobile is broken in twenty-two places and needs at least a week to repair." This was too much to be a hoax, and I could not doubt it. Nevertheless, I glibly said: "This is really unfortunate but there are other routes and if not I'll take the detour via Selma." "It wouldn't do you any good. The Vicksburg Railroad wouldn't let any trains go for four or five days because their bridges and trestles over the swampy areas have already begun to collapse. You can just be glad that you are here, since soon it will also be happening on the track running this way from Macon if this rain keeps up." "So we're cut off?" "Not entirely sir, the north-south road is said to be still in good condition but this, however, doesn't go your way if you're heading to Mobile. So shall I have your things brought to the hotel?" "Take the devil there but not my luggage. I'm not going to sit here in Montgomery in this dull, little town." "As you wish, but you wouldn't get further south or west even by horse. Try it and see." With that the man took leave and "overlay, sir" rang in my ear again just like it did three days ago in Jesup.

Overlay for the third time on just one single trip! Every day, in fact, for the last few weeks I have been careful about wasting time: I forcibly tore myself away from very interesting pursuits in Florida, which had barely begun, and because of this rush to conserve time I left Washington and many a pleasant day in the company of friends quickly made but all too quickly relinquished again. And now one day after the other passes by, scarcely of use either for relaxation or work but full of the aggravation and trouble that go with a lonely trip! I did a lot of swearing during these few minutes. When I was certain that I had to stay in Montgomery, I got rid of this unprofitable fit of anger and cheered myself up with the best consolation in an adverse situation—with making plans. I devised plans on how I would now pass and make use of this time. It didn't take long before I had decided immediately to take a room for a week in a boarding house, and soon after that decision was made, I was sitting at the well-furnished breakfast table of the Exchange Hotel in Montgomery. Now I laughed when I heard others complaining about the situation; I merrily went out into the rain and did not return until I had found a room and discussed and settled board and everything else down to the dollar and cents. Then I picked up my bags, moved over to the boarding house and stopped worrying about the railroad. In the evening, when I heard that steamboats would be coming up the river to make the connection with Mobile and the West, that no longer concerned me.

So here I was sitting in Montgomery, the capital of Alabama, and soon found once more that in a calm frame of mind you can find something to enjoy in every place. I quickly got acquainted with the group of people with whom I was boarding,* and found, even if the city remained cheerless, during daily outings that there were many attractive things in the nearby area to give me sufficient material to last me for weeks of work in diary entries and written sketches, and far too many worthwhile things remained unseen when I left the place eight days later.

The boarding-house society alone made the stay pleasant, for here I found elements the traveler doesn't easily come into contact with on the standard itinerary but which you have to get to know before beginning to form an opinion about the nature and character of a people. The family who ran the boarding house was that of a smith who held some kind of foreman's position in a railroad workshop, and the boarders were old and young workers of similar or lower position. The owner of the establishment could be called well-off, since he owned the spacious house and the adjacent garden, which unfortunately was only used as a cabbage field. On Sunday the others, his fellow lodgers, were at least outwardly very "gentleman like" when they put aside their work clothes, and at all times a notable sense of propriety prevailed amongst the group. Only one Irishman, an iron founder by trade, played the boor but was so dense and had such a comically thoughtless way of speaking that no one could get angry with him.

The ladies of the group attracted my attention. The smith's wife appeared to be barely thirty-five, although she was the mother of seven children, the oldest of whom was a sixteen-year-old daughter. She possessed a wholesome beauty, the likes of which one seldom finds here, and had such a cheerful disposition and such a bright mind that in discussion, domestic affairs, social events—in everything she was the dominant figure, which she by no means appeared to be striving for. She took great interest in all things that lay outside her everyday concerns without being any less able or industrious in her usual duties—in all,

*THAT IS THE WAY THE GERMAN-AMERICANS USE THIS CONVENIENT WORD. [ED. NOTE: THE ENGLISH INFINITIVE "TO BOARD" WAS ADOPTED AND TRANSFORMED INTO THE GERMAN VERB *BOARDEN*.]

a very delightful, well-balanced, happy individual. Her mother and half sister lived in the same house; the former was no less lively than her older daughter but was more retiring and inclined to domestic concerns; the latter, on the other hand, was the commonplace American woman—superficial, coquettish, physically poorly endowed from her doll-face down, and despite the fact that she was only twenty-one years old, so covered with makeup that you did not want to look at her—appearance was supposed to be everything but there was nothing behind it.

In their general character traits the smith's wife and her half sister were not unfamiliar types for me; many times I have had the good fortune to enjoy observing people similar in personality to the smith's wife at close contact and more often still from afar. One runs across the half sister's type by the dozen every day, and since women of this sort exactly resemble each other in their unattractive shapes, their impoverished affected intellect, their extravagant tasteless dress, and their demeanor, which is anything but natural or simple, one can quickly spot them from a distance.

It was interesting here for me to compare and distinguish and to recall earlier observations. These seemingly basically different natures have something in common: the vigorous striving after something better than the simple fulfillment of maternal and domestic duties allotted to them. The minority of women seek to go beyond these limitations by commendable work in the self-education of mind and spirit, while the overwhelming majority of women discard as many of the natural duties as possible and try to fill the gap with supposedly impressive but worthless things. The former are those whose excellent character alone justifies the American woman's privileged position—which is so intolerably misused by these others—and to whose significant influence on the family and society so many oasis-like phenomena in the desert of American life can be traced. They are not as rare as similar women are in Germany; most particularly they display their abilities more energetically and with more apparent skill and know better how to get what they are striving for. It would be going too far to want to go into the obscure depths of the women question here, even very superficially, but I only want to add the comment that, almost without exception, women here stand far above men in everything that one usually calls education or culture. An American man with a mind for learning that cannot be used to earn money—for literature or for any form of art—is a rare bird; usually he does not know enough how to develop and encourage this taste, and in the few cases where someone had the interest and time for them in his youth, all that was learned has remained rather incidental, gathering dust—withered and forgotten in the rush to make profits.

I was traveling with a man who one day recited "Des Sängers Fluch" ("The Curse of the Minstrel"), the next day "Odi profanum,"[2] and for a change the beginning verses of the *Odyssey* or something from Shakespeare, but I never thought he was educated; the beautiful lines were memorized and nothing more. With the women here the exact opposite is true. There is the necessity for them to be educated, and since it is customary here for women in all except the very lowest positions to have a great deal more leisure time than ours do, they really can learn a great deal if they bring the proper seriousness and interest to their studies and if they have enough good schools. Nevertheless, a person who desires to learn can do so, and many women use the opportunity to the best advantage. The general result is that the women know about more things that foster intellectual tastes and noble sentiments; these extend their field of vision, and therefore entitle them to speak up in good society and to converse on many subjects men know nothing about. It is easy to imagine then how this abnormal situation makes women dissatisfied in marriage and leads to an exaggerated opinion of one's self and causes them to misjudge their true position in life.

This incongruity is most evident in our house due to the strong personality of the wife, but it doesn't seem to be a disturbing element here because she is one of the few who, although off in higher intellectual regions, has not forgotten how to keep her feet on common ground. With youthful enthusiasm, she reads in the evenings after cooking during the day for her nine boarders and eleven family members. In only one place do these two aspects of her life conflict. The oldest son, a youngster of fifteen, works with the father and the oldest daughter helps her with the housework. That she is not able to educate these two better was very painful to her. She had heard a great deal about German schools and could think of nothing she would like to hear more than when I gave her further information about them and about the universities. How much she would have liked to give her children such an education! "Nothing goes the way I want," she said, "how sad to see this youngster who wants to learn so much that would open further possibilities for him standing at the anvil during the most advantageous years for learning." Her mother thereupon answered, "Be quiet, that is destiny"—the word surprised me, but she understood what it meant. She also wanted to hear about our confessional disputes,[3] but as I explained what they were all about she changed the subject. The mother then told me that a few years ago her daughter had converted to Catholicism out of sincere conviction.[4] These conversions, which were formerly very rare, have been frequent in the last decades, and as far as I can see are very often to be traced to the dissatisfaction of women with their fate. As everyone knows, one convent after the other is being filled up.

Thus we quietly spent eight days living together, and during this time I not only got to know these people but also a bit of the South in a way that until then I had not seen. Montgomery lies in the midst of a rolling countryside whose soil consists of a rather sand-and-gravel-free loam to a great depth. It is one of the most fertile areas in all Alabama, prime cotton land, and its value is considerably increased by the proximity of the Alabama River, which is still navigable twenty geographical (ninety-two statute) miles further upstream. And although the so-called prairies, much of them a marshy plain extending between the Alabama and the Appalachicola rivers, begin very near here, the

environs of these last foothills are still very picturesque, filled with steep ravines, little waterfalls, narrow passes, and abysses. It is covered by the most
beautiful forests that I have seen anywhere in the South. The clay soil gives the
area its varied sharp features, for through its two main qualities, softness and
tenacity, it promotes the formation of very tortuous beds even for the smallest
rivulets, and since this territory abounds in rivers and lakes, there is always
running water to be seen. Coming out of the land of still water, out of swampy
Florida, one again enjoys hearing the murmuring and rushing of quickly flowing brooks all around, and one notices twice as much what a cheerful, lively
touch this adds to any area, whether rich or poor, rugged or gentle.

The fertility of this clay soil is, as mentioned, very great; my landlord, who
formerly owned a farm in this district, had often produced over five hundred
pounds of cotton per acre, and yields of this size, if not the rule, were also no
rarity. With the emancipation of the slaves a general decline has also set in
here, and the best land is ten and twenty times less valuable than before. In
addition, frequent floodings, vermin, and low cotton prices have hurt, and "we
are having bad luck here in the South" is a current saying. But probably people
now feel every change and adversity more keenly because the main misfortune,
the disappearance of their old comfortable life style, has made them despon-
dent. I had an example of the typical indolence when I once asked why eggs
were so much more expensive here than in Florida, which is full of tourists.
"We have to import them from Tennessee," it was then explained. "What," I
asked, "such a rich and yet sparsely populated area imports eggs? You must
certainly be able to keep hundreds of chickens on your forty acres alone." The
answer was: "If it weren't for the Negroes—who steal every egg as soon as it is
laid."

Before the railroads opened up the interior of Alabama in the direction of
Mobile and New Orleans, there had been a lively steamboat traffic on the
Alabama River (near the estuary it is called the Mobile River), which did a
wonderful job carrying the area's enormous cotton crop down to the sea. Large
steamers went 100 geographical (461 statute) miles upstream from Mobile to
Wetumpka and used to stop in this area at more than two hundred places, that
is, at all the important plantations in the district. Now there is only one regular
steamship connection between Selma, lying to the southeast of Montgomery,
and Mobile. Since the break in service on the Montgomery-Mobile Railroad,
however, the steamers have been coming up the river more frequently again in
order to transport out of isolated Montgomery the goods and travelers who now
are unable to use any other means of travel south or west. The good people of
Montgomery were very happy when they saw the tall smokestacks of the steamboats towering over the levees again; the newspapers described every arriving
boat in the most rhetorical fashion, as is their way, and never tired of recalling
the wonderful times when often a dozen steamers lay at anchor before the now
nearly dilapidated warehouses and when barely enough ships could be brought
up to pick up the surplus of the "South's gold." Half the Negro population and

many curious whites besieged the wharf all day long in order to greet the old familiar boats and also to watch now and then the efforts of black teenagers who were riding around in skiffs on the broad swollen river trying to fish out driftwood.

On Sunday night the old boat *Peerless* came, and I entrusted myself to its decrepit hulk, although my acquaintances tried to persuade me to wait for more favorable circumstances. True, this steamer did not look exactly charming and the company did not appear to be the best, but for two days—that is how long the trip was supposed to last—both were good enough. I didn't scruple about making myself comfortable and once more soon noticed how powerful the process of getting accustomed to something really is. It is the standard of measurement for our comfort, through which all kinds of changes become easily accessible. When I grew tired and went to my cabin, I found my coarse bed first-rate, and it scarcely bothered me that the rain soaked through the blanket on my feet and that I had to fill out the covering for my narrow bed with a few newspapers.

Our ship was constructed in the manner peculiar to Mississippi steamers on rivers in this area: long, narrow, riding very low, a paddle wheel at the rear, two smokestacks next to one another, which are much higher than the ship and are slit and bend outwards at the top like an Indian feather headdress. Above the open lower deck, which houses the engine, the firewood, and the freight—predominantly cotton bales—the space for passengers rises on pillars consisting of a long room framed on all sides by a row of cabins, kitchens, a bar, and the like. The women gather in the rear part of the room, which can be partitioned; the men in the forward part where the stove, the bar, and the army of spitoons are located; and at the tables positioned between these two poles the educated, the self-complacent, the asocial, et cetera, read, bore themselves, grumble, or sleep, but are dislodged when the company has become a little heated by numerous card players. As a special attraction on our boat there is a very cheery pair of mockingbirds, which sit in their cage on the back table and sing untiringly. It gives the curious the opportunity, under the honorable pretext of a desire to learn and of a sense for music, to venture up very close to the ladies without offending propriety. Smoking is supposedly prohibited in the entire cabin, but this depends upon the wishes of the ladies. An open gallery runs around this cabin, extending into a very narrow space in the forward part of the ship, where in good weather the passengers can stand if it is not too obstructed with trunks and crates. Over the cabin there is a second smaller deck with the wheelhouse, the captain's room, and sleeping quarters for travelers. All the furnishings as well as the food, which unfortunately is included in the ticket price, are less than plain and rather should be called

14   TWO MODES OF TRANSPORTATION IN ALABAMA.

crude. Since the service is operated only by colored people, much is left to be desired in the way of cleanliness. Besides all this, the rain seeps into the sleeping quarters, the entire ship shakes and groans at every thrust of the engine, and now and then at a clumsy docking it rides in between the trees and underbrush, so that it crashes and clanks something terrible and everything screeches. In any case, in America they must be used to this, since they don't seem to want to improve it. Considering the generally primitive state of things here in the South, it would probably never occur to anyone to find fault with these conditions. In fact, just as it did with me at first, it would sooner evoke a feeling of recognition that at least they have been able to do as much as they have if it were not for this self-complacency of the Americans, which so often invites criticism. One comes across this self-complacency more frequently and in more unpleasant ways than in the North.

The scenery along the river while we steamed down the Alabama was on the whole the same as everywhere along the big rivers of the South: predominantly dense forest running down to the water's edge, few clearings, scattered log cabins, and now and then a larger wooden dwelling or warehouse. The water was loam-yellow. For a long stretch, a steep incline, at one point two hundred feet high, dropped right down to the water on both sides, then first on one and then on the other and again on both sides gradually descended to level ground. It consisted of a dark clay, which was full of cretaceous fossils that the people here called "soapstone."

Since the river was over its banks in all low-lying places, the area had a much wilder appearance than it would under normal circumstances. Many fields stood under water, and numerous log cabins still barely held out on tiny islands, the water having already reached some of them, which were now abandoned. From such an island our boat picked up some pitiful looking cattle and pigs, which had lived for several days cut off from all food on this confined spot. Many times it was impossible to land; they then brought the cargo and occasionally travelers aboard in small rowboats. At night by glaring torchlight this afforded the opportunity for some graphic scenes. I shall not forget the picture one night when a broad skiff full of Negroes stopped under the trees, which stood under water up to the branches: the ominous mixture of the rushing water in the bushes, the undulating movement of the smaller trees in the flood waters and of the calmer, broad shadows of the big sycamores and oaks, the torchlight in the dark branches and on the broad expanse of agitated water, the throwing out of the cable, the colliding and bouncing off, the sounds of cracking and the vocal confusion of people shouting.

Most of the trees on the shore stood deep in water, and many struggled in face of the tumultuous flood waters that whirled around them, their branches mimicking the despair of drowning persons; some were uprooted, others twisted all together. Since almost everywhere the trunks stood immersed, the particular characteristics of the branches, which gave the specific shape and color to the treetops, were more pronounced than in a normal situation. Most abundant and most impressive was the sycamore, the American plane tree, with its white, slightly gray flecked, broad outstretched boughs that together with the branches sketch some bold lines in the midst of its light, gray-green foliage.

Under these unusual circumstances, instead of forty hours, we needed two and a half days to reach Mobile, since we tarried at several places much longer than we should have. Arriving early in the morning, we had a good walk around the streets of the cotton city and then at once took the next train to New Orleans, which carried us through swamps abundant with flowers, through cypress forests and palm groves, past white dunes, and over inlets, and which in six hours—the first uninterrupted trip in six days of travel—finally brought us to the metropolis of the South.

CHAPTER FIFTEEN

New Orleans

ADVANTAGES OF THE SITE. PRESENT STATE OF COMMERCE.
MOUTH OF THE MISSISSIPPI. LEVEE CONSTRUCTION.

New Orleans, the major Southern commercial city of the United States and capital of the former French colony of Louisiana, lies on the left bank of the Mississippi about twenty geographical (ninety-two statute) miles above the estuary between 29° and 30° latitude. Since all the area in this region is already part of the delta formation, a flat swamp, and since the banks of the Mississippi only rise a few feet above the average water level, New Orleans is just as poorly located as a city, or more precisely as a dwelling place, as it is excellently located as a commercial site. This last-mentioned advantage has made up for all disadvantages. Only in the first years after the founding of the city (1718) was it abandoned because of flooding. Soon settled again, it has continually grown despite floods and sickness and is already one of the most important commercial cities of the world. By all appearances the city still has a growth ahead of it, which few others can match.

The advantages of its location are very apparent. Thanks to the Mississippi and its tributaries, it possesses waterways that reach up to the Great Lakes region and by way of the Ohio even into the Pennsylvania coal district, while one of the most fertile regions in the world, the West Indian islands and Central America, lies only a few days' journey away from its doors. Thus it is situated in the middle of two large and rich areas. On the one hand lies the interior of North America, rich in grain, wood, coal, and metals, on the other the West Indian and Central American countries with their never-ceasing harvests of tropical and subtropical produce; and in the city's immediate vicinity is one of the most important cotton growing regions as well as large tracts with high-yielding rice and sugar cane crops. It seems as if trade between such rich areas would make it necessary to found a large commercial city in between them, just about on the site of New Orleans, a city that, because of the exportation of all the produce coming into it from all sides, especially from the distant hinterlands, would have to be awarded one of the leading roles in world trade.

In part, this seems to be true. But a great deal of what was prophesied for New Orleans has not occurred, especially at the time when steamship traffic on the Mississippi and its tributaries began to increase so incredibly. In addition to New York, with which for quite some time now it has ceased to compete, it has also fallen behind St. Louis, Cincinnati, and Chicago in the interior. It is recovering so slowly from the effects of the Civil War, which hit it harder than any other city in the South, that it gives the impression of lacking a certain vigor and supply of energy, something unusual in North America. The interior of the United States has been opened up to the Atlantic Coast by railroads and canals to a much greater extent than one previously had foreseen. This applies especially to the most fertile and most densely populated states, while the area of the Missouri and that west of the Mississippi, which geographically are generally drawn towards New Orleans, have by no means developed socially and culturally as rapidly as, say, Indiana and Illinois. Naturally, this does not fail to have its effect on their predestined commercial capital. In short, so many of the states in the Mississippi basin that were once slave states, primarily Louisiana, are without exception ruined, impoverished, and because of political disorders and dishonest government are hindered in the development of their resources; this is all the more so since momentary disasters, like bad harvests, floods, clogging of the Mississippi estuary, appear to have conspired during the last few years to check the prosperity of this region and its main city. If one again looks over the natural advantages of the metropolis and its earlier very rapid growth in prosperity, then one would say that all these recent difficulties can only be a delay in the course of its development, since it is basically dependent on the progress of civilization in the middle and southern sections of North America, which, despite all individual deviations, is on the whole making definite progress.

With regard to the present state of commerce in New Orleans, the account in the *New Orleans Price Current*,[1] which is the only somewhat official publication of its kind, gives the following data for the business year ending September 1, 1873, to which I am appending some information drawn from various reliable sources.

As is well known, for years the staple commodity of New Orleans' trade has been cotton. This year 1,407,821 bales have been brought to the harbor; in 1868 the supply of bales had only come to 668,695, but in 1871 it mounted to 1,548,136 and in 1872 to 1,070,239. The latter fluctuations can be accounted for by the difference in the harvest from year to year. On the whole, the cotton trade has expanded significantly. The second most important article is sugar, which is the most important agricultural product in the state of Louisiana. In spite of good years since the war, the sugar crop has never risen to the level reached in the last antebellum years. At that time it varied between 200,000 and 300,000 hogshead (barrels containing 1,000 to 1,200 pounds) and in 1861 amounted to no less than 459,410. Since then, however, the best harvest was in 1870 with 144,881 and that of last year came to little more than 100,000 hogshead. For 1870, production of molasses resulted in over ten million gallons but for 1873 in only 8,898,064 gallons. Both these products go mainly to the northern and western United States, amounting in 1872 to 81,015 hogshead of sugar and 153,023 barrels of molasses. Rice is also a very important product of Louisiana's agriculture, and its cultivation was promoted especially during the last war because of the difficulties of supply from abroad. The largest crop ever harvested here was in 1870 and amounted to 100,748 barrels; that of 1873 produced 52,206 barrels (of 250 pounds each). In some places the rice crop is yielding more than that of sugar, and because of the great deal of swampy ground lying completely fallow around here, a steady increase in its production can be foreseen. The yield on one acre used for rice cultivation is five to eight barrels of white rice with a value of $7.00 to $9.00. Tobacco in significant qualities is also brought to New Orleans from various parts of the Mississippi basin and then for the most part is shipped to Europe.*

Today the supply coming into the city and the quantity then being shipped from there are by no means as great as they were fifty years ago, since this trade has been seriously hurt, almost destroyed, by the war and is only slowly making a recovery. In 1873, tobacco coming in amounted to 30,191 barrels, that going out amounted to 19,984 barrels; taken together they do not even reach a third of the total in 1860, the last year before the war. In 1873, produce from the West amounting to 1,046,124 barrels of flour, 6,097,522 bushels of corn, and 2,450,027 pounds of bacon came in, and of these products not more than approximately 20,000 barrels of flour, somewhat more than 800,000 bushels of corn, and 490,000 pounds of bacon were sent to Europe and to American harbors on the Atlantic. Some of this quantity went to Cuba and to other places in the Gulf area. But 45 percent of the imported flour, 55 percent of the corn, 29 percent of the oats, and 10 percent of the bacon, and so forth, remained in New Orleans, and one can estimate that on the average half of this produce is consumed in the city and its immediate environs. People who are experienced in this type of commerce complain, however, that the West is not growing enough or at least is not sending enough of its produce to New Orleans. Boats had been built especially for transporting grain, and now because of the lack of these goods they have to be used for some other transport purpose.

The "products of the West" such as flour, corn, bacon, and the like are often

---

*STORAGE IN THE WARM, HUMID NEW ORLEANS CLIMATE AND SHIPPING TO EUROPE VIA THE GULF IS SUPPOSED TO HAVE SUCH A BENEFICIAL AFFECT ON THE CURING OF THE TOBACCO LEAVES THAT THEIR QUALITY IS IMPROVED, AND CUSTOMERS FREQUENTLY EXPRESSLY REQUEST TOBACCO BROUGHT TO EUROPE "VIA GULF."

finding shorter and cheaper routes to Atlantic harbors via the railroads and canals than to New Orleans for which, precisely because of its connection to the interior by means of the Mississippi River, they had predicted a very rapid growth and a commercial significance that was to overshadow all other places. New Orleans has become the emporium for produce from the interior, but only for the Gulf region. The slow tempo in which the economic development of this region is moving, Texas somewhat excepted, has also impeded the development of its main commercial center more than one would have believed possible in the time before the railroads, during the heyday of the South's "peculiar" economic system, slavery. Nevertheless, there is no doubt that the South is vigorously striving to pull itself upwards, that even Central America and the West Indies, in spite of political troubles, are economically in the midst of making steady progress, and that the level of productivity coming from the American Southwestern and Midwestern states, from the area that drains into the Mississippi, can only steadily increase. Thus, without doubt New Orleans also has the prospect of certain growth ahead, but this can only be accelerated if the city abandons the idea that it is predestined to be the commercial capital of the Union and thinks more about what remains to be done rather than on the blessings nature has already bestowed on it.

Total exports in 1873 amounted to $104,000,000. Among the imports, whose value came to about $17,000,000, coffee, salt, and timber are of paramount importance. In 1873, 188,074 sacks of coffee were imported, almost exclusively from Brazil. This constitutes almost one-third of the entire importation of coffee to the United States. Salt was imported from Liverpool, 432,876 sacks, and from Turks Island in the West Indies, 93,500 bushels. Wood for building purposes comes from various places in Florida, Alabama, and Mississippi, and 7,000,000 cords of timber were sent to New Orleans that year.

In 1873 shipping traffic in the port of New Orleans was as follows: of arriving North American vessels, there were 73 steamers (64,432 tons), 196 sailing ships (131,319 tons), 104 foreign steamers (168,519 tons), and 428 sailing ships (255,342 tons). Of coastal craft, 204 steamers and 286 sailing ships came in with a total capacity of around 270,000 tons. Of the foreign steamers, 68 were English, 15 German, 12 Spanish, 8 from Costa Rica, 1 from Mexico; of the sailing ships, 187 were English, 107 Spanish, 61 Norwegian, 19 German, 18 Italian, and 16 French. There are three steamship lines running to New York, one each to Philadelphia and Baltimore, three to Liverpool, and one each to Hamburg and Bremen. New Orleans itself owns 5 ocean and 151 river steamers and 376 sailing ships with a combined capacity of 53,212 tons.

New Orleans, which for the most part owes its importance to the Mississippi but at the same time has to suffer a great deal because of the moods of the "Father of Rivers," naturally keeps watch on this vital artery with the greatest attention and follows all changes in its condition with an interest reminiscent in many ways of the close relationship of the Egyptians to the Nile, only with somewhat less gratitude and, as is natural, with more concern. The "news from the river" forms an important section in every newspaper. One time it's the condition at the estuary that's reported, at another the condition of or a breach in the levees, and at still another it's about a sand or mud bank. Shipping accidents, which by comparison probably occur more frequently on the Mississippi than on the most trafficked rivers of Europe, furnish a supply of exciting reports for the "news"[2] every week. Furthermore, the big cities in the river basin, notably St. Louis, have been brought so close together by the heavy traffic and have so many concerns in common that one takes an interest in their welfare as one does in the health of relatives. Then there is the Delta's maze of canals, lakes, and lagoons in the immediate vicinity of New Orleans, whose condition naturally always arouses interest. Even the many tributary rivers draw attention to themselves and are well known and much discussed— one rising while the other is falling—none of them flows past at any time without there being something worth noting about it. Thus in various ways this magnificent and influential natural phenomenon invites observation and study. The fact that the still relatively very small population living along the river banks is given more to exploiting it than studying it explains why up until the present people have known less about it than one would expect, based on its importance.

Actually there are problems that have occupied the attention of those people living along the Mississippi for decades. A portion of their well-being depends to some degree upon a solution to these problems, but the inhabitants, having failed to investigate them properly, still don't do anything about them. Thus frequent clogging of the outermost channels in the Mississippi estuary is an old problem. At the moment, people here and in Washington are again debating the remedy but have come to no definite conclusion. Deep-drawing ships often have to lie weeks on the mudbanks that always build up anew out in the channels. But with this soft mud, out of which a single big flood can create entire banks, dredging offers only a momentary gain. Some people are suggesting the building of a new shipping channel to the west of the natural channels in the estuary; other are talking about increasing the embankment along one of the old channels. This would provide the river greater velocity by which it could with little assistance maintain its own bed at the required depth. For many practical-minded people this seems the best remedy to this problem. On the other hand, there is the view, which seems more accurate, that the construction of a new channel system would only bring a slight improvement by spreading the difficulties out over several points. Right now the newspapers are full of what these two plans promise to do, and the prospect finally seems at hand that one of the two will be carried out[3] due to the Federal Government. But the fact that so little preference is being given to one plan or the other based on a scientific study of the facts is demonstrated by, in addition to the endless discussion itself, the appearance and serious consideration of weird plans, such as the one according to which mechanisms should be constructed to lift even the biggest ships up and over the mudbanks, and even more it encourages differences of opinion about the formation of these mudbanks themselves. Some people talk about volcanic activity, others about extrusion of deeper sediment by the weight of the constant addition of new strata. Although we read in one report that even the lowest shorelines, mudbanks, and the like have changed little since the time when the French drew the first maps of the Mississippi estuary, others talk of how the rise and fall in the earth's surface, and still others of how great floods, have molded the outermost delta area as if it were wax. At the moment, scientific knowledge of the facts is entirely lacking.

There is a similar problem with regard to building levees along the river, which in the last decades has caused flooding of a widespread area along its lower course on the average of every four years. Every year it makes a hole here and there in a few levees. Because of this, large stretches of arable land are in such a constant swampy state that the draining of these bogs alone would seem to make stronger protection for the riverbank area worthwhile. There is, however, no systematic construction of the levees, which are built only rarely according to principles based on a study of rivers. Instead of being planned with regard to topographical conditions, the extent and limits of the levees are often planned according to property boundaries, so that a coordinated effort is impossible. Frequently the protective measures, which a more prudent landowner or community has taken, are frustrated by the indolence of others. In times of flooding it happens only too often that some of the people living along the river bank, feeling themselves in danger, puncture their neighbors' levees, or, as has already happened many times, with weapons in hand they oppose any form of precautionary measures the government engineers consider necessary. Building most levees so close to the river's edge that with time they are whittled away by waves from the steamboats is a mistake only now beginning to be corrected, after the four Southern riverbank states reputedly have already spent around $50,000,000 for levee construction. In general it seems that, like all misfortunes, floods are now felt and feared here more than in the golden age of slave labor, when the plantations in the lowlands, despite the frequent floodings, were more productive than in those in the higher areas. Now along with a more costly and less reliable labor force and the overall impoverishment, the difficulty of recovering from the damage due to inundation has naturally increased.

Levee construction along the Mississippi, as far as it concerns the state of Louisiana, has been delegated to a company that has undertaken the responsibility of building fifteen million yards of levees at sixty cents a yard within four years. The state, which is known to be financially ruined, is paying 10 percent of the entire cost per year for a period of twenty-one years and is levying a tax of one-fifth of one percent for levee improvement.

MAIN STREET. BUSINESS AREA. RESIDENTIAL HOUSES. PARKS AND GARDENS. CEMETERY MONUMENTS.

New Orleans has an advantage over most cities I know of having Canal Street, its widest and most beautiful but also its busiest route, leading down to the Mississippi. This is important particularly for one's first impression. It was already the city's main artery when New Orleans extended only a few blocks to the east and west of it, and it has remained so with expanding conditions. It still intersects the middle of the "half-moon" form in which New Orleans has developed around the sharply curving Mississippi here, although for fifteen years now the city has been ten times its original size.* Being the starting point for numerous tramway lines (because of its position right near the train stations and the steamboat and ferry landing), running through the very business district of the city where in almost every one of the buildings along the way is a richly stocked emporium, and finally being, as already mentioned, centrally located, it is truly the main artery of the city.

In one way, of course, one has to measure its activity according to American standards; that is, one has to consider the number of people who travel along the street in the trolley cars. If one simply looked at the pedestrians and carriages, he would find less traffic than in many European cities of comparable size. But the horse-drawn trolleys greatly compress and speed up the flow in these nevertheless spacious streets, thereby making it naturally less conspicuous to one viewing it from the sidelines. You soon become accustomed to seeing such trolley cars rolling past every thirty seconds or sometimes even more frequently. They go their way quietly without crowding or confusion, and seldom does a carriage with one or two horses or a freight wagon get mixed up among them. Freight traffic generally uses the river, the canals, and a few side streets. If a blindman were to walk along the main street of this large commercial city for the first time, he might at times believe he was on a village street.

This street is about 70 paces (175 feet) wide and has a layout as practical as it is attractive, the kind one also sees here and there in other Southern cities. Along the houses on both sides of the street is a 6-pace (15-foot)-wide slab-covered sidewalk, joined to a somewhat lower-lying road 37 and one-half feet wide. However, a lawn lined with several rows of trees runs in the middle, while the tracks for the trams are laid along the sides of this green stretch. With few exceptions the houses on this street, as on all other streets of New Orleans, are by no means imposing buildings as in the Northern and Western metropolises of the Union but generally have more modest exteriors and are seldom

---

*BECAUSE OF THIS HALF-MOON SHAPE OF THE CITY LAYOUT, NEW ORLEANS CARRIES THE NICKNAME OF CRESCENT CITY.

more than four stories high. According to the American custom, a veranda-like projecting structure made of iron juts out over the entire width of the sidewalk and frequently runs up to the roof, so that it forms a broad balcony in front of every floor. Inasmuch as these projections connect with one another, they make a covered path of several hundred feet in length under which sightseers can walk up and down, undisturbed, in front of the large display windows in times of strong sunshine or rainy weather. Nevertheless, the inartistic construction of these projections, which lack any attractive arches or ornamentation of importance, certainly doesn't add any appeal to the houses. On the contrary, the projections themselves give those parts of the street sort of a fair-like character similar to that which one finds in many similar streets of New York and other American cities, although it's much more pronounced here. Such things as the many loiterers and flower and fruit vendors found under these projections and the glaring advertising posters put up on the houses themselves, as well as on the poles, reinforce the impression of crudeness. Only very remotely can one compare them with arcades. They are really transitory constructions that can be demolished without damage and then erected again without any great effort or cost. Like the iron buildings in New York, Boston, and other places, they give us just a little foretaste of the age of iron architecture, which is supposed to be in store for us.[4]

The intersecting thoroughfares, which run right and left off Canal Street, are narrow insofar as they belong to the old city, but they are seldom winding. Those that contain tall buildings and very lively business activities put you exactly in mind of the business streets of southern European commercial cities. Most of these streets, however, run out into districts where mean-looking wooden houses, often not bigger or more sturdy than fair booths, sometimes stand along evenly leveled alleys, sometimes along broad boulevards full of weeds and puddles, almost like a meadow. Were it not for the beautiful shade trees and the greenery of the gardens, then these would be dreary sections of town. Now, when everything is green and in bloom, one can indulge in the illusion that they represent garden suburbs with poorly kept-up summer homes. Often in the middle of the streets there are large culverts with lazily running, almost stagnant water—a fact that badly reflects on the health authorities of this city, which is so often afflicted with epidemics. I will not talk about the innumerable puddles, for the weeks I was there were unusually stormy and wet. Nevertheless, these puddles would not exist if the streets were built and maintained correctly. Street cleaning in all the American cities, big and small, I have seen up until now is at an astonishingly low level. People who know the situation for the most part excuse it by saying that here is an instance of how it is very difficult to prevent fraud on the part of the contractors. If they would allot small sums of money for this work, probably not much less would be done than when they act as generously as the welfare of the city seems to demand. Thus one could choose the lesser of two evils and keep a rein on the thieves by the most paltry appropriations possible, but of course, this is only feasible in circumstances that unfortunately do not happen often—when a "ring" of contractors does not allow itself as much from public funds as it intends to steal.

Unique traces of the former French administration have been retained in the names of the streets and squares. There is a Napoleon Avenue, Josephine,[5] Austerlitz, Marengo, and Jena Streets, a Bourbon and Dauphine Street, and certainly a few dozen famous Frenchmen from St. Denis to de Lesseps are immortalized here. That the nine muses, together with Apollo, Bacchus, the Dryads, the Naiads, et cetera, get to see their names posted upon the street corners is not common outside the boundaries of modern Greece and the land of Corneille and Racine, but here it is carried out with thoroughness. Here Erato and Thalia intersect Annunciation and Tchoupitoulas Streets, Terpsichore meets Chippewa, and Bacchus and Apollo meet Napoleon Street; St. Patrick Street runs two blocks away from the Dryads, and Pitt is near the Naiads. It's a regular melange. For their part the English have added a few of their men to the French celebrities, and the Americans have contributed names that have been used a thousand times—their Liberty, Pleasant, Franklin, Madison, et cetera, as well as a series of streets numbered 1 to 8, which under these circumstances is the most sensible. But I don't know whom to credit with the bright idea of naming some of the largest new streets, which come one right after the other in a row—Genius, Force, Virtue, Law, Hope, Benefit—and, not satisfied, also adding Agriculture, Industry, Commerce, Abundance, Arts Streets, and the like. Such a well-meaning man deserves a civic crown. If you come down from the abstract heights of these attractive and dignified streets into just Homer Street, which is in the suburb of Algiers, and pass near Ptolemy and Socrates Streets, it feels almost like coming down to lowly earth. Incidentally, the biggest bookstore in New Orleans doesn't have a copy of Homer in Greek on the shelf; this omission really lends importance to this other type of recognition, through street names. As regards the Germans, they have put up the names of their great men on this and that cozy tavern. Since the beer parlors are the places in which, according to ancient custom, they perform their libations from morn till very late, they have generally displayed pictures of their heroes in these places and, with the broad and tolerant *Weltanschauung* that belongs to them, seldom forget to add to the group some portraits of ladies, such as the four continents, the blondest of the blond, or the surprised, bathing, sleeping, or whatever other beauty.

Except for the cottages in which not only the poorest feel comfortable in this mild climate and which ultimately offer much healthier and more pleasant dwellings than the tenements, which are only seen frequently in the Negro quarters, every house has its veranda, which either runs around the ground floor and upper floor—most of the dwellings outside the business district are two stories high—or which, as is usually the case, forms only a kind of covered balcony in front of the second floor. They are seldom decorated with flowers, for floriculture does not seem to have many friends among the lower classes here. Rather, it seems to be conditioned by custom or fashion rather than by a question of taste, for in nearby Mobile the streets and houses are full of flowers, which with the mild climate and the good earth are so easy to raise. Every house, however, has a courtyard and many have gardens in front, alongside, or behind the house, and many times in these there towers a plane tree, an oak, magnolia, cypress, or even a tall palm tree.

Frequently in both the immediate and distant vicinity of the city the well-to-do have their country homes, which are almost always surrounded by beautiful gardens and seem to be built more in various European styles with all kinds of stucco and cast decoration, pillars, arches, and towers than in the North, where the inhabitants are more often attached to the wooden farmhouse with its simple vestibule. The gardens are actually more interesting than the houses they surround. Here you see the most beautiful magnolias, orange trees, pomegranate, Japanese persimmon,[6] the various southern varieties of oak, European plane trees, their American sister the sycamore, here and there date palms, and not infrequently banana trees. However, the latter unfortunately often suffer from frost and the people would obtain fruit more often from a smaller Chinese variety than from the large-leaved type, which they almost exclusively continue to cultivate and which, for example, is already doing quite well in Florida. On the whole, one notices much less of an abundance of southern plants than a preponderance of our conventional and cosmopolitan garden plants. One would expect that in such a place, so rich in flowers as the Gulf state area, and in a climate ideal for the acclimatization of warmth-loving plants from all subtropical regions of the earth, the number of garden plants would be considerably more, especially since many of our more unassuming varieties could be replaced by attractive indigenous ones of which there is no lack in the woods and fields. But that is the case only in very few instances. The scarlet red honeysuckle, the winding jasmine, and here and there the violet-blue tradescantia are the only ones I often saw transplanted from the woods to the gardens, and they certainly make worthy additions.

What could not be done if the flower gardens were something more than just a fashionable luxury, if people with basic imaginative taste and feeling for nature made a beginning and set up at least parts of the gardens as model exhibits of the local flora as in many of our parks! How strange it is that in Southern parks you very rarely see any of the plants, especially the climbing ones, which are one of the greatest ornaments of their forests! While in the North they cultivate only trees and bushes, here they eliminate every one of the local plants as being a weed and wouldn't even tolerate the exceedingly characteristic Spanish moss if they could get rid of it. If it worked, they would certainly bring fir and larch trees from the North and plant them in place of palm trees and live oaks so as not to deviate from the accepted garden model. They act so inanely here in such matters, and no mention is made of horticulture or of scientific gardening.

Nevertheless, even the most commonplace garden of this kind seen here is still better than the showy, so-called City Park, which is nothing more than a fenced-in swamp, where even before the heavy spring rains you have to vault from the base of one tree to another to get from one place to another and where only herds of cows, horses, pigs, and goats can move about with any relish. At the entrance, two rows of beautiful old live and water oaks are the only things resembling something of a park in the whole place. A board constitutes the bridge from this part to the swamp. Dickens really didn't exaggerate very much about many things when in *Martin Chuzzlewit* he created a picture of the American swampy city, the city of Eden.[7] If he had wanted to give it a park, he would only have had to copy this city park of the metropolis of the South. You seldom meet a human being in it. It only seems to be really fit for those weary of living to snuff out their lives in its shadows—something that actually happens rather frequently and in time will give the entire place a gruesome appeal, the only thing for the present about which it can boast.

The cemeteries are much more attractive in their own way; they really bear no comparison with the wonderful sites in other big American cities but are distinguished by unique-looking sepulchers and pretty garden layouts. Some very tiny ones are in the middle of the city, where they have gradually been completely surrounded by houses; others, newer ones, are more than a mile away and then are larger. The massive grave sites with above-ground mausoleums, often no smaller than a railroad signalman's cabin, constructed out of marble or stone painted to simulate marble and generally built in the form of a Greek temple, are conspicuous in both types of cemeteries. The cemeteries in the inner city are literally crammed full with these colossi and allow for only a few paths to wind between them. The inscriptions, however, are very scant of words, generally giving only names, dates of birth and death of the various members of the family who are buried together there. Frequently, some society will have such a communal burial plot; for example, in the St. Louis Cemetery there is a plot for the members of a Masonic lodge, one for those of a Spanish volunteer aid society, another for those in a German businessmen's club, and so forth. Further on, especially along the walls, there are tall brick constructions, completely unadorned rectangular shapes, which look like file drawers. There are four to six drawers, one on top of another, and thirty to forty of them in every row; some are still open, others newly walled up, and those that have already been filled for some time have been sealed with a marble slab bearing the usual short inscription. Here and there a bouquet, a plaster figure, or plaything made of seashells, or the like placed in front of the marble slab give a lively and colorful impression to these basically bare grave fronts, which are heavily laden with pearl or imitation flower wreaths and memorial plaques. But the inscriptions are seldom noteworthy. I only remember one that appeared worth recording. It had just recently been carved on the marker of a Polish woman who had died at fifty-one years of age and had already been dead now for sixteen years:

Pour sa mère sur cette terre
Le Bonheur a fui
Sans Retour.[8]

I instinctively looked around to see if the gray-haired little old mother were not tottering up the path. It was quite a sunny morning, the time at which such lonely mourners like to visit their graves. Certainly she liked to come here. But everything remained silent; only at the gate did I meet three American ladies all dressed up, with makeup on, who were carrying lilies in their hands, and looked ridiculous.

In one of the new cemeteries that lies beyond the city there is a marble war memorial erected in memory of the deeds of the Confederate Army. A soldier in combat dress stands on a tall pedestal at whose base the busts of Lee, Jackson, Johnston, and Polk[9] have been added, and the entire sculptured work has been set up on an attractively adorned hill. It bears no comparison with some of our better victory monuments and with time will be of even less value, since in other places they have also erected memorials of this type, more or less duplicates, and are still erecting them. Only the fine head of General Lee, even in this rough-hewed form, is a sight worth looking at. Incidentally, in Cambridge, Massachusetts, there is already a very similar monument to the troops of the Federal Army.

FLOODINGS. CLIMATE. SANITARY CONDITIONS.

Along with other important maritime commercial centers of the South such as Savannah and Mobile, New Orleans is situated far from the sea. It is almost 23 geographical (almost 106 statute) miles away from the mouth of the Mississippi but will scarcely ever have to fear the competition of a place built nearer to the sea, for farther downstream, although there is a little dry space here and there big enough for a planter's home or a storehouse, there is no place to be found large enough upon which to build a city. As noted earlier, however, it has to be protected from the Mississippi by an entire system of levees, for even a rise of a few feet in the water level endangers the low-lying city. Often a storm even blows water out of Lake Pontchartrain, one of the nearby lagoons, into the streets of the city, so that it stands there several feet deep. The frequent epidemics to which New Orleans is exposed, yellow fever above all, seem to indicate that the city has extended only as far into the swamp as is compatible with its vitality. All around, the land is swampy, and during the rainy springtime, you walk on the levees or the railroad track in order to get from place to place if you cannot go by water. The highways, which are few and in poor condition, stand partly under water. On many occasions I have seen the street in front of my windows, which is not one of the most low-lying ones, turned

15 "THE CEMETERIES ARE DISTINGUISHED BY UNIQUE-LOOKING SEPULCHERS" AND "TALL BRICK CONSTRUCTIONS, WHICH LOOK LIKE FILE DRAWERS." ST. LOUIS CEMETERY, NEW ORLEANS.

into a lake four to six times in one day when storm after storm passed over with sudden but very heavy downpours. I learned to understand the reasons for many precautionary measures, for example, the thick brick enclosures around the garden flower beds: otherwise the earth would be washed away very rapidly. Even traffic in the main streets and business area becomes difficult with any kind of heavy rain; for women it is impossible, but it offers the observer protected from the rain many a new, unexpected sight. There one sees horse-drawn trolly cars, which like neptunian chariots dash through water up to their axles, so that it foams, makes a hissing noise, and sends a spray over the passengers who on getting out have to make their escape onto the sidewalk through a breaking wave. You see cascading water rushing over dead cats on into a whirlpool of oranges, banana peels, corn cobs, and cottonseed; Scylla and Charybdis, lakes, inlets, islands—soon every street turns into an interesting aquatic world, and the Negro children romp around in the slimy puddles with a gusto that scarcely befits humans.

Since the very flat site of the city does not allow these frequent little floodings to run off quickly enough to carry the sludge along with them, they certainly do not do any good for health conditions, especially if they are followed by a fierce heat wave as usually happens in summer. But fortunately, New Orleans is for the most part so spread out and offers so many small, low-priced homes that this disadvantage is to some extent offset by well-ventilated, bright dwellings, and the relatively favorable state of the city's health, considering its location, can primarily be attributed to this situation.[10]

I have extracted the following information about these conditions from the annual report of the New Orleans Board of Health (1873): the annual number of deaths in New Orleans was 37.05 per 1,000, and if one subtracts the 972 fatal cases due to yellow fever, cholera, and smallpox, then 31.72 per 1,000. During this year, 505 died of smallpox, 241 of cholera, 226 of yellow fever. The total number of smallpox cases amounted to 1,300, cholera 259, and yellow fever 388. During the last seven years (1867–1873), yellow fever caused the following number of deaths: 310, 7, 3, 587, 54, 39, 226; smallpox 40, 14, 137, 528, 2, 29, 505. Cholera did not make any significant appearance. The first yellow fever case of 1873 was found on a ship from Havana in June, which seems to verify the opinion of those who claim that the sickness is a product of the tropics and has only been brought in here. During previous epidemics, the introduction of the disease had not been demonstrated. In any case, New Orleans, with its location and its environs already described, with its hot summers and late summers, which nonetheless do not exclude unpleasant changes in the weather,* with its drinking water taken from cisterns or from the Mississippi, and with its poor methods of street cleaning, appears to offer an excellent breeding ground for this plague. It looks like improvements in this regard are gaining ground only very slowly, and the impetus, which serious epidemics usually give, always seems to lose steam very shortly thereafter. Right after the epidemic of 1853 it seemed as if everything possible was going to be done to make the city a healthier place. But today, for example, street cleaning is perhaps worse than it was twenty years ago. In fact, it was proven that during last year's cholera epidemic there was up to 126 pounds of animal matter and up to 422 pounds of vegetable matter in the gutters along the length of one city block! Dead dogs and cats are not an unusual occurrence in the gutters of even the best streets, so it is not astonishing when the same report tells us that the dust in the streets contains 15 percent organic matter. The fermentation that must occur when after a few hot days it rains—one of the Southern downpours that churns up everything—is easy to imagine.

Apart from these troubles, New Orleans can take pride in having a rather pleasant climate, and even in summer the heat is supposed to be in no way oppressive because it is relieved by the cool winds coming from the river.

---

*THE AVERAGE TEMPERATURE FOR JULY IN 1873, A NORMAL YEAR, WAS 84°F., FOR AUGUST 82°, SEPTEMBER 79°; THE HIGHEST TEMPERATURE IN EACH OF THESE THREE MONTHS WAS 98°, 92°, 91° AND THE LOWEST 82°, 78°, 78°; THE RAPID CHANGES IN THE WEATHER OCCUR PRIMARILY IN SPRING WHEN SOMETIMES THERE IS EVEN FROST THOUGH THE TEMPERATURE HAS ALREADY GONE UP TO 86°; THE DAILY TEMPERATURE CHANGE CAN THEN BE AS MUCH AS 40°, AND EVEN IN JULY AND AUGUST IT CAN FLUCTUATE BY 20°F.

Nevertheless, the climate is still not as comfortable as in the Southern states on the Atlantic, for the location here is too far west and subject to the influence of cold north winds blowing in here over the broad flat continent. Thus, winters get considerably colder here than at the same latitude on the East Coast of the United States. People who have lived here for many years still wish to feel the perceptively relaxing effects of the Southern climate, and I noticed with astonishment how sensitive they had become to the somewhat cool mornings and evenings. With temperatures of 50°F. they didn't feel comfortable without a fire in the fireplace, while to us nothing can be more pleasant than thoroughly enjoying this invigorating morning and evening briskness.

Perhaps one factor contributing to the relatively good health of the population is that it is not easy for anyone who can do any work whatsoever to have to live poorly. More than enough produce from the interior and the West Indies comes through here, and the Gulf, together with its lagoons, sends in plenty of healthy fish and other edible marine life, while Texas, whose beef production few places can equal, lies next door. You get an extremely good impression of the abundance and quality of the essential and gourmet comestibles when you visit the markets, which occupy an important place in the life of New Orleans. A great many of them are scattered about the city in roomy, sometimes not inelegant, halls constructed of iron. In them they sell not only meat, fish, vegetables, and fruit but also all kinds of household wares, crockery, tin utensils, and material for making clothes, et cetera. Since in addition to all this the markets also include many little eating places and cafes and the buyers and sellers are predominantly Creoles and Negroes, each of them yelling, bawling, and laughing enough for ten, it looks just like the goings on at a fair at home.

The variety of beautiful fruits and vegetables alone makes a visit to such a covered market interesting, but the appearance and conduct of the people make it even more worthwhile. On the sidewalk before the entrance, for example, Indian women sit in a row with baskets full of big blackberries, which, just as we do with cherries when they suddenly appear in quantity, people eat every single day in pastry or as stewed fruit. These Indians are pitiful remnants of Atala's tribe,[11] who lead their gypsy-like existence out on the prairie, but clearly their blood is strongly mixed. They have yellow-brown facial coloring, broad faces with flat noses and thick lips. Their sad, shy manner contrasts sharply with the lively cheerfulness of the Negroes, mulattoes, and Creoles. They all have a cloth thrown over head and shoulders that they hold together in front of their mouths so that you see little of their faces. Their pitch-black hair, which often has a pronounced auburn sheen, is tied in a knot on the top of their heads and hangs straight down in the back. But they do not feel at home even in this very diverse crowd in which the darkest Negro moves comfortably, and even without any thought of their poetically celebrated past, their presence is for everyone a sight that arouses sympathy.

Upon entering, a mixed odor greets and stuns us almost more than the noise of the voices. It flows together from the fish counters, the fruit stands, and the coffee booths; just as you turn around, a very unusual one is added, perhaps the smell of the sauerkraut that the German gardener offers for sale beside his artichokes and tomatoes, or of the shrimp, the finger-long prawns whose season has just begun, or of pineapple, which the salesman has cut up in tasty-looking pieces. Round about the edge of the market hall, tables are set up at which many people are taking some refreshment. Mirrors run along the backs of the tables so that the diners with self-satisfaction can to a certain extent supplement the insufficient portion of their contentment with the dishes served. But they will be already half-satisfied if they only look at all the good things. What wonderful examples of culinary art! How nicely the brown-roasted, scaly skin of this pompano, which is almost one foot wide and three feet long, separates from the milk-white meat, and the strong bones glisten like mother of pearl; how skillfully it is cut into two halves; and how great the broth smells on which a whole layer of ruddy fat is swimming! Then there is the half-saddle of lamb, whose flesh is so tender that the ribs fall apart while the fat has been browned as hard as glass! Nearby are the cold chickens, whose rough looking exterior is too well known to prevent someone pleasantly anticipating what the insides are like; the excellent roast beef, the width and length of whose slices tell of immense portions; the plates of baked eggs, right from the oven; the banana slices on which the fat is still simmering sending up a fragrance to heaven, slices that in size and shape remind one of the *Kartäuserklösse*,[12] which we get on fast days at home; the rose-red crabs, which look much too ugly for their wonderful taste; finally the hugh bowls of oyster soup whose steam envelopes the tables in a romantic cloud. As connecting links for all these wonderful things arranged in a row, there are potbellied, shiny brass kettles full of coffee set up between every two tables; with four spigots three-quarters of the way up their sides, each is ready to dispense drink and looks like a many-breasted goddess of plenty.

Then you have to see them eating! A hungry Negro in front of a full plate is a sight for the gods. I love these fellows no matter how great their ignorance is or how rascally they can be sometimes, for the sake of the "silent love of life" that is featured in their laugh, their eyes, and in their entire demeanor. They are satisfied with their life and this is something very beneficial, since they are not just animals. But their "will to live" never expresses itself so clearly as when they have something decent to eat and especially an adequate amount of it. What pleasure! What an ability to pile it in and put it away! What don't those powerful jaws chew up; how the head, neck and shoulders, arms and hands do work! Judging by these performances, a calf would be a little thing for many a fellow. Quite a few also fold their hands and say a little prayer before and after successful completion of the task, and when you look at many of their faces and see that even in this very secular, noisy place they take their prayers very seriously, you believe you see something of a more noble childlike quality shining forth under the more animal-like nature.

Next to these unique restaurants the fruit stands offer the most interesting sights. Even during the colder season there is no lack of produce, for the West Indies, which supplies many of the things piled up here, is already deep in summer, while locally only the first fruits of the season, blackberries and perhaps some tomatoes, are ripe. Bananas, the cheapest and most nutritious fruit, are always available in huge quantities; they hang around the columns in their large, lemon yellow or brown-red bunches, now and then becoming black due to overripening. Taken from just one plant, many of these bunches are as heavy as thirty, forty or more pounds and contain several dozen of the cucumber-shaped fruit. Here they buy small amounts of bananas in quantities of a dozen for twenty-five to fifty cents, according to size, and at these prices you can see how the fruit trade must be one of the most lucrative businesses, for wherever they are grown, bananas are plentiful and their cultivation demands little room or effort; all the same, the present market price is still very little when you compare it to the excellence of the fruit.

As is well known, the whole interior of the banana is edible; it consists of a soft, sweet-smelling, doughy substance, and is, especially when fried in fat, an extremely tasty and nutritious food. After the bananas come oranges, persimmons, and pineapples, and of these only the persimmon has really found a home here; the orange is sold in smaller quantities than in Florida and is maintained more as a decorative tree in gardens, while the pineapple is properly grown only in the southernmost section of the United States, in southern Florida. These two fruits come in chiefly from the West Indies, a small part of the oranges coming from Florida and the surrounding area. That they make a really wonderful sight all stacked together in huge piles, not to mention what they taste like, is something everyone who visualizes these shapes and colors can imagine. The pineapple is definitely one of the most attractive-looking fruits in size, form, and with its yellow-brown, scaly, lozenge-shaped husk, tufted with a cluster of sword-shaped leaves on top, and everyone has something complimentary to say about the orange glowing brightly amidst the dark foliage. The persimmons, the variety known as Japanese persimmon, are not bad although they are neither as big nor as sweet as the somewhat similar medlar fruit coming in from Sicily.[13] They are, nevertheless, as big as plums, golden yellow like the latter with a somewhat frosty color tint and grow crammed together with often as many as twelve on the tough wooden stems. A great advantage is their low price, for a pound costs only ten cents, while a pineapple costs fifteen to thirty cents, a dozen oranges thirty to fifty cents. They are thus easily within financial reach of the children. Since, in its own way, keeping these little tormentors happy is here as everywhere in family circles a difficult and sometimes even irksome problem, a sort of social question in miniature, the existence of such an inexpensive and nutritious fruit in what is otherwise an area lacking fruit is a matter not to be underestimated and whose importance anyone who knows anything about daily living recognizes.

The smaller-sized produce available are: huge blackberries, similar sized strawberries, various sorts of nuts and chestnuts from the coconut down to the lowly peanut, the tamarinds, tough pods that are filled with the dark brown acidic pulp that we know from the *Tamarindenmus*[14] one gets at the apothecary—but these play a less important role here than the other fruits mentioned. They are regarded more as delicacies or trifles. On the other hand, vegetables are present in large quantities. Already large quantities of new potatoes, beans, peas, very beautiful white cabbage and lettuce heads, as well as artichokes, sweet potatoes (yams; our potatoes are called "Irish" in order to distinguish the two kinds), and tomatoes (paradise apples) are available. There are many Germans among the gardeners who sell these products, and our countrymen are supposed to be doing better than others in this work because of their industry and expertise. I frequently had the opportunity to hear their praises sung in American circles where their "being so well-off" was primarily ascribed to the fact that members of the family, especially the wives, do a great job in helping out. Obviously the Americans regarded this success, which they themselves don't usually have, with great wonder, for many times elsewhere I have talked to intelligent German gardeners and they all criticized the Americans for the lack of perseverance they display every time they try to cultivate a garden. As in the North, you could say the Germans constitute the best and largest number of gardeners here. In Charleston, Havana, and even in the middle of Florida they furnish perhaps half of the markets with their produce.

There is nothing especially worth mentioning about the flowers. Roses, violets, lilies, geraniums, verbenas, and the like are the most numerous just as they are in Germany, and you seldom see a tropical ornamental plant, like a cycadia or a scarlet sage, standing in between them. They make the most attractive bouquets out of roses, violets, and young cypress branches. The dark cypress green goes wonderfully with the lighter colors.

A Frenchman is shouting in three languages: "Belles fleurs à vendre! Schöne Blumen verkaufen will ich! Nice flowers to sell!" Another man in front of a sack full of fresh potatoes is singing: "My potatoes are very nice! O nice are my potatoes!" A third one is selling lilies, whose roots are wrapped in cabbage leaves so that they seem to be growing out of a head of cabbage; even the black servant girls have to laugh uproariously over his cry "Cabbage lily," and a large throng crowds around him to hear further explanations about the qualities and cultivation of this remarkable plant. At the same time, a mathematical expert with a horribly crafty Yankee face has set himself up with a big blackboard in front of the gateway and is gesticulating and shouting for a few dozen curious people to come nearer; he then works out the square roots of numbers with an astonishing speed. When he has the blackboard completely covered, he suddenly jumps down and stretches out his hand and cap for five-cent pieces before perhaps someone can get away without contributing. He doesn't make out badly, certainly much better than the singer and harp player. He knows his audience, to whom mathematical facility is still a bit of black magic with which one fleeces uninformed people with impunity. What he is proclaiming is like a gospel for the upper class of Negro society. Still not having quite understood it all, they follow him with wonder as he takes his stand on his back and goes to set up his mathematics class on another corner.

In general the colored people provide the dominant features of street life here; they are amply equipped with everything that is needed, primarily free time and inexhaustible mirth. As dealers of fruit, flowers, and confectionery goods, as bootblacks, porters, coachmen, and most often as loiterers with undetermined or actually no employment, they are found everywhere. In fact, they constitute the main body of people on the street, especially the women and girls who steadfastly saunter about from morn till night. The entire colored population exhibits a much more agreeable character than in any of the other ex-slave states where I have been able to observe it up until now. It has a considerably higher social position and doesn't consist for the most part only of the dregs of society as in other large cities of the South.

New Orleans has a larger colored population than Charleston or Richmond, but you would not believe it if the statistics did not say so—so much less is the distance separating these people from the whites. This is partly because of the great preponderance of mulattoes (who call themselves "yellow people" as opposed to the "dark" or "black people"), partly because of prosperity that prevails in these circles, and partly, though not least of all, because the French in Louisiana never set themselves off so strictly from their slaves and freed men as the Anglo-Americans did in the other slave states. To be sure, practically all the laws were also adopted here that were intended to exclude colored people from white society; but very often they were circumvented in a more humanitarian way than elsewhere. Even though prohibition against marriage between colored and white existed here, very often there were common law marriages between members of both races not infrequently leading to sincere relationships that benefited the good upbringing and well-being of the offspring. This is especially true for the quadroons, these people of mixed mulatto and white blood, who in intellectual gifts take no second place to the whites and whose women, with their wholesome physical good looks, are far and away ahead of the competition in what Americans consider beautiful in the female sex. I think I am impartial in this matter, but have to say that those slender figures of the American women, those narrow little heads with thin hair, and those pale faces with superintelligent eyes seem so unnatural and unhealthy to me that they have with time become unbearable. On the other hand, it seems to me that the healthy natural beauty of many colored women always has more of an advantage over that intellectualized beauty. The colored people have also been able to enter into every kind of business and trade and have found their French fellow citizen, who is inclined to live and let live, a more generous competitor than the tougher and more selfish American.

CHAPTER SIXTEEN

The Mississippi and Ohio

TRIP UPSTREAM. THE STEAMBOAT. BUILDING UP POWER BEFORE
CASTING OFF. RIVER SCENERY NEAR NEW ORLEANS. BATON
ROUGE.

On a clear golden evening, which came at the end of a hot April day, I left
New Orleans on the *John Kilgour*, one of the large steamboats traveling
between New Orleans and Cincinnati. They had told me it was one of the
fastest and most comfortable passenger ships on the river, but when I took a
look at its interior, it seemed to me so much more a cargo ship that I considered giving up making this relatively long trip on such a loaded down and
falsely labeled vessel. The lower quarters were jampacked with barrels, bales,
and boxes as is normally the case, but the superstructure above deck, which is
usually the area for the saloon, was completely blocked with chests, bundles
of plows, and other tools, and to protect this part of the ship from inclement
weather, big bunches of bananas were hanging in cramped rows around the
roof, looking as immobile in their linen wrappings as the big bats that hang
all folded up on the trees in South Asia. There seemed to be no room for a
person to pass. When I nevertheless cleared a path through these barrels full
of pineapples, the orange crates, and banana bunches, which by the way
exuded a very pleasant aroma, I found that the interior seemed to be somewhat better than the exterior. I stepped into a saloon that was a good 100
paces (250 feet) long, with fifty not too small, well-furnished cabins extending along its sides, and found that at least on the roof there was even consider-

16   ON THE LEVEE, SHOWING
THE INDIAN FEATHER
HEADRESS SMOKESTACKS ON
THE MISSISSIPPI STEAMER OF
WHICH RATZEL SPEAKS.

able room to get a little fresh air in good weather. Of course, the cleanliness
was not great, and the cabin windows were all barricaded with cargo; but I
knew that you cannot expect much from the river steamboats in the South if
you want to be satisfied to any degree. The boat was supposed to leave at 5:00
P.M. and reach Cincinnati in seven days.*

There was a great deal of activity on the wharf, since other boats going up the
river were also leaving at the same time, and amid endless noise and kicked-up
dust, hundreds of excited, yelling blacks were busily occupied loading the last
bits of cargo we were to take with us. For the most part it was cotton and tropical
fruit that were still being loaded. As a consignment of empty barrels was rolled
on, a friend who had come aboard congratulated me. "Now at any rate there
won't be any lack of life preservers should the boat explode." But, he added, "you
don't have to worry much about that since the ship is owned by the captain, who
will be more careful than so many others, who in the event of accidents at most
lose only their jobs, and then only for a short time."

*IN 1817, WHICH WE CAN REGARD AS THE FIRST YEAR OF STEAMBOAT TRAFFIC ON THE MISSIS-
SIPPI, THE SECOND SHIP THAT PLIED THIS RIVER NEEDED TWENTY-FIVE DAYS TO SAIL FROM NEW
ORLEANS TO LOUISVILLE. EVEN IN 1821, WHEN MORE THAN SEVENTY STEAMBOATS WERE NAVI-
GATING THE MISSISSIPPI, A TWELVE-DAY TRIP FROM NEW ORLEANS TO LOUISVILLE WAS A GOOD
FEAT.

I have already described a boat similar to the *John Kilgour* in my trip on the Alabama River;[1] but this one was considerably larger. It was 240 feet long and about 40 feet wide and had side paddle wheels, while those smaller boats have only one big paddle wheel at the back. Moreover, it is constructed with such a flat bottom that despite heavy cargo it draws only 6.5 feet of water, has room for freight and machinery on the flat deck (which looks like the deck of a ferryboat) and allows the saloon as well as the walkway that runs around it to be placed upon the tall pillars on top of which there is a still smaller cabin complex and the little wheelhouse. As on the other boat, both smokestacks are very tall and rather slender—the distance from their tops to the ship's deck is over 70 feet— and the entire ship has just as smoky and dirty a look about it. The woodwork consists of neither graceful nor meticulous workmanship. There is no comparison with an ocean liner or a Hudson River ship or even with boats like those I've seen in Florida. Formerly it was simply not customary to give the Mississippi steamboats the elegant exterior that elsewhere is a prerequisite. For a long time they, like most of their passengers, still shared something of the immaturity and roughness of the West's young culture. Now, since the trains make the trip from New Orleans to St. Louis and Cincinnati in less than two days, the throng of steamship passengers has dropped off considerably. However, they say in the last few years some very beautiful, elegant Mississippi steamships have been built, one of which is approximately 300 feet long and considerably more than 100 feet high. The only time that there are still many steamship passengers is when the railroads are damaged due to flooding, and that, by the way, is not all that infrequent.

As the time for departure approached, in the forward part of the saloon where the tobacco chewers, the smokers, and the card players usually gather, there were throngs of people like one usually finds only on an ocean liner embarking on a long transoceanic trip. A great deal of baggage came aboard along with the numerous passengers and those who came to say goodbye. At the same time, the number and noise of people engaged in business increased: those who still quickly wanted to dispose of a telescope, a pair of glasses, or a pocketknife; the newspaper boys; the women selling fruit; and other eager salesmen. These people know that for many individuals the beginning of a big trip not only creates an almost irresponsibly optimistic atmosphere, which sometimes really upsets normal standards of prudence and thriftiness, but they also realize very well that most travelers going up the river return with bags full of goods found in this trading center of Western produce, and that many people have earned their money very easily. The vendors are therefore twice as persistent and successfully so. One after another, the passengers put away a little supply of bananas and oranges in their cabins; the popular little penknives used as both toothpick and fingernail cleaner are sold by the dozen; even a revolver finds a buyer at the eleventh hour, and when the boat got underway and the crowding had subsided, half the travelers were concealing themselves behind the big pages of the *Picayune*, the *Republican*,[2] and other New Orleans newspapers.

We passed the long row of steamboats, then the flatboats, the simple wood, coal, or grain ships, which look like giant swimming cigar boxes, and finally the sailboats, which lay closely packed together. It had become quiet on the wharf, for it was already evening. In the streets that run from the center of town down to the river, only the last rays of the sun were shining, giving the thick dust, which was now settling down due to the calm that had descended, a luminous red color that glowed like fiery-red smoke, and giving a blinding incandescence to the windows, which couldn't have shone brighter had they been diamonds. The city, however, lies on the whole scarcely higher than the river and has few steeples of note, and thus offers no view from this side worthy of its size or importance, giving a bad impression with only dingy, windowless warehouses and railway freight depots along the landing area. Suburban homes and beautiful gardens, which to be sure form a part of such a metropolis, only appear farther up the river. There the suburb of Carollton begins. On the other (right) bank, the Mississippi has put the green meadows under water and only permits the trees and the nearest homes of the villages of Algiers,[3] Gretna, and others—places that really could be counted suburbs of New Orleans—to stick up.

As laboriously as the big steamboat, slowly puffing away, seems to make its way upstream, we nonetheless soon lose sight of New Orleans and its suburban dependencies. Scarcely one German mile (a bit more than 4.5 statute miles) from the city, on both sides we now come across the levees that protect the plantations from the water, which is driven up high against them. Beyond that we can already see the fields full of young sugar cane standing in long rows, every row separated by two furrows, running far inland until the thick forest cuts this view off at the horizon. In all of Louisiana and in large parts of Mississippi and Arkansas, the three states that lie along the banks of the lower Mississippi, this remains the predominant picture of the shoreline landscape: a levee rises about four feet above water level, behind this is low-lying arable land, and again behind this the dark strip of the thick woods is always present. But now large stretches of the cultivated land are under water, which extends deep into the countryside* like a shallow lake.

The evening glow, whose image in the water is broken up by the river's waves into a play of bright spots, stripes, and circles, is reflected in the flooded areas like one big golden mirror. In the twilight we cannot see the already half-washed-away homes nor the villages in which the waters have been standing ankle deep for weeks. Only large holes in the levees and here and there an

---

*AT THIS TIME (APRIL 1874) ON THE OPPOSITE SIDE FROM MEMPHIS THE STATE OF ARKANSAS WAS UNDER WATER UP TO TEN GERMAN (FORTY-SEVEN STATUTE) MILES INLAND FROM THE RIVER. [ED. NOTE: THE FLOODS OF SPRING 1874 CAUSED WIDE DEVASTATION ALONG THE MISSISSIPPI AND ITS TRIBUTARIES, AND BOTH GOVERNMENT AND VOLUNTARY AID WERE SENT FROM OTHER PARTS OF THE COUNTRY TO ALLEVIATE THE SUFFERING.]

uprooted tree can be made out. Everything looks like scenes of destruction. You would think that the Mississippi would be filled with wreckage, that you would hear the rushing sound of the terrible flood, which is still pouring in through the breaches in the levees over the countryside—but nothing of this can be heard or seen; rather, the picture is so peaceful that it makes one uncomfortable. We have heard so much in the last few weeks about the ravages of this river; now it looks as quiet as a mountain lake from which the tall mountains surrounding it keep away the storms, and in the evening it seems especially peaceful. Under the uniformly dark glassy surface, which spreads over it after the glow of sunset, you don't even recognize its muddy yellow color anymore. You don't see any waves like those the keel and the rudder of the ship plow up, you don't hear any water eddying or flowing past, at most you hear the gurgling breaking of the waves on the bank when we come close to the shore. You get the feeling that this river is too mighty to be able to carry out its work of destruction merely by convulsive outbursts like the sudden swelling of a glacier stream. It is like a man with immense strength who with a playful finger presses his opponent down without a muscle or an expression betraying that it in any way caused him the least bit of effort. Only once did I see its waters carrying out their destructive work as they drove an old cedar trunk, which had been caught in a break in the levee by its bulky maze of roots, deeper and deeper with the blows of the waves, now boring, now pushing, into the hole that in a short time would surely become a bigger breach. The cedar trunk went about its ruinous work so zealously that it looked like a living being, full of wickedness and malice; the trunk itself will soon be forced onto the land along with the flood, which will bury it somewhere in its mud.

The next morning we came to the old state capital, Baton Rouge, a country town that lies on the southernmost of the bluffs, which here and there rise out of the prairie-like flatlands of the Mississippi valley. Vicksburg and Memphis and many smaller places are also built on similar bluffs. These are alluvial formations, which around Memphis, for example, consist solely of yellow clay. On the highest point of the Baton Rouge bluff stands the capitol building, which is built in a sort of Gothic castle style.[4] A few years ago it was so completely burned out that it now does a good job of looking like an old ruin. The only thing is it now reveals too much of the red brick, the commonplace, poor quality mortar, and the deceptive modern exterior finish, and in any case it will never reach the venerable age of a genuine ruin. The Negro masters alone, who like nothing better than to collect objects they find, will energetically take care of that here. I have seen them taking a great deal of time and trouble fishing out driftwood, effort that if used for any regular work would have certainly been twice as profitable. In such matters as the example given here they are as useful as carrion-devouring birds.

Our ship was puffing heavily but went steadily on its way and had already accomplished the task of overtaking a big St. Louis steamboat, which had left New Orleans an hour before us—a task that even before leaving had been the most popular topic of discussion; I was only surprised that it didn't lead, as usual, to big bets being taken. A breakdown in the engine occurred, which caused an involuntary five-hour halt, but hopes of overtaking the steamboat were not given up. Every streak of smoke visible ahead of us was credited to the *City of Quincy*, and as we finally caught up to her on the third night, it really was a cruel disappointment that a sudden breakdown in the machinery again forced us to stop for a few hours. It wasn't the delay in the trip itself so much as losing the chance to overtake the rival that annoyed our people, who had counted on victory. Certainly many of them would have been very happy if the captains, following the grand tradition of Mississippi navigation, had gone all out for a dangerous boat race.

IMPRESSION MADE BY LARGE RIVERS. SCENIC CHARACTER OF THE MISSISSIPPI. SHORELINE FORESTATION. AGRICULTURAL CULTIVATION. CITIES ON THE SHORE. TRAFFIC ON THE MISSISSIPPI. POPULATION OF THE RIVER STATES. THE OHIO. ITS RIVERBANK SCENERY.

As a general rule, one can say that the immediate impression of large rivers falls far short of their true significance. Neither their destructive nor their creative work can be seen from their external appearance. Therefore, whoever approaches the Mississippi, for example, which we know is one of the largest vital arteries of America, a land rich in rivers, and expects to find a magnificent natural spectacle, will definitely find himself disappointed. A body of water strikingly wide only in a few places, in which the current is so little noticeable that by early morning light or at dusk you could believe yourself transported to a very quiet inland lake; low, almost completely forested shorelines, once in a while an island just as low or a reed bank that is just becoming an island, something halfway between a sandbank and an island—these are the sights it offers. Because of the Mississippi's unusually winding course, you seldom have broad vistas either upstream or downstream, and in the end the most impressive thing that remains is the length of time in which we have this river that always looks the same—wide, tranquil, and without change—fixed in front of our eyes. We have seen it look the same for four days and nights from the sea up to the mouth of the Ohio, and from this fact alone can comprehend what an overpowering, grandiose impression it made on the Europeans when they were carried in their fragile canoes towards the sea on its waves for the first time. From the estuary of the Ohio to that of the Missouri, which is still two days travel farther northwestwards, its features still remain the same, so that indeed you can call it one of the most magnificent rivers and at the same time the most remarkably monotonous one there is. Moreover, one has to supplement the impression of the various parts of the river with the help of a map and a topographical description in order really to keep in mind its dimensions and significance.

As is well known, the color of the Mississippi is yellow, not the thick, cloudy yellow characteristic of many other rivers but rather a brighter, half-transparent yellow, slightly tending towards grey. The mud particles, which give it this color, are so fine that you can leave Mississippi water standing for weeks in a glass without it becoming clear. At first, of course, a very small amount of the yellow powder goes to the bottom, but it still remains yellow, translucently cloudy. One soon gets to like this coloring, which generates beautiful effects, particularly at midday when the surface of the water reflects the blue of the sky in a silver-blue shimmer, while the sunlight makes the tops of the waves glow, so that despite its dull tone the water's yellow color shines wonderfully.

Because of the monotony of the landscape along the river, the passage of time and conditions at various times of day as reflected in the river offer greater interest and compensate for the lack of magnificent or lovely scenery along the bank with a wealth of engaging views. On the ocean one anxiously awaits the rise of the moon and the stars that brings with it a change in the heavens and on the surface of the water. As opposed to being on land, being on the ocean gives one an entirely different perspective of those unique things—the dawn's glow and the evening twilight, yes, even the cloud formations—which every day almost always seem the same to us. As time goes on it's like that here too. As soon as the sun has set, bush and forest on the shore become two low borders, which like hedges or fences enclose a shimmering roadway. Meanwhile, on the water's surface the golden glow, which reflects the deep yellow and red of the evening sky, spreads out over the water and often continues on into the forest whose floor is covered with water. Here the glow dances like thousands of will-o'-the-wisps on the waves breaking on the tree trunks. When the colors of the sky dim and gather more along the horizon, the surface of the water also becomes dull and only shows a reflection on the bigger waves originating from the sides of the ship. As for the rest of the water, it lies there like a dark crystal. Nothing of the cloudy color is noticeable, and you could believe that if right now a meteor shot across the sky and lit up the darkness, you would be able to see into this water right down to its very depths.

Now the moon appears behind the trees, causing new will-o'-the-wisps, this time like silver flames, to dance on the water below them. It begins to rise and transforms the play of the waves trailing behind the ship into either a boiling sea of molten incandescent silver in the distance or into a nearby mass of silver circles, curves, and dots, which are continually dissolving, reforming, and intertwining to create the most varied figures. This reflection is at times similar to the phosphorescence on the ocean but without the peculiar phosphorous shimmer and the light shining up from the deep that is characteristic of it. Towards morning the natural color of the river, the muddy, semitranslucent yellow, emerges again in order to become once more similar to a mirror as soon as the sun appears. Wherever the waves beat, in the light of the early sun it's as if a yellow liquid were boiling over a shimmering surface that, depending on the movement of the waves, appears to rise, open, or close.

The woods on the shoreline generally look the same all along the way. One sees solitary magnolias or live oaks here and there standing in fields or in front of homes. The former are recognizable by their dark green leaves and uniformly slender leafed tops. In the distance the bizarre tops of the cypresses, always densely covered with Spanish moss, frequently jut out over the smaller trees, primarily willows and aspens* and a few sycamores, which alone cover the edge of the river, the islands, and the flooded low-lying areas. This forestation seems to be very dense because of the bush-like willows and grows to be very high because of the aspens, which like most trees at home in the swamp are noticeably slender and grow straight up. But it never loses the character of a young forest because so many trees and bushes shoot up in the moist, rich, swampy soil that few of them can properly develop. Only the sycamores ordinarily grow into fully developed trees and more than all the others enliven the landscape along the banks with their white branches and the yellow-green color of their new leaves. Every one of them has a different shape because the branches are strong but few in number. The tree tops therefore are very transparent, and have a tendency to begin branching off very early, so that often heavy boughs branch off from the trunk right above the roots and shoot up straight as flagpoles, while at other times the entire trunk spreads out over the roots in four or five branches, or forks into two parts, so that you think you see a pair of trees in front of you. Nevertheless, the forestation along the river bank is mostly low, and wherever the willows prevail, actually looks more like bushes.

In Louisiana the lowlands along the Mississippi are under cultivation or at least bear traces of having once been carefully cultivated. Sugar cane and rice are the crops that are grown here and provide high yields. Here and there one sees a palatial-looking building and near it, without fail, a simple factory-like structure with two tall chimneys. The latter is the so-called sugarhouse where the cane is pressed and the juice is boiled away; the former is the planter's home. In the splendor and luxury that once existed here, the homes resembled many princely palaces of the Old World, but now they either stand deserted or

---

*A TYPE OF ASPEN, WHICH BOTANISTS CALL *POPULUS MONILIFERA* AND PEOPLE LIVING NEAR THE MISSISSIPPI CALL COTTONWOOD, IS PARTICULARLY CHARACTERISTIC AND MORE FREQUENTLY SEEN ON THE BANKS OF THE MISSISSIPPI AND ITS SUBSIDIARIES THAN ANY OTHER BUSH OR TREE. FROM HERE TO THE BORDER OF CALIFORNIA'S VEGETATION ON THE OTHER SIDE OF THE ROCKY MOUNTAINS, IT IS THE MOST COMMONLY FOUND SPECIES OF TREE, AND ALONG GREAT STRETCHES OF THE WESTERN PRAIRIES AND THE PLAINS IT IS ACTUALLY THE ONLY ONE.

their magnificence hangs loosely around their impoverished existence like a bright robe around an ailing, aged body. It is the unanimous opinion of all who know this area that the present appearance of the cultivated parts of Louisiana, especially those along the Mississippi River, is now almost the very opposite of what it was before the last war. Louisiana was the richest and best cultivated state in the South, and the plantations extended like endless gardens along the river and its numerous estuary branches and canals. Now a large portion of the land is in the hands of former slaves who leave it neglected, and another part can no longer be used because of a lack of people to work it. The miserable log cabins and wooden shacks where the blacks live are grouped around the half-dilapidated planters' homes. Everything, even the landing stages hanging half-torn away along the shore, even the terrible condition of the levees and the wretchedness of the cattle one sees grazing here and there, speaks of decay. The flooding, which now covers large stretches of once arable land, combines all these elements together into a very sorry picture.

In comparison to these ruins of a culture, the thinly populated stretches along the river in Arkansas, Mississippi, and Tennessee, which are still frequently in their natural state, were very refreshing sights. Even the most primitive natural state is more satisfactory than the sight of a culture that has been half-destroyed at the height of its growth, like the one that confronted us all along the way in Louisiana. To be sure, everywhere we landed we found bands of idling Negroes and whites who looked as if they had no knowledge of work but were ready to pick a fight, as if they had just returned from the war. Some of those whom I saw in Arkansas had a definite Latin look about them—dark complexion, black eyes, hair hanging down to the shoulders, tall with proud bearing. One could presume that Spanish or perhaps even Indian blood flowed in their veins. One family consisted of an old man, a younger man, and a young woman, who could also be taken for typical Southern types. The former two appeared very old-fashioned and picturesque with their tattered coats, high boots, and broad hats, while the woman, shielding her face with a long blue veil and wearing clothes as good as can be, looked very up-to-date and urban in her dress. They were in the process of emigrating and, judging from the condition and the small number of their belongings, were very poor. Nevertheless, the two men did not in the least look at the world with downhearted spirits but rather viewed it openly and even boldly; among all the people on the ship, I didn't see anyone who appeared as unconcerned and courageous as these. I thought, these people, if they wished to talk, could perhaps say along with the squatter in Cooper's *Prairie* "I have come . . . into these districts, because I found the law sitting too tight upon me, and am not over fond of neighbors who can't settle a dispute without troubling a justice and twelve men. . . ."[5] Of course, both of them were armed, for you can seldom be together with a rural Southerner for an hour without getting an occasional view of a revolver or a dagger.

Besides Baton Rouge, we also went past Vicksburg, Memphis, and Cairo on this trip. The first two places are situated on elevations, as I have already described. The fronts of a number of business concerns face the river, along with some modest summer homes, like those one usually finds in the environs of this type of city. But within, both cities, as far as I can see from a quick view, are dirtier than usual and are paved poorly or not paved at all but are nonetheless uniformly laid out with straight streets, as one is accustomed to seeing in American cities. I was informed by a young Swiss fellow, who got on in Helena (Arkansas) in order to go to the celebration, that just at that time the Germans in Memphis were having a May Day festival. He was looking forward to a lot of fun and dancing at the festival, for which he was "dressed to kill." Cairo, the first significant city in Illinois and an important railroad junction point, has a more prosperous look about it than the two Southern cities. Numerous ships lay anchored before the long row of warehouses extending along the shore, and despite the early hour there was already a great deal of activity on the railroad. In the vicinity of Cairo large steam-powered mills have the name "Egyptian Mills" affixed on them in letters clearly visible for a great distance. But not far away we read "City of Karlsruhe Hotel," which didn't quite help this attempt to add a further dimension to the illusion created around the venerable Egyptian city name.

Except for these cities and some smaller landing stages there was not much activity or traffic to be perceived. Several ships were anchored in Baton Rouge, Vicksburg, and Memphis, and quite a few in Cairo, but we seldom met more than one steamship per day, and on the entire trip saw no more than five flatboats. Since we were not yet in the summer season, when the ship traffic and general commerce from the interior to New Orleans is usually limited to only the most essential things, this was at any rate blamed in part on the all-round sluggishness of business about which the tradespeople on board were endlessly complaining.[6] On the whole, one can nevertheless say that traffic on the Mississippi has in no way increased to the degree that development of the states that are located in its river basin would lead one to expect. We see this phenomenon all over in the transportation life of the river basin, while the faster, more comfortable, safer railroad transportation is entering into competition with the riverboat traffic. This is particularly striking on the Mississippi, since one cannot doubt that its location and size and the nature of the entire river system that belongs to it make it one of the greatest promoters of transportation and communication of all rivers in the world. It is, in fact, the main artery of the most populated, richest, and most industrious regions of America. Its invariable abundance of water, its depth, its breadth, the relatively straight course that it takes, and the length of its navigable section make it the paragon of a large, natural means of transportation. Accordingly, its importance was extraordinary as long as the railroad had not yet connected the major cities of its basin.

The amazingly rapid development of Mississippi steamboat traffic, which had gone from two small steamers in 1817 to 220 with 40,000 tons already by

1832, must have aroused very great expectations at that time when settlements had scarcely reached the estuary of the Missouri River and were quite sparse along the middle of the Mississippi, in Tennessee and Arkansas. But the advances made in steamboat traffic, as important as they were, soon ceased keeping pace with the development of resources and the growth of population in this large river basin. I alluded to this fact in discussing the commerce of New Orleans,[7] which is naturally affected more than any other city by the increase and decrease in traffic along the Mississippi. The reason for the decrease lies basically in the length of time ship transportation requires as compared with the railroad. The situation that makes this problem particularly sensitive here is that New Orleans, at the inner edge of the Gulf of Mexico, catches up to the main lines of the large Europe-America-Europe traffic, all of which leave from the Atlantic Coast, only after first making the long and dangerous detour around the Florida peninsula. Together with the above-mentioned reason for the stagnation taking place in New Orleans, this situation helps explain why Tennessee, for example, despite its position on the Mississippi, for the last few years has been sending large quantities of cotton to Atlantic ports.

On the Ohio we are already coming into the sphere of influence of the more dynamic and active way of life that extends out over this broad land from the Atlantic Coast. The river takes us through an area that, measured by American standards, can be called highly civilized. Along its banks extend the most fertile and densely populated states of the West: Kentucky, Illinois, Indiana, and Ohio. Right at this point, where, as it comes out of the northern Alleghenies, the Ohio becomes navigable—at the gate to the Pennsylvania coal region as it were—there lies the important industrial city of Pittsburgh, and further downstream the significant commercial and manufacturing cities of Cincinnati and Louisville, both of which belong to the emporiums of the West. Further on lies Evansville, (22,000 inhabitants), and opposite the river's entry into the Mississippi lies Cairo (6,300 inhabitants), both important business and manufacturing centers. These are already entirely different situations than we found along the Mississippi where, except for New Orleans, the only significant places between the Ohio estuary and the sea were Vicksburg and Memphis, of which only the latter had a population of something over 40,000 while Vicksburg had only 13,000. Going further, if we compare the population of the various states along the Mississippi, we find Louisiana with 726,915 inhabitants, Mississippi with 827,921, Arkansas with 484,471, Tennessee with 1,258,520, Kentucky with 1,321,011, Illinois with 2,539,891, Indiana with 1,680,637, and Ohio with 2,665,260. If we add to this the fact that in the four states along the lower Mississippi the number of farms is 264,069 and the factories 10,684, while one finds 678,467 farms and 52,607 factories in the above-mentioned states along the Ohio, the markedly sharp cultural difference is obvious.

In addition to the very different topography of both river valleys, in accordance with the above-mentioned conditions, the scenery on the riverbank changes a great deal as soon as we turn into the Ohio River. Already on the Missouri side of the Mississippi the bank is elevated for long stretches and seems more extensively cultivated and more densely settled than in any of the more southerly sections, with the exception of southern Louisiana. Here on the Ohio it is usual to see uninterrupted cultivation of the valley's soil, which even now at high tide stands on the average just six to ten feet above the water, and the further upstream we go, the bright green of the wheat fields, the darker green of the oats, orchards in full bloom, and well-kept settlements, villages, and small towns supersede the lowland forestation, which absolutely predominated in the Mississippi valley.

Frequently where the river appears to cut itself off from the sea because of a bend, you have some villages in a semicircle or even a little town on the shore, and all around you see fields and gardens between the river and the valley's surrounding hills, which for some time now have no longer been as thickly forested as nature would have it. In the evening when the Ohio, which flows much more peacefully than the Mississippi, is smooth as glass and the whole picture stretches out in a somewhat placid mood, half-obscured, you could think yourself transported to the Weser[8] or to the Danube. But the illusion disappears as soon as the bank becomes low again and covered with swampy vegetation, or as soon as the hills come directly down to the water, so that there is no valley floor left. One immediately sees that the people here have just picked out the most convenient places to cultivate and to build houses, whereas villages on higher ground or those protected by embankments in the low-lying area, as in Germany, are simply not to be found. In fact, you seldom ever find single houses on the inviting, flat hilltops or on the promontories of the valley slopes. On the other hand, however, ship traffic is heavier here than on the Mississippi. We especially met many flatboats going downstream with loads of coal and others with iron ore (from Missouri) going upstream. The boats with the heavier iron ore were, so to speak, being shoved along by steamships, which have one big paddle wheel at the rear, and which usually have two very large flatboats secured to the front of them. The laborious heaving, towing motion of these misshapen conglomerates looks absolutely awful. Even when working their way through the waves without anything attached to them, these so-called stern-wheelers are very ponderous looking things. Every time the unshapely wheel creates a big wave out of the water, it looks as if it wants to lift the whole boat into the air from the back and if possible run by itself in the water.

In some places coal barges lay by the hundreds in long rows of pairs along the shore. We meet big and small freight and passenger steamers coming or going in every one of the bends, which divide the river into a series of detached scenes, and we find one or more of them at the landing of every little town that we pass by.

After the monotony of the Mississippi valley, the low hilly shore of this river is really refreshing. There isn't anything significant about it, but still there aren't the perpetual, endless parallel lines of the water level, shoreline, and bushes. As small as the hills are, valleys, even gorges, also dark cave entrances are still visible in which we can imagine there are all sorts of things, whereas with the Mississippi one has to have a really good imagination to picture its valley with its bushy river banks containing vistas other than the flat, low-lying, swampy scenery that we had constantly before our eyes. In this regard, landscapes that are not especially beautiful are like faces that are not especially beautiful: what attracts us most are the things that keep us guessing; they are all the more interesting the more our imagination is aroused by their features—to expound, to delineate, to expand on, and to follow up on them. If the tallest tops of a pine forest tower above an elevation that is nonetheless relatively level, it indicates there is a valley on whose slopes these trees are growing and that in our mind's eye we can give life to the floor of the valley with brooks, meadows, and fields and friendly, quietly secluded dwellings. It is the same when a mountain spur hides a valley of which we only get a fleeting glimpse as we ride by, when a road or even a railway line runs inland behind the ridge of the shoreline, or when a church tower looms above it. Fortunately, here along the Ohio there is no lack of beautiful scenic material along the banks to satisfy the most demanding wishes for filling in the background. I think what you often hear said is true: the Ohio looks more European than any other North American river.

Naturally the activity along the banks as well as on the river itself near the two large cities here is most impressive. Both are situated at sharp turns in the river, extend along the banks with elongated, narrow suburbs, have important localities lying opposite them on the other side of the river, and are recognizable at a great distance by the thick clouds of smoke and imposing bridges, which span the river with astonishingly daring arches visible from afar. Numerous steamships are anchored at their wharves, which are densely covered with barrels and bales. Both Louisville and Cincinnati have neither pretty nor imposing riverfronts; they impress at first only by the number of their buildings.

CHAPTER SEVENTEEN

The Three Major Cities of the West

FOUR LARGE TRANSPORTATION ZONES OF THE INTERIOR OF THE UNITED STATES. THEIR MAJOR CITIES. GRADUAL DEVELOPMENT. CINCINNATI. EARLIEST DEVELOPED OF THESE CITIES. SIGNIFICANCE OF THE OHIO FOR THE SETTLING OF THE WEST. OLD IMMIGRATION ROUTE. TWO WAVES OF IMMIGRATION. GROWTH OF THE POPULATION IN THE OHIO BASIN. SITE OF CINCINNATI. LAYOUT OF THE CITY. ARCHITECTURE. GENERAL IMPRESSION. INDUSTRIAL SIGNIFICANCE. COMMERCE. CINCINNATI'S IMPORTANCE FOR THE SOUTHEAST.

The interior of the United States, that huge expanse of plains, is bounded on the east and west by the two "backbones" of the continent, the Alleghenies and the Rockies, on the south by the Gulf of Mexico, and on the north by that low but huge plateau of the Canadian lake basin. For communication and traffic purposes it naturally divides into four large sections, which correspond to the four prominent topographical features of this region. Natural transportation units are formed in the North by the Great Lakes; in the West by the Missouri, the greatest western tributary of the Mississippi; in the East it is the Ohio, the most important of the eastern tributaries; and finally in the South, the Mississippi itself, which quite naturally forms the valley out of the fertile areas that lie along both of its banks up to the distant mountains. Not only do their tributary streams and rivers flow into them but also their traffic, which then find their way through the riverbed of the mighty Mississippi to the sea with its international connections. For the close relationship between transportation and urban development to exist, it is necessary for each of these natural transportation regions to have its own junction point. Moreover, the extreme demographic sparseness yet enormous activity of this young people, the huge quantity yet one-sided type of goods produced (which from the very start presupposes an active trading), the amount of commerce as well as the pace of the traffic all require these junctions be cities far surpassing any other settlements in the entire area. Actually we have seen four large cities in this section of the country that have developed with remarkable speed. We already know the one in the Mississippi region, New Orleans; it now remains for us to consider the other three: Cincinnati in the Ohio region, Chicago in that of the Great Lakes, and St. Louis in the Missouri region.

Of the three "Queens of the West," the honor of first place is easily due to Cincinnati as the first that came to have a significant importance for the young West. St. Louis followed her from that moment when the settlements on the Mississippi spread out over the Ohio region and extended up the Missouri and over the west bank of this river. The Northwest,[1] which for a long time was considered inhospitable, began to be populated when the area of the Great Lakes—instead of fostering intimate contacts with the less inviting, more slowly progressing Canada, to which nature had at first directed it—began to develop close ties by means of canals and railroads to the New England states and particularly with tremendously enterprising New York. What the Ohio meant to Cincinnati, and the Missouri and Mississippi to St. Louis, the Erie Canal and the railroads running to the Atlantic Coast meant to Chicago. Even more than Cincinnati and St. Louis, Chicago is a product of the last few decades, although it has in part already equaled the other two in size and importance and in fact has already surpassed them.

The geographic position of St. Louis at the confluence of the two major arms of the Mississippi and that of Chicago at the far end of that part of the Great Lakes chain that reaches farthest into the Midwest, readily show these sites to be important, commanding ones boding well for the future. They are locations that seem to be unique in these regions, precluding all competition, completely fulfilling the requirements governing the sites of large transportation and cultural centers. There is, however, nothing as positive to say about Cincinnati's location. Where St. Louis and Chicago are situated, major cities were bound to arise. Even if they did not develop from exactly the spot where they actually first began to grow and expand, they nevertheless found the right site somewhere in the immediate vicinity. We can really see how a number of embryonic metropolises have tried to spring up very close to one another in a small area there and that the simple common sense of the first settlers had clearly recognized the suitability of these two spots for the site of the major cities of the West. Cincinnati, on the other hand, for several decades was the metropolis of the West partly because of fortuitous circumstances, but in the course of time had to give up its leading position as these circumstances became less important, as is the way with such things.

If one looks at Cincinnati on the map, or better when one visits it and compares its location with that of the two other large cities on the Ohio River, Pittsburgh and Louisville, one becomes well aware that not only does it not have as advantageous a site as the two other metropolises, but that it does not even have the best location in the region it commands. It takes second place to St. Louis and Chicago because the river on which it stands plays a less significant role for traffic and transportation than do the bodies of water on which the other two cities stand, and Cincinnati itself lies a greater distance away from the region's gateways to international travel—the Hudson, the St. Lawrence, and the Mississippi. In addition, it is not even situated as conveniently for navigation on the Ohio as Louisville farther downstream, which is the last stop for unhindered big ship traffic. On the other hand, its industrial future is not as bright as that of Pittsburgh, which is further upstream, the last stop for all navigation on the Ohio, very advantageously placed in the middle of the extremely rich coal and iron region of Pennsylvania, and which radiates its influence almost equidistantly out to New York, Philadelphia, and Baltimore in the East, Buffalo, Cleveland, and Detroit in the North, and Cincinnati, Indianapolis, and Chicago in the West. Cincinnati, therefore, does not have the prospect of gaining the predominant position that the other two Western large cities certainly possess. It has to content itself with a more modest role and put up with the competition of newer, smaller, less famous cities, which for their part can think about placing themselves some day on the same footing with the former leading city of the West. But the significance it has already attained and kept for itself, and the rich and influential, although brief, history it has behind it, assure it a leading place among North American cities for a long time yet.

The reasons for the quick development and erstwhile great importance of Cincinnati are to be found above all in the role that was assigned to the upper and middle Ohio in the settlement of the West and in the history of this settlement itself. During the eventful years from 1770 to 1800, when for the first time the colonization of the West was energetically begun by the old Atlantic states and when the land between the Allegheny Mountains and the Mississippi was won for cultivation, two large streams of immigrants, the only ones from that period worth mentioning, were moving towards the middle Ohio region. One came from the Southeast from the states lying around the Chesapeake Bay, mainly from Virginia, and the other from Pennsylvania, New York, and the New England states. The former group occupied what is today West Virginia and Kentucky, which lie on the left bank of the Ohio, the latter at first penetrated into the area of the headstreams of the Ohio, moved from there down along the right or west bank of the Ohio, and then into the interior. This was in contradiction to the treaties with the Indians, which forbade white settlements west of the Ohio. Therefore, the settlement of the Ohio region took place only amidst constant fighting. Not until 1810, after the overthrow of the great chieftain Tecumseh, could the area on this side of the Wabash River be considered as having been fully wrested from the Indians,[2] while the entire territory up to the Mississippi and including Wisconsin could not be thus classified before the beginning of the 1830s.

Not without some truth did the traders describe the Ohio territory as a paradise to the Easterners so anxious to travel. Its mild climate, its excellent water supply, and its generally rolling countryside, with which its frequent alternation of natural forest and fields already foreshadows the attractive park-like landscape of the eastern prairies of Indiana and Illinois, all make this one of the loveliest and most fruitful areas of North America. For decades now it has formed the center of the farming states of the Union. One understands the practicality with which immigrants turned toward this region and why they for decades regarded the Ohio basin as their preferred goal. Only with the opening up of the Northwest by New York and the New England states did the migration flow change its course. The old immigration routes, which came from the three ports, New York, Philadelphia, and Baltimore, all headed towards Pittsburgh, and then together went down the Ohio Valley and from there, according to choice, either south, west, or northwards. The present-day main route for immigration, which takes the shortest way via Chicago to get from New York, the large assembly point for immigrants to the Far West and Northwest, was hardly used until forty years ago. It was only a footpath in comparison with the famous route towards the Ohio River. Thus, as it were, this beautiful area became a collecting place where throngs of humanity driven westward in unbroken and endless streams from the old Atlantic states and from distant Europe were merged. But what particularly accelerated the total occupation of this river basin was the standstill in colonization, which the long-drawn-out, uncertain conditions to the West and Northwest, in Indiana and Illinois, had brought about. The territory of what is today the state of Ohio, as well as West Virginia and Kentucky, had been taken from the Indians with relatively little trouble in numerous yet nevertheless small and sporadic battles. The somewhat more dangerous and important Indian wars for a time placed a block on the further expansion westward and northwestward. Later the immigration ceased flowing exclusively into the Ohio basin as it had formerly done and became diverted more and more toward the Northwest and Far West. One easily comprehends the total consequences of this situation when one sees that Kentucky, the area on the south bank of the Ohio, became the first state west of the Alleghenies in 1792, and that Ohio entered the Union as the second one in 1802, while Indiana entered only in 1816 and Illinois not before 1818. Moreover, the population figures also correspond to these developments. Ohio went up from 45,365 inhabitants in 1800 to 1,980,408 fifty years later, Indiana, which is only about one-sixth smaller in size, went from 4,875 in 1800 to 990,258 in 1850, and Illinois, which is one-ninth larger that Ohio, rose from 12,282 in 1810 to 855,384 in 1850. Last year Ohio had the third largest population in the Union and since then has been holding its own in the front rank.

One understands then how this early growth of the central Ohio region was bound to confer immense significance on the major city of the area. The predominant position to which Cincinnati was raised, until the entrance of the Northwest and of the Upper Mississippi region into the great cultural mainstream of North America, is to a certain degree only a reflection of the position unquestionably occupied by Ohio among the states, the Ohio River among transportation routes, and the Ohio land route among the great paths of immigration during almost the entire first half of our century. In this regard, a glance at the growth figures of the three large cities of the West will indicate an important aspect of urban and cultural history.

	Cincinnati	St. Louis	Chicago
1788	—	1,197	—
1800	750	—	—
1810	2,540	1,600	—
1820	9,642	4,598	—
1830	24,831	5,852	—
1840	46,338	16,469	4,470
1850	115,436	77,860	29,963
1860	161,044	160,773	109,260
1870	216,239	310,864	298,977

If anywhere, figures talk here. We see in the growth of Cincinnati the early significance of the Ohio region, which has been steadily gaining since the beginning of this century. St. Louis indicates how the central Mississippi area from the 1830s onward energetically entered upon this course and by its huge natural advantages for quick development was soon able to leave Cincinnati behind. Finally, Chicago, the newest, whose remarkably quick growth is even surpassing that of St. Louis, shows what the concerted effort of canals and railroads together with the advantages of an excellent geographical location is able to accomplish. From 1840 on, when for the first time these three cities coexisted, they grew from decade to decade in the following ratio: Cincinnati 1 : 2.4 : 3.4 : 4.6; St. Louis 1 : 4.7 : 9.7 : 18.8; Chicago 1 : 6.7 : 24.6 : 66.8.

Let us first return to Cincinnati, to the most venerable among these young queens. In addition to the general statements made above about its site, it must still be added that this site, topographically considered, is excellent. The hills along the Ohio, which above and below the city come down to the river, have left open a free space, an embayment, around which they fall back forming a semicircle. This embayment is fortunately no flat plain as such formations usually are but is a little plateau situated out of the reach of the often very serious and dangerously quick floodings of the Ohio River. A city would have hardly developed here on low ground. Indeed, this embayment is somewhat narrow, in fact really too narrow for a new metropolis that is trying to gain space in all the glens and on all the slopes of the surrounding mountains and that suffers from the heat and the clouds of smoke and dust the valley locks in, particularly in summer. The mountains, moreover, are formed from silurian slate, which, like the banded limestone of our triassic formation, crumbles easily and strongly tends to a build up of dust and debris.

With the increasing growth of the city, the residential areas are steadily extricating themselves from the basin-shaped valley and moving on up the surrounding heights and into the green valley of the Little Miami River, which flows into the Ohio near Cincinnati. What remains in the valley then, near the river, are the businesses, the shops, offices, warehouses and workshops of the merchants and tradespeople. These, however, will always have to put up with the confining situation, which, caused partly by the steep incline of some well-traveled streets and the rather narrow layout of the streets, is already becoming very unpleasant. The murky, soot-filled atmosphere, which comes from the use of bituminous coal by the numerous factories, makes this disadvantage all the more serious to someone coming from the big cities of the East, where generally the bright-burning anthracite coal is used. On the other hand, it is all the more airy and fresh on the surrounding heights. There several suburbs, "little residential cities," have been built in the midst of very lush meadows and numerous groves of trees, like in one huge garden and park. Cincinnati is trying to compensate for the cramped site of its most important section, its business district, with huge park sites in these pleasant surrounding areas.[3] One therefore hopes that Cincinnati will continue to enjoy its substantial prosperity so that it will always have the possibility of extricating itself out of the narrow rocky enclosure and at least move up to dwelling places on the cleaner heights.

The city is evenly laid out as far as the topography allows. The model of Philadelphia is not hard to recognize here. Even the naming of the streets reminds one of the Quaker City.* Also, the architectural character can be better compared with that of Philadelphia than of New York, just as the Pennsylvania influences have been the most powerful of all those from the old transmontane states that have played a role here. Similarly and no less clearly, Chicago shows through its dealing with New York and the New England states, as well as the history of settlement in the entire Great Lakes region, its very

---

*THE STREETS PARALLEL TO THE RIVER, I.E., THOSE RUNNING EASTWARD, ARE DESIGNATED BY NUMBERS, THOSE INTERSECTING THEM AT RIGHT ANGLES ARE GENERALLY DESIGNATED BY THE NAMES OF TREES LOCAL TO THE AREA.

close links to them.[4] Chicago's looks remind you of no other city in the Union as much as New York. Thus the rule is confirmed here that cultural influences, which go from east to west into the interior, have followed the latitude from which they started almost in a straight line.

In spite of its cramped location, Cincinnati has also copied Philadelphia in its preference for small dwellings, which wherever possible are only meant for a single family. It has not yet gotten to the point of presenting the display of magnificence that makes the main streets of New York, Boston, and Chicago look like streets lined with palaces. Of course, in the central parts, in the business sections, the tall, handsome granite and sandstone buildings are the prevalent type now, but in many other parts of the city the description that Monsieur Chevalier wrote when he visited it in 1832 still fits today. He said then:

> The architectural appearance of Cincinnati is very nearly the same with that of the new quarters of the English towns. The houses are generally of brick, most commonly three stories high, with the windows shining with cleanliness, calculated each for a single family, and regularly placed along well paved and spacious streets, sixty feet in width. Here and there the prevailing uniformity is interrupted by some more imposing edifice, and there are some houses of hewn stone in very good taste, real palaces in miniature, with neat porticoes, inhabited by the aristocratic portion of Mrs. Trollope's hog merchants,[5] and several very pretty mansions surrounded with gardens and terraces. Then there are the common schoolhouses. . . . In another direction you see a small, plain church, without sculpture or paintings, without colored glass or gothic arches, but snug, well carpeted, and well-warmed by stoves. In Cincinnati, as everywhere else in the United States, there is a great number of churches. . . .[6]

All this, just as it is described here, is still to be found in the outer sections of the city and stands out as the predominant feature in all the new cities and in the outer sections of the older big cities of the United States. The inner city of this Western queen, however, has already become a bustling, noisy, steaming, smoke-blackened industrial city.

Cincinnati's industrial significance will without doubt steadily win out over its commercial importance. Its geographical position does not permit it to compete successfully with Chicago in trade, as its inhabitants had formerly dreamed of doing, but it does have more advantages for industry than any other important city in the West. If one doesn't think it frivolous to make a prediction about these rapid and eventful developments here in the West, which have already so often caused all calculations to be cast to the winds, then with regard to Cincinnati one would least likely go wrong if he saw it as one of the future industrial centers of North America. Of all the Western states, Ohio is the richest in coal and iron. It alone has a considerable piece of the great Pennsylvania coal and iron ore deposits within its borders. Further west, the coal beds taper off, until in Illinois and Iowa they simply are often no longer worth mining, while in Nebraska and Kansas they run out entirely. In addition, a rapidly growing population is more readily able to augment the labor force of the factories than is the case farther to the west.

It is therefore not irrelevant that industry has already played a prominent role in Cincinnati's initial growth. It justifiably still bears its nickname and honorary title "Porcopolis," since the pork-butcher industry got started here, and it is together with Chicago still the center of the industry.

As early as the 1830s, people commented with admiration about the industrial activity of the citizens of this new city. At that time, however, there were no huge smokestacks exuding smoke within its boundaries as there are today, but it already did contain an astonishingly large number of middle-sized workshops, which supplied the West even beyond the Mississippi, then still caught up in the first wave of rapid settlement and development, with its needs for cheap agricultural tools and household utensils. In time, the workshops became factories, and already by 1870 one estimated that thirty thousand people were employed here in large-scale industry. In 1872–1873, Cincinnati exported $77,000,000 of "miscellaneous manufactures," $18,500,000 of whiskey, and $12,500,000 of pickled pork. The total of all exports for the same year was valued at $213,000,000, so that these three industrial products alone accounted for more than half of the export wares. However, for twenty years now, Cincinnati's exports as well as its imports have no longer been showing the energetic growth we have become used to seeing in Western cities. In 1854–1855 they amounted to $116,000,000; in 1872–1873 to $540,000,000, almost an increase of five times. For the West this is a slow rate. In the last few years, Cincinnati has eagerly taken advantage of the law of 1871, which declared the large commercial centers of the interior as ports of entry.[7] Direct imports and exports in 1873 surpassed those of 1872 by 142 percent. In addition to the important means of transportation it has in its rivers, its canals, and railroads, a new direct rail line of the Ohio-Chesapeake Railroad has been added, thus providing Cincinnati with closer lines to Virginia, which has begun to prosper again, and with it its seaports. In South Carolina they are also talking of laying tracks over the Alleghenies to connect the Ohio emporium with Charleston. But critical times and the poor financial conditions of the Ohio-Chesapeake Railroad, typical of most Southern railways, do not speak encouragingly for the rapid development of this project, which the benefit for this line obviously seems to warrant. Nevertheless, this plan is indicative of how important Cincinnati is becoming for the Southeast. A further support for this development is the fact that in 1872–1873 $11,500,000 worth of cotton was exported via Cincinnati. There is no doubt that Cincinnati has been assigned a most important role in the movement, which is trying to divert a large part of the South's products from the

Mississippi towards Atlantic ports. With its location relatively far to the east and its four railway lines to New York, Philadelphia, Baltimore, and Norfolk, Cincinnati already offers strong competition to transportation on the great water route and thereby also for the commerce of New Orleans. Since the North and South have begun to draw nearer to one another and economic differences between them have begun to level out, this position of middleman between the North and the West on one hand and the South on the other, which circumstances and the course of cultural development have marked out, is already clearly more a task for Cincinnati than for St. Louis.

SAINT LOUIS. CITY LOCATED IN THE CENTER OF THE INTERIOR. FOUNDING AND FIRST YEARS. PENETRATION OF THE ANGLO-AMERICANS. SIGNIFICANCE OF THE MISSISSIPPI FOR ST. LOUIS. INFLUENCE OF THE SOUTH. GRADUAL DISPLACEMENT OF THIS INFLUENCE BY THOSE COMING FROM THE EAST. INDUSTRY AND TRADE. GENERAL IMPRESSION. MISSISSIPPI BRIDGE. EDUCATIONAL SYSTEM. SOCIAL ATMOSPHERE.

We now come to St. Louis, the second oldest queen. The excellence of its geographical location has already been touched upon. Probably if someone were looking at the map of North America for one spot above all others that would be worthy of being the capital of this huge area, he would, after careful consideration of all the facts, find himself picking the place in the center of the larger eastern part of the continent where the main river of the West empties into the main river of the entire country, the Mississippi. Even though such junctions where navigable rivers meet are always naturally designated to be the sites of important cities, here, in addition to the importance of the Missouri and the Mississippi for huge sections of the United States, the central location of this confluence makes these environs a predestined site for a world metropolis. It lies almost exactly in the middle between four important cities, marking off the edges of the Mississippi basin by the four points of the compass: Pittsburgh in the East, New Orleans in the South, Denver (Colorado) in the West, and St. Paul (Minnesota) in the North.

The significance of this remarkable spot is increased by its location in the midst of the most fertile regions of North America, on the borders of the rolling countryside and the prairies, that is, between farming and cattle-raising areas, as well as its proximity to the estuary of the Illinois River, which forms a ready-made natural canal between the Great Lakes region and the Mississippi. The

French fur trapper Laclède,[8] who in 1764 founded St. Louis,* of course could have hardly had its future world significance in mind when he selected the site. The fact that the French governors who administered Upper Louisiana one after the other chose this place as the seat of government and that the settlement became populated relatively quickly shows that people recognized the advantages of the place. St. Louis is not the only example of a large city originating from some trading settlement or collection point for the fur trappers. Although there was little travel in what were then still wild regions, nevertheless, it was necessary for such a trading post to be sufficiently centrally situated in order to be easily accessible to the Indians who came long distances from every direction. Even New York and Chicago were originally only trading stations for bartering with the Indians. Because of the river fork created by the Missouri and Mississippi, St. Louis also had the added advantage that it could be easily defended on two sides against the Indian attacks from which such new settlements were not usually spared. The city was attacked by Indians in 1780, when a number of its inhabitants were killed, but that was the first and last time.

Just as all western North America, then called Louisiana, became populated very slowly under French and Spanish control, St. Louis, until it became part of the Union in 1803, remained a little village settlement that even after forty years of existence still had no more than 140 houses. The district of St. Louis had no more than 2,280 white men, all Upper Louisiana no more than 9,020. Of this last figure, three-fifths were Anglo-Americans, primarily people from Virginia, Pennsylvania, and the new Ohio territories, which had been colonized from these old states. With the exception of the roving fur trappers, the French population was concentrated in the built-up areas, while the Anglo-Americans were spread out across the land, usually as farmers. St. Louis lay on the route over which the American colonization of the West was then moving. At the time of the Louisiana Purchase,[9] the settlement already extended the entire length of the Ohio, which from the river's estuary to that of the Missouri is then no more than 45 German (208 statute) miles. But though the direct route west from the mid-Ohio region was shifted because of the warlike Indians in the area between the Wabash and the Mississippi, ever since the founding of St. Louis, ship traffic on the Mississippi had steadily expanded up to the new settlement.

---

*LACLÈDE HAD RECEIVED A PATENT FROM THE FRENCH GOVERNMENT TO TRADE WITH THE INDIANS OF THE MISSOURI AND FOUNDED THE SETTLEMENT OF ST. LOUIS WITHOUT KNOWING THE ENTIRE WEST BANK OF THE MISSISSIPPI RIVER HAD ALREADY BEEN CEDED IN 1762 TO SPAIN BY SECRET TREATY. IN 1768 SPAIN TOOK POSSESSION OF THIS "WESTERN LOUISIANA," AND VICE-GOVERNORS IN ST. LOUIS ADMINISTERED THE UPPER PART OF THIS PROVINCE. IN 1800 LOUISIANA, AND WITH IT ST. LOUIS, WAS RETURNED TO FRANCE AND IN 1803 FINALLY BECAME PART OF THE UNITED STATES.

Merchandise came and went by ship to and from New Orleans. When we learn that in 1804 St. Louis was sending out not less than $203,750 worth of its leading export products, furs and lead, we can assume that commerce on the central Mississippi was already by no means insignificant. The presence of river pirates between the Ohio and Missouri estuaries, against whom an expedition had to be sent from St. Louis in 1788, also testifies to this fact. In 1798 Spanish galleys loaded with troops traveled up to St. Louis. But only in 1815, when the first steamboat appeared on this part of the Mississippi, could it really be said that the route from the South and the East to the Missouri estuary was completely opened up. In 1816 the Louisiana territory (called Missouri since 1812) already had 60,000 inhabitants, by 1830 this figure had multiplied five times, and by 1840 fourteen times. St. Louis grew with it accordingly. In 1810 it had 1,400 residents; in 1830, 6,694; 1840, 16,469; 1850, 74,439; 1860, 160,773; and in 1870 310,923. One figures that by the next decade it will be way over the half-million mark.*

The fact that this population growth even before 1851, the year of the first railway line in St. Louis, was so significant clearly shows the influence of the great natural transportation artery, the Mississippi. The only place you can find such immense growth in states that lack such an important artery is when they are associated with the great expansion of the railroad network. It is true, for today eighteen railroad lines converge in St. Louis, but the number of arriving and departing steamships, which in 1871 amounted to 2,574 and 2,604 respectively, appears for the moment to show little trace of a decline in Mississippi navigation. It has to be admitted, however, that since the big business boom that followed the Civil War, this figure has remained rather stable, and, here as everywhere else, wherever railroads are becoming more numerous, tugboat traffic, which alone is in a position to compete successfully with the trains, is increasing in place of passenger and freight boats.

St. Louis has essentially become what it is because of the Mississippi, particularly in the first decades of its development, but it is steadily becoming less of a Mississippi city. Formerly, things were different. Belonging to a state that up until the Civil War had permitted slavery within its borders and where from one-tenth to one-ninth of its population were slaves gave St. Louis a strong similarity to cities lying further south in the broad, flat Mississippi valley, such as New Orleans, Vicksburg, and Memphis. In addition, it was even more evident that, because of the big river, St. Louis, which was bordered only on the south by a higher culture while being surrounded by the remote wilderness to

---

*IN 1872 A CITY CENSUS FOUND IT TO HAVE 428,126 INHABITANTS, A FIGURE THAT WOULD INDICATE AN UNUSUALLY HIGH GROWTH. BUT THESE MUNICIPAL CENSUSES ARE NOT ALWAYS RELIABLE. ANOTHER STATEMENT, THAT 1,559 NEW BUILDINGS WERE ERECTED IN THE SAME YEAR, DOESN'T SEEM TO CORRESPOND WITH SUCH A HIGH POPULATION EXPANSION.

the north and west, basically depended on the South for all its ideas, customs, institutions, business methods, et cetera. You have only to read the history of Missouri in the first third of our century with its slave hunts, duels, and paid political assassinations to imagine you were in Louisiana or Texas. During these times St. Louis was, as one might say, a Mississippi city not simply in the sense that it was a product of the river but rather because it was the most northern and western representative of the ideas and customs that uncontestably predominated in the Mississippi valley. This could exist as long as the immigration along the Ohio route came mainly from Virginia and Kentucky. But after Indiana and Illinois were settled by the New England and transatlantic immigrants who came directly from the East, these two basically different groups clashed right here in the Missouri territory. The efforts it took before the Eastern culture prevailed over the Southern one are shown from the political battles that preceded the Civil War by several decades.[10] There was soon no doubt which was the stronger. Nowhere was the outcome of the conflict more clearly demonstrated than in St. Louis, where even before the abolition of slavery, one surmised that this was certainly no longer the metropolis of a slave state. It was a bustling, industrious city, the center for commerce and industry for the Far West and Southwest, in short a city the likes of which you did not see in the other slave states. The Southern atmosphere disappeared here as soon as the immigration from the East began steadily to pour into Missouri and more importantly when a whole series of railroads established the connection to the East. Up until then St. Louis had not been able to make satisfactory use of this connection because of natural conditions in the area that lay in between them.

Today St. Louis is a city full of life along the lines of New York and Philadelphia, the largest industrial city in the interior of the United States, and probably the city with the most promising future of all three major Western cities. Instead of the rough, often detrimental influences that formerly came up the Mississippi valley, the healthier ideas and customs from the North and East are now making their way from here on down the valley. Among the many triumphs the scions of the inhabitants of New York, New England, and Pennsylvania have won with their wonderfully effective weapons—diligence, energy, and a sense of order—over both savage and civilized opponents, the moral conquest of Missouri is certainly one of the most laudable.

17   "THE SOUTHERN ATMOSPHERE DISAPPEARED HERE AS
SOON AS THE IMMIGRATION FROM THE EAST BEGAN STEADILY
TO POUR INTO MISSOURI AND A WHOLE SERIES OF RAILROADS
ESTABLISHED THE CONNECTION TO THE EAST." THE EAST
MEETS THE SOUTH, AS SYMBOLIZED BY THE EADS BRIDGE AND
THE MISSISSIPPI STEAMER, ST. LOUIS.

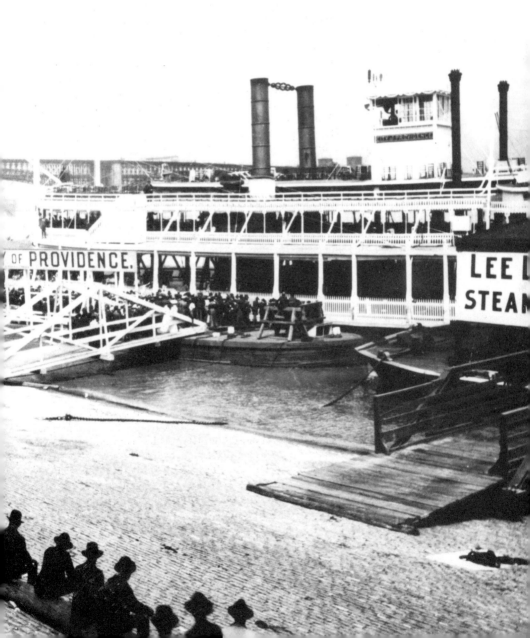

St. Louis, like all Western cities, is primarily a commercial town. It sends the so-called Western products such as salted meat, flour, and grain mainly down the Mississippi; more than half of this trade takes the water route. In return it receives a great amount of imported grocery goods and manufactured articles from the harbors of the East and South and distributes them throughout the region. In 1871, twenty-seven steam-driven mills produced 1.5 million barrels of flour, of which two-thirds went southwards; in 1871–1872, 500,000 pigs were prepared for market in the slaughterhouses; since 1861 this industry's output has increased twentyfold. In 1871 almost one million head of cattle, sheep, and pigs were brought in. On January 1, 1871, there were 120,000,000 feet of lumber stored in three lumber yards. Coffee shipped from here in the same year amounted to 149,000 sacks. In the area of large-scale industry, St. Louis holds third place among North American cities, coming directly behind New York and Philadelphia. It is estimated that in 1873, 41,000 workers were busy in factories and that the value of the products was $158,000,000. Between 1860 and 1870, capital invested in factories quadrupled. The iron industry is in first place with a production worth $5,500,000 (in 1872); in 1873 there were forty-three blast furnaces. In 1871, lead production yielded 17.5 million pounds of metal. The only one large sugar refinery produced 33 million pounds in 1872. Yearly, $15,000,000 to $20,000,000 worth of leather is produced. In 1871 there were 5,000 bales of cotton used in manufacturing, and in 1870 40,000 coils of rope were shipped out.

Since St. Louis is built on a gently rising slope, if one views it from the river, it stands there very proudly with its huge mass of houses and many steeples. But its waterfront is even less imposing than that of New Orleans. Granted, the wharves are graded and even paved for the distance of an hour's walk, but this entire section of the city is given over completely to business concerns and accordingly was constructed as anything but imposing-looking. One sees plenty of wooden shanties, warehouses, and taverns, and a cloud of dust and dirt hangs over the entire scene almost without a break. In order to get to know the better side of the city, one has to get through this outer shell. You only have to go a few blocks inland, say up to Fifth Street, to be convinced that they know not only work and business here but also comfort and luxury. One finds exactly the same kind of tall, luxurious house fronts with a great deal of ornamentation and large picture windows as in the corresponding big streets of Phildelphia or Cincinnati. They do not, however, look as expensive as those in New York or in revitalized Chicago, and only in a few sections do the streets of the residential areas present the clean, pleasant appearance they do in New York or Philadelphia. Planting trees along the streets is less common, the rows of houses are less symmetrical, often interrupted by empty spaces or little shacks, and even the houses themselves do not look as solidly built or as clean as the "brownstone fronts" in the other two cities. You do notice that you are in a new and very busy city. Something of the unfinished, of work done in a hurry, can be found in the architecture in almost every street. Thus, you have to admire all the more the social concern, which did not forget to include open squares and parks here. Lafayette Park,[11] which is located in the city itself and surrounded on all sides by houses, has one of the most attractive settings of its kind that I have seen in America. The public walkways in Shaw's Garden and Tower Grove Park[12] on the city outskirts are things for which Berlin could really envy this Western boom town. In addition, there is naturally also no lack of beer gardens in this western outpost of German culture and civilization.

The huge Mississippi Bridge,[13] which has been open to traffic since July 1874, far and away surpasses any other structure in the city. This bridge, which rests on four piers, has two levels, and spans the river for a length of 2,230 feet, adds the first real indication of magnificence or a big-city look to St. Louis, which otherwise manifests its greatness and significance simply by its large size. Owing to this structure, you now feel as if you have moved to a place with a cosmopolitan city atmosphere. Nothing indicates more clearly the importance that the trade with the East has won for the Mississippi city than this huge bridge connecting the city on the west bank of the river with the rail lines running from the east bank to the Atlantic Ocean.

In St. Louis, as in all American cities of the North and West, some of the most gratifying things to see are the institutions serving public education. The public schools are housed in fifty-eight municipal schoolhouses, which are by no means the worst looking of the city's buildings. I do not have in hand the exact facts about the number of private schools here, but they certainly cannot be small in a city with so many foreigners. In 1840 there were only two municipal schools. The two public libraries, Mercantile Library and Public School Library,[14] together contain seventy thousand volumes, and both have well-stocked newspaper reading rooms. The daily news is found in eight political newspapers, four English and four German.

In no other large Western city is the foreign-born element as self-reliant and relatively influential as in St. Louis. In 1870 there were 112,000 foreign-born inhabitants here, of which a good 100,000 were Germans. This group feels more comfortable and knows better how to live here at the more leisurely pace of the old country than in the other Western city where foreigners have gone, i.e., Chicago, where the number of Germans and Scandinavians taken together actually surpasses the Americans. For the German, Chicago is the city of business, of rush and push, while he sees St. Louis and Cincinnati as almost a second home where he attempts to enjoy and enhance his life in the manner of the homeland. All throughout the United States, St. Louis has the reputation of being the German El Dorado. Why is it that in Chicago he almost tries to outdo his Yankee neighbor in energy and enterprisingness, while in St. Louis he behaves so typically German? They say that the St. Louis climate relaxes one, while that of Chicago has a stimulating effect. Perhaps the reason is that in Chicago he lives with Americans who by nature are active, coming mostly from the New England states, while, as we have seen, St. Louis during its settlement and throughout its history did not exclude more indolent Southern influences.

CHICAGO. BEGINNINGS. ADVANTAGEOUS SITE FOR COMMERCE AND TRANSPORTATION. THE FIRST RAILROADS. DEVELOPMENT OF THE NORTHWEST. CLOSE CONNECTIONS TO NEW YORK. CONNECTIONS WITH QUEBEC. TRADE AND INDUSTRY IN CHICAGO. INHABITANTS' SPIRIT OF ENTERPRISE. GREAT FIRE OF 1871 AND RECONSTRUCTION.

Chicago's development, which includes a growth from 300 to 60,000 homes and from 3,000 to 300,000 inhabitants in the thirty-five years between 1836 and 1871, is even more unprecedented, more astonishing than that of St. Louis and Cincinnati. It is one of the modern miracles, which could become a myth for coming generations, and it could take the place of the deeds of gods and demigods in the young history of this people. In 1804 when the Federal Government had a fort built on the present-day site of this city, on the flat, swampy terrain where the Chicago River flows into Lake Michigan, not one white person lived in the entire region. In 1832, when all the settlers and their families in northern Illinois withdrew into this fort because of an Indian uprising, they totaled 700 people. Besides the fort, there were at that time, on the place where Chicago now stands, only a few taverns and general stores as are usually found in such places, shabby-looking cabins much like those we still see today in the West near military posts and Indian agencies. The city really began when thousands of workers arrived looking for work on the big canal between the Mississippi and Lake Michigan (the Illinois-Michigan Canal) which was begun during this period. In 1829 a town named Chicago, that is, a village with an area of three-eights of a statute square mile was first laid out; in 1833, during the first year of large growth, 150 houses (that is, log cabins) were built; in 1837 Chicago was designated a city and laid out anew, for which a space of ten square miles was then alloted; in 1840, when Cincinnati had almost 50,000 and St. Louis 16,500 inhabitants, Chicago had just reached 4,853; in 1847 the city needed to be enlarged again; and by 1850 there were 30,000 people living there. This was also the year in which the first railroad* was inaugurated in Chicago. With the opening of this line, the young city set out on the path that within twenty-five years would lead to her position as one of the largest cities of America.

Chicago is the most perfect example of a railroad city, the likes of which one could not find anywhere in the world. Twelve major lines and twenty-nine branch lines, in other words forty-one railways, run into Chicago. In addition to

---

*IT WAS THE CHICAGO AND GALENA UNION RAILROAD, WHICH RUNS TO DUBUQUE ON THE UPPER MISSISSIPPI.

the above-mentioned first railway line, in the course of the 1850s alone, eight other ones started out here. They were not motivated by inducements offered them to come here but were drawn by the city's good location and the enterprising spirit of its inhabitants, which turns out to have really increased because of the favorable site.* Five major lines now run from Quebec, New York, Philadelphia, and Baltimore into Chicago. It is also well known that Chicago has become the most important midway station, so to speak the border and resting point, between the eastern and western half of the great Continental or Pacific Railroad. When you add to this that in 1873 11,851 ships left Chicago's harbor carrying 3.25 million tons of cargo and that in addition to the great water route via Lake Michigan, one of the most important canals in North America, the Illinois-Michigan Canal,[15] comes into Chicago, a canal that forms the connecting link between the Great Lakes and the Mississippi, then you can get some idea of the importance for transportation this city has achieved in the twenty-five years since the railroad first appeared within its precincts.

The wonderful advantages of Chicago's site are not as striking as those of St. Louis, but it is impossible to overlook them. Its location on the shore of a great body of water as conducive to transportation as Lake Michigan would be to the benefit of any settlement, but Chicago has had the particular benefit of being situated at one of the natural starting and ending points for navigation. With a certain degree of necessity, ship traffic tries to penetrate as far as possible on the routes that are open to it, to use the waterways to the utmost extent possible, to use land means as a last resort, since travel by water is always cheaper and easier than land transportation. You could call this a natural law of transportation. Therefore, even in more important locations we still find that where a large shipping traffic is transformed into a great deal of land traffic, the juncture points are located at the far end of a lake or sea. One thinks of Trieste, Constantinople, Odessa, Poti,[16] and Petersburg. Chicago is such a transformation point for the Great Lakes region. Only via Lake Superior is there a waterway that leads further west, but this lies too far north in sparsely populated and partly still uninhabited regions. For the present, therefore, the southern end of Lake Michigan is the most suitable place to bring in the produce of the area from all points and load it on ships. Observers ascertained this so early that long before Chicago could even be called a city, they predicted a

---

*WHEREAS OTHER CITIES OF THE WEST, LIKE ST. LOUIS, CINCINNATI, AND MILWAUKEE, WERE PLUNGED INTO HEAVY DEBT THROUGH SUBSCRIPTION TO AND ENDORSEMENTS OF RAILROAD BONDS IN ORDER TO GET THE RAILROADS TO THEIR GATES, THE MOST IMPORTANT RAILROADS OF THE CONTINENT RIVALED EACH OTHER, AS IT WERE, IN JUMPING RIGHT INTO CHICAGO'S LAP. E. SEEGER & E. SCHLÄGER, *CHICAGOS ENTWICKLUNG* . . . (CHICAGO, 1872). [ED. NOTE: THE FULL CITATION IS E. SEEGER AND E. SCHLÄGER, *CHICAGO; ENTWICKLUNG, ZERSTÖRUNG UND WIEDERAUFBAU DER WUNDERSTADT* (CHICAGO, 1872), P. 6.]

future metropolis on this spot, and, as is very evident, one has indeed grown up here, exceeding all expectations.

Due to its location, Chicago is not only the metropolis on Lake Michigan but has become the main center of the entire Northwest, for the granaries of Illinois, Michigan, Iowa, Wisconsin, Minnesota, and also part of Indiana. One has to remember how extraordinarily rapid these states were populated in order to understand to some degree the growth of what is the natural commercial center of the area. During the period between 1840 and 1870, the population of Illinois grew from 476,000 to 2,500,000, that of Indiana from 686,000 to 1,681,000, that of Iowa from 43,000 to 1,195,000, that of Michigan from 212,000 to 1,184,000, that of Wisconsin from 31,000 to 1,055,000; Minnesota's population had not yet been counted by 1840, but in 1850 it totaled 6,100 and in 1870 439,000 individuals. Thus within thirty years we have in this area an increase from not quite 1.5 million to more that 8 million people. When you think of the work and success of such a rapidly growing population collected here at the focal point of this region, coupled with the enterprising spirit that the region's dominant ethnic group seems to possess in such a large degree, then everything miraculous about Chicago's astonishing development seems to disappear. Just as the flourishing of Cincinnati in earlier decades was a specific manifestation that at that time the flow of westward migration generally went along the Ohio, Chicago's growth is only the most impressive example of a whole series of events, which until now have made up the history of the settlement of the Northwest.

Just as the settlement of every region of North America has its own origins, character, and development, we also see unique traits appearing here. Among them, two have become important for Chicago: the construction of the railroads and the influence of New England. The settlement of the Northwest,[17] beginning in the 1830s, occurred just at the time of the first railroad construction, and therefore this region was the first of all the still unsettled territories to share, from the very beginning, in the benefits of the new means of transportation. Whether through the rapid transport of continually new crowds of immigrants, or through the possibility of expanded commercialization of the products the fresh soil so abundantly yields, the railroad was very prominent in promoting the settlement of the Northwest. Moreover, no section of the underpopulated Western states has as much transplanted New England stock as here. The Great Lakes region and the Northwest in general were for the real Yankees what the Ohio valley was for the Pennsylvanians and Virginians. Since it is generally conceded, and by none more than by the Americans themselves, that the New Englanders far surpass all the other groups of the North American people in all the gifts that help a country become civilized, the origins of the majority of the Northwest's first settlers are something that warrants noting. It is the German immigrant, however, who has had the second most important influence on the culture of the Northwest, for the opening up of this area to settlement and travel coincided with the increase and high point of German immigration to North America. German industriousness and intelligence, coupled with New England ingenuity and initiative, surpassed the colonizing capabilities of all other peoples or national mixtures. Despite this, Chicago is primarily a product of New England's enterprising spirit. The city contains a great number of Germans, but they belong chiefly to the class of manual laborers, and most German immigrants have shown a decided preference, as they do everywhere, for engaging in farming.

Another opportune coincidence in the development of Chicago was that it began at the very time when New York had secured her position against all rivals as the main commercial center on the North American East Coast. The Erie Canal, which creates the shortest connection between the territory around the Great Lakes and the Atlantic Coast, was the major factor in assisting New York to obtain this position. Besides the water link with this important canal, a link in which Chicago was pleased to see any extension, Chicago later had a direct railroad connection with Buffalo, with the canal's western starting point and then soon after, as we have observed, even with New York itself. It lies on the most direct line from New York to the West and in many ways has become an integral part of New York's economic network. Chicago collects the abundant products of the West in its granaries and warehouses and sends them to New York, which in turn takes care of processing these goods or distributing them throughout the country and abroad.

The close ties between both cities have resulted in Chicago considering every step that brought New York nearer to its goal of becoming a leading center of world trade as an extension of its own sphere of influence and its own prosperity. I have heard it aptly put: New York is the senior and Chicago is the junior partner in the Western business. Later it formed no less close associations with Boston, which in the last few years has been making the greatest efforts to direct a little stream of the huge Western passenger and freight traffic into its own harbor. But of even greater importance is the connection with Quebec, the city at the mouth of the St. Lawrence, which is just as favorably situated at the seaward end of the Great Lakes chain as Chicago is at the southwestern end in the interior. Once a canal had gotten around the great impediment to traffic presented by Niagara Falls, Chicago itself became accessible for small seagoing vessels, and one can no longer deny it the title of a maritime trade city, although it is still primarily a first-rate city in domestic trade. You have to remember in addition to all this that a canal also connects that part of the lake on which Chicago is situated with the Mississippi and thereby with the Gulf of Mexico.

One thing should not be forgotten. Since the Northwest began its impressive development, Chicago has taken the position of a building at an intersection, so to speak, along the highway to the West. Such places are just as prominent in world traffic as they are in the daily traffic in our city streets. The traffic that moves from the Northwest to the East and Southeast and vice versa is diverted from a direct route by the bodies of water in the Great Lakes chain and forced to make a detour. Naturally, they try to make this detour as short as possible, and that means hugging the shoreline so as not to couple one necessary detour with still another unnecessary one. One is easily convinced that Chicago's position on the south end of the greatest obstacle to direct East-West traffic makes it the natural transit intersection point for all the shortest routes that carry the traffic between the Northwest, East, and Southeast. Although many of them as would like to, none of them can deviate from this course without also deviating from their destination, so they still have to meet at this place.

Since the Northwest is the granary of the United States, it is only natural that Chicago is the largest grain market in the country. The grain trade, particularly in wheat, has expanded to such an extent in the last few years that Chicago has become the principal grain market for the entire world. In 1872–1873 what was up until then the United States' largest grain export amounted to 34 million hectoliter (96.5 million bushels). That year Chicago alone exported 32 million hectoliter (90.88 million bushels). The same year all of Russia exported 45 million hectoliter (127.8 million bushels). The value of breadstuff coming into Chicago during 1873 amounted to $65,500,000.

Chicago also has an almost equally dominant place in the meat business, which is of great importance to the hog-raising states of the West. In the years between 1871 and 1873, it exported no less than 163 million, 239 million, and 344 million pounds respectively of salted meats; and in 1871–1872, 1.16 million hogs were dressed for "packaging," whereas Cincinnati and St. Louis together did not reach that figure. The number of hogs brought in during 1873 totaled 4.5 million, cattle 761,000. In 1873, 90 million pounds of lard were exported, 11.5 million of suet, 11 million of butter, 31.5 million of wool, 32 million of hides, and 6 million of tobacco. Imports from abroad during the same year had a worth of $3,666,666; the value of trade with the coast and Canada amounted to $7,000,000. In New York, capital invested in factories increased in the ten years between 1860 and 1870 by 212 percent, Philadelphia by 238, and Chicago by 707 percent; this capital is estimated to be worth about $50,000,000 in 1873 and the number of people occupied in factory work during the same year to amount to 50,000.

There is no reliable information in the trade reports about Chicago's importance as a major Pacific Railroad depot for the trade between San Francisco and New York and for its own trade with the West. The hopes that Chicago would be North America's tea and silk emporium have, however, not yet been realized. As starting point for the only rail line that cuts across the western part of the entire continent, it has naturally become extremely important to this region. The spirit of enterprise here knows how to exploit these advantages; for example, it does more business with the mining state of Colorado than does St. Louis, which is much more favorably located for such trade. In the Western regions, the stretches of land most suitable for cultivation and development are generally located in the north, a factor that will be of great consequence for Chicago's dealings with the Far West.

As much as these figures and the rapid growth of Chicago, which they confirm, may speak for the enterprising spirit and the industriousness of its inhabitants, they are far less important than the testimony given by the behavior displayed by Chicago's inhabitants after the great fire of 1871. When discussing the Boston fire of 1872, I mentioned how little the inhabitants there, although hard hit, allowed themselves to be discouraged by the catastrophe. Chicago's reconstruction demonstrated an even more astonishing dauntlessness and perseverance among the people of this city. The misfortune was incomparably greater, but the indomitable spirit no less than in Boston. The fire raged in the wealthiest and finest districts, and the 17,450 homes that were burnt down easily represented 50 percent of the aggregate value of the 42,000 houses the city had at that time. In May 1874, when I saw Chicago, it gave me the impression of being the richest and most beautiful of all the large cities I have seen in the American West or South. The broad, pleasant streets, the palatial business establishments, the rich, quality homes reminded me of New York. This city has a very distinct aura of splendor and magnificence about it. You do not notice anything that indicates the city is so very young until you approach the more peripheral sections. There, of course, the prairie still frequently shines through between the simple, white-washed wooden homes, and one notices that, to begin with, the majority of the present inhabitants have neither time nor taste for solid luxury. But that the city center arose again so rapidly and so prosperously out of the ashes where the disheartened had imagined it would lie buried forever is an unparalleled event. It's hard to picture people like those who could say: "we built the city once; now we are going to help build it a second time." And they did what they said they would do. In the business districts, after a short depreciation of real estate, the former prices were being paid again for building plots. Commerce didn't flag for a second, and four weeks after the fire, the import and export lists showed higher figures than for corresponding periods in the normal year of 1870. While the wholesale trade had already been set up a few days after the fire in a "city" constructed of wooden planks along the shorefront, the sites for new, more durable buildings were also already being staked out, and by December 1, 1871, there were 212 business houses made of stone again under construction in the old business section. The result of this not feverish but sober, lasting recovery now stands before us as the most imposing city of the West. Such an accomplishment commands respect. When one hears of the wonderful generosity and great confidence of numerous creditors upon whom the city had to call, then you cannot help but be sympathetic. In fact, few events in American history portray the people in such an unclouded bright light or place them in a position enjoining such respect.

18 "THAT THE CITY CENTER AROSE AGAIN SO RAPIDLY AND
SO PROSPEROUSLY OUT OF THE ASHES WHERE THE
DISHEARTENED HAD IMAGINED IT WOULD LIE BURIED
FOREVER IS AN UNPARALLELED EVENT." CHICAGO, ONE YEAR
AFTER THE GREAT FIRE OF 1871.

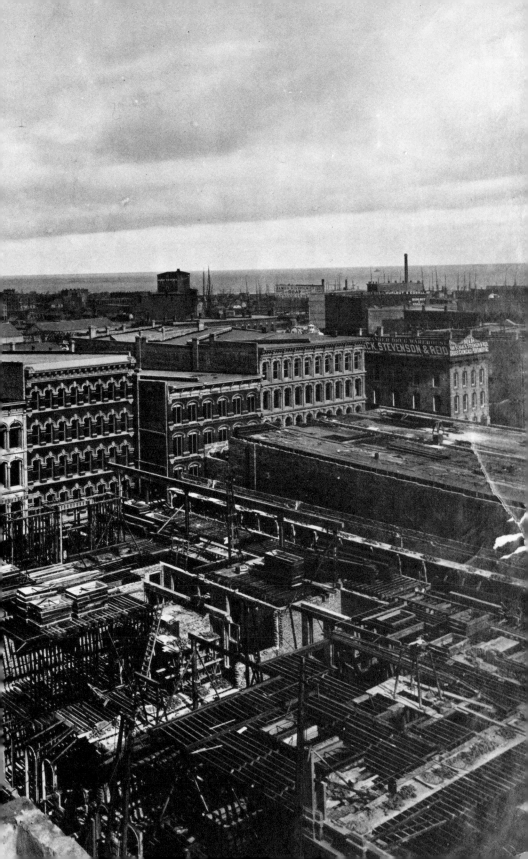

CHAPTER EIGHTEEN

Denver

A CITY THAT SPRANG UP OVER NIGHT. ITS DESOLATE LOCATION
ON THE PRAIRIE. PANORAMA OF THE ROCKY MOUNTAINS. ITS
EARLY HISTORY. BECOMING AN IMPORTANT RAILROAD JUNCTION.
EXTERNAL APPEARANCE. SOCIETY.

Denver, the capital of Colorado, is one of the most talked about wonders of the
West, one of the boom towns (*Pilzstädte*) that shot up overnight. In fourteen
years, having grown from a group of wretched log cabins in the midst of the
most desolate high prairie into one of the busiest cities of the West, it is indeed
an interesting phenomenon that should not go unnoticed.

Denver is neither as favorably nor as attractively located as one would
expect from the new capital of a territory, which they call the Switzerland of
America, whose settlement is so recent and actually occurred so rapidly because of the mineral wealth of its mountains. If it didn't have the wonderful
mountain panorama* before it, it would have the most dismal environs you

---

*AFTER A TWO-DAY TRIP FROM THE MISSISSIPPI VALLEY OVER THE GREEN, FERTILE PRAIRIE OF
KANSAS AND THE PARCHED, YELLOW STEPPES BY WHICH THE LAND IMPERCEPTIVELY RISES TO
THE PLATEAU, YOU SEE THE ROCKY MOUNTAINS FOR THE FIRST TIME LOOMING UP OFF IN THE
WEST LIKE EMBRYONIC LITTLE CLOUDS. FIRST THE SOUTHERN PIKES PEAK GROUP COMES INTO
VIEW, WHICH BECAUSE OF ITS ISOLATION, ITS LONG EXTENDED FORM, AND STEEP SIDES IS NOT
UNLIKE A LARGE, DISTANT ISLAND. IT APPEARES IN THE SOUTH WHERE IT EMERGES LIKE A
CREATION THAT HAS BEEN PUSHED OUT IN FRONT OF THE MOUNTAIN CHAIN RUNNING ALMOST
DIRECTLY NORTH-SOUTH. IT IS A WELCOME PRECURSOR, WHICH SEEMS TO PROMISE MUCH. ITS
LINES ARE OF SUCH WONDERFUL BEAUTY THAT YOU HAVE TO CALL IT MAJESTIC; ITS UPWARD
THRUST IS SO RESTRAINED, SO MEASURED, DESPITE ALL ITS BOLDNESS. WHOEVER HAS SEEN THE
WONDERFULLY BEAUTIFUL LINE OF MOUNT PELLEGRINO NEAR PALERMO KNOWS WHAT I MEAN,

could imagine. Seven geographical (approximately thirty-two statute) miles from the foot of the mountains, the city of Denver was built on one of the gentle elevations that helps form the rolling prairie; on one side it is washed by the South Platte River, which flows rather rapidly but is already shallow and

---

FOR IT IS VERY SIMILAR TO THIS MOUNTAIN GROUP. AT FIRST IT RISES STRAIGHT UPWARDS, AS IF INTENDING TO REACH A SUMMIT THAT WOULD SPAN THE CLOUDS. [ED. NOTE: MOUNT PELLE-GRINO RISES 1,990 FEET, TO THE NORTH OF THE CITY. OTHER GERMANS, J. W. GOETHE AMONG THEM, WERE ALSO IMPRESSED WITH THE VIEW OF MOUNT PELLEGRINO. SEE J. W. GOETHE, *ITALIENISCHE REISE* (ITALIAN JOURNEY, 1816–1817), PT. 2, SICILY.] THEN, BEFORE ONE NOTICES AND ON ONE SIDE BEFORE THE OTHER, IT STOPS WITH A GENTLE BEND AND NOW COMPLETES THIS STRIKING OUTLINE WITHOUT ANY SHARP RIDGE OR CLEFT AND WITH WIRY STRATA LINES THAT TEND TO RUN TOGETHER. THE OUTLINE REMINDS YOU VERY MUCH OF A LION WHO IS SLEEPING WITH LOWERED HEAD—SOMEWHAT LIKE THORWALDSEN'S LION NEAR LUCERNE. [ED. NOTE: BERTEL THORWALDSEN OR THORVALDSEN (1768 OR 1770–1844), A DANISH SCULPTOR, IS RE-GARDED AS A LEADER IN THE CLASSIC REVIVAL. IN 1820, THE FIGURE OF A MAJESTIC DYING LION, "THE LION OF LUCERNE," WAS SCULPTED OUT OF A WALL OF ROCK IN THE CITY TO COMMEMORATE THE SWISS GUARD WHO FELL ON AUGUST 10, 1792, DEFENDING THE TUILERIES IN PARIS AGAINST THE FRENCH REVOLUTIONARY MOB.] A REDDISH ROCK COLOR, OVER WHICH RUN DULL WHITE STREAKS AND PATCHES OF SNOW, IS EDGED ALL AROUND BY THE SOFT DARK GREEN MANTLE OF THE DEEP FOREST, OF THE MANY CREVICES, OF THE HOLLOWS, SO TO SPEAK, AND, AS WE APPROACH, GIVES THIS FORMATION A SOFT COLOR. THE GRAY-BLUE AND VIOLET MOUNTAIN SHADOWS SHINING THROUGH—A SIGHT FOR SORE EYES AND ONE THAT HAS BEEN GREATLY MISSED!—SPREAD A MODERATING EFFECT OVER THE WHOLE LANDSCAPE.

AS THIS BEAUTIFUL MOUNTAIN CONFIGURATION WAS COMING INTO VIEW, IN THE NORTH STILL OTHER SNOW-BRUSHED SUMMITS WERE APPEARING; THEY ARE ISOLATED PEAKS, WHICH YOU WOULD SCARCELY RECOGNIZE AS THE HIGHEST PEAKS IN THE MOUNTAIN RANGE WITHOUT SHARP OUTLINES TO INDICATE THEIR CRAGGY NATURE AND WITHOUT THE PROXIMITY OF PIKES PEAK—A GROUP OF IMPOSING SIZE AND HEIGHT IN THEIR OWN RIGHT. FIRST OF ALL, THEY ARE NOT AS POINTY AS THE ALPS—NO HORNS, NO NEEDLES, NOTHING EXTREME, EXTRAVAGANTLY BOLD, JAGGED, OR EVEN SOMETHING LEANING AT AN ANGLE IS TO BE SEEN; INSTEAD A TENDENCY TOWARD BROAD, BLUNT TOPS, LONG RIDGES, GENTLE GLENS, AND DIFFICULT PASSES THROUGH THE MOUNTAINS, EVEN WAVY LINES OF ROCK STRATA SEEM WITH FEW EXCEPTIONS TO BE THE RULE ALONG THE ENTIRE RANGE. STILL IN THE DISTANCE THEY LOOK IN THEIR BLUE AND GRAY HUES LIKE A HAZY SHADOW, WHICH BEGINS TO BRIGHTEN UP OR GROW DARKER WHEN THE SUN IS HIDDEN BY A THIN VEIL OF MIST. THEY ALSO SEEM TO BE WIDELY SCATTERED ABOUT ON THIS AND THAT SPOT ALONG THE WESTERN HORIZON WITHOUT ANY RECOGNIZABLE COHERENCE, NOW APPEARING, NOW DISAPPEARING, SOMETIMES COMPLETELY, SOMETIMES ONLY PARTLY, JUST LIKE THE PRAIRIE RISING AND SINKING, WITH MORE UPS AND DOWNS THAN A STORMY SEA. BUT AS THE CARS OF OUR TRAIN WOUND THEIR WAY UP AND DOWN THE CRESTS, MOVING STEADILY WESTWARDS, THE MOUNTAINS BECAME NOTICEABLY CLOSER, AND IT WAS ALREADY POSSIBLE FROM MANY HIGH POINTS TO CATCH GLIMPSES OF LOWER, DARKER MASSIFS, WHICH SERVE AS CONNECTING LINKS AND FOUNDATIONS FOR THE SUMMITS.

THEN THE PEAKS AND RIDGES FORMED GROUPS LIKE THAT OF PIKES PEAK, SO THAT TOGETHER THERE WERE FOUR GROUPS STANDING ON THE HORIZON—THE MOST NORTHERLY ONE WAS

full of sandbanks, creating none of the green oases here that you find farther upstream along its banks. On all other sides it is surrounded by the prairie, which even comes right into its streets with all the barrenness of a desert. There is no sight more striking than that of the outskirts of this city, where the streets are not laid out yet, and in the distance single houses or groups of houses with large desolate spaces between them stand around without any apparent principle or system on the completely untouched thistle and cacti fields of the prairie. Some of these are already trying to look attractive, knowing that the city someday will expand over this piece of wasteland; the majority, however, are more like simple cabins. Here and there the green plot of a vegetable garden is cut out of the gray-yellow soil of the steppe; high-sounding street names have been written in some places where no trace of a street exists, and for animation perhaps a herd of cows ambles along across the field. Nevertheless, hearing the bell of the streetcar in the distance or the roaring locomotive, one thinks how new this all is and what treasures are over there in the mountains or even here in the earth, and in the end, despite the dismal appearance, he consoles himself with hopes for the future.

All the same, I have to admit that it is easier for me to picture Denver as a ghost town, where the wolf and coyote howl and hot winds blow and little by little cover the ruins of a former, advanced culture with sand dunes, than to picture it as one of the queens of the West. One sees with pleasure one little city after another crowding about the banks of rushing mountain streams over at the foot of the green mountains, but to imagine a large modern city here in the steppe being turned into a man-made desert is an extremely unpleasant thought. Except for the poorly thriving cottonwood you scarcely see a dozen good-looking trees around the city, and anything grown by means of irrigation, even if it shoots up quite luxuriantly, still remains something artificial. These people will never see a fine shady forest around here. In addition, Denver almost always has a cloudless sky and a scorching sun despite its altitude.

LONGER THAN THE OTHERS, ALMOST A RANGE IN ITSELF AND IN APPEARANCE THE POINTIEST, MOST LIKE THE ALPS; THE MOST SOUTHERLY ONE HAD, AS ALREADY MENTIONED, THE MOST ATTRACTIVE SHAPE; THE TWO SIMILAR-LOOKING MIDDLE ONES, AS BIG AS THE SOUTHERN ONE, HAD DULL SHAPES, LESS INTERESTING TO THE EYE. THESE TWO ARE CLOSE TO ONE ANOTHER, WHILE THE NORTHERN AND SOUTHERN GROUPS ARE SEPARATED FROM THEM BY EQUAL AND CONSIDERABLY GREAT DISTANCES. BEYOND THEM YOU SEE THE MOUNTAINS STRETCHING TO- WARDS OPPOSITE ENDS OF THE COMPASS IN INDISTINCT, WAVY LINES, WHICH WITH SOME INSIGNIFICANT DEVIATION EXTEND THROUGH THE ENTIRE NORTHERN CONTINENT AND ON AGAIN IN SOUTH AMERICA FROM THE NORTHERN EDGE DOWN TO CAPE HORN. IT IS NOT WITHOUT SOME TRUTH THAT EARLIER GEOGRAPHERS, WHO COULD ONLY SURMISE THE RELATIONSHIP AND SIMI- LAR FORMATION OF ALL THESE ROCKY MOUNTAINS, SIERRAS, ANDES, AND CORDILLERAS, CALLED THIS CHAIN THE BACKBONE OF AMERICA.

These thoughts about this new city may seem cruel, but is it not shocking when we see a modern city, which appears to have a future, being built so foolishly in the desert? Certainly better places could be found only a few miles closer to the mountains, which would guarantee as good if not better a site for commerce and transportation. No sensible reason has been given for the choice of exactly this place. Pure chance! And yet in our day and age, which claims to have learned so much, this is the way settlements, which one expects will some day become major cities, are founded. In this regard the unlettered city founders in our own past had more sense and foresight. Nevertheless, be that as it may, there is no question that Denver is now flourishing. Ever since the Kansas-Pacific Railroad, which runs along the most direct route from the Rockies to the Mississippi, selected Denver as its western point of departure and ever since four other lines from the North, South, and West came together here, Colorado's capital has become the transportation center for the large area comprising western Kansas, the Rockies, and New Mexico, which is still mostly desert but rapidly becoming populated. The fact that it is thriving is the best proof that today the nuclei of large cities no longer develop as frequently because of the advantages of the site as they do because of the direction of the railroad lines. If it is farther from the foot of the mountains than one would like, it is still near enough to bring together without coercion all the lines of the road and railway systems that run through the mountains and to regulate without assistance the flow of traffic that comes and goes further in one direction or the other.

Its history is short and as yet contains no event that deserves to be preserved for posterity. And yet how a report about its founding and its growth really affects us! It is very rare that someone can describe to us, as it were, the first developments, the striking of roots, of an important community that someday would become one of our European cities as clearly as one can about this city's development. And when someone can, the attraction of watching it grow out of the rugged conditions of the wilderness and of seeing it spring up like a mushroom is still missing. The early history of almost all of our cities is shrouded in darkness, and so the detailed account we have of the earliest conditions in so many American cities by analogy, which prevails in such matters, throws a welcome ray of light on aspects of our own history whose shadows we cannot clear up any other way.

In 1857 the site where Denver now stands became a dwelling place for white men for the first time. A trapper with the ubiquitous British name of Smith[1]—a name so common in America that it alone sufficed to invest the first beginnings of the city with a certain allegorical even mythical character—built his hut here and lived alone until October 1858, the beginning of the gold rush, which in the middle of winter brought more than twenty thousand people to this mountain region that up until then had only been traversed by trappers. At that time, a General Larimer[2] built the first log cabin here. His name is immortalized in the name of a county and of a main street. At the same time, the first family arrived; in December the first Smith immigrated here from Santa Fe, New Mexico, and Blake and Williams opened the first store; and on February 1, 1859, Messrs. Murat and Smoke started the first hotel, the El Dorado. That same spring, rival newspapers, the *Rocky-Mountain News* and the *Cherry-Creek Pioneer*, saw the light of day, but immediately after the first issue the *Pioneer* gave up the ghost.[3] At the same time, the first sawmill was founded in the pine forest that lies southwest of Denver, and on May 7 the first mail coach of the Leavenworth and Pikes Peak Express Company arrived in Denver.[4] History does not state how many people it brought and how many it took away, but it can be assumed that the number of those who were trying to leave the territory would have been scarcely less than the arriving gold diggers, for the inhospitable land and the hard winter had disappointed many an expectation, and if we had accounts of the misery that was seen here in the winter of 1858–1859, dreadful scenes could be described. By this time the first child had been born in Denver, an Indian half-breed, and some people had died; a number had been stabbed, shot, or hanged, and in the autumn of 1859 the first couple was married here. With these events the new city was christened after a fashion. In March 1859, when the county officials were elected, there were already 375 votes cast.

However, in order not to make this bit of early history seem too simple, it has to be mentioned that at first the place was named St. Charles, that a second settlement with the charming name of Auraria was founded on the other bank of Cherry Creek, which empties here into the Platte River, that in November 1858, St. Charles received its present name in honor of Governor Denver[5] of Kansas—Colorado was part of Kansas until 1861—and that the first legislative assembly that met in the territory issued a writ of incorporation to both settlements, whereupon on December 19, 1859, the city of Denver came into existence. Presently then, it is in its fifteenth year.

From the very beginning, Denver, which became the end station of the post coach line that ran from Kansas over the prairie, also became the goods depot for the "Pikes Peak Gold Area" as they then called central Colorado after the mountain peak that was most conspicuous. It was just as preferable for the post coaches and freight wagons, as it would be later for the railroads, to come no closer to the mountains, with their rolling piedmont terrain, than was absolutely necessary. For them Denver was the most favorably located spot in this region, and we have them to thank, as well as the land speculators who had an interest in the rise of land prices, for Denver, and not one of the settlements founded at the same time at the foot of the mountains, becoming the capital of the territory.

Today Denver has around twenty thousand inhabitants. In 1870, the most recent year for which there are official figures, there were nine thousand people and almost fifteen hundred dwellings; since then no less than three hundred houses have been built per year. According to the report of the chamber of commerce, almost $12,000,000 worth of goods were sold here during the same year, $1,500,000 was deposited in banks here, and twelve life insurance companies took in $85,000, while fire insurance companies grossed $75,000. These figures, however, are likely to be only approximately correct and generally tend to be somewhat high.

What is there to say about the appearance of such a new city, where actually nothing is entirely finished? Cabins, wooden houses, and simple brick buildings predominate, and the few larger buildings look so isolated among the mass of nondescript little houses with large gaps of empty plots in between that they only increase the impression of incompleteness. The gardens that surround single homes are as new as the white poplars lining the streets, and even with all the greenery that the irrigation system brings out, they still cannot dissipate the bleak impression of the surrounding desert area. The streets are wide, unpaved, with raised sidewalks covered with plankboards and are already in places being used by horse-drawn streetcars. Some, those in which the leading shops are found, are rather busy. Teams of six and eight oxen, drawing wooden carts, miners on heavily laden mules or horses going "prospecting" (going in search of new mines, about which some wonderful reports have come from the San Juan region), and ragged, stupidly gawking Indians on small, overworked horses, are some of the more striking sights. Though not exactly frequent, whenever they do appear, they are all the more effectively characteristic of the place. Here and there one notices traces that the Denverites are trying to exploit the renown that Colorado has gained as a tourist playground and as a healthy area for those who have tuberculosis. There are several covered markets on whose main floors stuffed birds and mammals, Indian artifacts, and other curios are for sale at "fancy prices," and there is also no lack of establishments selling hunting and fishing equipment. Along every step of the way the still very scant literature about Colorado is brought to one's attention, and enticingly beautiful photographs of Rocky Mountain scenery are displayed.

A much more striking characteristic of the city's appearance, however, is the astonishing number of places where beer and hard liquor are sold. They indicate among other things the important role Denver plays in the life of the miners, who work hard for months in the wilderness, then, suddenly seized with the urge to live better, come down out of their canyons and in a few weeks spend every bit, be it little or much, they have earned. Those who have enough pass entire winters in Denver. Others, who are ultimately heading for the mountains, linger here where life is more pleasant until they have squandered the money they brought with them, whereupon they head off for work with all the more determination until the game can begin all over again. Moreover,

19   "WHAT IS THERE TO SAY ABOUT THE APPEARANCE OF SUCH A NEW CITY, WHERE ACTUALLY NOTHING IS ENTIRELY FINISHED?" PERIODIC FLOODING IN DENVER.

Denver, like all places on the frontier of American civilization, harbors more than enough riffraff, which is similar to having a bad wound in that it always has a festering border around it.

In front of Denver itself the Rockies rise up in a semicircle, completely filling the western horizon and send out spurs to the north and south. It is simple to explain, much simpler than for any Alpine scene, what they look like. The twenty miles up to the foot of the mountains are still completely prairie. At times it rises in smooth, steep surfaces and at times in stretches of rolling expanse until directly before the mountains it suddenly draws itself up in a display of hills that expand partly like ramparts and partly rise in conical shapes, and which all along the line form but a thin border in front of the mountains. Like the prairie, they are covered with short yellow-green grass; though treeless, they have only cragged peaks and ridges as if in rising they had taken along their broad, ample dress and only here and there wanted to make a hole in it. With frequent breaks, consisting of various but predominantly long horizontal formations, this fringe of hills runs all along in front of the higher mountains. On the south horizon, where the range seems to bend and form a semicircle like the one in the north, you clearly see this fringe gradually rising from the prairie, gradually passing on into higher mountains that, where we have the Rockies directly in front of us, seem suddenly to rise, as if on their own base, above the border of hills.

Behind this hill and mountain rampart, which emerges so suddenly out of the prairie, here and there, where it is tallest, towers the top of the high mountain range that lies still further to the west and is called the Snow Range.[6] Pikes Peak is still the southernmost of these elevations; then comes the multipeaked group of James Peak, and after this Grays and Longs Peak and some indistinct peaks off to the extreme north. They lie, with the exception of Pikes Peak, which is well out front, about fifteen to thirty statute miles behind the first mountain rampart. Where this is low, you first see thickly wooded mountains and then the snow-covered tops coming up behind them. To use the words "rising up" would be too much, since, as already stated, they seem to possess very few bold shapes. There is simply too much here in these mountains that is solid mass, too much running along continuously in the ridges and in the extremely shallow jagged lines. It is as if an upward movement, while still in a viscous state, began too early and came in conflict with a tendency to spread out in every direction and as if in the end the latter for the most part had won. Only the northernmost group, Longs Peak, is an exception. It rises on the north side in a long, unbroken, somewhat convex line and gives way with a shorter, steeper slope on the south to two low, rounded peaks, which then, along with a row of not as tame-looking peaks, extend to the south, where after some larger gaps Grays Peak once more takes up the rising movement.

CHAPTER NINETEEN

Travel on the Pacific Railroad

VARIOUS PARTS OF THE PACIFIC RAILROAD. RIDING INTO THE
BLACK HILLS NEAR CHEYENNE. WILDERNESS. MARVELOUS TREE
AND ROCK FORMATIONS. PREVENTIVE MEASURES AGAINST SNOW-
DRIFTS. EXTREMELY DESOLATE LANDSCAPE. SCANTY SCENERY.
VEGETATION IN UPLAND WILDERNESS. THE TRIP.

What one is accustomed to calling the Pacific Railroad for short is in no way, as
one would believe, a direct railway line from New York to San Francisco but a
complex of seven different, independent lines. Four of these are located east of
the Mississippi[1] and have already existed for many years; the other three, of
which the Western Pacific (running from San Francisco to the foot of the Sierra
Nevadas) is also older, together form what is known as the Pacific Railroad.
The most important and most difficult section of this line is traversed by the
1,680-kilometer (1,044-mile)-long Union Pacific running between Omaha and
the Great Salt Lake, whereas the Central Pacific forms the connecting link over
the Great Plains and the Sierra Nevada to Sacramento—1,190 kilometers (740
miles). From there the older Western Pacific travels the remaining 217-
kilometer (135-mile) stretch to San Francisco. During the last few years a
competing southern line, known as the Missouri-Pacific and Kansas-Pacific,
has been built for the eastern half of the Union Pacific and runs from the
Mississippi, actually from St. Louis, which is a much more southerly location

than Omaha. This line passes through Missouri, Kansas, and Colorado to Denver and from there on the north-south connecting line, the Denver-Pacific, until it joins up with the Union-Pacific at Cheyenne. Like the corresponding section of the Union Pacific, it runs across the entire length of the Western prairies, which rise so slowly that the almost 1,600-meter (approximately 5,250-foot) difference between St. Louis and Denver is negotiated, barring any significant obstacles in the terrain, entirely unnoticed. Only at Cheyenne, which you reach from Denver by climbing approximately still another 300 meters (985 feet) up over a very gradually rising high prairie, does the ascent into the mountains begin at 1,842 meters (6,043 feet) above sea level. The climb, however, is no longer that great since you reach the top of the pass at 2,513 meters (8,245 feet) (at Sherman Station). This part of the Rockies over which the railroad has been laid carries the name Black Hills.[2]

Near Cheyenne the land is a rolling prairie, an undulating landscape with short, dry grass, which you encounter everywhere, and looks, so to speak, like a slightly raised hem along the foot of the mountains. The train runs westward in almost a direct line toward the mountains, crosses or circumvents one swell in the ground after the other and confronts larger ones the higher it climbs. Suddenly, as if they had all contracted out of the rolling flatness into vertical shapes, they have unexpectedly become hills; rocky ridges appear on their sides, crags on their tops, and deep, chasmal, waterless, valleys separate them. Some of these are high and rough enough to be counted as worthy precursors of the snow-capped tops of Longs Peak, which tower over on the left. Lonely, scattered pines with poor growth, which here and there come close to looking like the Alpine dwarf pine, are growing in front of the rock face, in glens, in clefts, and other protected places; despite their stunted scrubbiness and poor condition, they are still a welcome change after the desert-like monotony of the high prairie. They also tell us that we are in the midst of mountains, although the prairie is scarcely an hour behind us.

The unusual rock formations cause the mind to conjure up marvelous images. You cannot help but notice them. Nearby they go unnoticed as well-known kinds of rock, but at a distance they catch and hold your attention by the innumerable striking formations—on the mountains they look like long rows of unfinished walls, like castles, and like ruins of churches and chapels, and in far-off valleys like pyramids, sepulchers, or when piled up, like cemeteries full of columns; on ledges they are like huts, dark mine entrances, terraces, or bastions. Except for the train, slowly treading its way up the mountain, everything is so devoid of human life, enveloped in the extremely gray-green cloak of dry grass, only occasionally interrupted by the pines whose dark twisted forms even seem enchanted. They would certainly seem to be trees but one would look around in vain for the shapes of trees. These are the gnomes of the tree kingdom.

As hour after hour passes there are only a very few new things to see in between long intervals in this monotonous picture. A flock of sheep with many black and white lambs, a water tower giving a drink with its long iron arm to the steam engine, deserted cabins standing with dirt piled high up to the roof,* several log cabins for the railroad officials, the shepherd—a boy sitting on a horse carrying a long stick and gun—his shaggy dog hurrying in front of him over to the flock, and several gray chipmunks leaping down an old streambed.

Farther on, inanimate objects appear; numerous snow fences, snow walls, and the first of those covered passageways made out of beams and boards, which later on in the Sierra Nevada run along for miles to protect the rail line from the snow. These are simple constructions, but, as I hear, they completely measure up to their requirements. The snow fences are roughly cut and made of wood. They stand very close to the tracks and often go back several rows, one after the other, and are placed in such an oblique fashion that they form a surface, which is something like a slanting roof against the snowdrifts blowing in from the side and which is naturally less susceptible to lateral pressure. The snow walls are rough-hewed walls made of fieldstones and are much more seldom seen than the fences. Finally, covered passageways, technically the snowsheds, are real tunnels made of wood, which are only used in the most exposed areas and run along for miles at a time.

Where the railroad comes down into the Sacramento Valley out of the Sierra Nevada, it runs through mountain landscape that offers the most wonderful scenery one can see anywhere from an American train. But because of the snowsheds it is exactly along this stretch that the world is literally boarded up, and only where perhaps a slat has broken off does one get a fleeting view of a green lake that lies below in the darkness of the pines, deep in the valley, of the first forests—the sight of which on the barrenness of the high plateau is doubly welcome—and waterfalls and rushing streams. No wonder everyone is so eager to dash outside to get a look around as soon as the train stops for a minute! However, the railroad covering is probably required here more than anywhere else between the Mississippi and the Pacific, for that side of the Sierras, the western one, gets the moist west wind coming straight at it, and while the interior gets too little snow and rain, here they often get too much. However, on the section on which we are now riding, on the eastern slope, the amount of snow is not the main reason for the large amount of protective equipment shielding the tracks, for even at Sherman, at the top of the pass, rarely more than a few inches fall; rather, the reason is due to the extremely strong winds that carry the snow down from the mountains into the valley and probably would blow it most frequently into drifts right in those natural cuttings that the railroad has to travel through.

The bare, rugged monotony of the mountain wilderness culminates at the

---

*THESE ARE CALLED DUGOUTS, AND BECAUSE OF THE SHARP WINDS ON THE PRAIRIE, THEY ARE FREQUENTLY SEEN THERE.

pass and remains the predominant characteristic of the scenery from now on until we arrive down at the Great Salt Lake, where nature is more generous to the surrounding area and where in several places an intensive cultivation of the soil has already led to good results. There are oases of lush grass and cheerful-looking willow and cottonwood shrubbery, and the largest of the plateaus, the one around Laramie, which has plenty of water, is of considerable size, about twelve German (fifty-six statute) miles long, but in the distance you always see the barren heights, and wherever the water does not reach right into the middle of the green meadow, the desert with its terrible aridness has again gained ground rapidly. In many places the soil must contain a great deal of salt, for even on the edge of many bodies of water, which frequently intersect the rail lines here and run from the south and flow into the North Platte River that in turn runs somewhat further north in an easterly direction to the Missouri, the vegetation is not much better than in the very arid upland areas. Naturally these streams are quite meager, especially in summer when they become barely visible trickles. A very good example of this can be seen in the case of Bitter Creek, along whose valley the train runs for awhile, where the water is so full of salt that one is wary of drinking it. Here was one of the most dangerous stretches for the many immigrants who before the completion of the Pacific line came with their families by horse and wagon, frequently in caravan fashion, through the desert to the promised land in the Far West.

Upon coming down from the pass, we see the snowcaps of Longs Peak outlined in deep blue and with very blurred contours on the south horizon; in comparison with the desolate character of the immediate vicinity it is a true delight. The contrast of the dreary colors with this, so to speak, gentle glow of the distant mountains is extraordinary, and one understands how a secret premonition of wealth and good living, even without all the traditional fabulous tales, drew so many over these desolate regions toward the mountains. There is no end to the things that can be written about these blue, towering, distant places and much could be wished into them.[3] Even the clouds that hang over them seem to suggest an entirely different fruitfulness than indicated by the saltworts and rough mat-grasses of this plateau!

For one day and one night the train rushed through this desert, which, except for the oases, only changes its look by slight color shadings, but whose basic character together with the rocks and pines always remains the same. Moving figures, however, gradually become more frequent. Some hunters are carrying captured antelopes on their shoulders, as the Good Shepherd carrying the lamb in the early Christian depictions. Soon afterwards antelopes in herds of twelve and twenty appeared more than once within shooting range of the train, actually trying sometimes to keep pace with it by big springing leaps. Covered wagons creep along the sand, drawn by skinny horses with cattle and goats following behind, urged on by the men of the group on horseback; the women and children peer inquisitively from under the cloth that is stretched out in a semiarch over the wagons. We pass by big and little station stops, where only seldom does anyone get on or off, and which consist of single cabins in the smaller places and several cabins all clustered together in the larger ones. The latter are always the center of local commerce and are therefore chockfull of every kind of merchandise and covered with announcements and advertisements, nor is there ever any lack of saloons. "If the temperate Chinese didn't compose the main body of railroad workers," one of the local people in Ogden told me, "then you would see a ginmill in every other house." One of these cabin clusters is called Como because of a sorry-looking little pond in the vicinity, which has been named after the Italian lake.[4]

I spoke of shadings in the coloration of the sparse vegetation covering this desert, and this is literally true, for its appearance changes considerably depending on whether the vegetation is denser or more scattered about. This may seem a slight distinction, but in this landscape, where the shapes and colors are so uniform, the very smallest change becomes a matter of importance. It is actually made up of the same plants as those on the high prairies: dry grass, ligneous lupin, artemisia, chenopod, saltwort, which often attain the size of low shrubs—generally dry, gray or yellow-gray bushes with few leaves. Oenothera with inch-long white pendent flowers, gilia with long scarlet tubular blossoms, fields of wild rye; sometimes juniper bushes add darker shading with their very lush green leaves, and brighter, more varied colors. Frequently though, the shading tends toward grays and yellows. Then the dry but still rather thick growth of grass groups itself in separate round patches, pressed together in hemispheric mounds, like the vegetation in the high Alps and the Polar regions, with the yellow of the sand still visible on all sides around these patches. Even these become less frequent in many places, finally disappear, and leave a very desolate wasteland. A stretch of desert continues for a bit and then one again sees green tints in the low-lying sections, thickets of wild rye, artemisia bushes, and in a deep, narrow ravine even a brook or little stream running between low, undersized willow bushes.

Being together so long helps a greater sense of sociability to develop here than one is used to finding on railroad trips; one can thus forget the desert through which he is traveling for a few hours. You also feel as on a ship, cut off from the outer world and relegated to the small circle of fellow travelers, most of whom remain together for three, and many for five and eight days. Fortunately, one is not so cramped for space in the parlor and sleeping cars as one would be in European railroad cars. He can go from seat to seat, from car to car, can set up a little table in front of himself to eat, read, or play cards, can wash and drink as much cold water as he desires. That promotes a sense of well-being and consequently a feeling of sociability. In these parts it is not difficult to make acquaintances, and since on an average there are always sixty to eighty people traveling on the express trains of the Pacific Railroad, everyone who is at least halfway sociable can find one or two people whose company is to his liking.

The logistical aspects of such a trip, seen from the view of the nontechnician, are simpler than one imagines. In European newspapers they have often described the so-called hotel trains,[5] which are not the normal trains, as the usual means of conveyance on the Pacific Railroad, and therefore the common impression is that every train is a hotel train. This is not so. On the contrary, the railroad companies set up restaurants, which are spaced out all along the entire route at which the train stops three times a day and in which you can usually get an acceptable meal for just one dollar. Only once did I find a so-called hotel car on a train—it was on the day train between Chicago and St. Louis, which leaves in the morning and arrives in the evening. Actually, as far as I know, hotel trains run only once a week from San Francisco and New York, and actually now that there are enough restaurants all along the route, they are really then only a gimmick. The amount of time saved isn't really worth it, since fuel and water have to be taken on board, and after six hours of being thoroughly shaken about, it is good for everyone to be able to give his stiff limbs some exercise again on firm ground.

A typical train, which leaves daily from Omaha or San Francisco, consists of one first-class car, one second-class car, a baggage car, and several sleeping cars. In second class there is a smoking section. Coming from Omaha, you change trains in Ogden (Utah) and in Sacramento, but coming from St. Louis via Colorado, you change in Kansas City, Denver, Cheyenne, Ogden, and Sacramento. The fares are subject to considerable change. In the summer of 1874, one paid $140 from New York to San Francisco, $118 from St. Louis and Chicago, $100 from Omaha, and $90 from Denver.

CONTRAST BETWEEN THE RAILROAD THROUGH THE ROCKY MOUNTAINS AND GERMAN ALPINE LINES. GENERAL DESOLATE CHARACTER. OASIS-LIKE ALPINE SCENES. TRESTLE WORKS. DOWN TO THE GREAT SALT LAKE. LAKE AT DUSK. AGAIN IN THE WILDERNESS. OASIS NEAR HUMBOLDT STATION. OVER THE SIERRA NEVADA. IN CALIFORNIA.

Because of their general aridness, the Rocky Mountains form a much less beautiful landscape than the Alps; at most, the wild, grotesque rock formations and the ravines or canyons that are for long stretches filled with these formations can be compared with the magnificent scenes in our high mountains. Nevertheless, one cannot fail to see that that section crossed by the Pacific line shows the mountains in their poorest, most monotonous, yes almost frightening aspect. Since most travelers go through the area without making a side trip, this one-sided impression is easily generalized, and therefore one frequently hears the most slanted, unbelievably underrated value judgments depicting the entire Rocky Mountain range as one big wasteland. This is extremely regretable, and I hope that the projected lines through Colorado and Utah and through Arkansas and Arizona to the Pacific will be realized very soon.[6] Along these lines, as opposed to that on the Pacific Railroad, the traveler will see the most beautiful parts of this so very diversely constituted mountain chain.

There is, of course, a great difference between the landscape through which our Alpine lines run and that of this first Rocky Mountain line. When I compare the summit of the Brenner Pass[7] with that of the Black Hills or the Humboldt Range, it seems to me that the Alpine scene, which in no way is the most magnificent or most beautiful, is the work of an infinitely rich and artistically creative imagination, whereas the ones here, even at the most breathtaking places, seem like rough sketches, like frames that are waiting to be filled in with shapes and colors. The immense abundance of lakes and rivers, the innumerable springs and little streams of the Alps are so much in evidence there, while here usually only a somewhat lighter, greener tone in the gray vegetation cover indicates a tiny amount of concealed moisture. Because of the predominantly dull lines in the mountain contours and the rock fields, which here and there seem to have been heaped up with indiscriminate ferocity, the emptiness and barrenness assume a crude, repellent aspect, but it needs only a more opulent coloring of vegetation to make it appear perhaps even attractive. Nudity here, just as with the human body, is a most demanding state of being; it is always repugnant except when the most attractive lines circumscribe it.

Several times things begin to look like Alpine scenes. But these similarities are only momentary. We descend from the plateau of the Black Hills to the basin of the Great Salt Lake through some canyon valleys that have some rather wild streams full of water rushing through them and green meadows and plentiful bushes on the valley bottom and slopes. Blue, snow-streaked Alpine peaks, which appear in front of us, narrow rocky valleys with a lush growth of grass on the banks of their brooks, which burst forth here and there out of the sides of the rocky embankments, the transition from plateau to hills and then to mountains, pines, which again are seen more frequently clinging to the rocky crevices—all announce our entrance into the Wasatch Range, the barrier that separates the desert highlands of the Wyoming Territory from the Great Salt Lake basin. When we go on through Echo and Weber Canyon, two valleys, whose rugged rocky fissures—for long stretches here the sandstone ramparts, towers, and pillars rise vertically for two thousand feet—only find their parallel in the wilds of the eastern Rocky Mountains of Colorado.

Here were the most dangerous spots for the railroad in the first few months after its completion, for you only find similarly difficult terrain on the western slope of the Sierra Nevada where it descends toward California. But for some time now the bridges have been as strong as anywhere on a Western line, the track bed secure and protected from falling debris. The so-called trestle works,

20   "ONE CAN ENTRUST
ONESELF TO THEM [RAILROAD
BRIDGES] HERE WITHOUT
FEAR, EVEN IF THERE IS A
HUGH DROP BENEATH THEM TO
THE VALLEY BELOW."
THROUGH THE MOUNTAINS OF
THE WEST BY RAIL.

viaducts that are cut out of seemingly very light beams, always look unsafe to those who do not know much about American railroads. But their ingenious construction makes them very reliable supports, and whoever has had the opportunity to travel, for instance, on Southern lines where one often crosses the swamps for miles on such trestle works, can also entrust oneself to them here without fear, even if there is a huge drop beneath them to the valley below.

The snow-covered mountains, which have been in front of us for some time with their dull, very flat pyramidal contours, sparsely forested but generally bare, are now off to the side and we are traveling along their slopes. The valleys between the rocks give way to wider valley floors with a wonderful grass matting and more peaceful bodies of water; the soil again produces flowers that remind one of the lush "bottoms" of the eastern prairies; it supports large meadows and fields of tall-bladed golden grain, and along the streams, willows and alder bushes, which are almost impenetrably entwined with creeping and climbing vines. As the Mormons on their journey to the Salt Lake came down from the wilderness of the plateau into these valleys, they compared the land that lay before them, not without some truth, to the Promised Land that was given to the Jews after their wandering through the desert.

Now the heavy string of cars glides down as if driven by its own weight towards the Great Salt Lake, which because of twilight was unfortunately only indistinctly visible. Before we reach it, a stop is made at Ogden and cars changed. From here the branch line runs down to the Mormon capital, Salt Lake City, which is two hours away. Leaving the Union Pacific we now come to the Central Pacific, and everyone is happy to have finished crossing one-half of the desert. We lose a few passengers who are traveling to Salt Lake City to investigate Mormonism or the silver mines. An unhappy, nervous lady from Ohio, who has traveled out here alone to learn about the prospects of a mining operation in which she has invested half of her savings, left us here with anxious misgivings. These poor, deceived people, who are inquiring about the whereabouts of their fortune—which has disappeared, never to be seen again, into some mining shaft that had very little silver in it—are not a rare occurrence in the Far West.

As the train rolls farther down the Weber River valley, we soon see the broad surface of the Salt Lake before us. The railroad runs right along its edge for a few miles, so that you can clearly see the reflection in the water of the mountains on the other side as well as recognize the darkish color of the water and the greenish shimmer on its surface. The valley with a uniform marshy grassland, runs up to the water and extends along this side of the lake with similar vegetation between the water and the mountains; on the other side, the mountains, whose semi-Alpine shapes and snow tops again remind you of the Rockies in Colorado, seem to come right down to the lake. The indistinct light of the last faint moment of dusk runs over the large liquid surface, where the wind does not stir up a ripple and which from afar looks like dull silver. The air is easier to breath, damper; the sky is full of clouds, hovering low, thickly clustered together with the blurry edges that indicate rain. Rain is beginning to fall as we again leave the lake and move up the valley, and before nightfall it spreads its gray veil in front of the bare yellow mountain range in whose valleys our trip will run for a further thirty hours. Awakening the next morning, we find ourselves in a still more desolate desert than the one we left yesterday, in a valley full of sand, rocks, and scraggly, grey bushes from whose downy branches and little leaves the clear morning sun distills a penetrating odor of vermouth—a highly novel but fitting addition to the desert character. The meadows, the bodies of water, the soft clouds, the rain of yesterday evening all seem like a mirage in one's memory now that the desert landscape has returned.

Has the train gone backwards? Everything that now appears and flies by, near by and distant, even the grey weeds on the ground, we saw yesterday. The landscape seemed more gentle then, but the difference is slight. We are again on a plateau surrounded on both sides by low, rocky hills, and in the distance by mountain ranges. In front and behind us they shut off the range of view only to disappear as we approach them behind the hills over which they tower on both sides. The summits are covered with snow further down than the ranges of the Rockies to the east, and that may be a good sign that we are closer to the ocean, which we are anxious to see. Soon the desolateness is interrupted by a cliff, a wall of rock, a rock cluster, soon a dark juniper tree, whose short branches are grouped close together on the trunk. There is nothing more to see except perhaps for the white salt ring around the edge of a dried-up pool. The shapes of the most distant, higher mountains, which already belong to the Humboldt Range, are scarcely different from anything we know of the Rockies. They are basically bastion-like rock massifs, which, although not very steep, also do not rise accompanied by many levels of foothills but rather consist of broad pyramidal forms with gentle contours. The clearly discernible sinuous and cracked bands of its strata and the lack of vegetation covering it give it a somewhat more rocky character than it would normally have on the basis of its relief and its contours. This mountain range always justifies its name of the Rockies. Once more, castles, walls, pillars, and rows of coulisses appear unexpectedly out of the gravel. If for the moment there aren't any rocks, then the hills themselves look like grandiose piles of gravel. The vegetation is so meager that it would scarcely change the character of the landscape if all this sand were baked together into rock by the sun and aridity.

In a few places where there is a little moisture but not enough to form salt or sodium carbonate pools, oases of green meadows appear in the course of the endless desert picture. Here the soil immediately verifies its innate fertility, and all year long yields great quantities of hay, thousands of bales of which we saw stacked up at some stations. These are sent near and far to mining districts, which here in Nevada, more so than in Utah and Colorado, are located in the most inhospitable sections. Without the importation of fodder from California and from these few oases, they would be completely incapable of surviving here. Near Argenta the railroad goes through such an oasis, which unexpectedly actually conjures up the picture of a swampy marshland rich in vegetation. What is very nice to see here are the broad dark green fields of rushes whose little brown tops sway back and forth like ears of grain, the pools and sluggish brooks on whose surface there is a covering of floating flowering polygonal shapes and thickly clustered algae, and finally lush sunflowers sheltered by the willows. But scarcely did we get to enjoy the new view when the land begins to rise again, becoming arid and salty, again producing artemesias and butterwort shrubs, those bitterly salty, grey, fibrous bushes.

Near Humboldt Station—you see this name everywhere, for mountain ranges, individual mountains, rivers, lakes, settlements, and famous springs— gorgeous corn and clover fields and an unexpected flower garden are to be seen, but you do not have to look far for the cause of this surprising, extremely rare phenomenon. In front of the station house a large spring is gushing forth, and it has been made into a fountain, which sends up a tall stream of the most wonderful mountain water. Even fruit trees do well with this moisture. The spring is the greatest sightseeing attraction between Utah and Summit, the highest place in the Sierra Nevada. The sons of the Celestial Empire, the yellow, methodical, grinning Chinese, who served the evening meal in the dining room of the railroad station, are for us newcomers equally worth seeing.

A magnificent sunset made a fine ending for the last day of our journey through the desert. Like the morning light and the rising of the moon and the coming out of the stars, it took on an entirely different significance in this wilderness, where there is so little to satisfy thirsty eyes used to more interesting views. In this sense the desert is like the ocean. There was a double sunset, or more accurately a double twilight, for on the western horizon a mass of clouds was just beginning to rise as the sun went behind them. The first twilight had almost faded all over as they broke up and swam along in the evening sky, which immediately became golden again like golden ships with purple sails.

During the night we had climbed further up in the valley of the Humboldt River and in the morning were near the pass, which at Summit Station[8] had an altitude of 7,017 feet. A wild mountain landscape had appeared in place of the desert. Snowfields below the peaks of the closest mountains were very near by, unruly streams crossed the railroad line, pine and spruce groves stood up on rocky slopes and in the crevices, which penetrated into the mountains between the walls of rock. We looked down into valleys where a sea of dark tree tops surrounded blue lakes and bright green fields while flocks were grazing on the slopes. The train dashed through mile-long snow tunnels, which limited the view, and passed all the wild mountain streams—the Yuba, the Bear, and the American River—which rush down from here to join the Sacramento River. Lower down came forests of strange-looking oak trees, long-needled pine trees with huge cones, an unknown type of cedar, and, tall white lilies, very similar to our garden variety, frequently standing in their shadow. This was now California scenery, and the clouds drifting by over us were coming from the Pacific Ocean.

As we left the mountains and arrived in the valley of the Sacramento and San Joaquin, miles and miles of cornfields wonderfully covered the land, and there was no lack of pleasant views of bustling cities and groups of farmhouses under shady oaks. Figs and grapes were offered for sale at every stop. Towards evening, after we had crossed the low mountains of the Coast Range, a cool sea breeze met us and after sunset the ferry took us over the arm of the bay that separates Oakland from San Francisco. Once again a world metropolis lay before us in a brilliant sea of light, and the desert was quickly forgotten.

CHAPTER TWENTY

San Francisco

SAN FRANCISCO BAY. ITS FAVORITE LOCATION FOR TRADE. SITE
OF THE CITY. COMMERCE AND TRADE.

At the spot where the Sacramento and San Joaquin, California's two main
rivers, come together and empty into the sea, a novel rock and sand dune
formation has created sort of a lagoon, which reminds one of many of the pools
of water that extend behind the dune-like strip of France's Mediterranean
coastline. Their position and shape are similar. There is an oblong bay, and it
runs parallel to the coast behind the outer coastline and empties out into the
ocean through a small opening. It is more than ten geographical (forty-six
statute) miles long and on the average two geographical (about nine statute)
miles wide. The southern part, which is separated from the northern one by a
narrowing convergence of the coastal strips and from the mainland itself, is
called San Francisco Bay, while the northern section is called San Pablo Bay.
The gateway to the sea for both bays is called Golden Gate. It bore this name
even before the discovery of gold in the Sierra Nevada, and the subsequent
immense export of gold granted it a very special right to such a name. San
Francisco is built on the inner side of the southern arm of the coastal strip that
the bay encloses. The entrance to the bay lies on the 37° 48′ northern latitude.

As always there is a complicated series of reasons for awarding this bay the
position of one of the best commercial harbors in the world and bestowing on
this city built on its shore the rank of a world commercial center. Above all, it
is such a good harbor as only nature could build, for the straits of the Golden
Gate, more than one geographical mile (4.5 statute miles) long, all along are
deep enough for the largest ships, and the bay, with its surface of more than
twenty geographical (ninety-two statute) square miles, offers anchorage for
innumerable ships. Moreover, because of its narrow and lengthy estuary and
the numerous islands it contains, it can be defended with relative ease. In
addition, it is just as admirably situated with regard to its own country as it is

to the foreign countries that border other parts of the Pacific Ocean, and therefore San Francisco has in part to compete and in part to trade primarily with those harbors. The bay offers California the benefit of the best harbor in the state. Moreover, since the Oregon coast has few harbors, only after the completion of the much more southerly situated harbor of San Pedro (recently named Wilmington),[1] which the Federal Government is building near Los Angeles, will there be some sort of second harbor worth speaking of between Puget Sound and the Mexican border. Furthermore, the Bay of San Francisco is the most centrally located harbor in California; and the fact that the state's two most important rivers empty into it further increases its importance. Here the river traffic as well as the most important transportation routes converge; the particular geographical features of the area on the whole compel these routes to follow the course of the more important rivers. The Sacramento River is at present navigable for steamships above Sacramento; the San Joaquin is navigable for about the same distance; and besides the large overland New York-San Francisco line, four additional local, i.e., Californian, railroad lines run to San Francisco.

When one tries to explain the relationship of San Francisco to the other harbors along the West Coast, the most striking fact is that the specific area, which produces marketable products and which seems to correspond with the borders of California, does not have a second harbor to rival it; furthermore, from the Strait of Juan de Fuca[2] south along the coast of the United States, Mexico, or Central America there is not a harbor to be found which is as spacious and at the same time as protected or which offers such easy entry as does San Francisco. The famous, old harbor of Acapulco,[3] which after San Francisco is probably the best along the entire coast, is only a little inlet compared to the California bay.

San Francisco's connections with the interior and the neighboring coast also help increase its importance. As the point of departure for the overland line to and from New York, it will not have to worry about competition for years; the North American traffic with Asia and indirectly also part of the European-Asian traffic will presumably not go via another place very soon, for you cannot imagine a more direct route between the most industrious and commercially active parts of Atlantic North America and the Pacific Ocean. However, the digging of the canal across the Central American isthmus, which has been projected for a long time, will allow direct sea traffic to compete with the overland route, but the development of the resources of the land west of the Great Salt Lake, most of whose incoming and outgoing metals and goods, so to speak, pass through San Francisco, should more than compensate for the expected loss from the canal, and passenger traffic as well as that of valuable goods will prefer the land route. Besides, this canal is still a long way off, which does not ncessitate practical consideration or conclusions for a while.[4]

All the same, you can certainly wonder whether the city itself could not have found a more suitable location on some other section of this natural harbor basin. They say it was only by chance that it grew up on this outermost tip of the neck of land. The first ships bringing supplies for the gold prospectors were directed, because of unfamiliarity with the then so little known locali- ties, to the old Spanish settlement of Yerba-Buena, which stood on this spot, instead of to the more favorably situated Vallejo. Vallejo was already one of the most important places in the entire province and would have offered not only a better climate than peninsular San Francisco but also a much better spot for the junction of rail lines because of its position in the Sacramento Valley. Up until just a few years ago it was still likely that one of the islands opposite San Francisco in the bay could be made into an artificial peninsula to serve as the end station for the most important railroad lines. At present the Pacific Railroad and the southern California line[5] stop at a provisional station stand- ing on pilings in the middle of the bay and are only connected with the city by ferries. For the time being, however, it seems as if that plan has been given up. The railroads are satisfied with the provisional railway stations and later on want to build a secure bridge over the bay at a narrow point in the southern part of the city.[6]

With regard to the present state of San Francisco's commerce, I am citing from the report of the *San Francisco Journal of Commerce* for 1873—the only compila- tion of any reliability—the following figures: exports during this year came to $29,711,311, while for 1872 they had been somewhat more than $6,000,000 less. More than $25,000,000 of this comes from the produce of California and the neighboring states of which wheat and flour with $21,000,000, wool with $6,500,000, and wine with $500,000 were the main items; after these came items with smaller figures: salmon ($250,000), mercury ($800,000), and preserved fruits, among other things. The majority of these exports went to England, which received almost $21,000,000 worth of goods from San Francisco. The re- mainder was distributed among the Eastern states, Mexico, China, Australia, Japan, Central and South America, and some of the island groups in the Pacific. Imports amounted to $7,000,000 from China, $6,000,000 from England, $4,500,000 from Mexico, and $4,000,000 from Japan. The total value of imported goods amounted to about $20,000,000 worth of foreign and $30,000,000 worth of domestic goods.

According to Hittell's *Resources of California*,[7] in 1872, 3,670 ships came into the harbor of San Francisco; their average tonnage was 330. The total tonnage of foreign ships amounted to 505,000, that of American ships from the Atlantic seaboard 96,000, and that of West Coast ships 634,000. There were 2,972 ships arriving from places on the West Coast, 122 from South America, 88 from Europe (of which 8 were German and 72 English), 77 from Australia, 80 from China and Japan, 68 from Polynesia, and 38 from the East Indies. The Pacific Mail Steamship Company, which has its headquarters in San Francisco, runs ten steamers with a total capacity of 39,000 tons two times a week on its Japan route, seven with a total of 19,000 tons two times a week on the Panama line, one with 13,000 tons to Honolulu, and four with 3,200 tons to San Diego.

The California-Japan line has a branch running from Yokohama to Hong Kong, and the steamers of the Panama line call at the most important harbors of western Mexico, primarily Mazatlán and Acapulco and to some degree also at the Central American ports. A British line maintains direct monthly connections with Hong Kong and a host of smaller steamers takes care of San Francisco's traffic with harbors lying farther north and south in California and those of Oregon, the Washington Territory, British Columbia, and on up to Alaska.

No less than commerce and transportation, California's industry also has its center in San Francisco. Of the $66,000,000 worth of items produced in the state this year, $37,000,000 worth was to have come from San Francisco.

SAN FRANCISCO'S FUTURE. SKEPTICAL OPINIONS. FAILURE TO MAKE AN ARCHITECTURAL IMPRESSION. SURROUNDING AREAS. DUNES. CITY PLAN.

With regard to that flattering opinion that San Francisco is assuming the position of a world metropolis, one must not forget that this position is not an active or, better expressed, a productive factor. That means, a city does not primarily become a metropolis because of its geographical location but rather because it knows how to exploit that location. World metropolises will develop on very few spots where the traffic flow between old, thickly settled regions converges or crosses but which are not dependent on the development of the hinterland. Singapore is perhaps the only example of this kind that can be cited for the current century. The case of San Francisco is quite different; its unquestionably exceptional position between two such great commercial areas as East Asia and North America is by itself alone incapable of guiding the flow of the international commerce of these regions through the Golden Gate, if the city itself through its own development does not offer a further incentive than just that which nature has provided to this superb location. With time, trade could find other routes, but San Francisco's development will always have a direct relation to the overall development of the Pacific Slope[8] in general and to California's in particular.

California's development will probably reach its limits because of the peculiarities of its climate and soil sooner than the areas to the north, Oregon and the Washington Territory, which in possessing all the important qualities for utilizing the natural resources are probably more similar to the most cultivatable parts of Central Europe than any other area of the United States. But today San Francisco is already much more than just the major city of California, and even if in less time than one can reasonably hope, a northern Pacific Railroad should run into Puget Sound,[9] this will not lessen its status as the "Pacific New York" as long as it has alert citizens who do not simply exploit the advantages of the location but through their own activity increase them.

The expectations are great; this is only natural. Since the people have really worked hard and honestly toiled to reach the current level, it is only reasonable that they look with pride on their accomplishments and hope only for the best for the city's future. I am not going to complain that I continually found the same old story about the metropolis of the future, the old phrases and exaggerations in every book and every pamphlet when I was looking for data and sound reasoning. It is rather obvious that San Francisco has a splendid commercial site, and the outlook for development that exists here—the thought of the fruits of civilization developing on the well-endowed coastal area, along the Sierra Nevada and Cascade Range, and of the close connections beginning to be made by new commercial routes between the oldest part of the Old and the youngest part of the New World, between East Asia and California—is enough to excite even a reserved individual to some wild flights of imagination. Nevertheless, in the end one gets tired of seeing these constant half-baked predictions about an unknown future, which give no time, particularly for the simpler minds, to brace themselves for the constantly new, perpetually futile, hypothetical projects. It is extremely unpleasant where it becomes, as here, a fashion or even a mania.

The strangest thing about the thoughts one has every time the slightest thing changes here is the general dissatisfaction with the development of the city. San Francisco could be larger, the trade more significant, and the population richer. In an otherwise good account of the city's development I read: "One easily understands that Chicago can be a city with only 75,000 inhabitants, but that San Francisco can have a smaller population than it has is hard to comprehend." One often hears similar things, for many people are not happy with the inhabitants whom they feel lack the grand spirit of initiative, which has made Chicago great; they accuse them of conducting business in a narrow-minded provincial way, and of neither adorning the new metropolis with large public works nor with the beautiful buildings that should not be missing from a city of its rank, and they voice other such similar complaints. But these people who are so annoyed don't take time to consider really how disparate this population still is—the generation that was born here is only now starting to come of age—how poor it is in terms of experience and traditions, how so much they set about doing here is still experimental, or how low the immigration figures have been for some years now with probably no chance of a large influx as long as those parts of America that are closer to Europe still have room for so many millions.

Perhaps those who say that San Francisco's appearance displays little of the beauty and splendor without whch we can hardly imagine a city of 200,000 inhabitants are more correct. With the exception of two or three blocks, California Street (the stock exchange and bank street) and Montgomery Street, where the largest hotels and shops are located, the streets are preponderantly lined with simple, mostly brick houses, which are painted gray or have weather boarding and which in the poorer sections of the city give the impression of being as temporary as the houses in the seminomadic prairie of the Far West. This is not compatible with a metropolis with such a great future, but one excuses it because of the earthquakes, which have caused considerable damage in San Francisco many times. The lack of churches of any note or other monumental pieces of architecture can be overlooked because of the city's youth and partly because of the lack of good building stone in its immediate environs. If some day this deficiency in good architecture is rectified, the immediate vicinity around the city will then be seen in all its beauty.[10]

In the meantime the general panorama is the prettiest thing about the city. One has the best view from the so-called Telegraph Hill, an elevated spot on the landhead on which the city is built. Here on sunny days, which I'll admit are few, you have before you the blue-green bordered surface of the bay with a garland of rounded, brown mountains around it. Like the shore, even the islands and foothills are rounded and brown, though many times not without some indication of what type of rock lies beneath the surface, as seen in the steep cliffs in front of them. One sees how the blue sea surrounds the land, stretching out like a narrow peninsula into the bay, and as one looks over the other crest of the hill, which turns away from the bay, one sees how it is covered with houses and gardens, how many other hills are similarly covered, and how around their feet a flat stretch of ground, which has been won back from the ocean, supports a thicker cluster of buildings than even the hill does. This is the business district. At the edge of this area are the long wooden warehouses, the wharves, and innumerable ships.

Above all, it is the bay that is the most beautiful. As we enter through the Golden Gate we immediately have the view of a spacious and safe harbor, for all around we see the rock and mountain rim of this magnificent basin. It is so close that we can distinguish the white line of the breaking surf along the shore; further away it is hazy, just like cloud strips along the horizon. There is space enough here. In the distance one can recognize several parts of San Francisco, above all the symbol of the city, Goat Island,[11] which can be seen from quite a ways away, and which is distinguished by its dark brown shrub covering against the brighter dunes and rocks on the shore. San Francisco is still partly hidden by a protruding hill; on its slopes on the other side there is a busy part of town, but the side facing us seems predominantly bare, full of dunes with only some scattered homes on it. Only when we have traveled beyond the point of this promontory do we catch sight of the long block of houses, which runs along three of the hills. Today (as is usually the case) the city, together with those parts of the bay closest to it, lies in fog, and the hills upon which San Francisco is built stand with their steeples and roof-topped crests like a multifissured rocky mountain behind a veil.

However, seen from close up, one of the attractive elements of the distant

21 "SAN FRANCISCO'S
APPEARANCE DISPLAYS LITTLE
OF THE BEAUTY AND SPLENDOR
WITHOUT WHICH WE CAN
HARDLY IMAGINE A CITY OF
200,000 INHABITANTS." VIEW
OF SAN FRANCISCO FROM
TELEGRAPH HILL.

view, the yellow sand dune that is visible wherever the brown underbrush is sparse, changes into one of the less pleasant features of San Francisco. You cannot go along any of the streets that run inland without finally coming to houses that are standing on sand hills or without wading through the sand, which has not yet been completely supplanted in the more outlying sections of the city by the plankboard walkways that are generally used in this country in place of our stone sidewalks. Not far from the central parts of the city we find the most novel-looking hills formed by drifting sand, and when you see houses build on these heavily eroded slopes, which is frequently the case, this is the final touch to the impression of nonsolidity you get from such a picture.

The city is not systematically laid out like the older American cities in the East and the South. Whoever has seen those cities is not surprised by anything in San Francisco as much as by the irregularities in its layout. The newest of all cities, it is in many ways the most irregular. This is attributable more to the layout than to the conditions of the terrain, for although the ground on which the city stands is more hilly than Rome's, still there is no other reason for so many dead-end streets, street corners built at acute angles, and streets that run straight along without a break other than the improvident caprice of the original city layout. As regards the hills and valleys, which run steeply up and down through the middle of the city, leveling them at least partially would have been comparatively easy, since they consist basically of drifted sand. But the unanimous complaint is that this city has never had a board of public works equal to its task or one that honestly protected the city's interests against those of individuals. But one must not forget as well that amidst San Francisco's growth and initial proverty, it was very difficult to develop great plans for the future and still harder to carry them out.

If one looks at the map of San Francisco, one has to conclude that the city is made up of three parts that had originally been planned differently or that it originated from the coalescing of these three different sides. It occupies a rectangular space on the corner of an equally rectangular tongue of land on which it is built. The section on the north side and that on the south side are covered with a grid of perpendicularly intersecting streets, which is the most outstanding feature of the plans of all newer American cities. But here, in between both sections, pushing itself in from the edge like a wedge, is an entirely different layout whose streets are much more widely spaced and meet those of the other two parts at obtuse and acute angles, almost always interrupting their course. In addition, in certain spots they bend and then run on in a direction that forms a right angle with the original direction. The layout at the inner end of this strange wedge looks most like that of both side sections; border between the northern section and the wedge forms the traffic artery of the city, Market Street. Most of the steamboat and railroad stations are located near the end of this street. This is destined to become the main street of the city and has already begun to supercede Kearny Street, which up until now has been the central street.

PECULIAR ATMOSPHERIC CONDITIONS. DUST. STREET LIFE. CHINESE. BACKWOODSMEN.

The weather conditions of San Francisco differ so greatly from those of the rest of California that it is as if a dozen degrees of latitude separated the main city from the rest of the state. It takes three hours, for example, to go from Sonoma to San Francisco, and one experiences a temperature change far greater than anything one has to get used to in traveling quickly over the Alps in a mountain train or in taking a night trip from Lyons down to Marseilles. If it is summertime in the Sonoma valley, a southern Italian heat prevails, as you would expect to find along this latitude, while in San Francisco there is a maritime climate in the extreme form of a damp fog or a cool wind. During July, there are days here on which in the morning and evening one could stand a good fire in the stove, and while it becomes oppressively hot when there is no wind or fog, towards evening on such a hot day it can become cold and then foggy during the night. One is not surprised at all in the middle of summer if he sometimes sees a lady in muslin, and at other times one with a fur jacket. The

first type of clothing can seem logical for the present moment, while within the space of an hour, so can the other. On one day, temperature changes of twenty-five degrees centigrade are not unheard of despite the overall equilibrium of the climate. Therefore, you seldom see people here in summer clothing. Almost everyone wears woolen clothes of equal weight in both summer and winter. The worthy farmer from the interior who comes dressed in linen and sombrero frequently has had the experience, as one rural journal put it: on first going out in the morning you shiver with cold despite the woolen clothes, the underwear, and the overcoat buttoned to the top. At 8:30 A.M. you undo two buttons of the coat, at 9:00 you unbutton it all the way, at 9:50 you take it off, at 10:00 you exchange your woolen jacket for a summer one, and at 11:00 you get out of all woolens and clothe yourself in summer wear. But by 2:00 P.M. you have to put on the woolens again, and around 7:00 P.M. you are again shivering despite the thick overcoat.

This change, which is satisfactorily explained by the unique location of San Francisco and the extremely damp and cold climate of North America's West Coast, would hardly be as perceptible if strong winds didn't constantly blow in from morning till evening from the bay; and these midday winds, together with the rapid temperature changes, would in their turn be tolerable if in the dunes, on and near which such a great part of San Francisco is built, they did not find excellent material to saturate the air with dust and carry whole clouds of sand across the land and into the bay. The sea air usually gives you an appetite, but the pollution in it makes the climate of San Francisco especially hazardous for people who have weak lungs. I heard more complaints than praise for the "bracing influence," the stimulating effect of the air in San Francisco. At any rate, it is not the right kind of air for high-strung individuals. The popular morning newspaper, the *Morning Call*,[12] once described such a wind with the following words: "Yesterday it was as windy and unpleasant as is humanly imaginable and as is humanly possible to endure. Clouds of dust swirled through the streets and darkened the air, and the amount of sand that forced its way through window crevices and over door sills was really terrible. The amount of soil that was blown from the city and San Francisco County out into the bay would, figuring land at its lowest price, make a nice piece of property for one family."

September, the warmest month in San Francisco, has a mean temperature of 32°C.; January, the coldest month, has one of 27°.[13] The average difference in

22   "IF ONE LOOKS AT THE MAP OF SAN FRANCISCO, ONE HAS
TO CONCLUDE THAT THE CITY IS MADE UP OF THREE PARTS
THAT HAD ORIGINALLY BEEN PLANNED DIFFERENTLY." GRID
PLAN OF SAN FRANCISCO.

temperature between the three winter and three summer months amounts to no more than 4°C. As in all California, the rainy season arrives in San Francisco in late autumn and in early summer makes room for the dry season. The fact that snow falls very rarely here and usually never stays on the ground for more than a few hours is understandable with such temperature conditions. Moreover, thunderstorms frequently do not come for several years at a time. On the other hand, earthquakes are not infrequent and sometimes occur with an intensity that causes considerable damage to the buildings and even injuries to human life. The earthquake of 1870, which destroyed numerous buildings along the harbor, created a panic right afterwards. Many people wanted to leave the city then, but in a few weeks the scare was forgotten, and that same year land speculation subsequently increased enormously.

Opinions about the agreeableness of this climate are even more divided because San Francisco is still not old enough for its inhabitants to have been able to form a clear picture about its effects on the human body. In any event, most of its merits are essentially of a negative type and even the negative virtues may not meet with unanimous acceptance. Not every German would be pleased to see his winter replaced by a wet, rainy season, even though he may be happy that the poor people here are virtually spared the problem of worrying about firewood and coal. The relief from the summer heat loses much of its merit, since it is caused to such a large extent by fog. Whether or not in the end the lack of summer relaxation and winter rest will lead to a similar strain on people's systems as occurs in the East with the rapid weather changes and prevailing dryness in the air, is a question I don't want to answer unconditionally in the negative. The new generation of Californians who were born here are actually supposed to be healthier than the youth in the Eastern states. In any event, the climate is taxing.

Street life in San Francisco produces possibly a still more varied impression than one might expect from its location and extensive commerce. As in all North American cities there is no lack of members of the black race in all shades here, and for the many thousand sons of the Celestial Empire presently living in the United States, San Francisco, with a Chinese population now of almost 20,000, is just as much the metropolis for them as it is for the Americans. The white population for its part, because of the heavy addition of Spanish and Mexican blood and the relatively large number of Jews, Italians, and French who live in and around San Francisco, has a more southern tinge to it than, for example, the population of New York, and sometimes it even seems possible to recognize this admixture by the garish colors of the clothes. The population statistics for 1870 indicate that among the 150,361 inhabitants of San Francisco there were 76,000 white native Americans, 74,000 foreign-born whites, 12,000 Chinese, 1,341 Negroes and those of mixed Negro blood, and 55 Indians.[14]

Now and then, sprinkled into this variegated, multilingual conglomeration one sees some of the more infrequent types of foreigners brought into port by ships. Several times I saw sullen-looking dark Malays, recognizable by the little black turbans and black, tightly girded caftans, full-blooded Mexicans with broad, brown, bony faces, real Indians, Japanese, and Russians. But the goings on are not all that colorful, for almost all of the Chinese are dressed in blue-black, or in grey, and the whites generally subscribe to the uniform fashion, which with slight variation is the same wherever European civilization has penetrated. I even saw some Chinese and Japanese moving about awkwardly in European dress.

The Chinese, who have assumed a very important place here, virtually continue with all aspects of that particular life style one would find on the banks of the Yangtze. Whenever they do not reside in the homes of their employers, they are crowded together in a few narrow streets, where they live so close together that they really give the streets that anthill-like appearance travelers have described as characteristic of large Chinese cities. At quitting time, there are no streets in the rest of San Francisco that even remotely resemble those of Chinatown with its teeming life, and the similarity in both the cut and color of the clothes of the average, equally tall Chinaman gives the scene a remarkably uniform character, something one is not at all accustomed to seeing in America. As long as the workday lasts, however, most of them are always busy. Through the open doors, one can see that in workshops they are washing, ironing, tailoring, rolling cigars, butchering the pigs, which supply them with their main source of meat, with remarkable care and deliberation. Along the street, one sees them sawing wood, carrying large bundles, collecting garbage, and even minding children. In the homes of the whites they perform all types of jobs that would be the duty in our country of the "all-purpose maids." Thus you cannot escape them anywhere, and everywhere they are busy in the same somewhat slow, careful, cautious yet diligent manner and always seem to be the same limited, passive beings with the same yellow, slant-eyed, expressionless, beardless dozen or so faces. You wouldn't expect it from their appearance, but as soon as they are among themselves they chatter like a bunch of geese, and their laughter and yelling never seem to cease.

What a contrast between this dull, stolid group and thousands of feverishly energetic people, with a feverish love of life, who come from the new states and territories of the Pacific Slope, of the various types of backwoodsmen, especially the miners, who constantly pile in and out of San Francisco and who like to come down from the nearby gold and silver regions to "Frisco," their little Paris, as soon as they have mined enough to risk a little gambling or at least be able to allow themselves a few days on a spree! You recognize these rough, adventurous figures, worn out half from toil, half from loose living, even though Hastings,[15] the clothing manufacturer, whose advertisements cover every rock and fence between Oregon and Mexico, has fitted them with the latest fashion. They are everywhere, in the saloons, the theaters, the stockmarket, where mining stocks are speculated on; and even if you are no physiognomist, you can recognize them by their tobacco chewing and immoderate spitting as well as by their drunken condition, which, similar to the nocturnal blooming of many plants, is wont with them to be a very natural condition associated with sundown.

Formerly these gold-hungry Westerners were the nucleus of San Francisco's population. Their wild recklessness did not fit the mold of an emerging metropolis, and they frequently clashed sharply with the more stable, property-owning, and well-bred classes. After the first decade of the city's history, they were overcome and now are themselves outsiders in the rich, large city, which has them to thank for its origin. San Francisco has not simply grown rapidly in wealth but also in education and cultured living, much more so than any of the other young cities of the West. One notes that the long distance "weeds out" the immigrants not only according to number but also to quality. A great deal of sediment remains deposited along the way, and the stream has become clearer as it flows down into the golden plains of blessed California. The rapid increase of wealth and comfortable living in this happily constituted, beautiful, fertile land modifies customary practices, while the location on the ocean, as well as the great tasks that it sets, expands the outlook and awakens many types of intellectual curiosity. There is a keen interest in intellectual life in San Francisco as demonstrated by Lick's foundations, the wonderful Bancroft Library, the newly founded Academy of Sciences,[16] and the public libraries. Some Californian authors have made a name for themselves even beyond the borders of the United States. Also they say that painting is more readily encouraged here than in other large cities of the West. It would be a wonder if the magnificent scenery, which California has in its Sierras, its coastal range, and its ocean, did not awake and foster a feeling for the beautiful and the grandiose.

CHAPTER TWENTY-ONE

Ruins

AMERICA IS AGING FAST. DEBRIS AND REFUSE LEFT BY MAN
ALONG THE PACIFIC RAILROAD AND IN THE MINING AREAS.
TRACES OF THE HAVOC OF WAR IN THE SOUTH. RUINS IN FLOR-
IDA.

America is young, but for a long time now it has no longer been the baby that
Europe once nursed so well. The nice little saying of Goethe, which talks about
a lack of ruins and monuments of basalt,[1] does not apply anymore; rather it
confuses many people's ideas. One has to keep in mind that even if civilization
here is young in years, it has lived all the more rapidly. Even if the features that
they have engraved here and there on the profile of this broad land are less the
respected features of true age than the traces of an earlier tradition, they are
nonetheless impressive. America learned from the Old World at the most opportune time, for in no series of millenia could it have been able to offer America
so many means for its rapid development as in the couple hundred years that
have elapsed since its discovery. Actually many people think that the process
of development has gone on too quickly and has prematurely formed all of the
unhealthy character traits of Europe's younger sister. Still, there is little use in
discussing such an opinion here.

To be sure, our castle and monastery ruins are different from those you find
here. The former are the funerary monuments of an age that has completely
disappeared, monuments of forgotten perceptions and of conditions difficult to
understand now. The sorrow they awaken is vague, like the feeling aroused by
a nameless grave or a gravestone whose inscription has worn away. It acquires
something of the general philosophical regret with which we look down from
more elevated heights on the world's everyday affairs and find them to be vain
and empty. But the imperceptively insinuating joy that we have in knowing we
still live and have survived as we stand in the midst of these mortal remains

often mixes something comforting with this sorrow. Great memories of proud, wonderful times and great trials of one's own people are connected with such ruins. How different these witnesses of a swift life! These don't comfort us because they are not grand enough nor lie sufficiently far enough in the past, for on the whole they clearly are destined to a decline that will occur just as rapidly as the life style that created them. They are significant examples, which highlight right before our eyes the impotence of man in the fight against nature, which in its quiet, powerful way is again winning out over man's handiwork. In any case, they demand our attention because of the close connection they have to both the life of yesterday and today.

It probably sounds odd to say that the huge construction of the Pacific Railroad has created a pile of ruins, ruins of towns, villages, and countless individual buildings, which now remain as debris all along the line, where oddly enough they alternate with the active centers of traffic this international trade route has summoned into existence here in the middle of the desert. In many areas where no settlements had existed, towns of a few thousand inhabitants grew up along the new line as it was being built and then, little by little, were abandoned again as the railway line pushed on further into the wilderness. Bear River City in Wyoming is one of the most prominent of these new deserted towns. Right by the railroad one can see a level spot, more deserted than the desert that surrounds it, with tumbledown mud walls, where the cabin outlines are often still recognizable, littered with scattered bricks, beams, boards, fence posts, and many smaller indications of civilization among which bottles and tin cans are particularly numerous. Innumerable oblong pits indicate the sites of former dugouts, i.e., semiburied cabins like those built as initial dwelling places all over the prairie for their warmth and protection against storms. In another place we can see a trackless railway embankment, which at one time ran into the settlement. Since this town stood at what was then the last stop on the Union Pacific Railroad, it was believed that it would become the basis of a permanent settlement. It had a few thousand inhabitants and even published a newspaper, the *Frontier Index*, but is now entirely deserted.

Lately some other towns have suffered a similar fate. The station at Wahsatch, which lies somewhat further west, formerly housed an engine house and railroad work shops as well as a restaurant where the trains usually stopped for half an hour. A little while ago all this was moved to nearby Evanston, and Wahsatch will soon be entirely deserted, since its scanty population will naturally move there too. It has happened this way in many places: something new, something big grew up and brought ruin and destruction along in its process of growth. Other "railroad towns" have made a comeback after first declining. An example of this is Cheyenne (in the Wyoming Territory), which in the first three years of the Pacific Railroad construction quickly grew to a city of four thousand people, and later declined again until it became the last stop on the line coming up from Colorado and the south. Now it is an important junction point and has a good future for itself securely in hand. In this way, life will probably again sprout from many of the ruins. In fact the coal and various ore deposits in the area have already been instrumental in creating some very respectable places and several branch railroad lines as well.

How many single ruins, even ruined or deserted towns there are already in the gold mining districts of California and Colorado, the Pennsylvania oil region, and the many other districts rich in ore! Without investigating the extent of these natural resources and the conditions under which they might be profitably developed, the enterprise always begins with feverish energy, builds enormous workshops and machine shops, brings in thousands of workers, and only realizes too late that even here one has to advance tentatively, building up, stone upon stone, if anything lasting is to be achieved. In young Colorado there is literally not one single mining district that does not have its deserted stamping mills or smelting works, and in some places they are very common-place sights. It is much the same in certain parts of Utah and New Mexico. When the peace and quiet of the primeval forest or the desert extends over such places, you get some very strange scenes. It can seem as if humanity has quit the field and given back to nature its old rights, which it now noiselessly but with powerful effect assumes again.

In the Adirondack Mountains, which run through the northern part of New York State, in a dark, wooded valley I once came upon such a place of deserted remains, the memory of which I shall never forget. We had been hiking all day through the mountain woodland; tired and hungry, and without resting, we continued on the path that was supposed to lead to an ironworks. We climbed up an elevation and then down into a high-lying valley, which tested our patience with a few unexpected ground swells and a new forest in which the branches sometimes hung very low and hit us in the face or on the ears, not exactly gently, if one had become lazy and did not protect oneself. From the last elevation point we saw two lakes lying far below us. Climbing down again, we went toward them over a brook, and with a satisfied feeling we got onto a wider path, which by its look had something civilized about it and was actually lined by a hedge here and there. We also came across a field of oats. After a while a hill came into view. On the side that faced us there was a broad building with chimneys on top. It looked old and gray. Our path led right up to this building, but when we arrived at the door, everything looked desolate, and a few houses that stood facing the other way on the opposite side of the hill were just as empty and looked as prematurely old as this one did. The pine

23 "HUMANITY HAS QUIT THE FIELD AND GIVEN BACK TO NATURE ITS OLD RIGHTS, WHICH IT NOW NOISELESSLY BUT WITH POWERFUL EFFECT ASSUMES AGAIN." A GHOST TOWN IN A MINING AREA OF THE WEST.

boards of the planking were already ice-gray, and here and there, one was loose or hung down; there were almost no whole panes to be seen in any of the windows, and the doors did not look as they usually do but were shut and covered over with planks, which someone had propped up against them. Bushes, young birches, pines, even a few cypresses were standing, as is usual in ruins, most frequently in places where a person who lived there would never have allowed them to be: right before doors and windows, on garden beds, or before a stone bench. The path here became as wide as a street, and led down the hill into the middle of a settlement that seemed to be even quieter though it was larger and had more varied types of buildings than what we had already seen. There was a broad street here, trees between thirty and forty years old, on the right a barn with an open door, which hung askew on its hinge, on the left a little schoolhouse, recognizable by its small steeple, further on a store, then small homes with barns and sheds, now and then a large workyard, then a warehouse in front of whose door lay heaps of charcoal. Thus the whole street went on and was overgrown with grass almost as in a meadow. No voice, no movement except in the white poplars and the mountain ashes on both sides, or when the wind coming along now in the evening sky from the direction of the setting sun rustled the weeds, which stood as tall as a man in the nicely enclosed gardens.

Finally there came a house that had no broken windows and curtains behind them; this one then had to be inhabited. True, no living creature stirred here either, but a loaded bird gun was leaning against the wall and not very old horse manure lay alongside the garden fence. It was the inn, the only inhabited house in the settlement. The guides knocked, called, and whistled; finally something animate came up the street, immediately alive with a cheerful stir: two dogs were chasing one another and their barking rang out clearly in the evening. Behind them came a big man with a weather-beaten face who became affable as he greeted our guides as if they were acquaintances. As Mr. Lamb introduced us, he pressed the hand of everyone of us in the vise-like grip of his right hand. He was the innkeeper; he led us to our simple rooms and then went to arrange for supper. After we had cleaned up and taken a rest and again stepped outside of the front door, a conveyance came down the deserted street and stopped before the building; a tall, thin woman, strikingly unadorned and simply dressed, in a very short skirt, unaffectedly sprang from the seat with the dexterity of one accustomed to doing so, threw the reins over the horse, and went with vigorous steps into the building. She was the innkeeper's wife and had picked up provisions in North Elba. Thus we now had met both guardians of this solitude, the only people who live here year in and year out.

That evening we heard the simple story of this deserted settlement: in many places in the valley iron ore was discovered, richer in quality and especially in quantity than in many of the deposits that are in the primitive rock of the Adirondacks from Lake Champlain to Schroon Lake. In 1826, when the mining development had already begun in several places, and when the area where we now were was still an Indian hunting ground scarcely known to white men, David Henderson,[2] the same person who later died on Lake Calamity, was then at the ironworks at North Elba, which were still quite new. An Indian approached him there, took a piece of iron ore out of his belt and said that the water in which he hunted beavers ran over a bed of this kind of iron ore. It was an unusually rich ore. Immediately a group of enterprising men banded together and entrusted themselves to the Indian's guidance, and on the second day they came to the place in the midst of the forest where the deserted works stand today. They found everything as the Indian had described it: a large embankment of iron ore over which the river ran, and in various places in the valley there were clear signs of a rich ore, which, as they used to say in accounts of that time, could supply the needs of the world for years to come. An unusual amount of water power and the large quantity of wood in the untouched forest round about seemed to remove any doubt about the great value of this deposit.

In order to prevent any delay, as well as any premature disclosure about the find, the group started out that night in the midst of a terrible storm, made their pathless way back, sent two representatives without delay to Albany with the Indian, for it was not advisable to let him out of their sight, and purchased a large piece of property in the Adirondack region, which at that time was almost all state property. Soon roads were laid through the wilderness, a settlement began, furnaces and forges built, and despite its remoteness from all traffic routes, the enterprise seemed to prosper in the best possible way. In 1850 the great blast furnace, which we first saw on entering the village, was finished. But the development of the iron industry in other parts of the United States that lay closer to canals and railroads, the rising importation of European iron, even the unfortunate death of Henderson, who had been the driving force behind the entire enterprise, made it seem advisable in the middle of the 1850s to cease work, and thus the auspicious and grand beginnings were abandoned. But the work stoppage will probably not last much longer now for in the Hudson valley the Adirondack Railroad is already running into the mountains, and it is coming up the Saranac valley to Lake Champlain to open up the wilderness around the lake and Canada. The entire rich area and all the machinery that was built during the thirty years of operation are still the property of the company, and this innkeeper has been placed here to keep an eye on things.

He and his wife were real American types. They had been in the Far West, were familiar with Colorado, California, and parts of the Midwest and apparently didn't feel uncomfortable in this secluded section. Both were able hunters, and during the long winter they went out on their snowshoes as often as possible to hunt deer and fur-bearing animals. They had tough constitutions. The woman was thin and slight from head to foot but also boney, and her face had an energy and a pair of cool, particularly sharp eyes, which made you think her capable of daring ventures. Slender as a girl and yet in no way femininely soft, she was the type that makes it difficult for one to say whether she was young or old, for there was no room in her firm features for stoutness or wrinkles, which come with advancing years. There seemed to be a sort of asexuality in this odd mixture of her physical characteristics. He was monosyllabic and serious, but showed no emotion, and still whatever he said was clearly and carefully chosen. They had no children.

Late in the evening another group of hikers arrived who had taken the way over from North Elba, which we wanted to see the next day; they were young men from New York and Boston, and their leader was a colored man, a mulatto, a quiet person who inspired trust. A man with African blood is leading whites on a pleasure trip through an area that a few decades ago was still Indian territory! How interracial contacts extend out into the world from this desolate and lonely spot!

The next day as the bright autumn sun rose over this curious place, the impression was even stranger than in the evening. There was the cricket chirping in the grass growing in the wide street; in another place the butterflies were flitting about the flowers undisturbed as if in a meadow; there in the morning, fresh with dew, this work of human hands looked so worn out, so dilapidated, while nature looked so powerful, so triumphant; here one saw how it once more entered its domain with full strength after a short period of time, after an imperceptively shorter time than it had taken in other places, even in Babylon and Thebes. We went into the houses and workshops, saw some attractive minerals from the iron mines in the store amidst broken boxes and glasses, viewed the book collection that had been procured for the benefit of the workers, entered the building that had housed the bank, and looked in the large ledgers that closed out everything on one day in the year 1856 with a thick, melancholic ink-line drawn diagonally across the page. We even visited the little school; it was intended for about thirty children, had been simply and nicely furnished, but now there was a serious gaping crack in the ceiling, and in the not too distant future it would be a complete shambles. Then we went up the stream that once powered the works, stood on the broad embankment of magnetic iron over which the water shot, and saw a place where the ore was mined in huge blocks like stone out of the wall of rock; then we passed rock outcroppings where the thick, black-grey ore veins were glistening in the sun and entered into subterranean areas that were hewed like rooms for the gnomes in the same glistening ore.

How the field of our thoughts and feelings expands, how everything seems to go on more peacefully in this place of quiet decay, where matter naturally strives to return to the old earth again. Here nothing is really hurried, here nothing forces anything else. It has been a long time since these objects were inhabited and used by humans, they are already going downhill and have nothing to offer us no matter how attractive they look, but are instead completely immersed in the process of becoming dust and ashes. There are so many different things and objects here, but they all mean the same. No matter from whatever aspect you look at them you see in all their shapes and forms only one trait in common: contours that after a short rise sink back again to where they began. When one stands in their midst, one thinks one sees the outline of these shapes connecting, intertwining, and soon everything around dissolving into general rising and falling wave-like contours. One movement, encompassing and making everything alike, appears in place of all this great diversity. Great words, like "eternal," "endless," "without beginning," and "sea of eternity" suddenly make sense and have meaning here.

The South has some other ruins to show. Unlike other wars, the Civil War was not a thunderstorm, which clears the air and together with the newly secured peace fosters new prosperity. It passed over the land like a hailstorm, demolishing much and damaging everything in its wake, which by sheer accident was not protected and in large areas even destroying growth for a long time to come.

Dilapidated plantation homes, often resembling country manor houses set in large gardens and surroundings, deserted churches, remains of Negro cabins, stables, barns, keep recurring today as permanent characteristics of the Southern landscape. One goes along a road, which barely maintains itself above the swampy surrounding rice fields by means of sandfill, gravel banks, and plankboards, and sees to the right or left a thick grove of large-trunked live oaks; and under the thick garlands of tillandsia, the so-called Spanish tree moss that hangs over all the branches, are scattered houses. One travels along a road constructed of logs or branches and finds that the cabins lack doors and windows, that at most two or three of them are inhabited by ragged Negroes, that the trees of the grove form a wonderful alley with four or six rows (although some are now out of line and lying rotting on the ground, others are shooting up here and there in no particular order), and that in the background stands a larger, weather-beaten house, which was formerly painted white but is now gray. This house, too, is not inhabited as it still should be and surely once was; a white tenant has two rooms in a side wing, the rest stands untended, and as I went up the walk, if I am right, I saw a few swallows direct their sweepback flight right into the windows. Or one takes an overgrown path in the woods, a path that sometimes can only be distinguished by the rotting planks and piles that formerly supported it above the damp ground; one comes upon a large clearing and sees a house in the middle of it with neither roof, windows, nor doors and stands there already a ruin.

In the vicinity of Charleston once, in the rather wild and deserted area of Goose Creek, along a path for strolling which ran through the sparse pine forest that covers the land there, I came to a clearing where activity was busily taking place. Twelve to twenty Negro men and women were occupied demolishing a house, the former home of a large plantation owner. They had just smashed in the back wall, gathered the bricks out of the rubble, and carried them off to their homes. On the same day I came to the so-called Goose Creek Church, standing in the middle of the forest on a little elevation entirely surrounded by live oaks and cypress trees. A wall runs around the little church and the little cemetery, and a tombstone from 1856 indicates the burial place of the old man who owned the nearby plantation and who was the last master. The chapel is just beginning to fall into ruin; doors and shutters were still closed to protect it from the wind and weather, but the mortar is falling from the walls, and in between the steps there is quite a bit of moss and some cypress shoots pushing up towards the light of day. Behind the hill on which the church or chapel stands is a fish pond that attracts masses of birds, and I have never heard so many mockingbirds harmonizing together in so many diverse ways as I heard in this place where on one morning as I sat on the church steps at least four of them were warbling and never tired from their competitive singing. The solitude around this deserted, venerable spot was almost forgotten with such cheerful activity going on. The abundance of life of the plants and animals, the power and joy with which it stirred, so full of promise on these first spring days, and pushed up towards the light of day seemed to surge like waves around the house of worship, and as I sat there and meditated, this picture became mixed with that of a deserted cabin I recently came upon on the Ashley River and out of whose windows a young oak, a healthy shrub, was extending its branches toward the light, while lying on the doorstep were such thick growths of black-berry runners that there was barely space to put a foot down. Soon the waves of life will hit the walls even more powerfully; they will look for ways to break up the inanimate stonework. But what will be there in a couple of decades other than debris inundated by green and brown vegetation and the flowering beauty of creeping and climbing plants?

When I was hiking on an oppressively hot March day through the pine forests above Palatka (in Florida), rather far inland where there is no longer any road or path, I came through thick scrub oak and palmetto brush to a strikingly open spot on the top of a sandy ridge. Here the only tree of any size was a bird cherry tree, standing there in full bloom, while little pines and oaks were growing up everywhere around it; the grass was not as tall as in the surrounding forest, and I was astonished not to see one single palmetto, since from the location and the soil I would have expected this tenacious weed, which grows in abundance all around, to be present. I threw myself under the bird cherry tree and looked up at the blue sky and the sun through its branches loaded with blossoms. A picture of perfect peace lay before me. From this spot I had the most beautiful view I had seen anywhere in Florida. One looked left and right and directly ahead over an unbroken wooded area that was dark because of the dominant pines, and only at the edge of the St. Johns River, which, wide and closed in on all sides, lay like a lake in the middle, was the area framed by the lighter colors of swamp vegetation and orange groves. It was a site possessing such a view that someone might pick it if he were trying to decide where to build a house in this area. I noted that the tree was as broad branched and had grown as shapely as if it had at one time been trimmed. Then I saw red carnations emerging out of the ground, which in this spot could only be growing wild, and on closer observation I noticed they were arranged in a circle around the tree and in a row along the edge of the taller grass. Had there been a garden in this desolate spot? I walked around and found that the clearing cut a rectangle out of the area of the taller trees and the tall wild grass; there were broken bricks around a hollow in the ground, and I recognized by the decaying stakes the outline of a house; then two tree trunks were found, cut off right at ground level and covered with the bright green shoots of the bitter orange tree; and strawberries, which usually do not grow so densely in these woods, were also discovered. Indeed, there had been a farm here, yet I did not learn anything concrete about when and why it had been abandoned. In another ten years all traces will have disappeared, just as the recollections of it have already faded from people's memories. It was probably someone from the North who came here to convalesce or for repose, and settled here in this solitude, one of those who builds farms on beautiful spots but who becomes tired of the rustic idylls to which their active life has not accustomed them or who die alone, and all that they have built with so much effort is often left to deteriorate entirely.

In addition, it is not hard to find entrenchments and battlefields from the Indian wars in Florida. In many places the walls of former Spanish missions or churches are still standing, and St. Augustine, which lately has become a much-frequented winter resort, is, as regards its older parts, a semi-decaying leftover from the time of Spanish and French control. In the last few decades these districts have improved tremendously and thus many traces of decay have disappeared. I heard tell, however, that in the 1830s along the St. Johns River you could find whole rows of neglected plantations, deserted mansions and sugar houses dating from the period of English colonial rule. The wild orange trees that one finds in the forests of Florida, which in turn have given rise to the widespread legend in these parts that this valuable tree is indigenous to the New World, also date from the same period.

However, enough of ruins and decay! They speak for themselves, for they also belong to life! Wouldn't it be odd if a river flowed along and didn't deposit any rock fragments? It may flow so quickly that its mobility fascinates you and masks the material that remains lying there, but this debris will only increase until it dams up the stream into a pool. Life is indeed not stronger than death.

Explanatory Notes

INTRODUCTION

1   Alexis de Tocqueville, *Democracy in America* (1835–1840); Michel Chevalier, *Society, Manners, and Politics in the United States* (1839); Charles Dickens, *American Notes for General Circulation* (1842); James Bryce, *The American Commonwealth* (1888); and Francis Trollope, *The Domestic Manners of the Americans* (1832).

2   For example, Henry Steele Commager, ed., *America in Perspective; The United States through Foreign Eyes* (New York, 1947), and Oscar Handlin, ed., *This Was America* (Cambridge, Mass., 1949).

3   For Ratzel's connection to Karl Haushofer and geopolitics, see Andreas Dorpalen, *The World of General Haushofer* (New York, 1942); Woodruff D. Smith, "Friedrich Ratzel and the Origins of Lebensraum," *German Studies Review* 3 (1980), 51–68; and James M. Hunter, *Perspectives on Ratzel's Political Geography* (Lanham, Md., 1983). On the misinterpretations of Ratzel, the popularization of his work in America by his best known American pupil, Ellen Churchill Semple, and the reevaluation of his work, see R. E. Dickinson, *The Makers of Modern Geography* (New York, 1969), chap. 5, where the author calls Ratzel "the greatest single contributor to the development of the geography of man" (p. 64).

4   Günther Buttmann, *Friedrich Ratzel* (Stuttgart, 1977). On the basis of some of Ratzel's letters and notes in possession of the family, Buttmann has constructed a more detailed account and a map of the route that the author took including places not mentioned in this book. Buttmann also gives added information about what Ratzel did in places he visited and about some of the people he saw. See his chap. 5, pp. 43–50.

5   In the fifteen to twenty travel accounts of the United States written by German-speaking travelers during the twenty-year period following the Civil War listed in the Harvard University Library, *Widener Library Shelf-list 11, American History*, 5 vols. (Cambridge, Mass., 1967), especially vol. 1, "U.S., description and travel, geography, etc.—individual works (by date)," pp. 862–866, Ratzel strangely enough is not represented. Most of these travelers do not visit as many sections of the United States as does Ratzel but restrict themselves to such places as the East Coast, the Plains, etc.; they deal in general impressionistic terms with selected aspects of American life—politics, religion, attitudes toward women; and they do not support their observations with the factual detail that Ratzel does. Perhaps the best known work on America from a later period than Ratzel's is that of Hugo Münsterberg who came to the United States as professor of psychology at Harvard in 1892 and wrote *Die Amerikaner* (The Americans) (1904) in order to help explain the American way of life to his fellow Germans. The English edition was also immediately appreciated by the English-speaking public for its insightful comments.

6   The *Illustrirte Zeitung* (Leipzig) 67 (1867), Nr. 1730, August 26, 1876, p. 181.

7   See Aleksandr Borisovich Lakier, *A Russian Looks at America*, ed. Arnold Schrier and Joyce Story (Chicago, 1979) for comments about Russia's knowledge of and interest in America during the mid-nineteenth century.

8   Henry Tuckerman, *America and Her Commentators* (New York, 1864), p. 302.

9   John A. Hawgood, *The Tragedy of German-America* (New York, 1940), pp. 57–58; Theodore Huebener, *The Germans in America* (Philadelphia, 1962), p. 122.

10   Tuckerman, *America*, pp. 301–302.

11   Cited in Bayrd Still, *Urban America* (Boston, 1974), p. 207.

297

12   Although Ratzel did pay visits to other tourist "musts" such as Niagara Falls (see Buttmann, *Ratzel*, p. 44), the falls were a purely natural wonder that did not fit in so well with his themes of dealing with cities and the relation of geography to urban development in the *Sketches*. Consequently, he eliminated descriptions of such places in the book.

13   For figures about urban population growth, see Adna Weber, *The Growth of Cities in the Nineteenth Century* (New York, 1891).

14   The German-Danish War of 1864, the Austro-Prussian War of 1866, and the Franco-Prussian War of 1870.

15   J. H. Clapham, *The Economic Development of France and Germany, 1815–1914*, 4th ed. (Cambridge, England, 1968), p. 155.

16   Geoffrey Barraclough, *An Introduction to Contemporary History* (New York, 1964), p. 46.

17   Comparisons are based upon figures and tables found in Weber, *Growth of Cities*.

18   Ratzel's interests in ecology seem to have been recognized by the German Democratic Republic, for that part of Ratzel's private papers located in Leipzig is housed in the Institute for Geography and Geoecology of the Academy of Sciences of the German Democratic Republic.

19   English statute mile = 1,609 meters. German geographical mile = 7,419 meters. German Imperial mile = 7,500 meters.

PREFACE

1   An historic region around Rome, Italy. Its borders are usuall considered to be the Sabatine Hills to the north, the Sabine Mountains to the east, the Alban Hills to the south, and the Tyrrhenian Sea on the west.

2   Although Ratzel at times throughout the text uses the term "North America" to mean the the entire continent, he usually is referring exclusively or particularly to the United States.

The cities, ranked in order of size, beginning with the largest, are: New York, Philadelphia, Brooklyn, St. Louis, Chicago, Baltimore, Boston, Cincinnati, New Orleans, San Francisco, Buffalo, Washington, Newark (N.J.), and Louisville. Ratzel is clearly referring here only to the United States, since by 1871 Montreal, Canada, also had over 100,000 inhabitants.

3   See Norman Foerster, *Nature in American Literature* (New York, 1923), especially the Introduction.

4   Large nature parks in Vienna and Paris respectively.

5   Opened in 1840, Greenwood Cemetery includes the highest point in Brooklyn (216 feet above sea level) within its borders.

6   The Eads Bridge (1874), designed by engineer James B. Eads who also designed the jetty system on the Mississippi River, was the first bridge built to span the wide southern section of the Mississippi and the first bridge to make extensive use of steel, or to employ the cantilever design. See also pp. 200–201, 243. The Louisville Bridge (1870) was built on twenty-five piers. The Cincinnati Suspension Bridge (1867), the largest single-span bridge of its class in the world at that time, was constructed by John A. Roebling, a German immigrant who came to the United States in 1831.

7   The Brooklyn Bridge, the first suspension bridge to use steel wire cables. Designed in 1867 by John A. Roebling. It opened for service in 1883 and was at that time the longest bridge in the world.

NEW YORK

1   In 1873 the Westchester County towns of Kingsbridge, Morrisania, and West Farms (that section of the county known as the Bronx) became part of New York City, the first addition to the city since 1731. The rest of what is today the Bronx was added to New York in 1895. In 1898 the Greater New York Charter incorporated Brooklyn, Queens, and Staten Island along with the Bronx and Manhattan into the city.

2   The Brooklyn Bridge, completed in 1883.

3   The most important of these buildings was the West Battery, constructed as a fort in 1807, renamed Castle Clinton in 1815, and serving, after 1824, as a place for public entertainment. In 1855 it became the immigrant landing station, and for the next thirty-four years saw the arrival of over eight million new Americans. The building was closed in 1890. Thereafter, the nearby Barge Office (now demolished) handled the increasing number of immigrants until the new depot on Ellis Island could be opened in 1892. Castle Clinton has now been restored as a fort and is a national monument.

4   Peace of Paris of 1763 ending the American phase, the French and Indian War, of the Seven Years' War in Europe. Treaty signed by Great Britain, France, Spain, and Portugal in which, among other things, France ceded to Britain all claims to Acadia and Cape Breton in Canada and all that part of Louisiana east of the Mississippi except for the Island of Orleans.

5   England's policy in the eighteenth century was to run the colonies primarily for the benefit of the mother country. After the end of the French and Indian War (1763), London saw an opportunity to reassert its authority and tap colonial sources of revenue. The policy took the form of such measures as a proclamation forbidding white settlers to go beyond the Appalachians (1763), the Sugar Act (1764), levying duties on sugar and molasses coming into the colonies from the West Indies, the Stamp Act (1765), establishing stamp taxes on newspapers and legal documents, and the Tea Act (1773), granting the tea monopoly in America to special agents of the London based East India Company.

6   See Ratzel's explanation and editor's accompanying note p. 261.

7   *Mundo Nuevo* (1871–1876). *Siglo XIX* may have appeared under varying titles as did many newspapers and magazines of that era.

8   Of course, many older buildings had been destroyed by fires, which periodically broke out in the city such as the Great Fire of 1776 or that of 1835.

9   See New York, note 16.

10   The New Post Office, located at the southern end of City Hall Park. Designed in Neo-Renaissance style by government architect A. B. Mullett, who did the Navy, War, and State Department buildings in Washington, D.C., it was completed in 1875 and demolished in 1938–1939.

Alexander T. Stewart (1803–1876). Emigrating from Ireland, he settled in New York and opened a small drygoods store (1823), which developed into the large retail store of A. T. Stewart & Co. He was a philanthropist and founded Garden City, Long Island (1869) as a planned community for moderate-income families. Ratzel is referring to Stewart's first large store, designed by John B. Snook and Joseph Trench, erected in the 1840s at the corner of Broadway and Chambers Street in Italianate style marble, and later known as the Sun Building. Stewart later built another larger cast-iron one located at Broadway and Ninth-Tenth Streets, which in 1896 passed into the hands of J. P. Wanamaker.

11   J. W. Goethe, *Faust*, Part One (1808), Scene: Before the Gate (*Vor dem Tor*):

> *Faust:*Aus niedriger Häuser dumpfen Gemächern,
> Aus dem Druck von Giebeln und Dächern,
> Aus der Strassen quetschender Enge. . . .

English translation: J. W. Goethe, *Faust*, Part One, trans. Philip Wayne (Harmondsworth, 1949), p. 60.

12   "The sage council, as has been mentioned in a preceding chapter, not being able to determine upon any plan for the building of their city,—the cows, in a laudable fit of patriotism took it under their peculiar charge, and, as they went to and from pasture, established paths through the bushes, on each side of which the good folks built their houses,—which is one cause of the rambling and picturesque turns and labyrinths which distinguish certain streets of New York at this very day." Washington Irving, *A History of New York from the Beginning of the World to the End of the Dutch Dynasty by Diedrich Knickerbocker* (1809), bk. 3, chap. 3.

13   See New York, note 15.

14   Since there was no city ordinance at this time desegregating public transportation, Ratzel is probably referring to an informal arrangement. State legislation was enacted for this purpose on April 9, 1873, forbidding the exclusion of any person because of race and color from "full and equal enjoyment of any accommodation, advantage, facility or privilege furnished by . . . common carriers, whether on land or water. . . ." New York State, *Laws of the State of New York, 1873* (Albany, 1873), 96th Sess., chap. 186, p. 303.

15   The experimental elevated railroad had a trial run in 1868 on Greenwich Street and later became part of the Ninth Avenue Elevated Railroad (1871). In the 1870s more elevated railroads were opened (the Third Avenue and Sixth Avenue ones in 1878). In 1870 the Beach Pneumatic Transit Co. opened an experimental section of tunnel running under Broadway from Warren to Murray Street. After serious objections to the project, it was abandoned. Nothing more was done with subway transportation until 1900.

16   Governeur Morris (1752–1816), senator, diplomat. Simeon DeWitt (1756–1834), state official, surveyor general of the State of New York (1784–1834). John Rutherford (1760–1840), politician. Three commissioners were appointed in 1807 by the state legislature to lay out the area north of 14th Street. They presented the Plan of 1811 providing for streets and city blocks for Manhattan up to what is now approximately 155th Street.

17   The section of Broadway above Fifty-ninth Street was known as the Western Boulevard or simply the Boulevard until 1899, when it became part of Broadway.

18   Ratzel seems to be thinking of the numbering in the older part of the city below Washington Square. Above that point the streets divide into an east and west section with the building numbers beginning at Fifth Avenue.

19   The legislation of February 26, 1866, established a state agency, the Metropolitan Board of Health, for the district of New York, to include Manhattan, Brooklyn, and Staten Island. It was felt that such an agency would be less influenced by the corruption or inefficiency that characterized New York City's administration at that time.

20   Croton Reservoir, above New York City, had been an important source of water supply for the city since 1842.

21   Compulsory education laws were not generally enacted and enforced in the United States until the beginning of the twentieth century.

22   Addition, subtraction, multiplication, and division.

23   The thaler (taler) was a silver coin used throughout German territories from the fifteenth through the nineteenth centuries. The Prussian taler became the most common taler coin for all Germany in the nineteenth century. After the founding of the Empire in 1871, the mark was established as the official monetary unit, but the taler was still recognized until 1907 as legal tender with an equivalent value of three marks.

24   Normal schools were schools primarily for the training of elementary school teachers.

25   The Free Academy of the City of New York, located on Lexington Avenue between Twenty-second and Twenty-third Streets, was founded in 1847 and in 1886 officially became known as the College of the City of New York.

26   Founded in 1805 by a group of philanthropists led by DeWitt Clinton and John Pintard.

27   In 1886 the number of women teachers in the entire German Empire was little more than one-tenth of all teachers, and this number had been increasing only in the previous few

years. John T. Prince, *Methods of Instruction and Organization of the Schools of Germany* (Boston, 1892), p. 2.

28   Thomas Hunter (1831–1915). An educator, he organized the first evening high school (1866) and founded Normal College of the City of New York (1869).

29   The temporary quarters were located in a commercial building at Broadway and Fourth Street. The lack of space and the noise from the horse-carriage traffic forced the school to move into its new home located at Park Avenue and Sixty-eighth Street. The original building at Sixty-eight Street was destroyed by fire in 1938. In 1869 the school was called the Female Normal and High School. Upon opening in 1870, the name was changed to Normal College of the City of New York. In 1916 it became officially known as Hunter College.

30   A historian of Hunter College supports Ratzel's observation by stating that the practical aspect was the principal selling point in promoting the cause of higher education for women. Daniel W. Patterson, *Hunter College* (New York, 1955), p. 9.

31   See Cambridge, note 13.

32   It is difficult to find a corresponding idiom in English. The sense of this one is: with a lot of money you just manage to make do; with a little money you're able to live comfortably.

33   See New York, note 25.

34   The Clionian Society (name later changed to Clionia), founded in 1851 at the Free Academy as a literary and debating society.

35   General Alexander S. Webb (1835–1911), president of the academy (1869–1902).

36   The philosophical faculty (*philosophische Fakultät*) at a Germany university is the humanities faculty, which offers programs of study including those leading to the doctorate and the more advanced *Habilitation*.

37   Columbia College was founded in 1754 and first located in the schoolhouse vestry of Trinity Church in lower Manhattan. That year it was granted its first charter as King's College. In 1784 the institution was reconstituted and changed its name to Columbia College. The affiliation of Columbia with the Episcopal Church of which Ratzel speaks was never an official one but rather a historico-traditional, cultural one.

38   In 1961 the municipal colleges were incorporated by an act of state legislation to form the City University of New York.

THE HUDSON

1   "The last towering ice sheet that slid down from the north over most of New York State, blocking the St. Lawrence outlet and making the Mohawk River and the Great Lakes drain through the Hudson, was split by the Adirondack heights; its southern portion was forced into a seaward progress between the high folded hills. It deepend the course of the great river as it moved." Carl Carmer, *The Hudson* (New York, 1939), p. 5.

2   In 1609, on his third voyage (not his first voyage as Ratzel states, although it was the first to the New World) aboard the *Half Moon*, Henry Hudson (d. 1611) discovered the Hudson River and sailed up as far as Albany.

3   Thomas Fulton (1765–1815), engineer and inventor, in 1807 successfully built and sailed a steamboat, the *Clermont*, from New York to Albany and back.

4   West Point has had a military past there since the Revolutionary War and has been continuously occupied by troops since 1778. The United States Military Academy, established by act of Congress, opened on July 4, 1802.

5   Former village on the Hudson, now part of Kingston.

6   Probably Ratzel's figure is a typographical or transcribing error, since the highest point in the Catskills actually measures over four thousand feet.

7   Thuringian Forest (Thüringerwald), a wooded mountain range in Thuringia, East Germany; the highest point is about 3,222 feet. Odin Forest (Odenwald), a wooded, mountainous region in West Germany between the Neckar and the Main rivers on the east bank of the Rhine River; the highest point is 2,057 feet.

8   Washington Irving, *The Sketch Book of Geoffrey Crayon, Gent.* (1819), "Rip Van Winkle." The sleep motif is an old folk theme of escape. Irving's immediate literary source was "Peter Klaus" in Johann Karl Christoph Nachtigal [pseudo. Otmar], *Volcks-Sagen* (1800).

9   In 1872 a Commission of State Parks was formed to inquire into transforming forest areas into preserved land for use by the public. In 1873 it recommended that a law be enacted to protect the natural forest. In 1885 Governor David B. Hill signed a bill into law, which stated that all land then owned or later acquired by the state in three Catskill and eleven Adirondack counties "be forever kept as wild forest lands." This "Forever Wild Law" provided for 34,000 acres in the Catskills and 681,000 in the Adirondacks to be set aside as forest preserve.

SARATOGA

1   Ratzel refers to the resort as "Saratoga," as was frequently done in everyday usage, although the correct name was "Saratoga Springs."

2   Baden-Baden, a health and tourist resort in West Germany at the northernmost part of the Black Forest, renowned for the curative powers of its springs as well as its many beautiful hotels, villas, walks, and parks. Interlaken, a health and tourist resort in central Switzerland on a stretch of land between the lakes of Brienz and Thun, famous for its clean air and magnificent scenery.

3   Theodore Thomas (1835–1905) founded the Thomas Orchestra in 1862; as its conductor, he led the orchestra in concerts in New York and later on tour. After a brief hiatus, upon the request of several influential New Yorkers, Thomas resumed his concerts in 1872 and continued until 1878. By common consent, the Thomas Orchestra in the 1870s was considered equal to the leading European ones. Thomas went on to become conductor of the New York Philharmonic Orchestra and later the Chicago Symphony Orchestra. He did more than any other American musician in the nineteenth century to popularize the music of the great European masters.

4   James Fenimore Cooper (1789–1851) was very well known in Europe. His *Leather-Stocking Tales* was widely read in Germany in both the original English and in German translation.

5   The French and Indian War (1755–1763) and subsequent wars with the Indians (Pontiac's Uprising, 1763). See also New York, note 4.

6   Sir William Johnson (1715–1774), a British colonial official. He was superintendent of Indian affairs "of the Six Nations and other Northern Indians" between 1756 and 1774, and active with his Indian allies against the French.

BOSTON

1   In his summary of the history of settlements in Massachusetts, Ratzel may have left the relation between the Pilgrim Colony at Plymouth and the Puritan colonies somewhat un-

clear. The Pilgrims were Separatists who founded a colony at Plymouth in 1620. During the 1620s, groups of Englishmen founded other communities around Massachusetts Bay. In 1630, under the auspices of the Massachusetts Bay Company, a large band of Puritans arrived. With the arrival of these colonists, the main settlement of Massachusetts began. Plymouth Colony was incorporated into the Massachusetts Bay Colony in 1691.

2   Thomas Hutchinson, *The History of the Colony and Province of Massachusetts Bay*, ed. Lawrence Shaw Mayo (Cambridge, Mass., 1936), vol. 1, p. 81. Volume 1 of the *History*, in which the relevant material here appears, was first published in 1764.

3   Edward Johnson, *Johnson's Wonder-Working Providence, 1628–1651*, ed. J. Franklin Jameson (New York, 1910), p. 247. First published in 1654.

4   Oliver Cromwell (1599–1658), Parliamentarian General in the English Civil War of the 1640s and Lord Protector or virtual ruler of England, Scotland, and Ireland from 1653 to 1658.

5   The Act of 1651, or the First Navigation Act, applied mercantilist doctrine to colonial trade. Designed to hurt Dutch shipping, the act mandated that all colonial goods be shipped in English ships owned, commanded, and mostly manned by British subjects.

6   The Navigation Act of 1660.

7   The decline in 1860 most probably was due to the financial panic of 1857 and those of the 1860s to the economic dislocations of the Civil War and its aftermath.

8   Aspinwall is now Colón, Panama; Batavia is Jakarta, Indonesia; Demerara is Georgetown, Guyana.

9   Dorchester is now a ward of the city of Boston.

10   A river in eastern Germany emptying into the Baltic Sea by Lübeck.

11   In the middle of the nineteenth century a massive landfill project directed development energies from the overbuilt and maze-filled older section to the orderly rows in the Back Bay area, making apparent some of the discrepancies Ratzel notes. In the 1960s a new massive project was begun in the center of the city, under the direction of the Boston Redevelopment Authority, to create great new open spaces in parts of the downtown area on a scale previously unknown in the city.

12   Hansa cities were cities belonging to the Hanseatic League, an association of north German towns and groups of German merchants abroad formed for the defense of their trading interests. The league experienced its heyday from the late thirteenth until the end of the fifteenth century.

13   Sir John Falstaff, the potbellied knight appearing in Shakespeare's *Henry IV* plays and *The Merry Wives of Windsor*.

14   In 1742 the original building was given to the city as a gift by the merchant Peter Faneuil. It was rebuilt in the 1760s and enlarged to its present form in 1805 by architect Charles Bulfinch, the nation's first professional architect.

15   The third church of colonial orgin, known as the Old South Meeting House, at the corner of Washington and Milk Streets. The present building was built in 1729.

16   The Boston Tea Party. Citizens disguised as Indians boarded the ships and dumped into the harbor the tea that was coming into the colony. The action was to protest the high duty levied by the Crown on tea.

17   David Pulsifer, *Guide to Boston and Vicinity* (Boston, 1871), p. 24.

18   The Old State House (1713), seat of the royal governor's council and colonial legislature until the Revolution. It was the site of the reading of the Declaration of Independence and is now a museum.

19   The Custom House (1837–1847), designed by Ammi B. Young. The building was one of the finest examples of Greek Revival architecture in America. Between 1913 and 1915, a thirty-story office tower was built over the dome, thus destroying the artistic unity of the building.

20   The new State House, located on a slope of Beacon Hill above the Common, designed between 1795 and 1798 by Charles Bulfinch.

21   John A. Andrew (1818–1867), who helped organize the Republican party in Massachusetts, was governor between 1860 and 1866, and a vigorous Civil War leader. Charles Sumner (1811–1874), U.S.senator from Massachusetts (1851–1874), leader of the antislavery group in Congress, took a prominent part in the impeachment proceedings against Andrew Johnson. He was a strong opponent of Grant's reelection.

22   Ralph Waldo Emerson (1803–1882), essayist and poet. Henry Wadsworth Longfellow (1807–1882), poet. James Russell Lowell (1819–1891), poet and essayist. Oliver Wendell Holmes (1809–1894), humorous essayist and poet. Henry David Thoreau (1817–1862), writer. Nathaniel Hawthorne (1804–1864), novelist. William H. Prescott (1796–1859), historian. John G. Palfrey (1796–1877), historian. George Bancroft (1800–1891), historian. Louis Agassiz (1807–1873), naturalist.

23   Ironically, today, because of its efforts to preserve and conserve its traditions and historical past and its reputation for elegant homes and rigid social code, it is sometimes called the most European of American cities.

24   Boston did have a reputation for being not only an intellectual center but also a focal point for various new movements. Henry James in his novel *The Bostonians* (1886) introduces the reader to some of the movements Ratzel mentions, such as women's rights, spiritism, and mesmeric healing. The Woman Suffrage Movement, which originated in the United States and Great Britain, culminated in America in the Nineteenth Amendment to the United States Constitution granting women the right to vote (1919).

CAMBRIDGE

1   *New England's First Fruits* (London, 1643), p. 12. Cited in Alexander Young, *Chronicles of the First Planters of the Colony of Massachusetts Bay from 1623 to 1636* (Boston, 1846), p. 551n. Ratzel in all probability used the Young work.

2   John Harvard (1607–1638).

3   Francis Bacon (1561–1626), English statesman, scientist, and man of letters. His works included *Essays* (1625) and *The Advancement of Learning* (1605). John Robinson (c. 1575–1625), along with Brewster, Bradford, and Cushman, organized the Pilgrims' emigration to America. He was the author of such works as *A Justification of Separation from the Church of England* (1610).

4   Increase Mather (1639–1723), member of a family of prominent Congregational clergymen known in seventeenth-century New England for their zealous Puritanism, intellect, and scholarship. He was the author of many religious works, sermons, and political and historical works.

5   Ratzel occasionally uses the city (Cambridge) to mean the university located there (Harvard) as is commonly done in Germany when informally referring to German universities.

6   Thomas Hollis (1659–1721), merchant in London and benefactor of Harvard College. He gave funds for a chair of divinity (1721), and mathematics (1727).

7   Elihu Yale (1649–1721), born in Boston, Massachusetts, in the employ of the East India Company from 1671, governor of Fort Saint George, Madras, India (1687–1692).

8   See Boston, note 22.

9   Karl Joseph Mittermaier (1787–1867), professor of law and politician. Rudolf von Gneist (1816–1895), professor of law and politician. Johann Kaspar Bluntschli (1808–1881), professor of law and politician. In the home Ratzel was visiting all three portraits were of law professors and politicians; two of them (Mittermaier and Bluntschli) had held chairs at Heidelberg, and an engraving of that city hung on the wall. This might indicate that Ratzel's host had at one time studied law in Heidelberg.

10   See Cambridge, note 5.

11   The Hasty Pudding Club, the oldest (1795) and very prestigious social club at Harvard. It was originally founded as a debating and literary society "to cherish the feelings of friendship and patriotism."

12   The Lawrence Scientific School, Harvard. The collections became the Museum of Comparative Zoology, the institution that Agassiz founded in 1859.

13   Louis Agassiz (1807–1873), born in Switzerland, was known for his research in natural history before coming to the United States in 1846. He became professor of natural history at Lawrence Scientific School, Harvard (1847–1873).

14   In 1873 Agassiz organized the Anderson School of Natural History at Penikese, an island in Buzzards Bay. The school, which was founded to pursue studies in marine research, had a great influence on science teaching in America and served as a model for other schools, but it did not survive his death.

15   Agassiz's second wife, Elizabeth Cabot Cary, whom he married in 1850, was a writer and educator in her own right and a promoter of women's education. His wife's commitment to the advancement of women may account in part for Agassiz's inclination to employ women in academic work; this was uncommon in Germany at the time, which would have caused Ratzel to take note.

16   The Astronomical Observatory, founded in 1843. The Peabody Museum of Archeology and Ethnology, founded in 1866 by a donation from the financier-philanthropist George Peabody (1795–1869). For the Museum of Comparative Zoology, see Cambridge, note 12.

17   Dissension between trinitarian and Unitarian partisans greatly disturbed the Congregational Church during the first half of the nineteenth century. Unitarian influence at Harvard continued to grow after Rev. Henry Ware, a Unitarian, was elected Hollis Professor of Divinity at Harvard College in 1805.

18   The German influence in American education was growing in the 1870s. In 1873, for example, the idea for the Johns Hopkins University was instituted and the school opened in 1876. It stressed an educational program emphasizing graduate study and research while deemphasizing the distinction between graduate and undergraduate study, and introduced the German seminar system into the curriculum. This program, some said, entitled Johns Hopkins to be called the first true university in the United States and served as a guide for the development of other universities.

19   Linonia and Brothers in Unity, literary societies at Yale University, founded in 1753 and 1768 respectively.

20   From 1701 to 1875, New Haven together with Hartford was the joint capital of Connecticut, hence Ratzel's mention of a state house there.

21   See p.50 ff.

22   See p.52.

PHILADELPHIA

1   The French and Indian War (1755–1763) between Great Britain on one side and France and its Indian allies on the other for control of much of North America.

2   For a brief discussion of Penn's plan, see John W. Reps, *Town Planning in Frontier America* (Princeton, 1969), pp. 204–223.

3   A description of Philadelphia's impact on urban development in Western cities can be found in Bayrd Still's discussion with excerpts from contemporary observers in his *Urban America; a History with Documents* (New York, 1974), pp. 99–103, and in Reps, *Town Plan-*

ning, pp. 222–223. It would have been interesting if Ratzel had commented on Philadelphia's grid plan as compared with that of a European one built under absolutist auspices such as Mannheim (begun in 1689) with which German readers were most probably familiar.

4   Market Street.

5   Broad Street.

6   Generally known as Independence Hall.

7   Ratzel reports this incorrectly to his German readers. The streets are not north but south of Chestnut with Locust and Spruce between Walnut and Pine Streets.

8   The author is referring to Broadway in New York, which by running southeast to northwest diagonally transects the grid plan of Manhattan. Approximately fifty years after Ratzel made this observation, Philadelphia moved to remedy the situation he mentioned. In 1917 the city began the construction of the Benjamin Franklin Parkway in order to cut across the grid and speed traffic from the center of the city to the East River Drive.

9   Those sections that developed beyond the original city, i.e., beyond or outside of Penn's grid plan.

10   Stephen Girard (1750–1831), financier-philanthropist, founder of Girard College, and active in Philadelphia's civic life.

11   See p. 118 ff.

12   The Greek Revival was popular in America in the 1820s and 1830s.

13   This Masonic Temple, located at Broad Street and John F. Kennedy Boulevard, was built between 1868 and 1873 by James H. Windrim.

14   The *Illustrirte Zeitung* (Leipzig), September 27, 1873, Nr. 1578, p. 229.

15   The City Hall was built between 1871 and 1901 by John McArthur, Jr.

16   The Eastern Penitentiary was built in 1829 by architect Jacob Souder and originally provided space for five hundred inmates. It was later enlarged and served as a penitentiary until 1970. Its design was an architectural expression of the Pennsylvania System, a penal philosophy emphasizing solitary confinement. Dickens, on his visit in 1842, was negatively impressed by the prisoners here and spent the greater part of the chapter on Philadelphia in his *American Notes* commenting on the life of the inmates. Charles Dickens, *American Notes for General Circulation* (1842), chap. 7, "Philadelphia and its Solitary Prison."

17   A translated paraphrase of "There are not many streams as the Wissahickon—none perhaps in this country, and few in the world." *The New Pocket Guide and Street Directory of Philadelphia* (Philadelphia, 1870), p. 21.

18   The Neckar River, 240-mile-long tributary of the Rhine, starts in the Black Forest and passes through Stuttgart and Heidelberg, entering the Rhine near Mannheim.

19   For a detailed contemporary description of the Exposition and its site, see *The Centennial Exposition* (Philadelphia, 1876); for a more modern account, see John Maass, *The Glorious Enterprise* (Watkins Falls, N.Y., 1973).

20   *Journal of the Exposition*, a weekly, Philadelphia, 1873–1874.

21   The Franklin Institute, a private, nonprofit organization for education and research in science, founded in 1824. It was a pioneer in systematic testing of the strength of materials and received the first U.S. Government contract for the study of steamboat explosions. The success of industrial exhibits sponsored by the institute led to the establishment of the Franklin Institute Science Museum in 1934.

22   December 15, 1836.

23   The University of Pennsylvania traces its origins to a charity school founded in 1740. In 1749 some citizens, including Benjamin Franklin, helped form an academy (opened in 1751) in connection with the school. Rechartered in 1755 as the College and Academy of Philadelphia, it became in 1779 the University of the State of Pennsylvania, the first institution in the United States to be designated a university.

24.   See New York, note 36.

25   James Hall (1811–1898), American geologist and paleontologist, supervised several geological surveys and was director of the New York Museum of Natural History (1871–1898)

at Albany. Because of difficulties with the state legislature over funding, Hall sold off parts of the collections he had amassed at the museum to various institutions throughout the country. The sale to the university probably took place earlier in the year that Ratzel visited Philadelphia, in 1873.

26 Frederick Augustus Genth (1820–1893) came to the United States from Germany in 1848 and opened a chemical laboratory in Philadelphia. He was professor at the University of Pennsylvania (1872–1888), specializing in the study of minerals and discovered twenty-four new types, one of which, genthite, is named in his honor.

27 Girard College, a private school providing elementary and secondary education, was founded in 1848 from the bequest of Stephen Girard. The school was to be free for "poor, male, white orphan children." In 1968, in response to a Supreme Court ruling, Negro boys were admitted for the first time.

28 The Mercantile Library, established in 1821 by local merchants and maintained by endorsements and membership dues. The building, designed originally as a market building, was taken over by the library in 1869. Since 1944 it has been part of the Free Library of Philadelphia. The Philadelphia Library, the Library Company of Philadelphia, organized in 1731 as a subscription library.

29 The Library of the German Society, founded in 1817.

30 *Saturday Night* (1865–1901?).

31 The *Public Ledger* (1836–1934), merged with *The Philadelphia Inquirer*.

32 The *Kölnische Zeitung* (1798–1945), a liberal oriented, highly regarded newspaper read throughout Germany, which traces its lineage back to newspapers regularly appearing since 1651. Ratzel originally wrote his reports on America, upon which this book is based, for this newspaper.

33 Col. M. Richards Muckle, head of the finance department of the *Leger*.

34 *The Public Ledger Building, Philadelphia* (Philadelphia, 1867), p. 16.

35 George W. Childs (1829–1894), publisher and philanthropist.

36 *The Public Ledger Building*, pp. 56–57.

37 Robert Burns (1759–1796), Scottish poet, enjoyed wide popularity for his verse, folksongs, and his at times satirical view of life.

38 Russell Jarvis (1791–1853), the crusading journalist and editor of the *Ledger*, left the paper in 1839 but later resumed his connection with it as a contributing editor.

39 Philadelphia had experienced several serious riots against Negroes during the 1830s and 1840s. In August 1834 there were three days of burning of buildings and acts of physical violence. Again in 1835 and 1842 there were similarly serious riots. Ratzel is most probably referring to the *Ledger*'s defense of the Negroes in its editorials of spring and summer 1838. The prejudice against the immigrants, of which he speaks, was mainly directed against Irish Catholics, who arrived in large numbers during the 1840s, and reached a peak in the ethnic riots of 1844.

WASHINGTON

1 The city was initially laid out according to a master plan of architect Pierre C. L'Enfant (1754–1835). L'Enfant provided a grand design with wide avenues and broad vistas, which gives the city a unique atmosphere of monumentality. For various reasons, L'Enfant's plan was modified and not continued and remained forgotten for most of the nineteenth century until revived by the McMillan Park Commission of 1901.

2 The Capitol Building, whose cornerstone was laid in 1793, was originally designed by William Thornton. Later architects included Benjamin Latrobe and Charles Bulfinch. Exten-

sions were authorized in 1850 with plans of Thomas U. Walter. Work was completed in 1863 in its main lines, with some further alterations taking place in the twentieth century.

3   At the intersection of New Jersey and New York avenues.

4   Constantino Brumidi (1805–1880), born in Rome, came to the United States in 1852. The frescoes in the Capitol (1855–1880) are his major work.

5   The Louisiana question was an aspect of the larger problem of Reconstruction in the South and the division between liberal Republicans and Democrats supporting home rule by the state's "best people" and the regular Republicans enforcing a Reconstruction policy. There were armed disorders with white Southerners forming the White League to resist the Republican state government. Federal troops had to be used to restore order in some instances. Tension continued throughout 1874, preceding the 1874 state elections. Finally, after the election, Congress imposed a compromise on Louisiana in order to bring peace.

6   *Landtag* (pl. *Landtagen*). The state legislatures of the German states such as the Bavarian Landtag, the Prussian Landtag, etc.

7   In referring to the Smithsonian, Ratzel uses the term "Institute," as it was informally known, throughout his description. Its official name is the Smithsonian Institution.

8   The Smithsonian was built between 1847 and 1855 during the Gothic Revival period in architecture by James Renwick, Jr. (1818–1895), who also designed such buildings as Trinity Church and St. Patrick's Cathedral in New York.

9   The great North American deer, now nearly extinct except in the nothern Rocky Mountains.

10   Spencer F. Baird (1823–1887), professor of natural history at Dickinson College, Carlisle, Pa. (1846–1850), served as Assistant Secretary of the Smithsonian Institution (1850–1878) and became Secretary in 1878.

11   James Smithson (1765–1829) never visited the United States while he was alive. In 1904 his body was brought from England to the Smithsonian Institution, where it now lies in a small chapel near the entrance to the building.

12   Agassiz founded the museum (now named in his honor) in 1859 at Harvard. He served as its curator during the final decade of his life.

13   The California Academy of Sciences, a privately funded institution in San Francisco, was founded in 1853 and is the oldest of its kind in the western United States.

14   Ratzel is allowing his patriotic feelings to carry him away here. To state that Germany and Austria had well over two times as many correspondents as France would be more accurate.

15   Emperor Wilhelm I (1797–1888), King of Prussia (1861–1888) and German Emperor (1871–1888).

16   King Johann (1801–1873), King of Saxony (1854–1873), known for his scholarly interests.

17   See *Check List of Publications of the Smithsonian Institution, July 1874*, especially p. 18.

18   Weather prediction had had poor results at least until the 1860s, causing some scientists to look on it with skepticism. Ratzel was therefore quite interested in learning what this Federal agency had been able to accomplish. The U.S. Weather Bureau was created in 1870 and assigned to the Signal Service of the War Department. It was to make use of the widespread military telegraph system in preparing reports on weather conditions from various parts of the country. In 1890 the Weather Bureau was separated from the Signal Corps and transferred to the Department of Agriculture. In 1940 it was again transferred, this time to the Department of Commerce, and is known today as the National Weather Service.

19   The National Weather Service and the National Archives have informed me that the map with the synopsis and probabilities for that date are no longer available. I could not cite the original language but have had to translate. Ratzel's German transcription back into English.

20   The Geological and Geographical Survey of the Territories (Department of the

Interior) was one of several Federal agencies engaged in geographical, geological, topographical, and scientific surveys of the United States. The commissions were combined and superceded in 1879 by the U.S. Geological Survey. The Geological and Geographical Survey of the Territories published annual reports by F. V. Hayden and others with slightly varying titles (1867–1879).

21   The White House was designed by James Hoban in 1792; work was completed on the building by architect Benjamin Latrobe during the first decade of the nineteenth century. Frequent renovations have taken place with a West Wing added in 1902 and an East Wing in 1942.

SOUTHERN CITIES

1   Resorts on the French Riviera.

RICHMOND

1   Palermo had a reputation for having a languid atmosphere and many idlers in the streets; beggars and thieves were numerous and visitors had to watch their purses.

2   Italian for alley.

3   The State Capitol (1785–1788) was modeled after La Maison Carrée, an ancient Roman temple at Nîmes, France. The Capitol was designed by Thomas Jefferson.

4   See Richmond, note. 8.

5   Robert E. Lee (1807–1870), Confederate general from Virginia, in February 1865 was appointed General in Chief of all Confederate armies. Jefferson Davis (1808–1889), president of the Confederate States of America. Thomas J. (Stonewall) Jackson (1824–1863), Confederate general from Virginia. James Monroe (1758–1831), a Virginian, fifth president of the United States.

6   There was much sympathy in Europe for the South's valor and its "underdog" position. Ratzel, although a strong supporter of German unity, came from southern Germany, with its long independent and particularist tradition, and could no doubt sympathize with some of the South's efforts just as he could appreciate the efforts of the individual German states such as Baden (where he was born) or Bavaria (where he was later to teach) to maintain some of their prerogatives against the centralizing tendencies emanating from Berlin after the founding of the Empire in 1871.

7   Two of the wars that paved the way for Prussia to unite Germany under its leadership. Prussia's victory in the Austro-Prussian War of 1866 caused Austria to withdraw from German affairs and form the Austro-Hungarian Empire (1867), while Prussia united all German states north of the Main River in the North German Confederation (1867) and formed military alliances with the remaining independent south German states. Prussia's victory in the Franco-Prussian War of 1870 allowed it to unite both north and south Germany in the new German Empire with the Prussian king, Wilhelm, as emperor and the Prussian minister-president as imperial chancellor. The defeat of France made Germany the paramount power on the continent.

8   A commandeered tobacco warehouse of Libby & Son, Libby Prison in Richmond was

used by the Confederacy from 1862 to 1865 mainly to house Union officers. Libby was most crowded between May 1863 and May 1864, when more than one thousand inmates complained of bad conditions.

CHARLESTON

1   More commonly known today as the Carolina cherry laurel.

2   China and Southeast Asia.

3   Broken bone or dengue fever is an acute infectious disease with sudden onset, headache, joint pains, and a rash caused by a virus transmitted by mosquitoes; it occurs chiefly in tropical and subtropical regions.

4   John Bachman (1790–1874), born in Rhinebeck, N.Y., was Lutheran pastor in Charleston, S.C. from 1815 on. Ratzel retains the German spelling for his name—Bachmann.

5   John J. Audubon (1785–1851), naturalist and artist, reknowned for his accurate paintings of the birds of America. Agassiz was professor of comparative anatomy and zoology at the medical college in Charleston from 1851 to 1854. Francis Lieber (1800–1872), educator, came to the United States from Germany in 1827, edited the *Encyclopedia Americana* (1829–1833), helped form educational policy at Girard College, Philadelphia (1834), and was professor of history and political economy at the University of South Carolina from 1835 to 1856 before going to Columbia College (now University) in New York. Although Ratzel is probably referring to Francis Lieber, he could also have meant Francis's son Oscar (1830–1862), who was a geologist and natural scientist.

6   German immigration to Charleston after the Civil War was slight, the mainstream going to other parts of the country with better economic possibilities. Consequently, the social life of the German community lost the unity of which Ratzel speaks. See Albert B. Faust, *The German Element in the United States* (Boston, 1909), vol. 2, pp. 406–407.

COLUMBIA

1   David Ramsay, *The History of South Carolina* (Charleston, 1809), vol. 2. Although there is no exact quotation from Ramsay corresponding to Ratzel's sentence, the sense of what he says can be found in paraphrase on pp. 435–436.

2   William Tecumseh Sherman (1820–1891), Union general famous for his "March to the Sea" through Georgia after his occupation of Atlanta in 1864. The events of the Civil War were followed very closely in Europe, and the leading figures were well known to newspaper audiences. European military men carefully studied the strategies employed in the war. Prussian general Helmut von Moltke, drawing upon the lessons of America's war, made stunning use of the telegraph and the railroad against Austria in 1866 and again in 1870 against France.

3   Wade Hampton (1818–1902), Confederate general, later governor of South Carolina (1876–1878) and U.S. senator (1878–1890).

4   In February 1874 a second Taxpayers' Convention, representing all but two South Carolina counties met in Columbia. It petitioned the U.S. Congress for relief from its economic difficulties and correction of administrative abuse and corruption. The people whom Ratzel

met here in Columbia were probably those exasperated with many of the problems they saw in the Reconstruction government of South Carolina.

The Grange (Patrons of Husbandry), an agricultural society, entered South Carolina in 1871 and was prominent for nine years in stimulating legal and social activities in favor of the farmer, laying the foundation of what developed into the Farmers' Alliance.

5   Robert B. Elliott (1842–1884), one of the first blacks to serve in the U.S. Congress. He was an ardent champion of civil rights and played an important role in the politics of South Carolina during the Reconstruction period.

6   Henry E. Hayne (1840–before 1920), politician, secretary of state for South Carolina (1872–1876).

7   Ratzel seems to be echoing an idea that was current in the thinking of the period and had the support of Lincoln. In August 1862 the president had called a group of prominent free Negroes to the White House and urged them to support emigration of their race to another country: "Your race suffer greatly, many of them, by living among us, while ours suffer from your presence. In a word we suffer on each side. If this is admitted, it affords a reason why we should be separated." The State Department made inquiries of South American governments and some African and Caribbean ones about taking American blacks. Although some blacks did go to Liberia, the plan for mass emigration never was actualized. John Hope Franklin, *From Slavery to Freedom*, 5th ed. (New York, 1980), p. 213.

SETTLEMENTS AND SPAS IN FLORIDA

1   In the 1870s, before the era of fully identifying specific diseases, the term "fevers" was applied generically to a wide variety of ailments. See New Orleans, note 10.

2   *Robinson Crusoe* (1719), a novel by Daniel Defoe (1660–1731), deals with a European marooned on a desert island. Its description of exotic and somewhat idyllic life on a desert isle, as well as Crusoe's adventures with his faithful native servant and friend Friday, made this book popular ever since it was first published.

3   The theme of Germans' interest in the sunny south frequently appears in German literature, as for example in J. W. Goethe's *Italienische Reise* (Italian Journey, 1816–1817) and Thomas Mann's *Der Tod in Venedig* (Death in Venice, 1913).

4   In 1763, at the behest of Catherine the Great, Germans began to emigrate to Russia. Groups of ethnic Germans continued to move to Russia until the middle of the nineteenth century. They generally retained their German language and many of their customs. Ratzel is referring here to one such ethnic German who had come from Russia.

5   Harriet Beecher Stowe (1811–1896) purchased a winter home at Mandarin in 1867, located on the St. Johns River near Jacksonville. Tocoi was then a station stop on the railroad line.

THROUGH GEORGIA AND ALABAMA

1   Nikolaus Lenau (1802–1850), Austrian poet, traveled to the United States in 1832 but returned the next year very disappointed with his experiences there. In the poem "Das

Blockhaus" (The Log Cabin) in *Neuere Gedichte* (1838), the poet describes his visit to an inn after a long day's journey. Supper ended, the men gathered around the fire and talked about business whie Leanu sat there sadly bored. Finally, as cited in the German lines, the poet tells how they all went to bed and how he remained alone drinking some wine without having to listen anymore to conversation in English about money matters.

> Und sie gingen zu Bett, ich blieb allein,
> Trank noch eine Flasche vom lieben Rhein,
> Als das englische Talergelispel schwieg.

2   "Des Sängers Fluch" (1814), a poem by Ludwig Uhland (1787–1862) was published in *Gedichte* (1815). "Odi profanum," the first ode in Book 3 of *Odes* (30–23 B.C.) by the Roman poet Horace (65 B.C.–8 B.C.).

3   Coupled with the Romantic Movement of the early and mid-nineteenth century and its attraction to an admiration for the Middle Ages, there was an increased interest in Roman Catholicism as well as an increase in the number of conversions to that faith.

4   Ratzel most probably explained the differences between the Roman Catholic, Evangelical Lutheran, and Reformed churches in Germany. He might also have taken the occasion to mention other recent events that dealt with religion and religious differences, such as the defection of the noted German theologian Ignaz Döllinger (1799–1890) and other disgruntled Catholics (who later became known as Old Catholics) from the Roman Church because of the proclamation of the dogma of Papal Infallibility at Vatican Council I (1870). More currently, he might also have mentioned the anti-Catholic policies of the Imperial German Government during the *Kulturkampf* (1871–1883), which was especially severe in Prussia.

NEW ORLEANS

1   The *New Orleans Price Current* (1822–1882).

2   Ratzel's descriptions of the Mississippi and activity upon it are remarkably similar to what Mark Twain was to do later in a more detailed, expanded form in *Life on the Mississippi* (1883).

3   In 1879 James B. Eads designed jetties at the river mouth, which deepened the channels. In the same year, responsibility for keeping the Mississippi navigable along its entire course and providing flood control was given to a Federal agency, the Mississippi River Commission.

4   Experiments in ferrous construction were in full swing in the first half of the nineteenth century. Iron structures were used not only for utilitarian work but also for traditional types of buildings. The mid-nineteenth century saw many cast- and wrought-iron buildings constructed in American as well as in European cities. The Dittenhofer Building at 427–429 Broadway in New York (1870) or the European railway stations such as St. Pancras Station in London (1866–1868) are examples of this style. Later on, however, steel, which improved on the possibilities of iron, was introduced into construction with the steel skeleton structure enclosed with stone, brick, etc., and in the twentieth century with steel reinforced concrete.

5   Derivation of street names: Josephine de Beauharnais (1763–1814), wife of Napoleon until the marriage was annulled in 1810. Austerlitz (1805), Jena (1806), Marengo (1800), scenes of famous victories by Napoleon's armies. Bourbon, name of the French royal family ruling France from Henry IV (1589) through Louis XVI (1792) and again from Louis XVIII (1814) through Charles X (1830). Dauphine, named after the French province of Dauphiné. St. Denis (d. 258?), apostle to the Gauls, first bishop of Paris and patron saint of France. Ferdinand

de Lesseps (1805–1894), French diplomat, chief engineer of the Suez Canal, and one of the initiators of work on the Panama Canal.

Apollo, classical god of the sun, light, music, healing, poetry, and prophecy. Bacchus, classical god of wine. Dryad, a deity or nymph of the woods. Naiad, a water nymph.

Pierre Corneille (1606–1684) and Jean Racine (1639–1699), classical French playwrights. William Pitt the Elder (1708–1778), British statesman and prime minister. Erato, Thalia, and Terpsichore, the muses of love poetry, comedy/idyllic poetry, and dance/choral song respectively. Tchoupitoulas, Indian word of uncertain origin, and Chippewa, an Indian tribe. Annunciation, the event commemorated by many Christian churches of the angel's proclamation to Mary of the Incarnation as related in Luke 1:28–35. St. Patrick (d. about 492), apostle to the Irish and patron saint of Ireland.

Some street names have been changed completely or have become part of already existing ones: Apollo is now Carondelet, Bacchus-Baronne, Force-N. Tonti, Genius-N.Galvez, Naiads (Nayedes)-St. Charles, St. Denis-Daneel, St. Patrick-S. Saratoga, Virtue-N.Rocheblave.

6   See New Orleans, note 13.

7   The hero of the novel, *Martin Chuzzlewit*, after finding no employment in London decides to try his luck in America. Upon arriving in New York, he hears of fortunes to be made out West and is taken in by a group of land promoters. He and his friend buy land in Eden, nothing more than a group of primitive cabins in a swamp. A year later, their hopes dashed, the two Englishmen return home. Charles Dickens, *Martin Chuzzlewit* (1843–1844), especially chaps. 21–23, 33–34.

8   For her mother, happiness on this earth has vanished without return.

9   Joseph E. Johnston (1807–1891), Leonidas Polk (1806–1864)—Confederate generals. See also Richmond, note 5.

10   In this era the dominant theory of disease causation was not contagious from person to person but rather from miasmas or vapors rising from low ground or decaying organic matter. This theory is emphasized in Ratzel's explanation here as well as his explanation of an example of illness in Florida, see p. 175.

11   *Atala* (1801), François René de Chateaubriand's romantic novel about the Indian maiden Atala and her beloved Chactas. One of the most famous of the Noble Savage stories, which were so popular in Europe at the end of the eighteenth and into the nineteenth century.

12   *Karthäuserklösse* (Carthusian dumplings), a simple pastry of doughnut-like consistency made with sugar, bread, eggs, and milk, formed into the shape of a ball, then rolled in sugar to provide sweetness.

13   Ratzel mistakenly refers to the Japanese persimmon as the Japanese medlar (*mespilus japonica*) or loquat, no doubt because among German-speaking Americans of that time the word *Mispel* (medlar) was used for persimmon as well as for the correct fruit of that name.

14   *Tamarindenmus*, puree of the tamarind fruit, sold in drug stores for medicinal purposes as well as for adding taste to beverages and food.

THE MISSISSIPPI AND OHIO

1   See p. 191 ff.

2   The *Daily-Picayune* (1837–1914), named for a Spanish coin valued at six and one-half cents. It was the first New Orleans publication that sold for less than a dime. The *New Orleans Republican* (1867–1878), the newspaper that supported the Republican party.

3   Algiers, now part of the city of New Orleans.

4   The Old State Capital (1847–1849), a Gothic Revival style building was designed by James H. Dakin, burned during the Civil War, restored in 1880, and then used until 1932.

5   James Fenimore Cooper, *The Prairie* (1827), chap. 5, speech of Ishmael Bush, the squatter.

6   No doubt the financial Panic of 1873 and its effects on business and commerce were also reflected in "the all-round sluggishness of business" about which Ratzel speaks.

7   See p. 197ff.

8   A river in western Germany, 273 miles long, beginning in Lower Saxony and flowing northwest to empty into the North Sea.

THE THREE MAJOR CITIES OF THE WEST

1   Ratzel uses "Northwest" not to denote what is today commonly considered the American Northwest, i.e., the area on the Pacific Coast, which includes Oregon and Washington, but rather what is known as the Old Northwest, approximately the area between the Ohio and the Mississippi rivers and the Great Lakes.

2   The Battle of Tippecanoe (1811) did disrupt the Indian alliances in the Old Northwest and broke the influence of Tecumseh and his brother, the Prophet, along the Wabash River, but the real overthrow of Tecumseh occurred in 1813 at the Battle of Thames River, Ontario, when Americans defeated and killed him.

3   In the 1860s, with 200,000 persons living in the basin near the river, Cincinnati was virtually the most crowded city in America. Park area then began to increase tremendously in the twentieth century with philanthropic donations of land for park use and increased public and government concern.

4   See Philadelphia, note 3 for not only Philadelphia's impact on Western cities but also New York's influence on Chicago.

5   Frances Trollope (1790–1863), mother of the novelist Anthony Trollope, lived in Cincinnati for two years (1828–1830) during her visit to the United States, which she described in *Domestic Manners of the Americans* (1832), chaps. 4–17, wherein she takes note of the importance of the pork business for Cincinnati.

6   Michel Chevalier, *Society, Manners, and Politics in the United States* (Boston, 1839), Letter 18, "Cincinnati," pp. 191–192.

7   United States, *The Statutes at Large and Proclamations of the United States of America* (Boston, 1871), vol. 16, 41st Cong., Sess. II, chap. 255, sections 29–38, pp. 270–272. The law was approved on July 14, 1870, but for all practical purposes it took effect in 1871.

8   Pierre Laclède (1724–1778), French fur trader and pioneer, came to America in 1755.

9   In 1803 the United States purchased Louisiana, which then included the area between the Mississippi and the Rocky Mountains, from France for 80,000,000 francs, thus doubling the size of the country.

10   These controversies included the problem of slavery in the territories, culminating in the Compromise of 1850 (California was admitted as a free state; the remainder of the Mexican Cession was to be divided at the 37th parallel into New Mexico and Utah, which would decide on slavery at the time of admission), the Kansas-Nebraska Act of 1854 (opening the two territories, Kansas and Nebraska, to settlement on the basis of popular sovereignty), the war for "Bleeding Kansas" (scramble for control between proslavery and free soil groups), and the Dred Scott Decision of 1857 (declaring the slave Scott not free by virtue of being taken into a territory where slavery had been prohibited).

11   Lafayette Park (1836) contains thirty acres of parkland, and is the oldest park in St. Louis and possibly west of the Mississippi.

12   Henry Shaw (1800–1889) came to St. Louis from England in 1819 and made a fortune in cutlery and real estate. He developed a plan (1866) for a huge garden and later donated land to the city for that purpose. Tower Grove Park was part of Shaw's country estate and is noted for the variety of its trees. Shaw's Garden (now the Missouri Botanical Garden) comprises seventy-five acres of gardens and buildings modeled after Kew Gardens in England.

13   The Eads Bridge, see Preface, note 6.

14   St. Louis Mercantile Library Association was formed in 1845 by St. Louis business-men who erected a library in 1851. The Public School Library was formed in the 1860s as a supplement to the public school system. It was free to teachers and staff, required a small fee from students, and was open to others by subscription. In 1874 it was made free to all users. It later became known as the Public Library of St. Louis.

15   The Illinois-Michigan Canal, ninety-six miles long, was opened in 1848 and runs from the Chicago River to La Salle on the Illinois River.

16   Least known of the cities mentioned by Ratzel here, it is located at the eastern end of the Black Sea in Georgia near the city of Batum.

17   See the Three Major Cities of the West, note 1.

DENVER

1   John Smith.

2   William Larimer (1809–1875), politician, led a party of gold-seekers to the Pikes Peak area. He also served as U.S. commissioner and judge of probate. During the Civil War he raised a regiment of volunteers in Colorado for the Union forces. Although known as General Larimer, the highest army rank he officially attained was colonel.

3   The *Cherry Creek Pioneer*, after one day of publishing, merged with the *Rocky Mountain News* (1859–).

4   The Leavenworth and Pikes Peak Express Company was launched by W. H. Russell and J. S. Jones to serve the region after the discovery of gold near Cherry Creek in 1858. The more famous Central Overland California and Pikes Peak Express Co., the parent company of the Pony Express, absorbed this line in 1860.

5   James W. Denver (1817–1892), politician, commissioner of Indian affairs (1857–1859), governor of the Territory of Kansas (1858), of which Colorado was then a part. He played a large role in restoring order in the territory.

6   The Snowy Range, part of the Medicine Bow Mountains, which are in turn an extension of the Front Range.

TRAVEL ON THE PACIFIC RAILROAD

1   Passengers traveling from New York to Chicago could take various lines running on the southern and shortest Allentown route, the Great Central route (including a stretch on a Canadian line), or the New York & Erie route. From Chicago to Omaha one could travel on the

Chicago & North Western, the Chicago & Rock Island, or, along with some other lines, the Chicago, Burlington & Quincy routes.

2   The Black Hills of Wyoming, as opposed to the Black Hills of South Dakota, are now known as part of the Laramie Range.

3   The idea of the American West and its frontier life was perhaps most successfully popularized in Germany during the second half of the nineteenth century by Karl May (1842–1912), who wrote many adventure stories about the American Wild West.

4   Scenic lake in the Italian Alps with many resorts in the neighborhood.

5   A hotel train was one that had a so-called hotel car or cars attached to it. A hotel car was divided into sections containing staterooms accommodating four persons, normal couch seating space, and a kitchen. The passengers booked in this car were served meals here while other passengers had to disembark at stops along the way to buy their meals. In 1867 this new dining feature was instituted with the new luxurious "President" model of the Pullman Palace Car.

6   Some of these lines were:

Colorado: The Denver and Rio Grande Line which was running here in the 1870s. The Santa Fe Line, running here in the 1870s.

Utah: several small lines, running here in the 1870s. The Denver and Rio Grande Western Line, running here by 1880.

Arkansas: The St. Louis, Iron Mountain, & Southern Line, running here in the 1870s. The Little Rock & Fort Smith Line, running here in the 1870s.

Arizona: The Southern Pacific Line, running here in 1878. The Atlantic & Pacific Line, running here in 1882.

7   The Brenner Pass, which today forms part of the boundary between Austria and Italy, was from earliest times a much frequented pass through the Alps, with an altitude of 4,497 feet.

8   Summit, California.

SAN FRANCISCO

1   Since 1909, the port and industrial section of Los Angeles.

2   Juan de Fuca Strait, between Canada's Vancouver Island and Washington State.

3   Acapulco, Mexico was settled in the 1530s and by 1600 was already an important link in the trade route between the Far East and Spain.

4   First attempts to construct the canal were undertaken by the French under Ferdinand de Lesseps, the chief engineer of the Suez Canal, between 1879 and 1889. After the French company went bankrupt, the United States purchased the French concession. Construction of a canal began in 1904 and the canal was opened to traffic on August 15, 1914.

5   The Southern Pacific Railroad, incorporated in California in 1865—it built south and eastwards.

6   There had been a long struggle for a direct rail connection for San Fancisco with the interior of the country. In 1871 the provisional solution of which Ratzel speaks, the Oakland Mole, a two-mile-long combination earth fill and trestle, was built out from the east shore. From that date until the opening of the San Francisco-Oakland Bay Bridge in 1936, most people entered the city aboard the transbay ferries.

7   John S. Hittell, *The Resources of California*, 6th ed. (San Francisco, 1874), chap. 6 (pp. 162–181) and p. 185.

8   In geographical terms, a slope is that part of a continent descending to and draining

into a particular ocean. Today instead of Pacific Slope we usually refer to this area as the Pacific Coast.

9   As early as the 1870s, the Northern Pacific had built lines connecting specific cities, but it was in 1883 that the railroad completed its line to its main western terminal, Portland, Oregon, and in 1887 direct main-line communication was established to run from the East to Tacoma on Puget Sound.

10   Of course, the disastrous earthquake and fire of April 18, 1906, which destroyed three thousand acres in the heart of the city, was still in the future. Thereafter the residents set about rebuilding their city on a more imposing scale, and the city now boasts a number of impressive buildings and homes, many forming a harmonious architectural unity.

11   Goat Island, renamed Yerba Buena Island.

12   The *Morning Call* (1856–1895); thereafter the name varies with the word *Call* in the title.

13   These figures seem much too high for San Francisco, which is renowned for its moderate climate year round.

14   The population Figures of all the individual ethnic groups taken together do not tally with the total here.

15   C.[Charles] C. Hastings & Co., a large store in San Francisco, which imported, manufactured, and sold clothing.

16   James Lick (1796–1876), financier and philanthropist, came to California in 1848 and made his fortune in real estate. In addition to other charities, he bequeathed $540,000 to found and endow a school of mechanical arts and $700,000 to construct an observatory on Mt. Hamilton as well as giving money to the Society of California Pioneers to preserve records of early California.

The Bancroft Library, started by Hubert Howe Bancroft, contains collections dealing primarily with Bancroft's field of interest: western North America, especially California. It consists of books, pamphlets, manuscripts, maps and periodicals. It was sold to the University of California in 1905 and is now located at Berkeley.

See Washington, note 13.

RUINS

1   Ratzel's reference is to a poem by Goethe, "Den Vereinigten Staaten" ("To the United States") (written after 1824). The pertinent section reads:

> Amerika, du hast es besser
> Als unser Kontinent, das alte,
> Hast keine verfallene Schlösser
> Und keine Basalte.

(America, you're better off than our continent, the old one. You have no ruined palaces and no monuments of basalt.)

2   David Henderson (1793–1845), iron mine manager, died in a hunting accident at Duck Pond, which was consequently renamed Calamity Pond.

Selected Bibliography

Buttmann, Günther. *Friedrich Ratzel*. Stuttgart, 1977.

Clapham, J. H. *The Economic Development of France and Germany, 1815–1914*. 4th ed. Cambridge, England, 1968.

Dickinson, R. E. *The Makers of Modern Geography*. Ch. 5, "Leaders of the First Generation: Friedrich Ratzel." New York, 1969.

Dorpalen, Andreas. *The World of General Haushofer*. New York, 1942.

Hantzsch, Viktor. *Ratzel-bibliographie, 1867–1905*. Munich/Berlin, 1905.

Hassert, Kurt. "Friedrich Ratzel; Sein Leben und Wirken." *Geographische Zeitschrift* 11 (1905): 305–325, 361–380.

Hawgood, John A. *The Tragedy of German-America*. New York, 1940.

Huebener, Theodore. *The Germans in America*. Philadelphia, 1962.

Hunter, James M. *Perspectives on Ratzel's Political Geography*. Lanham, Md., 1983.

Ratzel, Friedrich. *Kleine Schriften*. 2 vols. Munich/Berlin, 1906. In the first essay in this work Ratzel gives a brief account of his trip to and itinerary in the United States.

Sauer, C. O. "The Formative Years of Ratzel in the United States." *Annals of the Association of American Geographers* 60 (1971): 245–254.

Smith, Woodruff D. "Friedrich Ratzel and the Origins of Lebensraum." *German Studies Review* 3 (1980): 51–68.

Still, Bayrd. *Urban America*. Boston, 1974.

Tuckerman, Henry. *America and her Commentators*. New York, 1864.

Wanklyn, Harriet. *Friedrich Ratzel; a Bibliographical Memoir and Bibliography*. Cambridge, England, 1961.